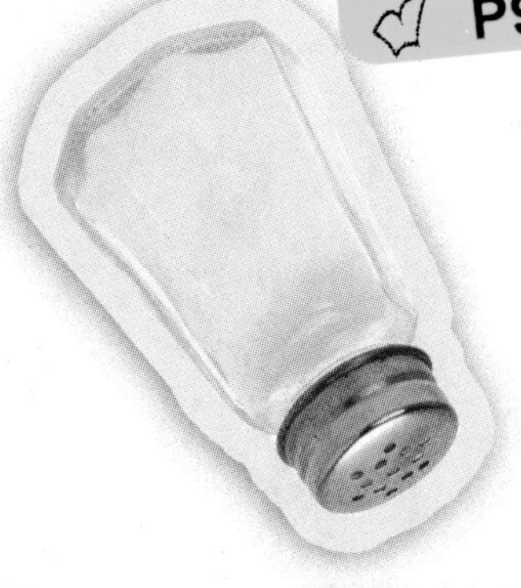

EVANGELISM Handbook

EVANGELISM *Handbook*

Biblical, Spiritual, Intentional, Missional

ALVIN REID

FOREWORD BY THOM S. RAINER

AFTERWORD BY ROY FISH

B&H ACADEMIC

NASHVILLE, TENNESSEE

ISBN: 978-0-8054-4542-8

Published by B&H Publishing Group
Nashville, Tennessee

Dewey Decimal Classification: 269.2
Subject Heading: EVANGELISTIC WORK—HANDBOOKS, MANUALS, ETC.

Printed in the United States of America
10 11 12 13 14 • 19 18 17 16 15

Contents

Foreword

It is the best of times for evangelism in America, and it is the worst of times. It is the best of times because there is a high receptivity to the gospel. According to our research, four out of ten non-Christians in the United States would welcome a conversation about Jesus with a Christian. That means that over 60 million people who are lost and without hope would like to know how to be saved and filled with hope. What a great opportunity! What a mission field!

But it's the worst of times as well. The American church is in serious decline. The passion for evangelism is less evident each year. Many church-going Christians will *never* share with an unbeliever the truth claims of the Savior. Never. Not one time. And many pastors and other church leaders are moving evangelism to the backburner of priorities. In fact, in one study we completed a few years ago, we found that 53 percent of senior pastors had not shared the gospel even one time in the previous six-month period.

It is the best of times, and it is the worst of times. The mission field is filled with opportunities for the message of the gospel to be heard, received, and affirmed. But the American church is largely and sinfully silent.

The publication of *Evangelism Handbook* could not be timelier. The need for every word in this volume could not be greater. And the priority for the message of this book could not be more urgent.

I have known Alvin Reid for years. We have been on the same platform in conferences. Our writings often end up in the hands of the same people. The courses we have taught are similar. And more than any of these, Dr. Reid's passion for the sharing of the gospel is what I admire about him the most. This man is not merely writing a book from the wealth of his intellectual expertise. He is writing a book from the passion of his heart. I love this quote directly from Dr. Reid in the book: "for me evangelism is not a job, it is the passion of my life. And the need of the hour is for the church to become more missional in its focus, a challenge for which I will give the rest of my life."

Don't think for a moment that *Evangelism Handbook* is just filled with passion and void of solid content. To the contrary, this book offers one of the best overviews of the discipline of evangelism that I've ever read. The first part is an incredible overview of evangelism from both a biblical and historical perspective. We are able to see why the message of the gospel is so important and why that message must be theologically and biblically sound. And we are able to walk through the history of the Church, looking at her evangelistic victories and her evangelistic mistakes.

The second part of the book reminds us of the critical need to be spiritually empowered to do evangelism. Dr. Reid powerfully examines how the spiritual disciplines can make a believer effective in sharing the message. In other words, he reminds us that, while the message is vital, the role of the messenger cannot be overlooked.

From history and theology and spiritual power, the book turns to the practical application of evangelistic approaches. And in the final section, Dr. Reid examines the missional focus of the church, offering incredible insights on how each local church should view its community from the same perspective as a missionary on a foreign field.

So there are many great truths, many great facts in *Evangelism Handbook*. But one thing that stands out in the book is Dr. Reid's passion for evangelism. That heartbeat, that spirit, permeates every part of the book.

The late Dr. Lewis Drummond, my mentor and my evangelism professor, said repeatedly, "Men and women, evangelism can be taught. Its truths are timeless. But more than anything, evangelism must be caught." It is that passion that Alvin Reid brings to this book, a passion that is caught.

I have read this book. I have caught the passion. May many more do likewise.

Thom S. Rainer
President and CEO
LifeWay Christian Resources

Acknowledgments

I never dreamed of becoming an author. During my freshman year in college, I received a B+ on every theme paper I wrote, convincing me I would never excel as a writer. Then a seminary professor wrote a comment on a term paper: "You are a very good writer." That statement changed my perspective, even though to this day I often question its accuracy! I enrolled in a writer's conference held at my seminary and published an article soon thereafter. I have been writing ever since.

I share this little glimpse about my writing for three reasons. First, it illustrates the power of words. The things we read do affect our lives. We can make a difference through what we write! Second, it shows an individual can change. My perspective about my ability to write changed through a simple comment. I pray that the words of this book will convince you that you *can* make a difference in evangelism—and, if you are not confident in your ability, that you can change. Third, we can misjudge our abilities. I do not consider myself a great writer, but I believe I can write. I had misjudged myself. Whether you are a pastor or a deacon, minister or layman, student or teacher, if you have doubts about your ability to make an impact for the kingdom of God, read on. You might discover that you, too, have misjudged yourself and the God who has called you to follow Him.

This book builds on my *Introduction to Evangelism* released in 1998, on the eve of my fortieth birthday. I turned fifty as this revision and major expansion was coming to completion. A conversation a few years ago began my journey that has become this book. My former student and current colleague Bruce Ashford and I enjoyed breakfast one day in my tenth year at Southeastern. He asked me a question that I could not let go. "What do you teach differently now about evangelism than when you taught me almost 10 years ago?" he asked. I mumbled something to the effect that I taught essentially the same. But inside my head I already had ideas spinning, motivated by troubling thoughts about the way the Western Church has practiced evangelism, about our failure to reach the hard-core unchurched, and about how we were losing youth faster than we could win them. This book culminates much of what I have thought about and learned over the last 10 years.

The gospel itself never changes. But culture, technology, and many other vital parts of life change all the time. Applying the unchanging gospel in a changing culture through churches that vary in degrees of effectiveness (more are actually ineffective) means we must adapt the unchanging message to unsteady times.

Like a good book, life is lived in chapters more than years. This book signals a new chapter in my life—a renewed focus on teaching and a passion for the gospel. Many have contributed to the various chapters of my life. While these words are mine and the many limitations and weaknesses of this book are mine, I have been aided by an abundance of friends and colleagues in its writing. In particular I have been assisted by several leaders in the field of evangelism and missional thinking through the contribution of articles throughout the book. These include Tom Johnston on how translators have utilized the word for "evangelize," Chuck Lawless on spiritual warfare, David Mills on practical helps for personal witnessing, George Robinson on effective short-term mission trips, Ed Stetzer on church planting, and David Wheeler on servant evangelism and evangelism to those with special needs. I am particularly grateful for my friend Thom Rainer for writing the foreword. Thom has been both an inspiration and an encourager for all the years I have been a professor. Finally, Roy Fish was my teacher and my mentor in PhD studies. He has been a hero for most of my ministry. Thanks, Dr. Fish, for writing the afterword.

My president, Danny Akin, and dean, David Nelson, have been the best folks with whom I could ever hope to work. I am grateful to them and to the trustees at Southeastern Baptist Theological Seminary for granting a sabbatical to complete this work. Denise Quinn helped with the typing of the manuscript. So many students contributed ideas and insights, and in particular my fall 2008 small group—Nathan Akin, Melissa Clift, Sabrina Crawford, Jason Delapp, Shaina Duncan, Brandy Griggs, Josh Reid, Walter Strickland, and Scott Talley—helped with feedback on the chapters on the cities, church planting, and paradigms.

More than anyone I thank the Lord Jesus Christ for such a great salvation we have the honor of sharing with others. Finally, I thank God for my wife, Michelle, and children, Josh and Hannah. They put up with a lot of my daydreaming, time away, and general hyperactivity. I love you all more than life. Anything I accomplish for Christ is a tribute to you three. Ministry is wonderful, but family is better.

Chapter 1

Things Must Change: The New Mission Field

The North American church is suffering from severe mission amnesia. It has forgotten why it exists.[1]

—Reggie McNeal

Have you ever been on a mission trip? If so, did you ever take such a trip to another country? Imagine for a moment your church gathered this coming Lord's Day as usual, but this day would be anything but normal. Today the entire congregation is loading buses following the final morning service. Passports in hand, you head to the airport and board as a group. Why? Your entire congregation is heading to a city in Asia where the gospel has never been proclaimed. You have decided as a congregation to do something adventurous, something quite revolutionary for your church.

Upon arrival your church begins to team up with nationals and missionaries to begin loving and serving the city, sharing Christ at every opportunity. Children are loved, lives are helped, communities are changed, and the good news is heard. After three wearying but

[1] R. McNeal, *The Present Future: Six Tough Questions for the Church* (San Francisco: John Wiley & Sons, 2003), 15.

gratifying weeks, your entire fellowship boards a jumbo jet and heads home, exhausted, jet lagged, but amazingly fulfilled.

Fast forward to Christmas season. Through video uplink, your morning services telecast live the leaders of the church you helped to birth in that Asian city. For the first time in the history of the world, a group of Christ followers wishes your church a merry Christmas from that city. Never in the history of man has this happened from this city, and you were a part of making this happen. Don't you think that would energize your church? No doubt many lives would be changed.

Here is the amazing news. Tomorrow morning your church can do the same thing. You do not need to board a plane to Asia to go on a mission trip. Every day believers across the United States awaken and step into the fourth largest unchurched nation on earth.[2] We are a mission field.

Mission trips are a wonderful thing. I have been on many across the U.S. and around the globe. But what if you thought of life as a mission trip? What if you and I and every believer in the West took the posture of a missionary and began to raise our children, approach our jobs, and look at our neighbors from the view of a missionary? It could be revolutionary.

Life is a mission trip. Take it! Cultivate that vision in your people and watch them begin to function like missionaries. And relive the book of Acts in your very lifetime. It will take a movement like that not only to reach the world but also to reach the West.

The World Has Changed, the Gospel Has Not

In the fall of 1989 my wife, Michelle, and I were commissioned as home missionaries with the Home Mission Board (now North American Mission Board) of the Southern Baptist Convention. My assignment: to assist the state Baptist convention in Indiana in evangelism, from training to youth work to hosting conferences and strategic planning. I was 29 at the time and pretty much ignorance-on-fire. I was concerned because our state convention had declined for 10

[2] http://www.revivalandawakening.org/call.html (accessed October 18, 2008); http://www.ptwm.org/pages/ezines.asp?Magazine=REVIVAL+Magazine%3A+Seeking+the+Reviving+Presence+of+God (accessed October 18, 2008); http://www.reachamerica.org/about.htm (accessed October 18, 2008); http://www.baptistcourier.com/281.article (accessed October 18, 2008).

straight years in evangelistic effectiveness and thankful because my executive director gave me a long leash (not a good idea).

We tried lots of things, some of which actually worked. We took a big twelve-foot cross and signed up churches to help carry it from the state border near Chicago to the southeastern corner near Louisville. I carried it 26 miles myself. Now I scratch my head a little remembering those days where zeal often burned hotter than light, but that little exercise actually did encourage more than a few churches to do something more than sit in a building. We changed our youth conference and watched it grow from a few hundred to almost two thousand in three years. We trained many to share their faith. And, for the next few years, we grew in evangelistic effectiveness annually, no doubt because the power of God can even work through ignorant young leaders who truly love Him and the gospel.

That three-year term in Indiana taught me a lot. I had never lived outside the south until then. I began to realize how much churches in the south assumed that people really ought to be in church. I began to meet large populations in which no one gave a second thought about Christianity. I saw large church buildings with a handful of believers because so many had been planted by southerners who moved north to the "Rust Belt" for work in the 1950s. These churches, and there were more than a few, became spiritual forts for the southern believers to continue their particular version of Christianity. Most of them were ineffective in reaching the people who lived in northern Indiana. When those who built these churches began to move back to the south, the buildings remained large, but the congregations shrunk. It bothered me that all these churches failed when it came to reaching the people around them.

I have watched from then until now the waning impact of the church on society in the West. Certainly there have been wonderful examples of effective ministry. Some today act as though the conventional church of our day has made no positive impact, which would be inaccurate. But neither would it be inaccurate to say that in my lifetime the church has lost much ground for the gospel in the West.

That we are in decline as Christians in the West is simply undeniable. From 1990–2000, the U.S. population increased by 11 percent while membership in Protestant denominations declined by 9.5 percent. The Methodist church reported in 2007 its lowest membership totals since 1930.[3] Even the Southern Baptist Convention, known for its conservative and evangelistic heritage, has seen historic decline in evangelistic effectiveness and more recently a drop in total membership. But the picture is bleaker than that. From the 1950s until now the SBC has averaged just over 384,000 baptisms annually. But in that same period of time the U.S. population has doubled in population from 152 million to 305 million. We are not keeping up with the population growth. Not even close.[4]

I could give far more statistics than these, but you can see the point. This book seeks to challenge and to equip students and leaders to build on the best of what the church has been doing, and to form a renewed passion for a movement of God to change our culture through the power of the gospel. It builds on an unchanging biblical foundation with a view to reach this culture in a contextualized way. Just because a given church was effective 20 years ago with a certain approach does not mean that same approach will reach its present culture today! We do not need a new gospel for a new day. Truth does not need to be revised or amended. But neither do we need an outdated or ineffective approach to sharing the timeless gospel in our day.

We must find a renewed passion for our Lord. Our task as followers of Christ is to be living witnesses, to take the timeless message to a particular time and place in a timely manner. We would do well to lash ourselves to the unchanging Word, to learn from the best (and for that matter, the worst) of the past, and to become ambassadors of Christ for our time. From a biblical foundation, I will seek to walk the reader through key spiritual resources, while emphasizing the intentional nature of our witness. But in addition to this, I will spend much time exhorting the reader to move to a new posture for proclaiming the good news. The posture can be summarized in the word "missional."

If we keep doing what we are doing, we will keep getting what we are getting. A fundamental shift must happen in established churches and must be in the DNA of new churches. Throughout this book I will speak much of Christianity as a movement to be advanced rather

[3] http://www.christianpost.com/article/20080327/sbc-urges-members-to-combat-u-s-church-decline.htm (accessed October 18, 2008).

[4] See http://www.lifeway.com/lwc/article_main_page/0%2C1703%2CA%25253D167523%252526M%25253D201280%2C00.html (accessed October 18, 2008); http://www.sbc.net/redirect.asp?url=http%3A%2F%2Fwww%2Enamb%2Enet%2Fatf%2Fcf%2F%7BCDA250E8%2D8866%2D4236%2D9A0C%2DC646DE153446%7D%2FBaptism%5FIndicators%5F2000%2Epdf&key=baptisms&title=Baptism% (accessed October 18, 2008).

than an institution to be maintained. We must recover the apostolic yearning to advance the gospel to the ends of the earth. The shift that must occur can best be summed up in one term: missional. Missional means a lot of things to a lot of people. So before I say more, let me define what I mean by the term.

The Missional Shift

The American church has enjoyed a position like few in history. From a favored status with a decided home-field advantage in the culture, the church today enjoys less influence than in previous times. No longer can we merely put up a sign that says "Visitors Welcome" in front of a church building or hold an evangelistic meeting expecting people in the community or the church to change their calendars for several days. We can complain about that and mourn the loss of impact, or we can look at the early church who had no standing in the culture, had no buildings to invite people to enter, and yet so lived the gospel in the culture that they turned the world upside down.

We can add without subtracting. Without losing the best of our heritage and the bedrock of truth, the church can move forward in our time; without surrendering time-tested approaches that continue to be used of God, we can add new insights to help us in effectively reaching people for Christ. But we must change our posture as the people of God as much as Paul changed from preaching Jesus the Messiah to Jews in Pisidian Antioch (Acts 13) to preaching Jesus as the one true God to Gentiles in Athens (Acts 17). We need a God-intervention not unlike the Great Awakening that swept Britain and the American colonies, sweeping multitudes into the kingdom and birthing new approaches in evangelism, missions, and church planting. We need theological renewal in a consumer culture not unlike the Reformation. In short, we need a biblical, spiritual, intentional, and missional movement.

The terms "missional" and "missional church" were first used by a group of North American missiologists and practitioners called the Gospel and Our Culture Network (GOCN). These leaders gathered to seek ways to apply in the North American context those implications gained from missionary thinker Lesslie Newbigin. After returning from decades as a missionary in India, Newbigin realized how secularized and pagan Western civilization had become. He argued that we in the West must see our world as a mission field, and that the church must adopt the posture of a missionary as we relate to culture. That approach has been slow to gain acceptance in the Western church as a whole. But that reality is changing as a generation of younger leaders of the church understand and embrace this idea.

So what exactly do I mean by "missional"? Ed Stetzer and Mike Dodson defined the term:

> In its simplest form, the term "missional" is the noun "missionary" modified to be an adjective. Missional churches do what missionaries do, regardless of the context. . . . If they do what missionaries do—study and learn language, become a part of the culture, proclaim the good news, be the presence of Christ, and contextualize biblical life and church for that culture—they are missional churches.[5]

A simple way of thinking about "missional" is this. Evangelism means to share the good news of Jesus Christ to a lost person. Missions means getting to know a people and their culture to be more effective in sharing Christ. Missional means that I, though living in the West, take the posture of a missionary. This will include attractional evangelism, which the conventional church in my lifetime has done pretty well. But it will mean adding a focus on building churches where believers sees themselves as missionaries in the culture, sharing Christ and living out the implications of a Christ-following lifestyle at every level, and raising children to do the same. I recall a time in my tradition when the focus was to help every member discover he or she is a minister. Authors were writing books on the topic "Every Member a Minister." I believe the better focus would be "Every Member a Missionary." I will unpack this idea throughout the pages of this book.

What are the marks of a missional church? A missional church focuses as much or more outside its fellowship (and thus outside the walls of the building!) as it does on the inside. Missional believers think of themselves as being sent into the culture as ambassadors for Christ. The typical conventional church today magnifies what happens inside its fellowship and often even more inside a building (which is not the church, by the way). The missional shift will help believers see the importance of living Great Commission lives 24/7 as opposed to thinking of church as a place. We often use "church" as

---

[5] E. Stetzer and M. Dodson, *Comeback Churches* (Nashville: Broadman and Holman, 2007), 4.

an adjective (church service, church clothes, church activities) when the term "missional" would be the better choice for an adjective. Best to leave "church" as a noun.

Stetzer and Dodson identified the following as marks of a missional church: (1) Incarnational—"missional churches are deeply entrenched in their communities. They are not focused on their facilities, but on living, demonstrating, and offering biblical community to a lost world."[6] (2) Indigenous—this means "taking root in the soil of their society and reflecting, appropriately, their culture."[7] They note how hard this is for established churches since they already have a culture of their own and find it hard to change when what they find meaningful no longer communicates to a changing community around them. Instead of expecting lost people to become like the church culture, missional churches "are driven by Scripture, but people from the community see people like them—just radically different in the way they live."[8] (3) Intentional—"In missional churches, biblical preaching, discipleship, baptism, and other functions are vital. But worship style, evangelistic methods, attire, service times, locations, and other matters are determined by their effectiveness in a specific cultural context."[9]

A Timeless Gospel Proclaimed in a Timely Manner

I came to Christ in 1970 as an eleven-year-old boy at a young church in Alabama touched by the Jesus Movement. I witnessed rapid growth, changed lives, and new ministries for the gospel in a short period of time. I saw a loving congregation welcome people who did not fit in with those inside the congregation. I sensed the presence of God in power. I know at least in a small way how the work of God in revival can bring many people to a radical transformation in a brief time. I have never recovered from witnessing the remarkable passion for Jesus seen in those young hippie freaks once they became Jesus freaks! A strong youth ministry showed me the impact youth could have on a church. In college, I spent a summer as an itinerant evangelist, and I have preached almost 2,000 events in churches, at colleges, and other venues in the years since. I learned to share my faith in

---

[6] Ibid., 5–6.
[7] Ibid., 6.
[8] Ibid.
[9] Ibid., 7.

college by doing street evangelism and have been trained in most of the programs of our time.

My pilgrimage has included time as a pastor, interim pastor, minister of music and education, as well as in denominational staff positions in two states. Evangelism has always played a critical role in these areas of service. My wife and I served as home missionaries in Indiana. As a consultant in evangelism, I have had the privilege of teaching evangelism and sharing Christ in several foreign countries on four continents. While my personal tradition is that of a Southern Baptist, I have enjoyed ministry with many groups of believers over the years, from Pentecostal to Presbyterian, from Free Methodist to Independent Baptist, from Nazarene to Church of God, and from Campus Crusade for Christ to the Fellowship of Christian Athletes. All have taught me about the many ways God has blessed His people with the honor of sharing His great news. I taught evangelism at a university and now teach at one of the largest and most missions-focused seminaries in the world. I have also been privileged to serve on a number of interdenominational committees and organizations. My point in sharing this is to say that for me evangelism is not a job; it is the passion of my life. And the need of the hour is for the church to become more missional in its focus, a challenge for which I will give the rest of my life.

We learn either by contrast—facing opposing views to our own—or through confirmation—by being encouraged to stand on what we believe. Preachers and teachers are supposed to comfort the afflicted and afflict the comfortable! My primary focus in this book is the latter. After all, the Western church has to be the most comfortable in history, which is part of our problem. Most people who read this book will already know more than enough to be effective in evangelism. I seek to give you a vision that you can do that to which God has called you. However, I do hope to challenge the way you think about evangelism and to challenge the paradigms we sometimes accept uncritically.

Here are some convictions you can stand on with confidence.

1. *Men and women are without hope until they receive salvation through Jesus.* Therefore, we must evangelize *urgently.* People apart from Christ are lost (Luke 15), dead in sins (Eph 2:1), under sin (Rom 3:9), and under condemnation (John 3:18). Immanuel Kant once declared that David Hume, the skeptic, awoke him from his dogmatic slumber. Surely a skeptical

world, living in fear, often without hope, should awaken us from our apathy!

2. *Many people are ready to respond to the gospel.* Therefore, we must evangelize *regularly.* Paul told Timothy to preach the word in season and out of season—or when we feel like it and when we don't! In 1995, I had the privilege of joining the faculty at Southeastern Baptist Theological Seminary. Prior to that I taught at Houston Baptist University. Before leaving the university, I made an appointment with several students, including some whom I felt needed to hear the gospel. One was a young lady named Audra. I shared Christ with her. This was new to her, although she had gone to church services a few times. I gave her a gospel booklet, asking her to read it again.The first week after beginning my work at Southeastern, I got a letter from Audra. She wrote, "On August 9, I opened my heart to Christ. . . . A big thanks goes to you." She even photocopied the tract to give it to another person who needed Christ. The point is that Audra needed someone to tell her how to be saved. The reason many people aren't Christians is that no one has told them how to be saved.
3. *Believers are commanded in the Bible to evangelize.* Therefore, we must evangelize *obediently.* Billy Graham has said the number-one reason we should witness is because God says we should. We will explore other motives for our witness, but we should not ignore this simple truth. Obedience matters to God. In this day of "consumer Christianity," which focuses on meeting our needs, obedience has become low on the priority list of many believers.
4. *Most believers want to witness but do not.* Therefore, we must evangelize *purposefully.* I have been in hundreds of churches over the past decade. I am amazed at the number of believers who want to witness, who want to make a difference, who long for their lives to matter. They are afraid, or do not know how, or have been too busy doing good things to participate in the best thing—winning people to Christ.
5. *The gospel is the greatest message we could ever tell.* Therefore, we must evangelize *confidently.* As a student in a Baptist university, I was discipled by a Presbyterian. One day he asked me a simple question that changed my life.

"Alvin," he said, "what is the best thing that ever happened to you?"

"The day I was saved," I heartily replied, with my Sunday school smile.

"Then, Alvin," he continued, "what is the best thing you can do for someone else?"

The answer was obvious. Yet I was immediately embarrassed at it because I knew my life did not reflect the joy of introducing others to the Jesus whom I knew so well.

6. *We must rethink the way we understand and practice evangelism.* Therefore we must evangelize *missionally.* A shift from only an attractional-based evangelism to include missional-incarnational approaches will be a theme throughout the book.
7. *We must understand the spirit of the times.* Therefore, we must evangelize *holistically.* Evangelism is less a technique and more a lifestyle, less a method and more a movement. The Western church has been in decline for longer than we would like to admit. The notion that we should simply do what we have been doing, only better or with more passion, must be rejected. The idea that the key to the future is a new method that meets the times misses the point. Separating evangelism from the life of the believer in a compartmentalizing manner must not happen. Einstein was right when he said insanity is doing the same thing over and over only to expect different results. We must take the timeless message and communicate it in a timely manner. Do you really believe the greatest thing you can tell another person is the good news about Jesus? Then tell someone!

A vortex of change and ideas challenge church leaders today. I like a challenge; this book is my best attempt to take on the challenge of leading the church to a more effective and comprehensive evangelism without abandoning the gospel.

Overview

I hope to take you on a journey—a trek from Creation's dawn to contemporary times, walking where giants in Scripture and history laid a path that will guide us forward. I seek to tell a story about *The*

Story we are privileged to share. Our journey begins with a look at what the journey is about; part I is an overview of biblical, foundational matters and how the church has practiced these in history. Our culture may have gone the way of relativism, but truth has not changed. Before talking about how to share Christ, we will spend time examining just what it is we share: the message of the gospel—walking through the Bible, examining the great message of redemption, stopping to learn from Jesus, Paul, and the early church along the way, taking snapshots to form an album to guide our perspective of reality today. We will explore the garden of truth, considering vital theological matters related to our witness. We will walk through the valley of history, learning from both the mistakes and the victories of the church as she advanced this great movement of God from the time of the early church until our day.

In part II we cast our sails across the ocean of spiritual growth, charting our course through pitfalls that can hinder or help our witness, features too often overlooked. We can no more be effective witnesses without the Spirit than a boat can sail without the wind, so the work of the Spirit begins our course. Prayer's role in evangelism strengthens us as the stars at night reflect His infinite might. Our testimony aids our witness as the map guides our way. We will see the place of character in our telling of the good news, as our lives must reflect the reality of a changed life as the sea reflects the sun. Finally, spiritual disciplines give us the ongoing fortitude to stay the course through the storms of this world until we reach our destination.

Part III takes us on a journey toward intentionality, recognizing theory is of little effect if we are not intentional in our application of it. We head up the treacherous path through the mountain range of contemporary effectiveness. Many have lost their way in these parts, falling off the cliff of overemphasis on relevance on the one hand or tumbling over the ledge of traditionalism on the other. Mountain climbing warrants both nimble feet, being able to adjust to the terrain, and a strong back, careful not to give in to fads. Capable leaders, like tested guides who lead people to hike the Himalayas, must guide our journey. We will climb to the summit of effectiveness not by blazing a new trail haphazardly or by going down older paths long considered unreliable. Instead, we will look at practical topics like personal and mass evangelism and the work of the church in the gospel with confidence and creativity. Blazing new trails of church planting will take us forward.

Finally, we will journey through the forest of Today and the missional focus of the church. If we will reach our destination, we will move from an attractional-based witness focused on the church as an institution to a missional approach from the view of the church as a movement. From examining paradigms that must be changed to reaching various groups from the unchurched to children and students to helping those blinded by false faiths, our journey will end at the place that is really the beginning—with a vision to reach the world with the gospel! I have enjoyed taking this journey myself. I hope you will as well.

Questions for Consideration

1. Have you been on a mission trip? If so, were you more likely to share Christ on the trip than you do in your daily life?
2. Have you ever considered living life in a missional manner, seeing life as a missionary would? What would it take to live that way?

PART I

Biblical

The invitation of Jesus is a revolutionary call to fight for the heart of humanity. We are called to an unconventional war using only the weapons of faith, hope, and love. Nevertheless, this war is no less dangerous than any war ever fought. And for those of us who embrace the cause of Christ, the cost to participate in the mission of God is nothing less than everything we are and everything we have.[1]

—Erwin McManus

A man named Simelvise was born in 1818 into a world of dying women. In Simelvise's day, one in six women died in childbirth. His desire to know the reason for the high death rate led him to become a physician. He discovered that these women were dying of something called "childbed fever." He decided to find out what was causing it. Studying the way the doctors worked in his day, he discovered something that we would consider appalling. When the doctors began their shift, they often went first to the morgue to do autopsies. Because they did not understand germs and bacteria, they did not wash their hands as they moved to the maternity ward. As they delivered children, they were killing the mothers.

Simelvise began to experiment with washing his hands. He encouraged his colleagues to wash their hands in a chlorine solution. Immediately the maternal death rate dropped from one in six to one in fifty among their patients.

Many physicians remained skeptical of this simple solution. Finally, Simelvise spoke to a convention of his colleagues: "This

[1] E. R. McManus, *The Barbarian Way* (Nashville: Thomas Nelson, 2005), 5.

fever is caused by decomposed material conveyed to a wound. I have shown how it could be prevented. I have proven all I have said. But while we talk, talk, talk, gentlemen, women are dying. I'm not asking you to do anything world shaking, I'm asking you only to wash. For God's sake, wash your hands." But they laughed him to scorn. Philip Simelvise died insane at the age of 47 with the death rattle of a thousand women ringing in his ears.[2]

Could it be that our Lord is saying to the church today, "You are so busy talking, talking, talking about secondary issues. While you talk, the world is dying." We have a message whose truth is even more valuable than the news that could save a generation of mothers. We have the good news that can change lives for eternity!

Part I surveys foundational issues necessary to rescue the world from hell. The Bible serves as both our anchor and our bedrock for ministry. We must build an altar upon which the light of the gospel can burn. We dare not hold up a faint flicker in the face of the yawning darkness of our day. Instead, we must raise up a blazing inferno of biblical truth, stoked by the fuel of biblical fidelity, theological orthodoxy, and the perspective of church history.

[2] Taken from a chapel sermon by J. Avant at Southeastern Baptist Theological Seminary, December 3, 1996.

Chapter 2

A Movement Not a Method: The Message We Share

There is one thing stronger than all the armies in the world: and that is an idea whose time has come.[1]

—Victor Hugo

I travel a lot, and in my travels I fly often. Every time I pass through the metal detector at airports, I set it off. I then have to go through the process of personal screening. I stand in a glass cage hoping one of the security personnel hears the cry "male assist!" in time to get me through the process without missing my flight (airlines do not care that I have a PhD; when it is time to go, they leave with or without me!). When the attendant comes, I know the drill: sit down, right leg up, then left leg, stand up, arms extended with palms up, turn down the waistband, and then they do a pat down, which is pretty much a total invasion of my personal space. I am so accustomed to it by now it doesn't bug me, since I have been experiencing this since 2001.

[1] Cited in M. Frost and A. Hirsch, *The Shaping of Things to Come: Innovation and Mission for the 21st Century Church* (Peabody, MA: Hendrickson Publishers, 2003), 165.

Why do I set it off? Because in 1998 I discovered I had a cracked hip and had to receive a titanium hip replacement. That will ruin your whole day, by the way. Notice I received the replacement in 1998, but did not start setting off the metal detectors until 2001. Why is that?

Because beginning in September of 2001 airports turned up the sensitivity of the metal detectors. Something happened to cause that, something everyone who reads this book will remember—9/11. You see, several years before then a 6'7" Arab named Osama Bin Laden got more than a little provoked at the infidels of the West. He convinced grown men to come to the United States, spend years learning to fly airplanes, knowing they would kill themselves that infamous day when, using no weapons except box cutters, they turned commercial jets into missiles, killing thousands.

Bin Laden changed the way we live. And he did it without a massive army, without a nation under his charge. How did he do it? He started a movement, a movement that a small number believed in to the point they would spend years preparing to kill themselves for their cause. I am not commending the movement that has spread around the world as global terrorism. I am simply making the point that history has witnessed radical changes in society both for good or bad because of movements.

But go back 2,000 years. Look closely and you will see a band of believers, a den of disciples numbering no more than 120 people. Meeting in a large upper room, they had no military might, no economic power, nor representatives among the cultural elites of their day. But they had one Lord, one faith, one Spirit, and one mission. And you are reading this book because your life has been changed by the movement they started.

Christianity is a movement to be advanced, not merely an institution to be maintained.

Movements change the world. At her best the Church can be described as a movement advancing through history. The story of evangelism in the history of the church is the story of a movement spread by people so consumed with love for their Lord they could not help but spread His message. Unfortunately, the history of the Church demonstrates more than a few times that the movement became lost in the institutions it created. But again and again, through reform movements or revival, or new missions advances and church-planting movements, believers unleashed evangelism in new and effective ways. Today the Church in the West stands in dire need of such a movement, a movement driven by a heart for the gospel.

What Is Evangelism?

Appearances are deceptive. Adding to a church roll does not in itself indicate biblical evangelism. Swelling numbers in a worship service does not guarantee the gospel is being preached. Talking about evangelism does not mean effective evangelism is occurring. What is evangelism? How can a person or church tell whether evangelism is biblical?

Karl Marx once said that the person who gives the definitions controls the movement. Evangelism means many things to many people in our day. Before we can go into any substantive discussion of evangelism, we must discover what the term means. Today the institutionalism of the conventional church has created a culture in which evangelism, if practiced at all, is done from a perspective that emphasizes greatly the work of the "professional clergy" and the work done within the four walls of the church building. If evangelism will be effective again in the West, we will move from an unbiblical clergy-laity division (if anything, we are all clergy, for we are all called to minister). Much will be said about this later, but ministers in the local church are to equip all believers to be about the ministry of serving Christ and sharing Christ (Eph 4:11–12).

What Evangelism Is Not

Before we can examine what evangelism is, let us consider what it is not.

The Mute Approach

People with this view suggest that evangelism is simply living a good, moral life. Certainly effective witnesses should live a moral life, a life worthy of our calling. But some believers go so far as to say that their lives will reflect Christ, so their words are not needed.

But if people look at you and see you are a good, moral person, how will they know Jesus is the reason? Might not a good Buddhist appear the same? They might think you just got a raise in salary. How will they know if we don't tell them? "How can they hear without a preacher?" (Rom 10:14). Evangelism includes who we are, but it is more.

The Numbers Game

Some people see evangelism as church membership recruitment. This is the "scalp-hunting," "belt-notching," or the "sheep-stealing" approach. "Scalp-hunting" is more accurate because I am not sure that churches steal sheep as much as they grow greener grass! But we must admit that some folks are more interested in getting a notch on their evangelistic gun belt than they are in people's lives. They are more interested in recognition for their numbers than faithfulness to God.

Years ago a pastor told me as the evangelism leader that his goal was to lead his church to be the biggest church with the most baptisms in the state. I was not impressed, and I am convinced God was not impressed. To seek to be the biggest or the best often springs from a heart of pride rather than obedience to God.

Professionals Need Only Apply

According to this view, evangelism is a job for specialists only. Many believers who are convinced of the importance of evangelism are equally impressed that the pastor, staff, and itinerant evangelists are to accomplish the task. As long as we get the fish (unbelievers) to the big fish tank (the church building), the professional fisherman (the preacher) will catch them. This familiar story reminds us of the need for all to fish:

> Now it came to pass that a group existed who called themselves fishermen. And lo, there were many fish in the waters all around. In fact, the whole area was surrounded by streams and lakes filled with fish. And the fish were hungry.
>
> Week after week, month after month, and year after year, these who called themselves fishermen met in meetings and talked about their call to fish, the abundance of fish, and how they might go about fishing. Year after year they carefully defined what fishing means, defended fishing as an occupation, and declared that fishing is always to be a primary task of fishermen.
>
> Continually, they searched for new and better methods of fishing and for new and better definitions of fishing. Further they said, "The fishing industry exists by fishing as fire exists

by burning." They loved slogans such as "Fishing is the task of every fisherman." They sponsored special meetings called "Fishermen's Campaigns" and "The Month for Fishermen to Fish." They sponsored costly nationwide and worldwide congresses to discuss fishing and to promote fishing and hear about all the ways of fishing such as the new fishing equipment, fish calls, and whether any new bait had been discovered.

These fishermen built large, beautiful buildings called "Fishing Headquarters." The plea was that everyone should be a fisherman and every fisherman should fish. One thing they didn't do, however. They didn't fish.

In addition to meeting regularly, they organized a board to send out fishermen to other places where there were many fish. The board hired staffs and appointed committees and held many meetings to define fishing, to defend fishing, and to decide what new streams should be thought about. But the staff and committee members did not fish.

Large, elaborate, and expensive training centers were built whose original and primary purpose was to teach fishermen how to fish. Over the years courses were offered on the needs of fish, the nature of fish, where to find fish, the psychological reactions of fish, and how to approach and feed fish. Those who taught had doctorates in "fishology," but the teachers did not fish. They only taught fishing. Year after year, after tedious training, many were graduated and were given fishing licenses. They were sent to do full-time fishing, some to distant waters which were filled with fish.

Many who felt the call to be fishermen responded. They were commissioned and sent to fish. But like the fishermen back home, they never fished. Like the fishermen back home, they engaged in all kinds of other occupations. They built power plants to pump water for fish and tractors to plow new waterways. They made all kinds of equipment to travel here and there to look at fish hatcheries. Some also said that they wanted to be part of the fishing party, but they felt called to furnish fishing equipment. Others felt their job was to relate to the fish in a good way so the fish would know the difference between good and bad fishermen. Others felt that simply letting the fish know they were nice, land-loving neighbors and how loving and kind they were was enough.

> After one stirring meeting on "The Necessity for Fishing," one young fellow left the meeting and went fishing. The next day he reported that he had caught two outstanding fish. He was honored for his excellent catch and scheduled to visit all the big meetings possible to tell how he did it. So he quit his fishing in order to have time to tell about the experience to the other fishermen. He was also placed on the Fishermen's General Board as a person having considerable experience.
>
> Now it's true that many of the fishermen sacrificed and put up with all kinds of difficulties. Some lived near the water and bore the smell of dead fish every day. They received the ridicule of some who made fun of their fishermen's clubs and the fact that they claimed to be fishermen yet never fished. They wondered about those who felt it was of little use to attend the weekly meetings to talk about fishing. After all, were they not following the Master who said, "Follow me, and I will make you fishers of men"?
>
> Imagine how hurt some were when one day a person suggested that those who don't catch fish were really not fishermen, no matter how much they claimed to be. Yet it did sound correct. Is a person a fisherman if, year after year, he never catches a fish? Is one following if he isn't fishing?[2]

Evangelism involves everyone in the work.

Cop-out

Some believe that if the church is filled with sweet people and things are going well, evangelism just happens. Evangelism is not everything we do in church. Intentional, focused witness matters. Not everything in the church has to be explicitly evangelistic. In fact, many things won't be. However, I have seen too many churches call certain events or emphases evangelistic when they are not. Churches should give attention to explicitly evangelistic emphases and distinguish between those activities that are designed for evangelism and those that are not.

The worst example of this was a church where I preached years ago. The small rural church had baptized no one in years. The pastor showed me the crowning glory of his ministry—they had added a steeple! He called it "church growth." There is nothing wrong with a

[2] D. Robinson, *People Sharing Jesus* (Nashville: Thomas Nelson, 1995), 21–22.

steeple, but the adding of a physical structure enhances evangelism only when it leads to the evangelization of lost people!

Evangelism is the communication of the gospel by saved people to lost people. It is not inviting people to church or getting people to be religious. Evangelism, in its essence, is none of the above.

While pastor of the First Baptist Church of Pasadena, Texas, Darrell Robinson told the congregation he could not reach the masses for Christ; instead, it would take all the members' involvement. He particularly challenged the leadership, including the Sunday school director, Women's Missionary Union director, and others to participate in a lay witness training seminar. The WMU director told Robinson, "Pastor, I will come to the WIN Lay Evangelism School. I will learn how to teach our women to witness. But you must know this. I cannot witness myself. I have tried and failed. But I will learn how to teach others."

After the four nights of training, this woman's team and all the others went into the community to witness. She did not have the opportunity to witness. But God had given her a burden through the training for her beautician. At her next appointment she sat in the chair, flipping through an evangelistic tract.

The hairdresser asked, "What are you reading?"

"I'm reading a little booklet about Jesus. May I share it with you?"

They read through the booklet, and the hairdresser was interested, expressing her desire to be saved. How did the WMU director respond? She freaked out! She left, drove to the church, and rushed into Robinson's office in tears. She told her pastor the situation, pleading with him to go draw the net. Robinson said he would go, but only if she went as well. The two plus another man from the church visited the hairdresser and her husband. Within 30 minutes, both had given their lives to Christ! Then the new believer said something that changed the WMU director's life.

"You have invited me to church," the hairdresser said. "You have invited me to Sunday school. You have asked me to come hear your pastor preach. But you have never told me about Jesus. Why?"

The WMU director made a commitment to Christ at that moment to tell others about Christ. She eventually led her hairdresser's son, a neighbor, and then her own father to Jesus. From that time on, she continued to share Christ faithfully. She later noted three reasons she had failed to witness. First, she did not know God expected every

Christian to witness, thinking it was a job for specialists. Second, she didn't think she had a valid testimony. It was not sensational, so she thought no one would be interested. Finally, she simply did not know how. She needed someone to teach her.[3]

Biblical Terms

The Green Bay Packers had just lost to a team they should have easily defeated. Coach Vince Lombardi, football in hand, told his players, "Men, today we will get back to the basics—this is a football." Understanding the basics in evangelism begins with, and never moves past, the Word of God. A variety of terms demonstrate fully the New Testament teaching about evangelism.

Communicate Good News

The basic word for "evangelism" in the New Testament is the term transliterated into the English as "evangel" (noun) or "evangelize" (verb). The verb form is seen several ways. The term *euangelizō* means "I communicate good news." You can see the prefix *eu*, which means "good." Think of other words that begin with *eu*: "eulogy"—a good word spoken of someone at a funeral; "euphoria"—a good feeling. The main part of the word *evangelism* contains the English term "angel," a messenger. So to evangelize is to tell a good message. In the New Testament, the term implies a good message, as in a victory. While some people might attempt to make us feel as though evangelism imposes on the privacy of others, let us never forget we are telling the good news—Jesus has conquered sin, death, and the grave!

This verb form is found 33 times in the New Testament and is common in Luke's Gospel, the Acts, and Paul's Epistles. Often it is translated as "preach the gospel!" It is normally in the middle voice, which means, "I, myself, tell the gospel." Some examples of this verb (emphasis added):

- "The Spirit of the Lord is on Me, because He has anointed me to *preach good news* to the poor" (Luke 4:18).
- "For Christ did not send me to baptize, but to *preach the gospel*" (1 Cor 1:17).

The noun form is *euangelion* and is found 76 times in the New Testament. It can be translated "gospel," "good news," or "evangel."

[3] D. Robinson, *Total Church Life* (Nashville: Broadman and Holman, 1997), 177–78.

It emphasizes not just any good news but a specific message. Paul particularly used this term a great deal. Our primary message is the specific news that Jesus died and rose again. Paul told the Corinthians: "Moreover, brethren, I declare to you the gospel which I preached unto you" (1 Cor 15:1 KJV). He then summarized the gospel with the death, burial, and resurrection. There are two essential issues that confront every person: sin and death. On the cross Jesus dealt with the sin problem; in the empty tomb He defeated death. We have good news to share!

We see the verb and noun forms in Rom 1:15–16: "So I am eager to preach the good news to you also who are in Rome. For I am not ashamed of the gospel, because it is God's power for salvation to everyone who believes, first to the Jew, and also to the Greek."

We must recover evangelism as telling good news!

Another interesting use of this term is the expression *euangelistēs*. It is found three times in the New Testament and is translated "evangelist." Philip is called the evangelist (Acts 21:8). Ephesians 4:11 calls the "evangelist" (note, not evangel*ism*) one of the spiritual gifts. Paul exhorted Timothy (and all ministers) to do "the work of an evangelist" (2 Tim 4:5). So evangelism means we have a specific, victorious message to tell.

We need to make evangelism GOOD NEWS again. We seem to think it is bad news; otherwise we might talk about the gospel more. My friend Tom Johnston teaches at Midwestern Baptist Theological Seminary and has a background in French. He discovered years ago that our translations over the centuries have translated "evangelize" not as "share good news" but as "preach," which only causes believers to think more of our witness as something to be done by formal preachers. He also recognized that the Holman Christian Standard Bible, the one used in this text (and my preference), broke ranks with history and correctly translated this verb (see, for instance, Acts 8:25,35; 11:20). Accuracy in translation is important here because some may assume evangelism is solely the work of "preachers" by reading "preach" instead of "tell the good news."

Herald a Message

A second term is *kerussō* and its related forms. This verb form means "to proclaim in the manner of a herald." It implies the declaration of an event. The verb form is found 61 times in the New Testament. While not always referring to proclaiming the gospel, often it is used in that regard. In fact, at times *kerussō* and *euangelizomai* are used as synonyms, as in Rom 10:14–15. On 12 occasions the expression *kerussein to euangelion,* "preach the gospel," is found in the New Testament, showing the close relation between the terms.

The noun *kerygma* is found eight times in the New Testament. It means "the proclamation." This term has received special attention in the modern era due particularly to C. H. Dodd's book, *The Apostolic Preaching and Its Development.*

Witness or Testify

Notice the words translated *martureō* (verb) and *marturion* (noun). Today we think of a martyr as someone who died for the faith. The Greek word *martyr* literally means "a witness." The term is similar to the English word, for a witness was someone who gave testimony to things they had experienced. Peter declared, "We are unable to stop speaking about what we have seen and heard" (Acts 4:20). But a witness gave testimony through words and actions. Many early believers died because of their commitment to Christ, leading to the expression *martyr* to describe such faithful witnesses. For many early Christians, it was better to die than to stop testifying about Christ.

The reason many believers today do not attempt to share their faith is because they have gotten over their salvation! The early believers did not—indeed they could not—get past the radical transformation they experienced through the gospel.

Become Disciples, or Christ-Followers

Mathēteusate is the main verb in the Great Commission passage, Matt 28:19–20: "Go . . . and *make disciples*." The verb in this passage is an imperative, a command. The Great Commission is not the Great Suggestion! We are not merely to proclaim good news; we are to make disciples.

It is interesting that these terms can be seen in Great Commission passages in the Gospels and Acts:

- good news, gospel (Mark 16:15)
- proclaim (Mark 16:15; Luke 24:47)
- witness (Luke 24:48; Acts 1:8)
- make disciples (Matt 28:19)

On Defining "Evangelizing"

Thomas P. Johnston[1]

The late David Bosch, noted 20th-century missiologist, explained the general uncertainty in developing a precise definition of "evangelizing": "It remains difficult, however, to determine precisely what authors mean by evangelism or evangelization. Barrett lists 75 definitions, to which many more could be added. Broadly speaking, controversy prevails in two areas: the differences (if any) between 'evangelism' and 'mission,' and the scope or range of evangelism."[2]

Variations in defining "evangelizing" cover most of the theological world. However, if Bosch and friends could only read the word "evangelize" in their English (or German) Bibles, then some of their scholarly uncertainty may be assuaged.[3] The importance of using the English verb "evangelize" in Bible translation came to my attention over 20 years ago. In 1986, while concluding a course on "Introduction to Personal Evangelism" in the Netherlands, I had a brief but poignant discussion with the professor who was to teach the next modular course on follow-up and discipleship. He bantered, "Evangelism is found in the Gospels and the Book of Acts, but it is not found in the epistles." While puzzled at his comment, I could not answer his linguistic and methodological challenge. Years later I noticed that Paul actually did use the verb "evangelize" (Greek εὐαγγελίζω) 21 times in his epistles (with an additional two uses in Hebrews).

The 1987 book by David Barrett, *Evangelize! A Survey of the Concept*, commented on Wycliffe's use of the verb "evangelize":

> In 1382 in England, John Wycliffe completed the first translation of the whole Bible in the English language, using the Latin Vulgate. In the earlier of his two extant versions, Wycliffe translated almost all usages of the Latin *evangelizare* (and hence the Greek *euangelizein*) into the new English word "euangelisen" (in some orthographies, "evangelisen").[4]

---

[1] Written by T. P. Johnston, associate professor of Evangelism at Midwestern Baptist Theological Seminary; document in the hand of Alvin L. Reid, February 12, 2008.

[2] D. J. Bosch, *Transforming Mission: Paradigm Shifts in Theology of Mission* (Maryknoll, NY: Orbis, 1991), 409.

[3] It must be made clear that the word "evangelize" will always be the focal point of debate as it is the methodology that differentiates a historic Evangelical view of salvation from many other competing views. Each view of salvation with its corresponding ministry methodology has its own approach to the definition of "evangelizing." Thus a common scholarly definition is not only unlikely, but also virtually impossible.

[4] D. B. Barrett, *Evangelize! A Historical Survey of the Concept* (Birmingham, AL: New Hope, 1987), 22.

Further research revealed that Wycliffe's 1382 First Edition used the verb "evangelize" 36 out of the Latin Vulgate's 43 uses.[5]

As it turned out, in the 1388 Second Edition Wycliffe, revised after his death, 33 of the 36 uses of "evangelize" were changed to "preach" (all but Luke 1:19; 8:1; 16:16). Barrett explained that the change from "evangelize" to "preach" continued through William Tyndale's translation and "has been perpetuated in all subsequent [English] Bible translations up to the present day."[6] Moreover, the translation of the Greek εὐαγγελίζω as "preach" has a 600-year history in English Bibles, lexical materials, and commentaries, not to speak of books on practical ministry.

Barrett's helpful volume came to my attention while I taught at a French Bible school in Quebec. I noticed that my French translation (Nouvelle edition de Genève, 1979) used the verb "evangelize" twice (Acts 8:25,40). It was not until lexical study fifteen years later that I became aware that the Greek verb εὐαγγελίζω ("evangelize") was found 54 times in the Nestle-Aland critical tradition (55 in the Majority Text).

Researching 16th-century French translations led to a breakthrough:

- The 1522 French Catholic Jacques Lefebvre (strictly translated from the Latin Vulgate) used the verb "evangelize" 37 times
- The 1534 French Protestant Olivétan (translated from the Greek) used the verb "evangelize" 13 times
- The 1560 Protestant French Geneva (slight revision of the Olivétan) used the verb "evangelize" 24 times.

The 1560 French Geneva was a significant Protestant Bible as numerous Bible colporteurs were burned at the stake for bringing it into France, and it became the basis for the English Geneva and for Protestant Bibles in other languages. The question then follows, who added the 11 uses of the verb "evangelize" between the 1534 Olivétan and 1560 Geneva? In my research, three people revised the French Olivétan: Clément Marot, Théodore de Bèze, and John Calvin. It is amazing that these Reformers saw the importance of the verb "evangelize" to such an extent that they reinserted it into the French text.

[5] A two-column critical comparison of the two Wycliffe text histories, the 1382 First Edition and the 1388 Second Edition, was compiled by J. Forshall and F. Madden, *The Holy Bible, Containing the Old and New Testaments, with the Apocryphal Books, in the Earliest English Versions Made from the Latin Vulgate by John Wycliffe and His Followers* (Oxford: University Press, 1850).

[6] Barrett, *Evangelize!*, 22.

Unfortunately, the English Geneva had no uses of "evangelize," while the verb continues to be used in some French and Portuguese translations.

Among the 11 additions of the verb "evangelize" to the Olivétan were four of the six uses of the Greek verb εὐαγγελίζω in Galatians 1. Consider the power of the word "evangelize" in verses 8–9:

> *Or quand bien nous-mesmes, ou un Ange du ciel, vous evangelizeroit outre ce que nous vous avons evangelizé, qu'il soit execration. Ainsi que nous avons déja dit, maintenant aussi je [le] dis derechef, Si quelqu'un vous evangelize outre ce que vous avez receu, qu'il soit execration* (Galatians 1:8–9; Bible de Genève).[7]

> But when even we ourselves, or an angel from heaven, should evangelize you other than how we evangelized you, may he be excretion. As we have already said, so I say once again, if someone is evangelizing other than what you received, may he be excretion (Galatians 1:8–9; trans mine).

This passage in Galatians was important for Martin Luther. When he read his Bible before 1517, he read the Latin Vulgate, which used the verb *evangelizare,* a direct transliteration of the Greek. Imagine Martin Luther nailing the "95 Theses" on the Wittenberg Door against the evangelism methodology of Johann Tetzel, who was selling indulgences for the forgiveness of sins. When Luther looked at the Book of Acts, he found a completely different methodology for evangelizing—preaching the Gospel! It was God's use of "evangelizing" in Galatians 1:8–9, coupled with Tetzel's false evangelizing, that led Luther to protest Roman Catholicism's false methodology of evangelizing, thereby initiating the Protestant Reformation.

Yes, the verb "evangelize" is a powerful word. Since 1382 two English language Bible translations have one use each of the verb "evangelize": the 1884 English John Darby (Luke 3:18; by the way his French translation used "evangelize" 21 times) and the 1899 English Douais-Rheims (Luke 8:1). However, the 2000 Holman Christian Standard broke ranks from six centuries of virtual censorship of the verb "evangelize" in English Bibles by using the word six times (Acts 8:25,40; 14:7,21; 16:10; Rom 15:20). What a breakthrough![8]

---

[7] Bible de Genève; available at http://biblegeneve.com/nt1669 (accessed June 26, 2006).

[8] For further information, please see my entire set of notes on defining evangelizing (94 pages) available free at www.evangelismunlimited.org.

Perhaps the contemporary uncertainty in defining "evangelizing" will be aided as readers of the English Bible can now begin to see the word in its biblical context. Consider, for example, five of Paul's uses of the verb "evangelize" in the book of First Corinthians (all italicized for emphasis):

1. For Christ did not send me to baptize, but to *evangelize*, not in cleverness of speech, that the cross of Christ should not be made void (1 Cor 1:17, trans mine).
2. For if I *evangelize*, I have nothing to boast of, for I am under compulsion; for woe is me if I do not *evangelize*. For if I do this voluntarily, I have a reward; but if against my will, I have a stewardship entrusted to me (1 Cor 9:16–17, trans mine).
3. Now I make known to you, brethren, the gospel by which I *evangelized* you, which also you received, in which also you stand, by which also you are saved, if you hold fast the word by which I *evangelized* you, unless you believed in vain (1 Cor 15:1–2, trans mine).

Let's acknowledge, unleash, and obey this powerful verb![9]

[9] Ibid.

There are other words used at times in regard to evangelism, such as *laleō*, "I speak," or the times we read of Paul "reasoning" with others about the gospel, but the above are central to understanding the New Testament meaning of evangelism. Other expressions give insight into the message of the early church also. Followers of Christ were called to be fishers of men (Matt 4:18–22; Mark 1:16–20), salt of the earth (Matt 5:13); light of the world (Matt 5:14), fruit-bearers (John 15:8); and ambassadors (2 Cor 5:20).

Definitions

On the basis of these biblical terms, and considering the practice of the early church and of our Lord, we can determine a succinct definition of evangelism. Here are some definitions to consider:

Anglican

"To evangelize is so to present Christ Jesus in the power of the Holy Spirit, that men shall come to put their trust in God through Him, to accept Him as their Saviour, and serve Him as their Lord in the fellowship of His Church."[4] The last phrase was originally "serve Him as their *King*" but has been changed since its inception in 1918.

Lewis Drummond

Drummond, who taught evangelism for many years at The Southern Baptist Theological Seminary and Beeson Divinity School, as well as serving as president of Southeastern Baptist Theological Seminary, wrote many books on evangelism. He gave an excellent definition of *evangelism*:

> A concerted effort in the power of the Holy Spirit to confront unbelievers with the truth about Jesus Christ and the claims of our Lord with a view to leading unbelievers into repentance toward God and faith in our Lord Jesus Christ and, thus, into the fellowship of His church so they may grow in the Spirit.[5]

D. T. Niles

One of the most familiar, simple definitions came from D. T. Niles: "One beggar telling another where to get food [or bread, as some put it]." This definition is helpful in that it emphasizes the humility necessary for the believer to have when witnessing. We are not better than those to whom we witness; we have met Jesus, and He has changed us. The reason many unsaved people think those of us in the church *are* "holier than thou" in our attitude is because too many of us *are* holier than thou. However, this definition is weak in that it says nothing about the content of the bread that we share. Taken in its larger context in Niles's book, the definition is stronger; left alone, this comprises an incomplete definition.[6] If we forget what the "bread" is, as many have, we may have humility, but no message.

---

[4] *Commission on Evangelism* (Westminster, England: The Press and Publications Board of the Church Assembly, 1944), 1.

[5] L. Drummond, *The Word of the Cross* (Nashville: Broadman and Holman, 1992), 9.

[6] See D. T. Niles, *That They May Have Life* (New York: Harper and Brothers, 1951), 96.

The Church Growth Movement

The church growth movement influenced many in the latter half of the twentieth century. It offered a three-tiered look at the process of evangelism.[7] The three components are these:

- P-1, *Presence.* For example, agricultural, medical missions.
- P-2, *Proclamation.* Presenting the gospel in an understandable manner.
- P-3, *Persuasion.* Second Corinthians 5:11 encourages hearers to respond.

An analogy for this definition is a house. In *presence evangelism,* people's needs are met; they see a demonstration of the gospel, and, therefore, a foundation is built on which the gospel can be communicated. Because the church growth movement began on the mission field, its importance is obvious. Cross-cultural issues must be considered in a viable presentation of the gospel. Increasingly, in a post-Christian or even an anti-Christian culture in America, presence evangelism has a place. Servant evangelism (covered later) fits in nicely in our context. *Proclamation evangelism,* to continue the house analogy, allows the light of the gospel to penetrate through the windows. People not only need a foundation, but they also need direction. The gospel can never be presented by a demonstration only; there must also be a proclamation. Finally, *persuasion evangelism* leads people into the relationship they need with Christ. One can live in a house and not be family; by persuading people to follow Christ, we are inviting them to join God's family.

There are strengths and weaknesses to this definition. The weakness comes when believers define evangelism at the P-1 level only. We must build bridges, but we must also do more. Still others stop at the P-2 level. This definition is complete when we see it as a whole. That being said, it is positive in that when we are stopped short of a complete presentation of the gospel, we know we have at least provided some aspect of the gospel that the Holy Spirit can use. In other words, we should always seek to present Christ through presence, proclamation, and persuasion; but when we cannot, we can be thankful that on some level we have presented Christ.

---

[7] "Evangelism: P-1, P-2, P-3," in *Evangelism and Church Growth,* E. Towns, ed. (Ventura, CA: Regal Books, 1995), 212–16.

Campus Crusade for Christ

For many years the definition of evangelism by this parachurch group has been: "Presenting Jesus Christ in the power of the Holy Spirit and leaving the results to God." This definition has guided the witness of Campus Crusade for Christ, the largest parachurch organization on earth and one of the most evangelistic groups in Christian history. More recently, Darrell Robinson, in his book and seminar, *People Sharing Jesus*, has used this definition.

This simple definition has been liberating for a generation of witnesses. It emphasizes the vital role of the Holy Spirit in the witnessing encounter. It also recognizes that our job is to share Christ; God alone converts people. Too many believers fail to witness because they define successful witnessing as harvesting only, yet the New Testament says a great deal about planting and watering as well. As a friend once said to me, we must get people as excited about *fishing* as they are about *catching*. While our ultimate goal is always to win people to Christ, this definition reminds us that God expects us to be faithful. This is something that every believer can do.

I am convinced that God is less concerned about the number of people we win than the number of times we share the gospel. We cannot control the response of those to whom we witness; in fact, if a person is saved, it is because God saves them, not us! But we do have control over the number of times we share our faith. It is certainly appropriate for a church to set evangelism or baptismal goals; however, in the case of the individual believer, a better goal to set is the number of times to share the gospel with others.

> *I would define evangelism thus: Sharing the good news of Jesus Christ by word and life in the power of the Holy Spirit, so that unbelievers become followers of Jesus Christ in His church and in the culture.*

This takes the pressure off of us to win a certain number and allows us to share the pure gospel without compromise. But there is a better reason: *If* we share Christ often enough, we *will* lead someone to Christ! I have seen this over and over again in the lives of students who are required to do witness reports. *The reason many Christians have never won anyone to Christ is because they have witnessed very little. My prayer is that in the pages to come you will be encouraged and instructed in evangelism to the point that you will spend the rest of your life advancing God's movement on this earth.*

Questions for Consideration

1. How would you define evangelism?
2. How does your definition compare to what you have read?
3. What are your unchanging convictions concerning evangelism?
4. How are these convictions seen in your daily life?

Chapter 3

Why Do We Do the Things That We Do? Motives for Evangelism

If you want to build a ship, don't summon people to buy wood, prepare tools, distribute jobs, and organize the work; rather teach people the yearning for the wide, boundless ocean.[1]

—Antoine de Saint-Exupery

Why do you do the things you do? Why do you like certain books and not others, prefer one type of automobile to another, or enjoy certain people while avoiding others? We all have preferences in everything from sodas to music to sports teams. And, we have varying levels of passion for each. Why do we do the things we do?

Why are you reading this book? Are you passionate about the subject (hopefully), in awe of the author (hardly), forced to read it for a

[1] A. Hirsch, *Forgotten Ways: Reactivating the Missional Church* (Grand Rapids: Brazos Press, 2006), 27.

class (likely), or looking for a remedy for insomnia (my books are good for that)?

Enough questions, but I do think given the recalcitrance of so many believers to share their faith, the question of why we should be interested in sharing the good news matters. As our culture moves farther away from a neutral or positive attitude toward Christianity, the question of why matters more.

Evangelicals have made much of the vital place of evangelism. We have created an amazing array of approaches to tell the world about our Savior:

- Citywide "crusades"
- Church meetings from the creative to the cheesy, from vacation Bible school and wild game dinners to block parties and gimmicks, like the church that offered a chance to win a free car to visitors over a six-week period, which caused more than a few members and staff from neighboring churches to decide to visit!
- We have training methods with creative acrostics like EE, CWT, FAITH, WD40, ESPN (okay, I made up the last two).
- We have devised ways to get believers to become a contagious Christian, have a purpose-driven life, and even to make evangelism explode!

Surely there should be a connection between our motive and our methods. Why share Christ? Too much emphasis on evangelism has to do with the how-to. I mentioned in chapter 1 that Christianity is a movement. The best way to know your movement is in trouble is when all you do is create how-to manuals! For people to have a lasting commitment to something as personally challenging as evangelism, we need a clear understanding of the why before proceeding to the how.

Motives for Evangelism

Motives for witness can be categorized in a least two categories: the perspective of God and the perspective of man.

From the Perspective of God

While many motivations exist to share Christ and will be considered, the fundamental motive for all we do must start with God Himself. The Western church has too often seen Christianity as a means to personal fulfillment, a way to find "your best life now." I often remind my students that if you cannot preach what we do in Somalia or China where believers are oppressed, you should not preach it in the West because we are safe!

Many believers demonstrate a lack of passion for the gospel stemming from a consumer ethic. After all, sharing Christ will bring rejection. The gospel, no matter how winsomely you share it, will be a stumbling block to some and scandalous to others (see 1 Cor 1:23). So if you or I are driven by a Christianity that is fundamentally about our happiness, we will hardly be motivated to be rejected, which will happen if we share Christ faithfully.

The Character of God

Our motive for sharing Christ should start with God, not with either believers or those apart from Christ. As my friend Mark Liederbach puts it, "The supreme motivation for evangelism, then, finds its genesis in who evangelism is about and all other forms of motivation find deep and rich grounding and proper expression from that point alone."[2] Liederbach then quotes Michael Green on the motivation of the early church to witness in the face of persecution:

> There can be little doubt that the main motive for evangelism was a theological one. [The early Christians] did not spread their message because it was advisable for them to do so, nor because it was the socially responsible thing to do. They did not do it primarily for humanitarian or . . . utilitarian reasons. They did it because of the overwhelming experience of the love of God which they had received through Jesus Christ. The discovery that the ultimate force in the universe was Love, and that this Love had stooped to the very nadir of self-abasement for human good, had an effect on those who believed it which nothing could remove.[3]

I discovered this in my own life as a young, idealistic evangelism leader. At 29 I was given the responsibility of leading the Indiana State Baptist Convention in evangelism. I took that role very seriously, praying much for a greater love for the lost. I saw no change in the practice

[2] M. Liederbach, "Ethic Evaluations of Modern Motivations for Evangelism" (paper presented at the annual meeting of the Evangelical Theological Society; Valley Forge, PA, November 16, 2005).

[3] M. Green, *Evangelism in the Early Church* (Grand Rapids: Eerdmans, 1970), 236.

of my witness, however, until I focused less on the lost and their need and more on my Savior and His love. That motivated me!

As we will see in the next chapter, we cannot separate the Great Commission in Matt 28:18–20 from God's command in Gen 1:26–28. When we grasp the amazing reality that the God of creation invites us to worship Him, that motivates us to see others become such worshippers as well. We share Christ because God is glorious, like no other, and we can share this amazing news with others. We have shrink-wrapped our concept of God to a few brief statements while over and over in Scripture we encounter His majesty.

The Love of God

God desires that people be saved (Luke 15:2; 2 Pet 3:9). During my first year in Wake Forest, we had one of the most severe winters in decades. Snow and ice were our constant companions. One week, after days of no first-grade classes for my son, Josh, he and I sought to rescue our family from cabin fever by renting a video. While I searched for a tape, he perused the video games. Unknown to me, Josh saw a man through the window walking up the sidewalk in a coat like mine. He left the store in pursuit of the person he thought was me.

Realizing the man was not his dad, Josh panicked. He walked farther up the sidewalk, being so afraid that I had disappeared that he forgot to consider going back to the video store. By this time, I realized he was not in the store, and I got nervous. Several minutes passed, and Josh was nowhere to be found. I prayed for my son's safety. Josh was outside a store, crying and praying. About that time, two ministers from our church found him. We were so glad to be reunited. Why was I so concerned about Josh? Because he is my son; he means more than life to me. His lostness hurt me deeply because I love him so much. One need only to turn to John 3:16 to see that our Father in heaven wants lost people to be saved. Or read Rom 5:6–8 or any number of New Testament passages. The need of a lost world resulted in the death of the Son of God.

Delos Miles reminds us of the place of evangelism in the plan of God: "Evangelism is not an isolated side show of history."[4] Evangelist D. L. Moody imagined every person he met as though that person had a large "L" in the midst of his forehead. Moody considered people lost until he knew they were saved!

[4] D. Miles, *Introduction to Evangelism* (Nashville: Broadman and Holman, 1981), 138.

The Greek word for "lost" is from the *apollumi/apololōs* word group. It describes a thing not used or claimed. Luke 15 describes what it means to be lost—the lost sheep, the lost coin, and the lost son. All signify value, something worth finding. In the case of the sheep, lostness meant being subjected to being taken by a wild beast or stolen by a thief, or wandering away and starving. In the case of the coin, it meant that it would not be able to fulfill its purpose for being created. In the case of the lost son, it meant wasting his inheritance, wasting his life, and missing the intimate relationship of his family.

Miles noted the progressive nature of the son's lostness. First, he rebelled against his father and sold his birthright for money. Second, he left home for a faraway country. Third, he wasted his money in a riotous life. Fourth, he faced a severe famine. Fifth, he became more like the hogs that he fed than the man that he was.[5] When the New Testament refers to people as lost, it is not a derogatory term. It means people are of value. In fact, people are worth the life of Jesus, the Son of God (Luke 19:10).

Personal evangelism is primary in the plan of God to reach lost people. This is obvious in the practice of the early church. Jesus won Andrew, who told Peter (John 1:40–42). Jesus won the woman at the well, who told others in the city (John 4:29). Therefore, personal evangelism is the single most effective way to reach the world for Christ. Every class taught at our seminary in the field of evangelism places personal evangelism at the heart of all we do. In our required courses, we expect our students to attempt to share Christ one-on-one each week.

Why is evangelism important? Because, it is important to God! He did not spare His Son for you and me! Should not our priorities be similar to his?

> *William Booth,* founder of the Salvation Army, to the king of England: "Sir, some men's passion is for gold, other men's passion is for fame, but my passion is for souls."
>
> *A. T. Pierson:* "There is a secret fellowship with God where we get His heavenly fire kindled within. . . . To linger in God's presence until we see souls, as through His eyes, makes us long over them with a tireless longing."
>
> *Oswald J. Smith:* "Never will I be satisfied until God works in convicting power and men and women weep their way to the

[5] Ibid., 141.

cross. . . . Oh that He would break me down and cause me to weep for the salvation of souls."[6]

From the Perspective of the Believer

When we properly see evangelism's motives come from the character of God, other motivations matter as well. John Piper observes: "Missions exists because worship does not."[7] Understanding that helps us to see other motivating factors that may be secondary to the wonder and worship of God but are at the same time both biblical and helpful.

Obedience

The God we serve expects His children to fulfill His purposes. In our consumer culture, where even the church has a "what's-in-it-for-me?" attitude, we must raise the standard of serving God out of a heart of obedience. I have made it a practice for all but about three years of the last two decades to read the Bible through each year. After almost twenty years of reading the whole counsel of God's Word, one thing that jumps out as critical throughout the Scriptures is the importance of heeding and obeying what God says. Again, the Great Commission is not the Great Suggestion.

Liederbach refers to this as the deontological motivation. He notes that motivation by duty, when rightly placed underneath the worship of God, has merit. It also has dangers; if one misapplies the motivation, it can become legalism. After all, telling someone to do something because "you are supposed to" is a better motivation for a child who has much to learn than an adult who should understand duty. A greater motivation should captivate the imagination of worshipers of the King of kings! But we do need to be reminded at times there is an "oughtness" to our faith. Rules matter; relationships are better. I expect my children to obey me, but I hope they do so out of love and respect for me over a mere sense of duty, particularly as they mature.

Andrew Murray said there are two kinds of Christians: soul-winners and backsliders. A born-again child of God cannot take seriously his or her relationship to Christ without dealing with the issue

---

[6] Quotes taken from W. Duewel, *Ablaze for God* (Grand Rapids: Zondervan, 1989), 108, 111, 116, respectively.

[7] J. Piper, *Let the Nations Be Glad: The Supremacy of God in Missions* (Grand Rapids: Baker, 1993), 11.

of evangelism. Evangelism is important to those of us who follow Jesus because of the critical role that obedience plays in our spiritual growth.

James Eaves, one of my evangelism professors at Southwestern Seminary, used to say that two barriers keep many Christians from going further in their walk with God: tithing and soul-winning. Why? They affect two things that matter so much—our comfort in material things and our reputation. Crossing these barriers requires faith, without which it is impossible to please God (Heb 11:6).

Remember Samuel's conversation with Saul? Saul disobeyed God and spared the king. Then he kept some of the livestock as well. When Samuel confronted Saul, what did Saul do? He blamed the people for his own disobedience. How did Samuel reply? "To obey is better than sacrifice" (1 Sam 15:22). But he went further: "For *rebellion* is like the sin of divination" (1 Sam 15:23). Unfortunately, we consider really bad sins those that other people commit. But Samuel said disobedience puts us in the same boat with those involved in the occult. Is any sin worse than disobedience of God?

But there is a positive side to this. I believe many believers want to obey Christ. They want to grow spiritually. Many don't witness because of their sense of inadequacy. The good news is that any believer can be obedient. We may be varied in gifts, abilities, and time, but we can all obey. And only God knows the impact we can make.

Let me give you a little quiz.

- Who was the theological advisor to Martin Luther, inspiring him to translate the New Testament into German?
- Who was the Sunday school teacher who led Dwight L. Moody to Christ?
- Who was the elderly woman who prayed faithfully for Billy Graham for over twenty years?
- Who funded William Carey's ministry in India?
- Who encouraged the apostle Paul in a Roman dungeon as he wrote his last letter to Timothy?
- Who discovered the Dead Sea Scrolls?

OK, did you pass? Had it not been for those unknown people, church history might tell a different story.

Jim Elliot, the martyred messenger of the gospel to the Auca Indians, once called missionaries "a bunch of nobodies trying to exalt Somebody." If God uses you as a Melanchthon (not a Luther), as a

Kimball (not a Moody), as an Onesiphorus (rather than a Paul), it's OK. The bottom line: God will use you if you make yourself usable. It's the "nobodies" whom Somebody chooses so carefully. And when He has selected you for a task, you are a somebody, never a nobody.[8] Be encouraged! You can obey God, and this book will offer many insights into how He will empower you to do so.

My hunch is that you came to Christ because of the impact of other people. While only the death of Jesus can provide for our salvation, we owe a debt to those who shared the message with us. Paul declared, "I am a debtor both to Greeks and to barbarians, both to wise and to unwise. So, as much as is in me, I am *ready* to preach the gospel to you who are in Rome also" (Rom 1:14–15 NKJV). "Ready," *prothumon*, literally means "on fire." Roy Fish says Paul had "holy heartburn." Our own sense of gratitude for the witness of others should encourage us to have that same impact in the lives of others. The Lord warned the prophet Ezekiel that he was accountable to warn others of their sin (see Ezek 33:8).

Spiritual Growth

When we witness, we take giant steps toward spiritual maturity. Christian growth is linked to discipline and surrender. We need Sea of Galilee Christians. The Sea of Galilee flows into the Jordan River. It is beautiful, filled with fish. The Jordan flows into the Dead Sea but not out. The Dead Sea is stagnant, lifeless, self-contained. Nothing is more pathetic than Christians whose lives are characterized by spiritual navel-gazing—totally introverted. Too many believers seem bored to death with their faith. Taking no risks, doing little for eternity, focusing on preserving their institution, there is no wonder so many live lives empty of passion!

Sharing Christ motivates a person to study Scripture because of the issues raised by lost people. It burns with a burden for people blinded by the gods of this world, eliciting a desire to pray. In my experience, some of the most exciting, dynamic, and evangelistic believers are those who began witnessing soon after conversion. One of the best things you can do for a new believer is to involve him immediately in sharing his faith.

Our lives should be marked by gratitude for salvation. Jesus taught that he who is forgiven much loves much (see Luke 7:47). Paul's

---

[8] Adapted from C. R. Swindoll, *Growing Strong in the Seasons of Life* (Portland: Multnomah Press, 1984), 87–88.

unashamed courage about the gospel in Rom 1:16–17 is linked to his sense of indebtedness. When the focus stays on our great God and His work of salvation, gratitude can spur us to good works, as we often see, for example, in the Gospels. But like obedience, our gratitude can create a "debtor's ethic" if we are not careful. We can believe we owe God and must work to repay the debt, creating an unbiblical, works-based attitude.

Eternal Rewards

Christians will be rewarded at judgment based on our service to God (1 Cor 3:11–15). Paul also tells us we will all stand before the judgment seat *(bēma)* of Christ (2 Cor 5:10–11). In this judgment of believers, we will give an account of how we served God. This is a judgment of service, not salvation. Our salvation comes by the complete mercy and grace of God. But we are to serve Christ with a goal of growing effectiveness (Phil 3:12–14). Paul writes that the things we have done will be judged to be good or evil (2 Cor 5:10). The word translated "evil" can also mean "worthless" or "trivial."

I like to use the analogy of standing before the Lord with a DVD of my life. First, the Lord shows a documentary of my life, demonstrating how I served Him. Then, a second tape is viewed. This tape depicts what my life *would have been* had I served the Lord with all my heart. My aim is that the two tapes will not be too different! This thought motivates me almost daily to faithfulness.

Further, the rewards we receive are not measured by human accounting. Greatness is related to serving the Lord, especially when no one is looking. That's really the test of greatness. On a cold, wintry night, Paul Keating was walking home in Manhattan's Greenwich Village. The twenty-seven-year-old saw two armed men assaulting a college student. A much-admired photographer for *Time* magazine, Keating had every reason to avoid trouble. He was outmanned, the student was a stranger, and he had nothing to gain. Yet he tried to rescue the young student. The victim escaped and ran to call for help. Paul Keating was found dead on the pavement from two gunshot wounds. The city of New York posthumously awarded Keating a medal of heroism. Mary Egg Cox authored an apt eulogy at the ceremony: "Nobody was watching Paul Keating on the street that night, nobody made him step forward in the time of crisis. He did it because of who he was."[9] If we are faithful in witnessing, who we are

[9] M. Lucado, *The Applause of Heaven* (Waco: Word, 1996), 74.

transcends the things that we do. The reward for such a life cannot be measured in this life alone.

Evangelism and Unbelievers

The reality that all outside of Christ are without hope for salvation and face certain judgment should move believers to witness as well. Liederbach refers to this as the utilitarian motive. Again, this motive should flow from the goodness and greatness of God, and when it does we can develop a biblical burden for those outside of Christ like Paul had in Rom 9:1–3. Living witnesses proclaim the gospel by personally sharing, through preaching, and by ministering to others so they will hear our words. We are God's plan A, and God has no plan B. If we see that as a great honor, that this God who created the universe would use the likes of you and me in this great endeavor, it properly motivates us. If we focus on the consequences too much, it becomes motivation by guilt. "If I don't share, they may not know." At one level that is exactly right (Rom 10:14: How will they hear without a preacher?). However, we must balance that reality with the awareness that each person will give an account for himself to God. If unbalanced, this otherwise healthy motive can lead to an ends-justifies-the-means attitude that unintentionally robs God of the glory due His name.

People are the objects of divine love: "For while we were still helpless, at the appointed moment, Christ died for the ungodly. For rarely will someone die for a just person—though for a good person perhaps someone might even dare to die. But God proves His own love for us in that while we were still sinners Christ died for us!" (Rom 5:6–8). We are created in the image of God, and according to Jesus, one soul is worth more than all the accumulated wealth of the world (see Mark 8:36).

Christopher Hancock came to Southeastern Seminary for a lecture series. At the time he served as vicar of the Holy Trinity Church, Cambridge, England. In the 1980s, Chris was a member of the faculty at Magdalene College, Cambridge. When he moved into his office, one formerly occupied by a theology professor, he noticed a dull, brown rug. The bookshelves were a wretched pale green. He had the shelves repainted, but the awful rug remained. He asked that the rug be removed, but the request was repeatedly denied. One day he saw the theology professor who had used the office earlier. Chris commented about the wretched rug. "It belonged to C. S. Lewis," the professor remarked. Suddenly the carpet's value increased! Then a rug expert valued the Persian rug at $250,000! Do we treat lost people for whom Christ died like an old rug? Is there anything more valuable than a soul?

Future Joy or Future Judgment

Only God knows the long-term impact of our witness. We know the eternal significance, for there is heaven to gain for those changed by the gospel. In this life, every believer in Jesus can be used by God to touch the lives of others. When Billy Graham was converted under the ministry of evangelist Mordecai Ham in a crusade in Graham's hometown of Charlotte, North Carolina, no one knew for certain he would become the great evangelist of the twentieth century. Before his conversion, however, Billy's father and a group of godly businessmen prayed that "out of Charlotte the Lord would raise up someone to preach the Gospel to the ends of the earth."[10]

Evangelist D. L. Moody is another example. How could Edward Kimball, the Sunday school teacher who led Moody to Christ, have ever known the potential of the uneducated, young shoe salesman? How could that preacher, a stand-in on a frozen winter day at the little Methodist chapel, have known the impact of the young Charles Spurgeon when he challenged the youth to "look to Jesus"?

Not everyone we lead to Christ will have the impact of these men, but some will. Never underestimate the impact an individual can make for Christ. Every person was created for a purpose—a purpose that will never be realized apart from a relationship with God through Christ. The most significant aspect of that purpose is stated in the Westminster Catechism: "to glorify God and enjoy Him forever."

Mike Woody gave his testimony at the 1997 meeting of the Southern Baptist Convention in Dallas, Texas. Woody had spent years in jail and had basically wasted his life. At one point he prayed, "God, show me you are real." A Christian cellmate tore his Bible in half and gave it to Woody. Ultimately he came to Christ and began to win others. Now, released from prison, he leads a significant ministry to street people and others in Fort Worth. Listen to his discovery: "I never dreamed I could be part of something good in the lives of other people." Mike Woody has learned the potential of one lost soul.

There is another side to the good news. Hell seems so far from our culture, but it is close to the heart of Scripture. The most consistent

---

[10] D. Lockard, *The Unheard Billy Graham* (Waco: Word, 1971), 13.

preacher on the subject of hell in the Bible was Jesus Himself. He taught, preached, and ministered with an awareness of the lostness of people and the reality of judgment.

Lostness means emptiness. Lillian Veles, who also gave her testimony at the 1997 Southern Baptist Convention, came to Christ from a life of sin. "Every time I spoke to myself," she recorded of her life before Christ, "I only heard myself. But after I came to Christ, there was God in my life." The emptiness, the lostness, was replaced by intimacy with God.

While more will be said in a later chapter about the reality of hell, suffice it to say that helping others to flee the wrath to come has been a motivating factor in the lives of many. John Wesley formed entire societies for those who sought to follow Christ and flee impending judgment. Jonathan Edwards warned his listeners of the "justice of God in the damnation of sinners" and the plight of "sinners in the hands of an angry God."

A Starting Point for Motivation

Jim Eaves taught me a simple exercise that has helped me to demonstrate the lostness of people. We have lost that sense of utter lostness a person faces apart from Christ. Let me encourage you to try this in your place of ministry. It is best done in a Wednesday or Sunday evening service or in a small-group study.

Have the group turn to Ephesians 2. Then divide them into two groups. If you have a large number, make several small groups and divide them into two categories. Have the first group read Ephesians 2 to note every reference related to this statement: "What It Means to Be Lost." It is staggering to see all the references in only one chapter in the Bible. Have the second group examine the same text to discover "What It Means to Be Saved." After giving the groups 10 to 15 minutes to study the text, have them report their results, using an overhead, marker board, or a chalkboard to report the findings so all can see them. Draw two columns to compare the groups. Make a list of the statements, which will include the following:

- Dead in trespasses
- Walked according to the world
- Disobedient

- Lust of the flesh
- Children of wrath

As they do this, note the stark, destitute state of lost people. Remind them that their neighbor, who may be a good, decent person, is "without hope," "at enmity with God," "far off," and so forth. That family member who seems so moral is "dead in sin"; those coworkers who give to charitable causes are "without God" unless they have met Christ. I have used this many times, and it has proven to be very effective in raising people's awareness about the lostness of people.

Then list "What It Means to Be Saved." The difference between the two lists is striking. Remind the people that there should be just such a difference between saved and lost people today—not because we are better but because God has changed us! This should result in a greater sense of gratitude for salvation.

Questions for Consideration

1. What motivates you to speak about Jesus to others?
2. What keeps you from being motivated to witness?
3. What keeps your church from being motivated to share Christ?

Chapter 4

The Mission of God: A Missional Reading of Scripture

A missional hermeneutic, then, is not content simply to call for obedience to the Great Commission (though it will assuredly include that as a matter of nonnegotiable importance), nor even to reflect on the missional implications of the Great Commandment. For behind both it will find the Great Communication—the revelation of the identity of God, of God's action in the world and God's saving purpose for all creation. And for the fullness of this communication we need the whole Bible in all its parts and genres, for God has given us no less. A missional hermeneutic takes the indicative and the imperative of the biblical revelation with equal seriousness, and interprets each in the light of the other.[1]

—Christopher Wright

[1] C. J. H. Wright, *The Mission of God* (Downers Grove, IL: InterVarsity Press, 2006), 61–62.

A pastor search committee interviewed a recent seminary graduate. The candidate was young, and the committee wondered about his level of Bible knowledge. The chairman of the committee asked the student, "Do you know the Bible?"

"Of course," he replied, "I just graduated from seminary!"

"Then tell us a story of the Bible—how about the 'Good Samaritan'?" replied the chairman.

"No problem," said the pastoral candidate.

"There was a man of the Samaritans named Nicodemus. He went down to Jerusalem by night, and he fell among the stony ground, and the thorns choked him half to death.

"So he said, 'What shall I do? I will arise and go to my father's house.' So he arose and climbed up into a sycamore tree. The next day the three wise men came and got him and carried him to the ark for Moses to take care of him. But, as he was going into the eastern gate into the ark, he caught his hair in a limb, and he hung there for forty days and forty nights. Afterward he was hungry, and the ravens came and fed him.

"The next day he caught a boat and sailed down to Jerusalem. When he got there he saw Delilah sitting on a wall, and he said, 'Chunk her down, boys!' They said, 'How many times shall we chunk her down, until 7 times 7?' 'No, not until 7, but 70 times 7.'

"So they threw her down 490 times, and she burst asunder in their midst, and they picked up 12 baskets of the fragments that were there. In the resurrection, whose wife will she be?"

The committee sat stunned. They conferred briefly, then the chairman spoke to the seminary graduate. "Well, young man, we are going to recommend you as our next pastor. You may be young, but you sure know your Bible!"

The frightening thing is that I have told this story in churches, and they didn't get it! Faithful understanding of the Bible is critical to evangelism.

One of the reasons evangelism has waned in its place in the contemporary church comes from the way we have compartmentalized it into a program or department in a local church, or an occasional activity in the life of the believer. This starts from the very way we see Scripture. If for you or me the commission to tell the good news to the world comes only from a few passages in the Gospels and the start of Acts (as vital as those are), we can easily push the witness of the church to the side. But what if the message of redemption, and the spreading of that message, was central to the whole of Scripture? Our approach to Scripture has much impact on the conclusions we draw. We must give much attention to understanding the whole counsel of God's Word, not just an occasional story here or memory verse there.

The Bible gives us our authority for evangelism. Drummond notes the close relationship between redemption in the Bible and contemporary evangelism. "If redemption truly is the heartbeat of the Bible, the church's responsibility of sharing the message of salvation rests right at the center of her ministry."[2] A direct correlation exists between one's view of Scripture and one's commitment to evangelism.[3] A high view of Scripture leads to a deep commitment to reaching people! We must acknowledge and obey the Word of God. Some neglect the authority of Scripture with tragic results. Some who respect the Bible neglect its teaching. We must affirm both its authority and its sufficiency.

Evangelism in the Pentateuch

Although Jesus declared the Great Commission in the New Testament, evangelism's song rings throughout Scripture. The theme of redemption forms the melody sounding throughout the Word of God, from creation to consummation!

Oxford scholar Christopher Wright recalls his childhood when he attended great missionary conventions. There the walls were covered with banners declaring great missionary passages—Matt 28:19–20; Isaiah 6; Acts 1:8; and so on. Those verses burned in his heart and mind a passion for the gospel. Something different happened when he attended Cambridge to study theology. He found a serious disconnect between those passages from the missionary conventions and his theological studies, which ignored those texts. "*Theology* was all about God—what God was like, what God had said and done, and what mostly dead people had speculated on all three," he observed. "*Mission* was about us, the living, and what we have been doing."[4] The two subjects never seemed to be linked.

[2] L. Drummond, *The Word of the Cross* (Nashville: Broadman and Holman, 1992), 67.

[3] See J. Avant, "The Relationship of the Changing Views of the Inspiration and Authority of Scripture to Evangelism and Church Growth: A Study of the United Methodist Church and the Southern Baptist Convention in the United States Since World War II" (PhD. Dissertation, Southwestern Baptist Theological Seminary, 1990).

[4] Wright, *The Mission of God*, 21–22.

Wright stated that the chief reason why this spiritual schizophrenia that splits theology and mission even exists is because we do not read the Bible as a missiological text. He argued that we should speak less of a "biblical basis of missions" (as if the missional endeavor of the church was just one of many possible things the church can be involved in) and more of the "missional basis of the Bible." This is a point worth pondering. Is *mission* one of a cafeteria of disciplines vying for the interest of ministers, scholars, and believers? Would we be right to, as some have done, make the telling of the news of redemption simply one compartmentalized part of the church, based on essentially one passage (Matt 28:19–20), or is there more?

An Old Testament theologian, Wright stated, "I wanted [my students] to see not just that the Bible contains a number of texts which happen to provide a rationale for missionary endeavor but that *the whole Bible is itself a 'missional' phenomenon.*"[5]

"The Bible renders to us the story of God's mission through God's people in their engagement with God's world for the sake of the whole of God's creation." * *—Christopher Wright*

* *Wright,* The Mission of God, *21–22.*

Wright argued that the very hermeneutic by which we interpret the Bible from Genesis to Revelation, from creation to consummation, is mission. I think he is correct. So as we journey all too briefly through the Scriptures to see the place of evangelism in its pages, I believe the theme of redemption and the sharing of that theme is a hallmark of the Bible, not a few verses at the end of the Gospels.

Could it be that the very way we have approached the Scriptures is part of our problem? Could it be that the separation of our witness from all of life stems more from an institutional reading of the Word, rather than reading it as our guide for advancing the movement of God? As my friend Mark Liederbach and I put it in *The Convergent Church,* when the church fails to emphasize the missional thrust of its purpose, or does not connect it to the final end of glorifying God, "the result inevitably will be a loss of moral vigor, a decline in motivation for outreach, a gradual waning of passion through time, and often an increase of squabbling over nonessentials and divisions related to the trivial."[6]

---

[5] Ibid., 22.

[6] M. Liederbach and A. L. Reid, *The Convergent Church: Missional Worship in an Emerging Culture* (Grand Rapids: Kregel, 2009), 144.

The book of Genesis demonstrates our need for a Savior. The first question in the Bible demonstrates the evangelistic heart of God: "Adam, where are you?" From creation onward we see the missionary heart of God. These words from Mark Liederbach illustrate succinctly the importance of the whole Bible in understanding the Great Commission:

> The Great Commission of Genesis 1:26–28 overlaps perfectly with the Great Commission of Christ in Matthew 28:18–20. The relationship with God through Christ is not only the reestablishing of the proper foundation of our personal lives but it also becomes the missional purpose of our life together and existence as the body of Christ. Every moment of our personal lives is meant to be a convergence of personal worship of the King and personal effort to expand his kingdom. Every moment of our life together as the body is meant to be a convergence of corporate worship of the King and a communal effort to enjoy and expand his kingdom here and blossom in it in an ever-increasing eternity of joy.[7]

I taught Old Testament at Houston Baptist University in the 1990s. I recall how some students who had never read the Bible responded to the creation account in Genesis. They tended to comment on its brevity and its beauty. We see in Genesis 1 a panoramic overview of the world God made—perfect, designed, interrelated, and wonderful. Genesis 1:26–28 shows man to be the pinnacle of creation, being made in the image of God. Further, God gave man a task, unlike the rest of Creation, to "be fruitful, multiply, fill the earth, and subdue it" (Gen 1:28).[8] We see a more specific focus on man in the narrative of Genesis 2. God gave Adam a "helper" in Eve and placed them in the garden of Eden "to cultivate it and keep it" (Gen 2:15 NASB). What does this last phrase mean? John Sailhamer argued that this means more than simply the physical labor of tending the ground: "Man is put in the garden to worship God and to obey him," Sailhamer observed. "Man's life in the garden was to be characterized by worship and obedience."[9]

---

[7] Ibid., 132.

[8] Read about this in greater detail in Liederbach and Reid, *Convergent Church*, 120–36. I am indebted to Mark Liederbach for his analysis of this passage.

[9] J. H. Sailhamer, "Genesis," in *The Expositor's Bible Commentary*, vol. 2, *Genesis, Exodus, Leviticus, Numbers*, ed. W. C. Kaiser and B. K. Waltke (Grand Rapids: Regency, 1990), 45.

We find Adam and Eve in the garden, the pinnacle of creation, ready to worship and serve God like nothing else in all creation. I have a friend who uses animals to demonstrate the wonder of creation. As he explains the unique features of an alligator or an owl that allows them to function uniquely in this world, my friend repeats the mantra, "Animals do what they were created to do, and they do it well." He then notes the impact of the fall as recorded in Genesis 3 by noting that the only thing in creation that does not do what it was created to do is man. Why? Man, who was created in the image of God with the capacity to worship Him chose instead to sin and rebel. Thus, the creation account in Genesis gives us much more than an introduction to God's Word; it actually relates to the gospel and this to our effective proclamation. When Paul began to explain the wonder of salvation in Romans he begins with creation (read Romans 1: our versions of the "Roman Road" in witnessing tend to leave this out). We must increasingly proclaim the good news in the larger sense of the story of redemption—creation, fall, redemption, and consummation. Such a broader look at the gospel will give us a greater appreciation for its majesty and help us to communicate better in an increasingly biblically illiterate world.

This reality causes us to face an important fact. If worship of the Creator stands as the *created purpose* behind life, if it is to be the drive behind each and every act of our lives, if it is the future and final glorious fulfillment of all creation, then it is imperative that no one be without opportunity to join us in this journey. Witness and worship go together! Likewise it matters that no corner of creation be exempt from exposure to the glory of God. Thus, the mission of our life must be continually shaped and reshaped by the mission of God, the very thing God created Adam and Eve for: worshipping God and spreading that worship to the uttermost reaches of creation. Our desire should be to see the nations worship, as we read at the end of Scripture:

> After this I looked, and there was a vast multitude from every nation, tribe, people, and language, which no one could number, standing before the throne and before the Lamb. They were robed in white with palm branches in their hands. And they cried out in a loud voice:
>
> Salvation belongs to our God,
> who is seated on the throne,
> and to the Lamb! (Rev 7:9–10)

Thus, a close connection lies between God's purpose in creating the universe and this commission Jesus commanded His church to pursue. All nations are to have the opportunity to worship the King of kings. God's people must spread this news, and it is indeed good news! From the beginning, God desired that His people would fill the earth with the worship of His great name. We now have the possibility not only of personally experiencing a right relationship with God and proper orientation toward the purpose of our existence, but we also see the purpose for how to live both individually and corporately.

In the words of Piper, "Worship, therefore, is the fuel and goal of missions. It's the goal of missions because in missions we simply aim to bring the nations into the white-hot enjoyment of God's glory. Missions is not the ultimate goal of the church. Worship is."[10] I would only add that we cannot have one without the other. Both matter throughout the pages of the Word and in our lives today.

Genesis 3:9 shows a redeeming God seeking His estranged creation. The first 11 chapters of Genesis reveal why man is so important to God and why the salvation of humanity becomes the dominant theme of Scripture. Even when God judged Adam and Eve for their sin, we see His grace. The *protoevangelium,* Gen 3:15, shows the early sign of the gospel: "I will put hostility between you and the woman, and between your seed and her seed. He will strike your head, and you will strike his heel." This singular verse is pregnant with New Testament truth. The passage relates to evangelism in at least five ways:

1. The expression "he will strike your head" shows the grace of God in that the Father gave a promise to Eve that her seed would triumph.
2. The same phrase initiates the promise of the ultimate defeat of Satan, remembering that one of the reasons for Jesus' incarnation was to "destroy the works of the devil" (1 John 3:8 NKJV).
3. Salvation comes through a mediator. This mediator will be directly related to humanity, being the "seed of woman."
4. This salvation comes through the suffering of the seed of woman, whose heel will be bruised.
5. Salvation is available to the whole race, for Eve is the mother of all living. All racial prejudices and bigotry should end with this passage, for if Eve is the mother of all living, then we are

[10] See Liederbach and Reid, *Convergent Church,* 132.

> all kin. In the earliest pages of the Bible, we find ample evidence for the necessity of cross-cultural evangelism.

The fall changed things:

> Prior to human sin and the fall, the task of spreading God's glory to all the earth was simply and inherently bound up with the life and experience of Adam and Eve. Because of sin, however, the human heart is no longer naturally inclined toward the heart of God or the fulfillment of his agenda. Even in the lives of God's people, the task of spreading God's glory to all the earth is constantly in danger of being pushed aside in favor of personal desires, comforting traditions, selfish longings and ambitions, and theological systems that fail to integrate the pursuit of God's glory with the aggressive proclamation of the good news of Jesus Christ.[11]

The flood gives us another picture of evangelism. In the midst of a godless people, Noah lived righteously. The ark is a picture of God's desire to save the world, for the righteous were not taken in the deluge. Further, the grace of God shines in the brightness of the rainbow. God delivered the righteous, even as He will deliver any person made righteous through the atoning work of Christ. What a glorious gospel we share!

By the end of Genesis 11, the reader can see the devastation of sin: murder, intrigue, idolatry, rampant ungodliness, and the judgment of God. Beginning with Genesis 12, we read of God's unfolding plan to redeem humanity. Abraham is told all humanity will be blessed through his seed. One Gospel writer tells us succinctly that Jesus is "the Son of Abraham" (Matt 1:1). Certain themes resound with the redemptive intent of God.

In Exodus we see further gospel truth. The Exodus event became the great salvific moment in the Old Testament. It is recalled over and over again throughout the books of the Old Testament, reminding the people of God's power to save. It was not by accident that Jesus also traveled to Egypt as a child and came out as well. Nor did Luke accidently use the word "exodus" in his account of the transfiguration of Jesus. Luke tells us Jesus discussed with Moses and Elijah His *exodus* (Luke 9:31 NLT), referring to His death and resurrection that would allow us to pass, not through a sea, but from death to life.

---

[11] Ibid., 130.

The covenant at Sinai was where God told His people they were to be a "kingdom of priests" (Exod 19:6). A priest was to point others to God, intercede on behalf of others, and teach the redemption of God to all people. The fact that Israel did not always fulfill this command did not take away their obligation to tell the nations about the only true God.

The Commandments (the Law) gave the standard of a holy God. Galatians tells us the law shows us how we need the gospel. Even as a person cannot be saved apart from recognizing his lost state, we cannot comprehend grace apart from the standard of the law of God. However, merely keeping the Ten Commandments cannot save. Even in the Old Testament, they were given to God's covenant people.

In Leviticus, the sacrificial system modeled the means of redemption. Hebrews 9:22 tells us that without the shedding of blood there is no forgiveness. The sacrificial system paved the way for the ultimate sacrifice, Jesus, the Son of God. The Day of Atonement, held once annually for forgiveness of sins, was replaced by the atoning work of Christ.

In Numbers, we see a picture of God's work of redemption in the bronze serpent (Numbers 21). What a beautiful shadow of the work of Christ on the cross. The proud, stubborn people of Israel were bitten by poisonous snakes. The cure was simple: look upon the bronze serpent. Most did, but a few were too proud—and they died. In the same way, Jesus compared the bronze serpent to His work on Calvary, for as the people of Israel had only to look and live, today we need to believe on Jesus to live (John 3:16).

The Historical Books

As we move from the Pentateuch to the time of conquest, the promise-fulfillment motif becomes more apparent. Central to the Old Testament message was this idea of promise and fulfillment. God promised Abraham a special land; it was ultimately fulfilled in Joshua's time. Joshua, the Hebrew equivalent of the Greek "Jesus," was the man who delivered the people *into* the land of promise; Jesus delivers us *out* of the kingdom of darkness.

The Prophets

The Book of Jonah demonstrates God's mercy to any nation that repents. Jeremiah speaks of a new covenant, the covenant provided by the death of Jesus (see Jeremiah 31). Ezekiel gives us a stern warning: "Nevertheless if you warn the wicked to turn from his way, and he does not turn from his way, he shall die in his iniquity; but you have delivered your soul" (Ezek 33:9 NKJV).

The prophetic records give ample witness to the importance of passion in proclaiming the word of the Lord in any generation. Messianic passages abound with prophetic glimpses into the redemptive heart of God. Scores of passages give light, but only a few select passages can be offered here.

- Isaiah 7:14: "Behold, the virgin shall conceive and bear a son" (NKJV).
- Isaiah 9:6 speaks of the Wonderful Counselor, Mighty God, the Everlasting Father, the Prince of Peace.
- Isaiah 53 describes the Suffering Servant, giving a picture of a vicarious sacrifice.

The prophets spoke God's word in the face of tremendous opposition at times. Our zeal for God should move us to speak out for Him. Imagine for a moment that you have a small child, a little girl. She is playing in the road, unnoticed by you. Your neighbor Bill looks up from his yard work, only to see a tractor trailer bearing down on your daughter. Bill runs to the scene, pushing your child to safety just in time. She is scratched and scared but unhurt. But Bill was not so lucky. He awoke the next day in a hospital bed to the diagnosis that he would never walk again.

How would you feel about Bill? Would you not rush to the hospital to thank him, to ask him if there were anything you could do for him? Suppose you did visit him, and he said, "No, thanks, but I'm OK. My family is here. I will make out all right."

But then suppose he looked at you and said, "There is one thing you can do for me. Would you mind telling just five people over the next several years about my actions to save your daughter? It would mean a lot to my family."

You would probably respond to Bill, "I have already told everyone I have met about what you have done! I will speak of you for the rest of my life!" The Old Testament showed us our need for a Savior, and it pointed the way for Him. Now that we know Him and thinking of all He endured for us, can we truly be silent?

A "Whole Bible" Approach to the Great Commission

My colleague Mark Liederbach gets this. He teaches ethics, not normally a subject associated directly with evangelism in our compartmentalized world. But he is very much a Great Commission Christian. He summarizes well the teaching of Scripture as it relates to redemption and our telling of that great story.[12]

One simply cannot understand the Great Commission apart from a reading of all Scripture. An understanding of the mission of God from all of Scripture can be summarized with the following:

1. *Everything begins in God and is to return to God.*[13] Understanding this undergirds any theological system, any system of ethics, any evangelistic strategy, or any evaluation of culture. God created, God sustains, God redeems, and God will consummate history as we know it.
2. *Human existence must be understood as theocentric, not anthropocentric.* "In Christian theology, particularly that of Augustine and Aquinas," Liederbach writes, "this idea of *exitus et reditus* asserts that proper theology must begin with discussion on the existence of God, then the creation and fall of human beings, their salvation through Christ, and finally their return back to God in death and resurrection. It is foundational to understanding that the universe is theocentric, not anthropocentric."[14] Our perspective on the world and the church begins with the assumption that the focal point is God, not us as individuals, our family, our church, or our denomination.
3. *Individual life stories must conform to God's story.* Because the whole of Scripture from Pentateuch to the Apocalypse holds God alone in the central place in the universe, all of our personal life stories must yield to the higher, grander, more wonderful story that God tells throughout the Scripture, and in which alone our life finds any meaning (the metanarrative). Christianity is not just one story as a part of many stories, from Genesis, through the wilderness wanderings, into the time of the kings and the exile, until the time of Christ and the

[12] Ibid., 133–34.
[13] Ibid., 134.
[14] Ibid., 132.

birth of the Church; it is The Story. Most of us live our lives, and approach the Bible, to find how to make God's agenda fit into ours. This idolatrous thinking must be reversed and must affect the way we think about and do church. My son read the great books of the Western world as part of his college studies, from Augustine's *City of God* to Plato's *Republic*, from Aristotle's *Nichomachean Ethics* to Dante's *Divine Comedy*. He enjoyed the readings more than he had anticipated. Why? Because these books have great ideas, which is why they continue to be studied in fine schools. Great ideas endure. There is no greater idea, no more compelling message, than the gospel! "Our agendas and our stories will not enflame the hearts of men and women to follow hard and live greatly. Similarly, any compromise or capitulation on the uniqueness of the gospel story as the sole means of salvation serves only to dilute the passionate existence we were meant to live," Liederbach and I argued. "The gospel of Jesus Christ is the grand story of the universe. It alone rightly captures the imagination and fires the soul for greater things. This is the story we must learn, live in, and seek to tell often and well."[15]

4. *A higher affection must motivate a life lived for God's glory.* When we truly see God's beauty and majesty from the creation through the Old Testament story and throughout the New Testament, when we grasp His greatness and our place in His plan, we can see the relative insignificance of other things that would vie for our attention and affection. "It is through a Spirit-filled meditation on the Word of God here and now that we can find our affections transformed and purified. The more one tastes of this kind of beauty, the deeper our hearts will long for more."[16]
5. *A life of worship should compel us to invite the lost to join us.* As we see all of Scripture in its grand message of redemption and the invitation to be worshippers of God, evangelism becomes less a burden and more the joyful proclamation of the good news that others, too, can worship this great God! Evangelism becomes nothing more than inviting people to join us in being and doing that for which we have all been created!

[15] Ibid., 133.
[16] Ibid.

Thus, worship from God's intention in the beginning serves as the impetus for evangelism and the purpose of our mission.

6. *The corporate worship of the church ought to change the culture.* When believers as individuals, families, and churches together live a life of worship, even as we were intended to do before the fall and are able to do now because of the cross, individuals and the culture are changed as a result.

We have the most amazing story to tell in history. But it is a story that begins in Genesis, not the Gospels. And it is still worth telling today.

Questions for Consideration

1. Have you ever thought of evangelism as being linked to the Old Testament, or have you only seen it as a few verses in the New Testament?
2. How do worship and witness go together?
3. Which if any Old Testament passage helps you better to understand the Great Commission?

Chapter 5

Jesus and Paul

Life was in Him, and that life was the light of men. That light shines in the darkness, yet the darkness did not overcome it.

—John 1:4–5

The Old Testament from Creation to the dawn of Christ's birth prepared for the "fullness of time" when He would provide the salvation promised by the prophets and longed for by the saints of old. His followers would be able to worship Him in Spirit and truth and take His commission to the nations. Following the ministry of our Lord, we see the apostle Paul as chief among equals who can teach us much today about sharing our faith by our lives. We often learn more effectively by watching others. Evangelism is caught as much as it is taught! Being a follower of Christ means to seek to be like Jesus. We can learn much from His example, as well as that of Paul.

Evangelism from the Life and Work of Christ

The Incarnation Was Evangelistic in Its Intent

Paul records the significance of the coming of Christ: "But when the completion of the time came, God sent His Son, born of a woman, born under the law, to redeem those under the law, so that we might receive adoption as sons" (Gal 4:4–5). The angel told Mary to name her firstborn *Jesus,* for "He will save His people from their sins" (Matt 1:21). Jesus is the Greek form of the Hebrew name *Joshua,* meaning "God is savior."

The Bible is clear as to why He became flesh:

- "But the angel said to them, 'Don't be afraid, for look, I proclaim to you good news of great joy that will be for all the people: today a Savior, who is Messiah the Lord, was born for you in the city of David'" (Luke 2:10–11).
- "For even the Son of Man did not come to be served, but to serve, and to give His life—a ransom for many" (Mark 10:45).
- "The next day John saw Jesus coming toward him and said, 'Here is the Lamb of God, who takes away the sin of the world!'" (John 1:29).
- "For the Son of Man has come to seek and to save the lost" (Luke 19:10).

The coming of Christ demonstrated the evangelistic heart of God.

In the first century AD Rome had emerged as the dominant world power. No nation could stand against its might. From the Atlantic eastward to the Euphrates, from the Sahara to the Danube, the Roman Empire personified the word "dynasty." Palestine existed as one tiny state under the heavy boot of Rome. Augustus, the cynical Caesar who demanded a census to determine a measurement to enlarge taxes, was declared a god following his death. Who could have noticed a couple making an eighty-mile trip south from Nazareth? What difference could a carpenter and a teenaged girl make compared to Caesar's decisions in Rome? Who cared about this Jewish baby born in Bethlehem?

God cared. Unwittingly, mighty Augustus became an errand boy for the fulfillment of the words of the prophet Micah. He was a puppet in the hand of God, a piece of fuzz on the pages of prophecy. While Rome was busy making history, the One whose life split time—by whose birth we date our calendars—arrived. The world didn't notice. History had seen Alexander the Great, Herod the Great, and the great Augustus, but the world missed it when the One who flung the stars into the heavens was born. History missed the coming of its author. But now, we know, He is the one John called "the Lamb slain from the foundations of the world."[1]

His Earthly Ministry Modeled Evangelism

Our Lord Demonstrated an Evangelistic Passion

He showed unusual compassion for people. The "people of the land," or ordinary Jews, were often disdained by the Pharisees. But Jesus looked at them with compassion. Following an intense time of ministry in which He visited all the cities in Galilee, He was moved with compassion for the people "because they were weary and scattered, like sheep having no shepherd. Then He said to His disciples, 'The harvest truly is plentiful, but the laborers are few. Therefore pray the Lord of the harvest to send out laborers into His harvest'" (Matt 9:36–38 NKJV).

The word translated "compassion" in this passage comes from the Greek term *splanchnon.* The word refers to the viscera, the intestines, and means a deep hurt. When we are willing to feel the pain of lost people, to understand the depth of their sin and the gaping chasm of hell before them, we are close to sensing the compassion of Jesus.

Jesus Practiced Mass Evangelism

He preached the gospel of the kingdom to the masses. The message of Jesus was succinct: Repent and believe the good news of the kingdom of God (see Mark 1:14–15). The kingdom of God, the rule of God over all creation, has received little attention by evangelicals. This is due in large part to the emphasis earlier in this century by more liberal theologians who minimized the future hope of heaven. One example was the realized eschatology of C. H. Dodd. On a practical level, the preaching of the "victorious Christian life" in recent decades among evangelicals has received great attention. There is victory in Jesus, but the focus on *believers* living victoriously rather than focusing on *God*—as Jesus did in His preaching of the gospel of the kingdom—should be balanced. The focus of our Lord's preaching

[1] Adapted from C. R. Swindoll, *Growing Strong in the Seasons of Life* (Portland: Multnomah Press, 1984), 34–35.

was less on the benefit of the hearers than the honor of the One on whom the message was centered.

Jesus Taught the Importance of Evangelism

Jesus taught the *priority* of evangelism. He taught that salvation is the greatest thing in the world. His parables of the pearl of great price and the treasure in the field illustrate this (see Matt 13:44–46). Jesus taught the *love of the Father* for one lost soul. Luke 15 demonstrates the love of God as seen in the lost sheep, the lost coin, and the lost son. In fact, the only time God is pictured in a hurry is when Jesus describes the father hurrying to meet the returning prodigal son. Jesus also trained *others* to evangelize. Before He gave the Great Commission, Jesus sent out the Twelve and the seventy. Robert Coleman's book, *The Master Plan of Evangelism,* cites the role of Jesus in training His followers to witness.

Jesus Practiced Personal Evangelism

There are over 40 accounts in the Gospels of Jesus' personal evangelism. Studying these accounts demonstrates several truths. Jesus could adapt His presentation to different audiences. He obviously knew people well. He was sensitive to His Father's leadership. He was urgent and persistent. And even our Lord did not reach everyone with whom He shared. The following illustrations help us to see how Jesus evangelized people.

First, Jesus *sought* people. In Luke 19, we read how Jesus sought Zacchaeus. He intentionally set out to meet him and even made an appointment to meet him at the tax collector's house. He met Zacchaeus where he was as he sat in a tree (v. 5). He identified with a sinner, regardless of the consequences (v. 7). Jesus further convicted Zacchaeus of his sin. Finally, this account shows us Jesus did not just *meet* sinners; He sought to *save* them (vv. 9–10). Who are you currently seeking for the cause of Christ? Do you have names of people for whom you are praying, people with whom you are establishing friendships who do not know Christ? I recently took part in a survey of pastors. One of the questions asked the pastors how many times they had an unchurched family in their home and how many times they were in unchurched friends' homes in the past year. Several of the pastors' commented how the survey made them realize what a low priority they put on seeking those without Christ.

Next, Jesus was *approachable.* In John 3, we read of Nicodemus approaching Jesus by night. Nicodemus was searching for truth (v. 2).

The reply of Jesus was direct. He boldly confronted Nicodemus (v. 3). A dialogue ensued concerning the gospel, but no immediate change was indicated (vv. 4–21). However, there is evidence of Nicodemus's possible change (see John 7:50–52). He brought gifts to anoint the body of Jesus after His death (see John 19:39). Are you approachable? If a lost neighbor, family member, or coworker suddenly began to think of spiritual things, would they think of you as the person to speak with about their questions?

Third, Jesus *made the most of every opportunity.* While every example of the witness of Jesus is critical, His encounter with the Samaritan woman in John 4 is especially enlightening. Compare Jesus' approach to this broken and ostracized woman to the way He spoke to Nicodemus in John 3. Nicodemus crept in at night, was a religious leader, and flattered Jesus. Jesus replied to him directly, admonishing him to be born again. Jesus tended to be very direct with openly religious people, by the way.

But He approached the woman of Samaria with great care and kindness, despite her failure and sin. She had after all been married and divorced five times and was currently living with a man. Yet Jesus spoke to her in a way that compelled her to consider His truth. His witness can be summarized as follows:

- *Intentional*—He had to go to Samaria (4:4) even though centuries of enmity existed between Jews and Samaritans. Even though weary from the journey, our Lord made time to speak to others.
- *Conversational*—He built rapport with someone very different by finding a common need, for water (4:7).
- *Respectful*—though the Son of God, a Jew, and a man, He spoke kindly to her, asking for her help (4:7).
- *Directional*—He quickly moved from trivial matters to spiritual issues, relating the water at the well to living water (4:10–15). In addition, He refused to be sidetracked by discussions of worship (4:19–24).
- *Convictional*—He did not deny her sin, but sensing her brokenness He did not dwell on it either (4:16–18). We must be careful to know when to challenge people at the point of sin when they are self-righteous, and when to show the grace of God when they admit their need for God.
- *Confrontational*—While not a popular word today, our Lord ultimately confronted her with the truth of who He is (4:26).

She ultimately had to decide whether or not He was the Messiah she sought.

- *Missional*—Not only did Jesus share His message in a missional context, but she immediately became one of the first missionaries in the New Testament, telling others of the Christ (4:28–30). Ironically, His own disciples missed the missional moment, thinking only of physical needs (4:27–38).
- *Attitudinal*—Finally, note Christ's attitude toward people. Jesus had at least three general dispositions toward three groups. To the common people, broken and wearied by sin, He consistently showed compassion (as noted above). To the religious crowd, particularly the hypocritical and the legalists, He often demonstrated anger or unacceptance of them. Read Matthew 23 and see His denunciation of the Pharisees, for example. Finally, toward those who would follow Him, He expected nothing less than absolute surrender (Luke 9:23).

His Death and Resurrection Embody the Message of Evangelism

Our primary need is not education; thus, Jesus' ministry was not essentially about teaching. He came for one main purpose: to die for our sins. Some people speak of those He came to save—the lost—as "pre-Christians." Such a term smacks more of political correctness than biblical fidelity. It is a presumptuous term, considering the New Testament's emphasis on lostness. I have a friend who refers to unbelievers as "delayed" believers, since every knee will bow and every tongue eventually will confess He is Lord (Philippians 2). But Luke 15 implies people without Christ are lost.

However, the word "lost" implies value. People are worth the death of the Son of God! Recently, as I sorted through the mail, I saw a flyer with the picture of a missing child. The number to call caught my attention: 1–800-THE LOST. Certainly no one sees the word "lost" as negative in that setting. Should we not have the same urgency for people separated from their Creator? Without the death and resurrection of Jesus, the good news we preach would merely be another story passing through history. But the death of Jesus makes the difference!

Jesus Christ did not come to give us a moral example of how to live. He did not come just to teach us how to live. He came to die and to live again so that we could die to sin and live—eternally.

How Jesus Taught Evangelism

The eight characteristics of how Jesus taught evangelism to His disciples, from Robert Coleman's *Master Plan of Evangelism:*[1]

1. *Selection*. Men were His method: "His concern was not with programs to reach the multitudes, but with men whom the multitudes would follow."

2. *Association*. He stayed with them: "His disciples were distinguished, not by outward conformity to certain rituals, but by being with Him, and thereby participating in His doctrine."

3. *Consecration*. He required obedience: "[The disciples] were not required to be smart, but they had to be loyal. This became the distinguishing mark by which they were known."

4. *Impartation*. He gave Himself away: "His was a life of giving—giving away what the Father had given Him."

5. *Demonstration*. He showed them how to live: "Surely it was no accident that Jesus often let His disciples see Him conversing with the Father. . . . Jesus did not force that lesson on them, but rather He kept praying until at last the disciples got so hungry that they asked Him to teach them what He was doing."

6. *Delegation*. He assigned them work: "Jesus was always building His ministry for the time when His disciples would have to take over His work, and go out into the world with the redeeming Gospel."

7. *Supervision*. He kept checking on them: "Jesus made it a point to meet with His disciples following their tours of service to hear their reports and to share with them the blessedness of His ministry in doing the same thing."

8. *Reproduction*. He expected them to reproduce: "Jesus intended for the disciples to produce His likeness in and through the church being gathered out of the world."

[1] R. Coleman, *The Master Plan of Evangelism* (New York: Fleming H. Revell, 1972), quotes taken respectively from 27, 42, 51, 61, 71, 72, 79, 89, and 97.

His Commission Demands That We Evangelize

Each Gospel narrative and the Acts have a Great Commission passage:

- "Go, therefore, and make disciples of all nations, baptizing them in the name of the Father and of the Son and of the Holy Spirit, teaching them to observe everything I have commanded you. And remember, I am with you always, to the end of the age" (Matt 28:19–20).
- "Then He said to them, 'Go into all the world and preach the gospel to the whole creation'" (Mark 16:15).
- "And repentance for forgiveness of sins would be proclaimed in His name to all the nations, beginning at Jerusalem. You are witnesses of these things" (Luke 24:47–48).
- "Jesus said to them again, 'Peace to you! As the Father has sent Me, I also send you'" (John 20:21).
- "But you will receive power when the Holy Spirit has come upon you, and you will be My witnesses in Jerusalem, in all Judea and Samaria, and to the ends of the earth" (Acts 1:8).

How much more significant are the words of our Lord? Jesus Christ knew when He uttered the words above He was about to ascend to heaven. He was in control of the events. This reality only adds to the magnitude of His final directive to His followers. What did He tell us to do? Not to build buildings or social ministries or great worship services or discipleship courses. All these are noble and vital. No, He told us to be witnesses—something every believer can be and do.

The Ministry of the Apostle Paul

Although the gospel spread through the witness of all believers, we would swing the pendulum too far if we neglected the vital role of key leaders of the early church. In particular we would do well to study the life of Paul.

Paul Was a Prepared Witness

Prior to His Conversion

Saul of Tarsus was being prepared for his future ministry. Schooled in Judaism, he studied under the great rabbi Gamaliel. Reared in Tarsus, he was born a Roman citizen. Bright, zealous, and knowledgeable in Greek thought, this man was destined to make an impact. His conversion also prepared Saul to become Paul the apostle.

By His Conversion

Paul's radical conversion has been misunderstood. Some who have not come to Christ expect a "Damascus road" type of conversion. While salvation is life changing, few people have experienced such a powerful conversion. In Paul's case, it was expected and necessary. He certainly never got over it! He never forgot what it meant to be lost, calling himself the "chief of sinners."

By His Commission

"But the Lord said to him, 'Go! For this man is My chosen instrument to carry My name before Gentiles, kings, and the sons of Israel. I will certainly show him how much he must suffer for My name!'" (Acts 9:15). Paul received his own version of the Great Commission, and with that he set the pace for the spread of the gospel across the Mediterranean world. Although Paul was the apostle to the Gentiles, he consistently preached to the Jews as well. The most overlooked feature of his commission is the admission by the Lord that Paul would suffer greatly for the sake of the gospel.

Paul's Practice of Evangelism

Paul Was a Passionate Witness

Evangelism for Paul flowed out of his passion for God. Imagine for a moment that you are in heaven as God scans Palestine. He is looking for a man, not just any man, to lead in the gospel's spread to the Gentile world. He passes over Peter, although this fiery fisherman was a key leader. He overlooks James and John, the best of the inner circle of the disciples. In fact, none of the Twelve are chosen. Neither are any of those who followed Jesus during His earthly ministry. The thousands of early converts are skipped as well. Even the seven deacons, though significant in their own way, fail to meet God's standard to be *the* point man for the gospel's spread to the Gentile world.

Instead, the Father scans Palestine to find the most passionate, jealous, surrendered individual in the region. Never mind that the man is a stiff-necked Pharisee or even that he is currently engaged in persecuting God's children. *That* could be changed! There he is,

Saul of Tarsus, relentless in his efforts to stop the church, acting in his mind in the name of God.

Suddenly, there is a bright light. The man falls to his knees, blinded. He hears a voice, and history is forever changed because of him. I have a hunch the passionate nature of Paul played a key role throughout his years of ministry. Paul's effectiveness as a leader cannot be understood apart from his zeal. His call guided his life.

What is your mission statement? I think Paul's could be summed up like this: "to know Christ and to make Him known." Paul was single-minded. He became arguably the greatest Christian and the greatest soul-winner (the two go hand in hand) in history. He could not be stopped. When faced with death, Paul did not blink. "To die is gain" (Phil 1:21 NIV), he said. When allowed to live, he boasted, "I am not ashamed of the gospel of Christ" (Rom 1:16 KJV). When made to suffer, he remembered, "That I may know him [Christ], and the power of his resurrection, and the fellowship of His sufferings" (Phil 3:10 KJV), and "I consider that the sufferings of this present time are not worthy to be compared with the glory which shall be revealed in us" (Rom 8:18 NKJV).

Paul Was an Intentional Witness

The evangelism of Paul cannot be understood apart from the man—his call, his zeal, his sacrificial obedience. Upon this strong foundation, several methods were built.

Personal Evangelism

Paul consistently shared his faith with individuals. In Acts 13 we read of his witness to the proconsul. Acts 16 tells us of the witness of Paul to the jailer at Philippi. Later he shared personally with Agrippa (Acts 25:23–27). In Paul's life, as in any church or individual Christian, personal evangelism was the basis upon which all other methods were developed.

Mass Evangelism

In the book of Acts, we also find at least nine references to messages preached by Paul. In 1 Cor 1:23, Paul reminded the believers at Corinth of the centrality of preaching the cross.

Household Evangelism

At Thessalonica, Paul used a house as a base to share Christ. In Philippi, Lydia's home became a doorway for the gospel.

Apologetic Evangelism

In Acts 18:4, Paul "reasoned" in the synagogue at Corinth. Acts 17 records his defense of the gospel at Mars Hill. In later years, the work of the apologists and polemicists would not only strengthen the faithful in times of persecution but also lead to the conversion of many.

Miracles and Evangelism

In Acts 13, we read of a sorcerer who was blinded, followed by the salvation of the proconsul (see also Acts 19:11–12). Although the miraculous played a part in the evangelism of Paul and other early Christians, there are numerous occasions in which Paul preached Christ without miracles. In Antioch, Lystra, Derbe, Thessalonica, Berea, and Corinth, there is no mention of miracles. God can use the miraculous to reach some people, but we must be careful lest we make the miracle of conversion secondary to lesser miracles such as healing. Conversion is the most significant supernatural event anyone can experience.

Educational Evangelism

One of C. H. Dodd's errors in *Apostolic Preaching and Its Developments*[2] was his sharp distinction between the *kerygma*, or evangelistic proclamation, and the *didache*, or the teaching ministry of the church. Teaching was also a part of evangelism. An obvious example of this approach came when Paul visited Ephesus, teaching at the lecture hall of Tyrannus. Part of his approach to sharing Christ included educating his hearers in the truth of the gospel. In a culture increasing in biblical illiteracy, we must do the same.

Paul also gave instruction concerning evangelism to believers. He told the Philippians that the gospel was so important that even those who preached out of impure motives were doing valuable work (Phil 1:15–16). The most significant teaching of Paul on evangelism is the charge he gave to Timothy. Paul told Timothy, and thus all seeking to

---

[2] C. H. Dodd, *Apostolic Preaching and Its Developments* (Grand Rapids: Baker, 1982); first printed in 1936.

minister for Christ, to preach the Word "in season and out of season" (2 Tim 4:2 NKJV)—when you feel like it and when you don't! Further, he instructed Timothy to "do the work of an evangelist" (2 Tim 4:5). In Paul's mind, under the inspiration of the Spirit, the evangelistic mandate was to be a central part of the ministry.

Literary Evangelism

One might think in our day that the practice of literary evangelism began with Bill Bright's *Four Spiritual Laws* or Billy Graham's *Steps to Peace with God.* Not so. Paul's treatise to the Romans gives a brilliant explanation of the gospel message. Beyond the ministry of Paul, the Gospel of John was written with an evangelistic intent (John 20:31). Mark's and Luke's accounts were written at least in part for evangelistic purposes as well. Paul also wrote letters that sought to evangelize as well as to encourage.

Church Planting

Because Paul preached where the gospel had not been heard, he planted churches where he went. One cannot understand the evangelistic effectiveness of Paul only by his preaching; church planting formed an essential part of his strategy.

Urban Evangelism

Paul consistently went to the great urban centers. Asia was reached with the gospel message from the base established at Ephesus. We could learn much from Paul concerning the importance of reaching the cities. More will be said about that in a later chapter.

Follow-up

Paul utilized a follow-up strategy we would do well to emulate. First, he typically visited those he had won to Christ. His missionary journeys normally retraced the steps of his preaching and evangelistic ministry. Second, Paul wrote letters to encourage young believers. Read 1 Thessalonians as one example. He also sent others, such as Epaphroditus, to encourage the believers as well. Finally, he prayed consistently for those he had won to Christ.

Paul understood well what he said when he recognized that the gospel is the power of God to salvation (Romans 1). I have seen its power many times. While teaching a required New Testament class at Houston Baptist University, I was conscious of the fact that some students in my class were not Christians. Without preaching at them, I tried to demonstrate the clear message of the New Testament throughout the course. I prayed that the course would be more than another academic exercise for the students. I became humbled by the comments written at the end of a final exam. One student, a married woman about 30 years old, had never said a word the entire class. On her exam, however, she wrote these words: "Because of this class, both my husband and I have been saved and baptized, and we now read the Bible together every night and are active in a church. Thank you for this class!" There is indeed power in the gospel.

Questions for Consideration

1. What struck you most about the evangelism of Jesus? Of Paul?
2. What areas in your own life most resemble the life of Christ or the example of Paul?
3. What area needs further growth in witnessing?

Chapter 6

The Birth of a Movement: Evangelism in the Acts

> *It was a small group of eleven men whom Jesus commissioned to carry on his work, and bring the gospel to the whole world. They were not distinguished; they were not well educated; they had no influential backers. . . . If they had stopped to weigh up the probabilities of succeeding in their mission, even granted their conviction that Jesus was alive, and that his Spirit went with them to equip them for their task, their hearts must surely have sunk, so heavily were the odds weighed against them. How could they possibly succeed? And yet they did.*[1]
>
> —Michael Green

The early believers faced big obstacles. They had no New Testament canon, no established organization, and few clearly defined leaders. They faced hazardous persecution, and they were greatly misunderstood. Still, the spread of the gospel had its allies as well. As Paul aptly put it, Jesus came in the fullness of time—or at just the right time (Gal 4:4). The sovereign God of the universe had

[1] M. Green, *Evangelism in the Early Church* (Grand Rapids: Eerdmans, 1970), 13.

ordered events to prepare the way for the Great Commission. What helped the gospel to spread?

Preparation for the Gospel

For one, there was the universal peace provided by Rome, or the *Pax Romana.* Michael Green said it well, "The spread of Christianity would have been inconceivable had Jesus been born half a century earlier."[2] Rome controlled the entire known world at the dawn of the first millennium AD. Beyond the peace enforced by Caesar Augustus through his mighty army, the continuous expansion of roads aided the spread of the good news. I have seen the remains of Roman roads as far north as England, and they can still be traversed after many centuries.

Before Rome's political peace, *Greek culture* paved the way as well. Alexander the Great's conquests and concomitant process of hellenization produced a common language—Greek—across the Mediterranean region that the various cultures could speak. One can hardly underestimate the impact of a common tongue on the preaching of Christ by early missionaries.

The *Jewish faith* gave the early believers a heritage upon which to build. The first Christians knew the Old Testament Scriptures as their Bible. Further, the Jewish diaspora in the centuries before the birth of Jesus resulted in the establishment of synagogues across the Roman Empire. The synagogue not only provided a place for Paul and others to begin presenting Christ on missionary excursions but also provided a model for corporate worship in the early church.

A *spiritual vacuum* and *political unity* helped to set the stage for evangelization as well. "Politically and religiously," states F. F. Bruce about the first century, "the world was ready for the gospel at that time as it had not been before."[3] The world today is ready for the gospel as well! Bruce commented further on the significance of that period:

> The greater part of the civilized world was politically united, but the old classical religions were bankrupt. Many people had recourse to the popular mystery cults in their search for liberation from evil powers and assurance of well-being in the

[2] Ibid.

[3] F. F. Bruce, *The Spreading Flame* (Grand Rapids: Eerdmans, 1995), 24.

> after-life. Others . . . were attracted to the Jewish religion, but it labored under the disadvantage of being too closely tied to one nation. When the Christian message began to be proclaimed among the peoples of the Roman Empire, it showed a capacity to satisfy both the craving for salvation which the mystery cults professed to meet and the ethical ideas which, as many Gentiles believed, were realized in the Jewish way of life even more than in Stoicism.[4]

In the grand drama of redemption (creation, fall, redemption, consummation), the coming of Jesus was central to the plan of God in history. To this day, we date our calendars based on His incarnation.

A Strategy Develops

The church spread both spontaneously and strategically. The spontaneous growth came as the early believers, consumed with the Holy Spirit and conviction, went everywhere speaking of Christ. But a strategy developed on several levels as well. Later I will describe in more detail the concept of a *missional witness*, but for now observe the simple, twofold strategy of the early church. The New Testament plan for evangelism was and is one of *total* evangelism. The faith of the early Christ-followers could be described as missional from its beginnings. Evangelism never found its way into a program or committee assignment or became compartmentalized to a day of the week or a particular group; rather, it formed part of the warp and woof of the fabric of the early church. The strategy has been summarized under two headings, which when taken together give us a template for evangelistic focus both then and now.[5]

Total Penetration

Total penetration means the goal of the church is to reach everyone for Christ. Jesus made this clear:

- Go into *all* the world and preach the gospel (Mark 16:15).
- *Make disciples* of *all* nations (Matt 28:19–20).

[4] Ibid.

[5] To my knowledge, Leighton Ford was the first to use the following terminology. R. Fish taught the concept in my seminary days, and D. Robinson popularized the approach in his book *Total Church Life*.

- Repentance and remission of sin should be preached in His name to *all* nations (Luke 24:47).

Applied specifically, it means each congregation seeks to reach its area with the gospel. From the birth of the church until now, one can hardly conceive of a true understanding of the church apart from zealous evangelism.

Three important groups during the first century were open to the gospel: (1) Jews, (2) Proselytes (non-Jews who kept the laws of Judaism), and (3) God-fearers (non-Jews attracted to the monotheism of Judaism but who did not obey all its laws and were not circumcised).

Of the more than 6 billion people in the world today, approximately one-third have not heard of Jesus Christ. A popular soft drink made a commitment a few years ago that all the world would have a drink of their cola. Their goal was the total penetration of the world with their product. Starbucks Coffee in less than 20 years has crisscrossed the globe. I have personally seen Starbucks in London, Paris, ChiangMai, and Bangkok. Worldwide, people recognize the golden arches of McDonald's restaurants more than the cross of Christianity. Penetrating the world, the whole world, must remain our passion. Penetrating the culture with the gospel must take precedent over getting people into our buildings.

Total Participation

Total participation means involving every believer in evangelism. Jesus expects all believers to be involved in spreading the gospel. Everyone who receives the Holy Spirit is to witness (see Acts 1:8). Increasingly on a large scale, evangelicals are taking this mandate seriously. Emphasis by various mission groups on reaching the 10/40 window—referring to the section on the globe representing the most unchurched people groups—has raised awareness of the challenge to take the gospel to all peoples.

While I affirm such lofty goals, the more critical issue on a practical level is to apply the same philosophy of reaching the world and getting every single church in the world committed to the strategy. It is much easier to put together a grandiose plan to communicate the gospel to the whole world than to get individual churches committed to win specific areas to Christ or to motivate individual believers to win their neighborhoods to Christ. The New Testament pattern of evangelism involves beginning with Jerusalem, where the believers were, and reaching out from there. We see this played out in the Acts of the Apostles. We must continually ask ourselves if the contemporary church has remained faithful to involving all believers who know Christ in sharing with all those who do not know Christ.

Evangelism in the Acts

Over the years I have read hundreds of books in the field of evangelism. Many have been helpful, a few have been wonderful, and others have been disappointing. When asked to name the greatest book I have ever read on evangelism, I immediately reply, "the Bible." More specifically, the book of Acts gives more insight into the evangelistic work of the early church than any other source. How did the early church accomplish its task?

The Thesis of Acts

Acts 1:8 lays the foundation for the entire book. Luke's narrative describes how the early believers, through the Holy Spirit's power, witnessed in expanding areas. You see the concept of total participation for total penetration in the very thesis of the book. The *purpose* for each believer: "You are my witnesses." The disciples asked about the signs of the times, but Jesus responded by telling them to be soul winners, not stargazers.

The *personnel* involved in witnessing is noted in Acts 1:8 and demonstrated for the next 28 chapters—all believers. The apostles, laity, men, women—all kinds of people—took the good news to others. William Carey faced a belief among fellow churchmen of his day that the Acts 1:8 mandate was only for the early church. The High Calvinists of Carey's day said that if God wanted to save the heathen, God would do so. Thankfully, Carey's view won the day. Due to his influence, modern missions was born in the late eighteenth century. It grew into one of the greatest missions movements in church history.

The *power* needed to win the world is the Holy Spirit. Some modern believers live as though there is a form of spiritual entropy at work in which the power of God is waning in the face of cultural rot. Not so! God is still at work today as He was working in the lives of the early believers.

See what the Holy Spirit did in the early church. Take Peter, for example. What caused Peter to change from the cowardly, denying disciple we see in Luke 22 to the courageous preacher described in Acts 2? Peter got an old-fashioned dose of the Holy Spirit!

If the book of Acts tells us anything about evangelism, it is that the Holy Spirit is central to the fulfillment of the Great Commission. The book of Acts could rightly be called the "Acts of the Holy Spirit" because the key person in the book is the Holy Spirit. Jesus ascended, another Comforter came, and He empowered believers to do the work of the early church.

Features of the work of the Spirit in Acts:

1. Four times the Spirit speaks in a direct quote, and in every case He says "Go": Acts 8:29–35; 10:19–20; 13:2 (where He set apart Saul and Barnabas for formal missionary work); and 28:25–26.

2. Consistently, when the Spirit filled believers, their immediate response was to share Christ: Acts 2:4,11; 4:8,31; 6:3,7; 9:17,20; 11:24; 13:9

Finally, this verse gives us the *plan* of the early church. They witnessed locally but had a vision that extended globally. The term "glocal" has been used in recent days, referring to the church being equally local and global in its witness. That epitomizes the vision of the early church. Note that the twenty-eighth chapter of Acts ends abruptly. Why? Because it's still being lived. You are the twenty-ninth chapter of Acts. I'm the twenty-ninth chapter of Acts. All believers are the twenty-ninth chapter of Acts. Give this vision to your church. We are still part of what God began 2,000 years ago. The canon is closed, but the church still grows.

The Witness of the Believers in Acts

Several aspects of evangelism in the early church are worthy of close examination.

All Believers Witnessed Personally in the Culture

The idea of a course or seminar on personal witnessing would have been foreign to the first believers. Witnessing was one of the defining marks of authentic Christianity. Even on the day of Pentecost, known for Peter's great sermon, personal witnessing permeated the city, as noted by Conant and Fish:

> It is widely imagined that those three thousand converts (Acts 12) were brought to Christ by Peter's sermon alone, but nothing could be farther from the truth. The private witnessing of all the disciples culminated in the public witnessing of one disciple and brought the results of that day. In other words, if the private witnessing had not preceded Peter's sermon, there is not the least likelihood that any such results would have followed.[6]

On the day of Pentecost in Acts 2 all the believers spoke about the mighty acts of God. So all 120 people were sharing the gospel (see Acts 2:11), and then the crowd got together, where Peter preached to them. In Acts 4:29–31 we read of the church at prayer following the threats of Jewish officials. They prayed not for persecution to cease but for God to give them all boldness. As a result, they *all* were filled with the Spirit and shared Christ (v. 31, not just the church leaders). Following the persecution that came after Stephen's martyrdom we read that all the believers were scattered by persecution with one notable exception: "except the apostles" (see Acts 8:1–4). What did all these believers, who were obviously not apostles but regular rank-and-file Christ-followers, do? They went everywhere sharing Christ! This idea is picked up in Acts 11:19 and following. These same laypeople, including men of Cyrene and Cyprus, spread the gospel to Antioch, leading to a shift in the advancing Christian movement, for we will read in Acts 13 that the first formal missionaries would be sent not from Jerusalem but from Antioch.

The early deacon Stephen was a witness, and Philip was even called an evangelist. Virtually every time believers in Acts were involved in some kind of verbal activity, they were witnessing, praising God, and gaining favor among the people. Examples of personal evangelism in the book of Acts are numerous. Notice the witness of Philip to the eunuch (Acts 8), Peter to Cornelius (Acts 10), and Paul to the proconsul (Acts 13).

Part of the problem we face in understanding the witness of the early church comes from translation. For example, in Acts 8:35, when most English versions say Philip "preached Jesus" to the eunuch, the

---

[6] R. J. Fish and J. E. Conant, *Every Member Evangelism for Today* (New York: Harper and Row, 1976), 11.

Greek word is actually the word meaning "share the good news," not "preach."

Similarly in Acts 11:19–23, the men who went everywhere speaking about Jesus were not preaching formally in the modern sense but were sharing Christ personally. While we may see that both "preaching" and "sharing the good news" each refer to communicating the gospel, the average reader of Scripture can easily assume "preachers" are the ones who should be doing the witnessing. In fact, many assume just that.

> **Acts 8:35:**
>
> KJV: *Philip "preached unto him Jesus."*
>
> NKJV: *Philip "preached Jesus to him."*
>
> NASB: *Philip "preached Jesus to him."*
>
> **More accurately:**
>
> NIV: *Philip "told him the good news about Jesus."*
>
> HCSB: *Philip "proceeded to tell him the good news about Jesus."*

Today, personal evangelism in the church is the exception, not the rule; in Acts, the opposite was true. The Great Commission has experienced a great reversal. We must recapture a commitment to aggressive, missional, unashamed personal evangelism! We have to recapture the vision that when the message of the Christian faith has spread most effectively, it has done so by informal missionaries, what we would call "laity," simply talking to others about Jesus. This idea is being recovered today by the growing focus on missional Christianity. That is how they did it in Acts. That is how they did it in the early centuries. That is how the gospel spread in times of many spiritual movements and awakenings. And that is how it must spread today.

If preachers alone could reach the world, the world may have been reached! God has and will use preachers, but God's plan then and now is living witnesses. Why do some big-budget movies bomb while some lesser-known movies surprise the critics? Word of mouth. The early church was captivated by their message because Jesus had captured their hearts. When this took place, they simply had to spread the word. They were so transformed by the gospel of grace that their response took on a missional fervor. Likewise, if and when we are freshly captivated by the gospel, we will talk about Jesus.

Harnack said, "We cannot hesitate to believe that the great mission of Christianity was in reality accomplished by means of informal missionaries."[7] None of the first disciples of Jesus came from the clergy of their day, so we should not be surprised that the gospel spread primarily through "amateur" witnesses. Michael Green assesses the first-century church and in so doing gives an indictment of the American church:

> In contrast to the present day, when Christianity is highly intellectualized and dispensed by professional clergy to a constituency increasingly confined to the middle class, in the early days the faith was spontaneously spread by informal evangelists, and had its greatest appeal among the working classes.[8]

History gives the same witness. In times of great awakening, personal evangelism receives renewed fervor. One of the more overlooked features of the leaders during past revivals is their commitment to personal soul-winning.

Only Some of the Disciples Preached to Crowds

One can see that all believers practiced personal evangelism. But notice that public proclamation of the gospel was vital as well, and was practiced by far fewer believers. Peter, Stephen, Paul, and others preached—not all believers.

The public preaching of the gospel was undergirded by personal witnessing, as evidenced in Acts 2. Early Christian believers had no church buildings. Today we suffer from the "edifice complex," an overemphasis on buildings and budgets with little attention to people and passion. In the early church, preaching in the open air was the norm, not the exception. When George Whitefield and John Wesley began preaching in the fields with great effect in eighteenth-century England, they were criticized for using such a lowly approach. But they were only following the example of the early church!

Believers Lived Their Faith and Pursued Their Mission Daily

I am afraid that our version of Acts today, were we to tell the story of the contemporary church, would focus greatly on our Sunday services and the events at our buildings. On the contrary, the focus in the first century was not weekly in a building but daily in the culture:

---

[7] Green, *Evangelism in the Early Church*, 172.

[8] Ibid., 175.

- Acts 2:46–47—concluding his first summary statement of life in the early church, Luke uses the term *daily* two times, indicating this was central to their understanding of church.
- Acts 3:2—Here we read of a lame man over 40 years of age, who had been crippled his entire life. He was *daily* laid at the temple gate. When he saw Peter and John heading off to pray, he asked for their help. Now they could have said, "We're busy. We'll come back after our services are over." But they refused to let their important spiritual activity keep them from touching a life in need. As a result he experienced physical healing and eternal salvation, and his witnessing led to multitudes hearing the gospel. Peter and John did not have to wait until Sunday to help this man. As missional worshippers, they did not let their corporate prayer service attendance hinder their witness and ministry in the culture. They did not need to check their iPhone to see if they had time to care.
- Acts 5:42—facing persecution and threatened to be silent, the apostles *daily* preached the good news.
- Acts 6:1—the early church ministered to others *daily*.
- Acts 16:5—the churches grew in number *daily.*
- Acts 17:11—the Bereans searched the Scriptures *daily.*
- Acts 17:17—Paul reasoned *daily* in the marketplace.
- Acts 19:8–10—Paul shifted his strategy from a weekly focus in the temple to a *daily* focus in the culture and had arguably his most effective and lasting ministry.
- Acts 20:18,31—Paul argued that his ministry was consistent *every day* he was among the Ephesians.

They Reached People and Formed Churches

Today a strong focus on church planting has grown in the American church and globally. That is a good thing, and I have added a whole chapter on church planting later because of its importance. However, some obsess over church planting and have very little emphasis on reaching the lost. Read the book of Acts to see the early church's strategy for church planting. They never lost sight of the Great Commission. Effective church planting never loses the focus on reaching the lost, even as "congregationalizing" takes place. Too often when church planting endeavors see some fruit in evangelism, the focus prematurely moves away from outreach to building a support structure. Of course the early church did not have disgruntled or other members from existing churches to deal with, so keeping the focus on the gospel may have been a little simpler. But today, church planters can become tempted to take anyone who wants to be part of the new church, including "mature" believers from other churches, and count them as part of a successful church plant. If one is not careful, however, the new church may end up reaching the very people who will keep the church from reaching the lost.

Mark Liederbach and I said the following in *The Convergent Church:*

> Maybe that is why we are televising our weekly services in an effort to use the medium of television to reach tiny audiences of the convinced, while MTV has created an entire subculture via cable television that exerts expanding influence on American culture, especially among the younger population (that would be the group not sitting by the TV anticipating the next televised Sunday service). We are not intending to minimize the vital place of corporate worship. . . . But what we are saying is that we believe it is a tragedy that we evangelicals are far better at emphasizing Sunday morning services than we are at mobilizing missional worshipers to invade their world the rest of the week.[9]

They Declared an Unchanging, Timeless Message

One of the most debated aspects of the book of Acts centers on the question of whether there was a fixed pattern in the early church's gospel preaching. C. H. Dodd's work, *The Apostolic Preaching and Its Developments*, claimed there was a noticeable pattern. This pattern included: (1) Jesus inaugurated the fulfillment of messianic prophecy, (2) He went about doing good and performing miracles, (3) He was crucified according to God's plan, (4) He was raised and exalted to heaven, (5) He will return in judgment, and (6) therefore, people should repent, believe, and be baptized.[10]

Many scholars agreed with Dodd. These included Martin Dibelius, A. M. Hunter, and C. T. Craig. There is some disagreement among them on the basic points of early Christian preaching, but they concur that a core of content can be seen.

---

[9] M. Liederbach and A. L. Reid, *The Convergent Church: Missional Worship in an Emerging Culture* (Grand Rapids: Kregel, 2009), 288.

[10] Summarized in R. H. Gundry, *A Survey of the New Testament* (Grand Rapids: Zondervan, 1981), 75.

Scholars in recent years have increasingly disagreed with Dodd's findings. It is fair to say that the message was clear to all in the early church, but the application of the message varied. Perhaps Green, in his survey of early church evangelism, said it well when he stated that the proclamation of the early Christians was "united in its witness to Jesus, varied in its presentation of his relevance to the varied needs of the listeners, urgent in the demand for decision."[11] What is abundantly clear in Acts is that a consistent message is proclaimed throughout.

They Gave Testimony to the Gospel's Impact on Their Lives

The objective message of the cross and Jesus' resurrection permeated the witness of the early church. With this objective truth, they added the more subjective element of their personal testimonies. The message of the cross, when paired with a changed life, is still the most formidable weapon for storming the gates of hell.

One of the most moving verses on evangelism in the Bible is Acts 4:13. Peter and John had been arrested by the Sadducees for preaching the message of the cross and Jesus' resurrection. The religious leaders described Peter and John as *unlearned* and *ignorant*. But they could not explain the apostles' changed lives. "They marveled," we are told, and "they took knowledge, that [Peter and John] had been with Jesus" (KJV). The testimony of these men gave evidence of the reality of their message. The question for us is, "How long does a person have to speak with us before he or she recognizes that we have been with Jesus?" When the authorities threatened Peter and John, Peter replied, "We are unable to stop speaking about what we have seen and heard" (Acts 4:20).

For these early believers, the objective message of the gospel was so dynamic in their lives that they would die for the Christ they preached. Their lives were so radically changed that they were willing to live for Him as well as tell others the story of their changed lives.

Little Chad was a shy boy. One afternoon in late January, Chad told his mother he wanted to make a valentine for each one of his classmates. *I wish he wouldn't do that!* she thought. She knew how the children ignored her son. Her Chad was always behind them when they walked home from school. Chad was never included. Nevertheless, she decided she would help. She bought construction paper,

[11] Green, *Evangelism in the Early Church,* 66.

glue, and crayons. For three whole weeks, night after night, Chad made 35 valentines by hand.

When Valentine's Day arrived, Chad was excited. His mom, fearing his disappointment if he received no valentines, told Chad she would have his favorite cookies baked and ready when he came home from school. *Maybe that will ease the pain a little*, she thought.

That afternoon the kids were later than usual. Chad's mom had the cookies and milk on the table. Finally she heard them coming, laughing and talking with one another. And, as usual, Chad was in the rear. She feared he would burst into tears as soon as he got home. His arms were empty, she noticed, and when the door opened, she choked back the tears.

"Mommy has some warm cookies and milk for you."

Chad just marched right on by, and all he said was, "Not a one . . . not a one."

Her heart sank.

And then he added, "I didn't forget a one, not a single one!"[12]

Chad was so focused on giving that he had given no thought to receiving. He had something to share, and so do we!

They Shared Christ in the Face of Tremendous Obstacles

The greatest outpouring of the Spirit in history came on the Day of Pentecost. When great revival comes, everything goes well, right? Well, if that is your view of revival, you had better stop asking God for it. No, when God works, Satan rears his ugly head. The early church faced an array of internal and external obstacles, but they turned these obstacles into opportunities for God to work. Nothing could stop their passion for soul-winning.

Inward Obstacles

Hypocrisy. Hypocrisy is not a twentieth-century phenomenon. Ananias and Sapphira (see Acts 5) lied about the circumstances surrounding their material gifts. Peter confronted the obvious sin; an evangelistic church must be unafraid to confront known sin. The book of Acts is the story of the greatest evangelistic spiritual awakening in history. But consider the difficulty the early Christians faced. The problem with Ananias and Sapphira was hypocrisy. Have you ever had hypocrisy in your church?

---

[12] C. R. Swindoll, *Improving Your Serve* (Waco: Word, 1981), 92–93.

A pastor friend faced a crisis in his church. He discovered a staff member was involved in immorality. While being sensitive to the man's family and being as gentle as possible, he and the church confronted the sin, dealt with it, and the staff member was removed. The church later experienced a deep and powerful revival. If the church had failed to confront sin, it would have been robbed of some of the power of God.

Ministry Needs. Acts 6 tells us of the neglected Hellenistic widows. Notice the complaint of the widows was about a real need. Not everyone who brings up an issue is a complainer; a growing church must deal with legitimate needs. The apostles were hindered from doing their ministry, so the church dealt with the issue by enlarging the organization. However, it was not simply changing the structure by setting apart who we think were the first deacons that solved the problem. The selection of Spirit-filled leaders made the difference.

The widows were saying, "We're being neglected." Peter didn't say, "Would you be quiet?" He said, "You know, there's a problem here. Let's appoint some deacons so we can serve the Lord in the ministry of the Word and prayer, and you can serve the tables and take care of these ministry needs."

Theological Convictions. Theological matters also played a key role in the evangelism of the early church. The Jerusalem conference described in Acts 15 dealt with a theological issue directly tied to evangelism: Did Gentiles have to become Jews to be Christians? From that day onward, the evangelistic effectiveness of the church has often depended on how it deals with matters of theology. Evangelism is more than methodology. We must deal with theological concerns in order to be effective in evangelism.

Outward Obstacles

Beyond the *inward* obstacles, the church also grappled with *outward* persecution. Note these three examples.

Threats. The Sadducees arrested Peter and John, ordering them not to preach anymore. How did the apostles respond? First, they courageously *preached* the gospel (Acts 4:8–12). Then they *testified* concerning their unwillingness to be silent (Acts 4:20). Finally, upon their release, they *prayed* with other believers (Acts 4:23–31).

In their prayers, they began by acknowledging God's sovereignty (Acts 4:24). They also acknowledged God as Lord of creation and history. When the early believers prayed, they prayed for *boldness*

(Acts 4:29). Notice the answer: "And when they had prayed, the place where they were assembled together was shaken; and they were all filled with the Holy Spirit, and they spoke the word of God with boldness" (NKJV). Now *that's* praying!

Physical Beating. Acts 5 tells us that persecution moved from threats to actual physical abuse. But notice the response: They rejoiced "that they were counted worthy to suffer" (Acts 5:41). Joseph Tson, who was persecuted greatly in Romania before the collapse of Communism, said most American Christians have not faced enough persecution to be counted worthy of suffering.

Martyrdom and a General Persecution. Stephen paid the ultimate sacrifice for his conviction about the gospel (see Acts 7 and 8). When John Wesley preached one time, his opponents ran an ox through the crowd. He wrote in his journals about having his mouth bloodied and still he kept on preaching. We must understand that the gospel is worth any cost.

Paul Brand and Philip Yancey wrote a stirring book entitled *Pain: The Gift Nobody Wants.* It's about leprosy and pain in general. Brand describes a leper colony in India and the main leper colony in the United States, in Louisiana. The main problem with leprosy is that it causes you to lose your feeling. Some people in these leper colonies kept losing fingers and ears, and they didn't know why. They put a camera in their dormitories. They discovered that while these people were sleeping, rats would chew on their fingers. The lepers didn't even know it. They couldn't feel.

The point of the book is that there is something worse than pain—the inability to feel pain. Those lepers would give anything to feel pain. The three most prescribed drugs in America today are classified as antidepressants or pain relievers. We try to blot out our pain, even in the church! We must understand that there is no service to God without pain. His desire is not to give us comfort but to build the character of Christ in us.

They Were Willing to Adapt Their Approach When Necessary

Too often in our day we confuse methods with the message. While their message never changed nor should we change it, the application of the message changes with different audiences. Most of the time in Acts we read of the gospel's spread to Jews. Therefore, the early Christians did what makes sense—they pointed to Jesus as the Messiah for whom the Jews sought. But sometimes they encountered

Gentile audiences and thus changed their approach. Our much more varied world requires such contextualization as well. Here are two clear examples:

- Acts 17—Paul at Mars Hill. When speaking to a Jewish audience, Paul and others focused on Jesus as the Messiah. But when he spoke to pagans in Athens, he made no mention of any Messiah, for whom none of them were seeking. Instead, he began with their idolatry and interest in creation to move from general revelation to special revelation. So, when dealing with those who understood the (Old Testament) Scriptures, Paul went from Scripture to their cultural situation. When dealing with those ignorant or unconvinced by the Scriptures, he began with creation, which fit their culture, and moved to Scripture.
- Acts 19—Paul changed his strategy when the Jews to whom he preached in the synagogue became hardened to the gospel. He moved from the religious institution, the synagogue, to the culture, a school of Tyrannus. He specifically taught daily, and as a result he stayed longer and influenced more than anywhere else (see 19:8–10).

My colleague George Robinson has spent extensive time working with church planters globally and in the U.S. He developed a simple matrix based on Acts 1:8 for a church to use in evangelizing its community.[13] This simple approach at penetrating a culture with the gospel can assist churches to build an evangelistic DNA like that of the church in the Acts.

The Acts Missional Strategy Matrix

	Matrix Terms Defined
Jerusalem	Any location within the daily sphere of influence of your community of faith.
Judea	Any location outside of the daily sphere of influence of your community of faith, but shares a common worldview.

[13] Used with permission by George Robinson.

	Matrix Terms Defined (Continued)
Samaria	Any location outside of the daily sphere of influence of your community of faith that has a slightly differing worldview, but shares some commonalities.
Ends of the Earth	Any location outside of the daily sphere of influence of your community of faith that has a radically differing worldview with few, if any, commonalities.
Prayer & Advocacy	Any activity of promotion through education, prayer or financial commitment.
Project	Any on-site activity with pre-determined goals that are completed in a single visit.
Partnership	Any on-going activities (both on and off-site) for the achievement of a specified set of goals shared between your community of faith and other Great Commission Christians in the area. Upon completion of shared goals the partnership may be dissolved or redefined.
Adoption	A lifelong commitment to a specific location or people. This commitment involves a relationship that involves, but is not limited to any predetermined set of goals.

Target area →

Level of Commitment ↓

	Jerusalem	Judea	Samaria	Ends of the Earth
Prayer				
Projects				
Partnership				
Adoption				

Striking the Match—Implementing the Strategy

Remember, one of the obstacles to successful church is a step-by-step approach. One way you could implement the Acts Matrix is to identify key leaders within your church who will lead a target group. To do so you would have a "Jerusalem Team," a "Judea Team," a "Samaria Team," and an "Ends of the Earth Team." The responsibility of each team would be to identify ways in which your church is already involved in their target area and move the church toward multiplication in that area.

Make sure you do not focus only on your "Jerusalem"—keep in mind what God did to the first church when they made that mistake! Start where you are and move outward, and soon you will find a church-planting vision permeating your local church body. Where are the weaknesses of your church according to the matrix? Where are your strengths?

Questions for Consideration

1. How can you help to implement a comprehensive Acts 1:8 approach in your church?
   Take a few minutes to consider how the New Testament strategy for evangelism applies to your church field. If churches could just get this concept—total penetration and total participation—what an impact we could make across America. What if every believer in your community—youth in the public schools, moms in neighborhoods, businessmen in the workplace—sought to touch their sphere of influence for the sake of the gospel?
2. What if like the early believers we all lived like missionaries advancing a movement?

Chapter 7

History I: Second through the Eighteenth Centuries

> *Perhaps the tragedy of our time is that such an overwhelming number of us who declare Jesus as Lord have become domesticated—or, if you will, civilized. We have lost the simplicity of our early faith. Beyond that, we have lost the passion and power of that raw, untamed, and primal faith.*[1]
>
> —Erwin McManus

As a university professor, I heard many stories about college students struggling with two major concerns: money and grades. That's why I love this story of a college coed told by Chuck Swindoll. After a long struggle, she finally wrote an ingenious letter to break the news to her parents:

> *Dear Mom and Dad,*
>
> *Just thought I'd drop you a note to clue you in on my plans. I've fallen in love with a guy named Jim. He quit high school after grade eleven to get married. About a*

[1] E. R. McManus, *The Barbarian Way* (Nashville: Thomas Nelson, 2005), 12.

year ago he got a divorce. We've been going steady for two months and plan to get married in the fall. Until then, I've decided to move into his apartment (I think I might be pregnant).

At any rate, I dropped out of school last week, although I'd like to finish college sometime in the future.

On the next page she continued:

Mom and Dad, I just want you to know that everything I've written so far in this letter is false. NONE of it is true. But Mom and Dad, it IS true that I got a C in French and flunked Math. It IS true that I'm going to need some more money for my tuition payments.[2]

Creative! Poor grades and an empty pocketbook fare better with Mom and Dad than illegitimacy and a bad marriage.

Perspective is exactly why studying history is so important. History helps provide a foundation and a perspective for contemporary ministry. Santayana's well-known dictum that "Those who cannot remember the past are condemned to repeat it" is sage advice. But the reverse should be heeded as well, for we can learn much to instruct and inspire us from the movement of God in history.

The Spread of Christianity Following The First Century: How Did They Do It?

That question recognizes the remarkable rise of Christianity in the face of virtually insurmountable odds. Indeed, Rodney Stark's subtitle to his book *The Rise of Christianity*[3] made the point well: "How the Obscure, Marginal Jesus Movement Became the Dominant Religious Force in the Western World in a Few Centuries." While obtaining actual numbers of Christians in the Roman Empire in a time before computers and the modern obsession with numbers proves difficult, I think Alan Hirsch is close to the mark when he estimates the growth of the faith from around 25,000 in AD 100 to around 20,000,000 by AD 315.[4] Stark assumed a population of the empire by AD 315 of around

[2] C. R. Swindoll, *Growing Strong in the Seasons of Life* (Portland: Multnomah Press, 1984), 71–73.

[3] R. Stark, *The Rise of Christianity* (New York: HarperOne, 1997).

[4] A. Hirsch, *Forgotten Ways: Reactivating the Missional Church* (Grand Rapids: Brazos Press, 2006), 18. See also R. Stark, *The Rise of Christianity: A Sociologist Reconsiders*

60 million, noting that others including Harnack believed that by then Christians were actually the majority, perhaps as many as 33 million.[5]

Hirsch notes a similar time of remarkable growth closer to our time—the rise of the church in China. Estimates before the religious purge of Mao Tse-tung hover around 2 million believers. After the lifting of the Bamboo Curtain in the 1980s, Westerners were amazed to discover at least 60 million believers in China, with some claiming as many as 80 to 100 million![6] While the percentage of Christians to the empire remained smaller when compared to the Roman Empire, in China with well over a billion citizens there, the remarkable growth at a time when the Communist government sought to obliterate such religious belief is nonetheless amazing.

The Western church today tends more toward stagnation than life, but this has not always been the case. It should not surprise us that in each of these cases Christianity's growth came as a marginalized and often persecuted system.

Stark argued the early church grew not primarily via miraculous events or mass conversions but through social networks of many believers communicating the message, for movements that continue to grow "discover new techniques for remaining open networks, able to reach out and into new adjacent social networks."[7] Movements that die become closed to outsiders, unwelcoming, and disconnected, forming their own subculture without need of others. Thus the institutional church, when it becomes inward focused, plants the seeds of its own destruction in its efforts to focus more on its subculture than those in need of Christ. More about that in pages to come.

Second and Third Centuries

A Spontaneous Expansion

Just how did the gospel spread in the centuries following Christ's resurrection? Did the church expand mainly through evangelists who gave all their lives to spread the good news? Did the gospel simply spread naturally through culture by the witness of common folk whose

History (Boston: Princeton University Press, 1996), 6–13. Hirsch gathered his numbers mainly from Stark. I personally believe the numbers were greater at the end of the first century.

[5] Stark, *Rise of Christianity*, 10.

[6] Hirsch, *Forgotten Ways,* 20.

[7] Stark, *Rise of Christianity*, 20.

lives were changed by its power? The answer would be both. And the answer would be more than that. There were "full-time wandering missionaries," who, as Origen put it, "wander not only from city to city but from town to town and village to village in order to win fresh converts for the Lord."[8] The early historian Eusebius wrote of evangelists who went to places where the gospel had not been preached, preaching the gospel and appointing pastors as they went.[9]

At the same time, however, all believers seemed to carry the message as did believers in the Acts. Green observed how "Christianity was from its inception a lay movement, and so it continued for a remarkably long time."[10] He brilliantly summarized the expansion of the church via common believers:

> But as early as Acts 8 we find that it is not the apostles but the "amateur" missionaries, the men, evicted from Jerusalem as a result of the persecution which followed Stephen's martyrdom, who took the gospel with them wherever they went. It was they who travelled along the coastal plain to Phoenicia, over the sea to Cyprus, or struck up north to Antioch. They were evangelists, just as much as any apostle was. Indeed it was they who took the two revolutionary steps of preaching to Greeks who had no connection with Judaism, and then of launching the Gentile mission from Antioch. It was an unself-conscious effort.[11]

He added how the gospel likely was spread:

> They . . . went everywhere preaching the good news which had brought joy, release and a new life to themselves. This must often have been not formal preaching, but the informal chattering to friends and chance acquaintances, in homes and wine shops, on walks, and around market stalls. *They went everywhere gossiping the gospel;* they did it naturally, enthusiastically, and with the conviction of those who are not paid to say that sort of thing.[12]

A continuity is seen from Jesus calling Peter and Andrew and the unknown woman at the well, to Philip and the eunuch and Peter with

---

[8] As cited in M. Green, *Evangelism in the Early Church* (Grand Rapids: Eerdmans, 1970), 168.

[9] Ibid., 169.

[10] Ibid., 173.

[11] Ibid.

[12] Ibid., italics added.

Cornelius, to Pantaenus's witness to Clement of Alexandria and Justin's witness to Tatian.[13] While the gospel spread so much by nameless believers who knew nothing more than to tell the good news, leaders were also needed to guide the church theologically and heroically into the future. Such were some of the early church fathers.

Key Early Leaders

Polycarp, bishop of Smyrna, is best remembered for his courageous martyrdom. This second-century church father found himself before the proconsul, standing in the arena. The proconsul ordered the elderly saint to recant his faith in Christ. Polycarp replied, "Eighty and six years have I served Him, and He never did me any injury: how then can I blaspheme my King and my Savior?"[14] When threatened with wild beasts, Polycarp remained undaunted. When threatened with fire, he answered: "Thou threatenest me with fire which burneth for an hour, and after a little is extinguished, but art ignorant of the fire of the coming judgment and of eternal punishment."[15]

> "They went everywhere gossiping the gospel."
>
> —Michael Green

Polycarp was sentenced to be burned at the stake. But the fire didn't burn him. Finally, he was pierced with a dagger. He was praised not primarily for his courage but because his death was "altogether consistent with the Gospel of Christ."[16] Polycarp also led in the advancement of the gospel to new lands. Irenaeus recorded Polycarp's role in sending Pothinus to Celtic Gaul as an evangelist.

Ignatius, bishop of Antioch, wrote an epistle to Polycarp, identifying himself as a witness for Jesus Christ. These early church fathers saw evangelism as central to the Christian faith.

Irenaeus was a disciple of Polycarp. His work *Against Heresies* refuted the Gnostic heresy that threatened to sap the evangelistic fervor of the early church. The writings of many Christian thinkers served the gospel well in the formative years of the church, from Origen's *Against Celsus* to Augustine's *City of God*. While in Rome, Ire-

[13] Ibid., 224.

[14] Polycarp, "Epistle to the Philippians," *Apostolic Fathers,* vol. 1 of Ante-Nicene Fathers (Grand Rapids: Eerdmans, 1988), 89.

[15] Ibid., 90.

[16] Ibid., 94.

naeus heard of the horrible persecution in Lyons, in which the famous martyr Blandina was killed. Wild animals, beatings, molten copper, and other atrocities caused Blandina's martyrdom. Many believers in Lyons were revealed as worthy of the martyr's crown.

Irenaeus came to the city to be bishop, and eventually the city was declared to be Christian. Tertullian's famous statement written a few years later that "the blood of the martyrs is the seed" of the Christians was apparent in Lyons. Irenaeus eventually dispatched missionaries to other areas in Gaul and beyond.

The apologist Justin Martyr, another second-century saint, stood fearlessly as a martyr. His writings defended Christianity. This Christian philosopher also saw evangelism as a priority:

> At last [Justin] became acquainted with Christianity, being at once impressed with the extraordinary fearlessness which the Christians displayed in the presence of death, and with the grandeur, stability, and truth of the teachings of the Old Testament. *From this time he acted as an evangelist, taking every opportunity to proclaim the Gospel as the only safe and certain philosophy, the only way to salvation.*[17]

Born about 205, Gregory Thaumaturgos evangelized the city of Neo-Caesarea. The saying was that when Gregory came there, only 17 Christians could be found; when he died, there were only 17 pagans. His name means "miracle worker," referring to the miracles attributed to his ministry.

As the years passed, the church followed the pattern of Old Testament Israel, gradually substituting passion for God with ritual. In the centuries after the New Testament era, the sacramental system developed. It focused more on the practice of certain forms in the church rather than a relationship with Christ lived in the world. Evangelism particularly suffered as the sacraments of baptism and the eucharist replaced the message of the gospel.

Early Movements

Montanism emerged in the late second century in response to the growing formalism in the church. The movement was named for Montanus of Asia Minor, who was characterized by a mystical

[17] Ibid., "Introductory Notes to the First Apology of Justin Martyr," 1:297. Italics added.

demeanor and a focus on the Holy Spirit and the imminent return of Christ. The most notable adherent of Montanism was Tertullian. Montanists denounced the growing distinction between clergy and laity in the church.

Novatianism arose from the influence of Novatian, leader of a spiritual reform movement in Rome in the third century. Taylor declared, "His zeal for the gospel brought him many honors."[18] Novatianism was a reform movement against the growing worldliness in the church.

Donatists, named for Donatus, arose after the persecution by the Roman emperor Diocletian (284–305). Donatists opposed those who recanted the faith when faced with persecution. Donatists emphasized godly living and disciplined Christianity.

The fight to keep evangelism as a priority in the face of ritualism is with us still. Green wrote:

> Unless there is a transformation of contemporary church life so that once again the task of evangelism is something which is seen as incumbent on every baptized Christian, and is backed up by a quality of living which outshines the best that unbelief can muster, we are unlikely to make much headway through techniques of evangelism. Men will not believe that Christians have good news to share until they find that bishops and bakers, university professors and housewives, bus drivers and street corner preachers are all alike keen to pass along, however different their methods may be. And they will continue to believe that the church is an introverted society composed of "respectable" people and bent on its own preservation until they see in church groupings and individual Christians the caring, the joy, the fellowship, the self sacrifice, and the openness which mark the early church at its best.[19]

Growth in the Face of Persecutions and Plagues

One should not underestimate the impact of the changed lives of unbelievers to impact a pagan culture. One of the underestimated facets of early church history concerns the massive plagues that hit the empire. During the reign of Marcus Aurelius beginning about

[18] M. Taylor, *Exploring Evangelism* (Kansas City: Nazarene Publishing House, 1964), 77.

[19] Green, *Evangelism in the Early Church*, 275.

AD 165, a plague devastated the empire, taking the emperor as well. Another came around AD 251 with similar effects. About 260, in his Easter letter, Dionysius wrote a tribute to the believers whose heroic efforts cost many of them their lives. Pagans tended to flee the cities during plagues, but Christians were more likely to stay and minister to the suffering: "Most of our brother Christians showed unbonded love and loyalty, never sparing themselves and thinking only of one another," Dionysius observed, adding, "Needless of danger, they took charge of the sick, attending to their every need and ministering to them in Christ, and with them departed this life serenely happy."[20]

Reading this from a comfortable home in the West, I wonder if we can share in the difficulty of the persecuted church by our willingness in the West to forsake comfort in order to minister to those in dire need, whether it be AIDS patients or giving ourselves more to those who suffer in our culture, whether by illness or poverty. Dyonisius would agree: "The best of our brothers lost their lives in this manner, a number of presbyters, deacons, and laymen winning high commendation so that death in this form, the result of great piety and strong faith, seems in every way the equal of martyrdom."[21]

I fear that sometimes we in the West can feel a bit of self-pity that we do not suffer as believers do in places like Saudi Arabia and China. Of course, some relish our ease of life and pursue a prosperity gospel long on narcissism and short on sacrifice. But if Dionysius is right, there is yet a way to be valiant for Christ in any culture: seek the marginalized, the disenfranchised, those no one cares about, and love them and be Christ to them. Consider the example of William Booth, the founder of the Salvation Army. Each Christmas, there was a tradition in London: the churches would send out representatives to the streets to invite the poor to the celebration, and thousands thronged there. Anglicans would begin by announcing: "All of you who are Anglicans come with us." Catholics would join in: "All who are Catholics come with us." The Methodist, the Lutherans, and others would follow suit. When all the invitations were made, many more people milled about. At that point, William Booth would shout to the people: "All of you who belong to no one come with me."[22]

At the same time seasons of persecution, as mentioned above in the lives of Polycarp and others, galvanized the church, causing her to focus on essentials. I have spoken to those from the persecuted

[20] Stark, *The Rise of Christianity*, 82.

[21] Ibid.

[22] W. Kallestad, *Entertainment Evangelism* (Nashville: Abingdon, 1996), 53.

church in our day from other lands. They never seem to quibble over the color of carpet in a building or argue much about musical styles. Sadly, as the church came to power in the Roman Empire, it also seemed to lose its passion for sacrifice, and the impact of the gospel suffered as well.

Some have seen the rise of Christendom as a reality from Constantine's time (285–337) onward as ushering in the triumph of Christianity. Actually, it began an era of institutionalism and doctrinal deviation unprecedented before that time. Constantine "destroyed [Christianity's] most attractive and dynamic aspects, turning a high-intensity, grassroots movement into an arrogant institution controlled by an elite who often managed to be both brutal and lax."[23]

From about Augustine's time (354–430) until the Reformation, evangelism suffered. However, there were faint stars that lit the distant skyline of the West. The Reformation paved the way for the remarkable evangelistic expansion across the globe. In the modern era, several great awakenings and global missions expansion ushered untold multitudes into the kingdom of God.

The Middle Ages

One can trace the health of the church throughout history by its commitment to evangelism. One can also trace the lack of health of the church by observing its decline into institutionalism. The Dark Ages were so named for many reasons. But from a spiritual vantage point, one can see the twilight of evangelistic conviction and work throughout much of the established church during this era. The rising dominance of the Roman Catholic Church brought a theological shift from biblical authority alone along with a rise in ritualism.

The shift in focus from the New Testament gospel to the sacraments in the church blunted the spread of the true message of salvation. Still, God always has a people, a righteous remnant of the faithful. Certain individuals prove worthy of mention.

Ulfilas (318–88) reached his own people the Goths in the fourth century AD. Barbarians along the Roman Empire's northern border captured many Romans and enslaved them. Ulfilas was won to Christ by the witness of Roman Christians who had become slaves. He won many of his own people to Christ, translating much of the New Testament into the Gothic language.

---

[23] R. Stark, *For the Glory of God* (Princeton: Princeton University Press, 2003), 33.

Patrick evangelized parts of Britain in the fifth century. He was kidnapped from his native Scotland and taken to Northern Ireland by marauding pirates. After his capture, he recalled the teachings and prayers of his godly mother and was converted at age 16. His six years in prison bred a desire to see his captors converted, along with all the Irish. Patrick established over 365 churches and reached well over 120,000 people for Christ.[24] He is now honored as the patron saint of Ireland.

The person responsible for evangelizing much of Scotland in the sixth century was Columba (521–97). Converted at age 21, he and twelve priests left Ireland for Scotland in 563. Columba ministered chiefly on the island of Iona, laboring there for the Lord for 34 years. Others would come to Iona to be equipped, then would go forth bearing the good news.

Near the end of the sixth century Augustine of Canterbury (545–605) evangelized Britain. Not to be confused with the more famous Augustine of Hippo, he nevertheless had a significant ministry. Traveling to the British Isles in 597, Augustine and his companions won the ruler Ethelbert to Christ. The king told Augustine his people would not "hinder your preaching and winning any you can as converts to your faith."[25] The king gathered the people daily at one point to hear the gospel. Augustine established a ministry center named Canterbury where he eventually became the first archbishop. Many Angles and Saxons came to Christ through the outreach of Augustine.

Boniface preached the gospel first in Germany and Belgium. He earned the title "apostle of Germany" and became the first archbishop of Mainz. So successful were his efforts that he was questioned by the Pope in Rome. His ministry experienced what modern missiologists call "people movements"—a movement of entire communities to Christ at once. He chopped down a sacred tree devoted to the pagan god Thor. When nothing happened to him, he reached many people with the gospel. Boniface died as a martyr at the hands of pagans in 754. Historian Latourette said of him, "Humble, a man of prayer, self-sacrificing, courageous, steeped in Scriptures . . . he was at once a great Christian, a great missionary, and a great bishop."[26]

---

[24] Taylor, *Exploring Evangelism*, 95.

[25] N. E. Schneider, *Augustine of England* (New York: F. M. Barton Co., 1944), 126.

[26] K. S. Latourette, *A History of Christianity: Beginnings to 1500,* rev. ed. (New York: Harper and Row, 1975), I:349.

The Reformation Period

Evangelism on the Eve of the Reformation

In the face of the ritualism and worldliness so common in the Catholic Church at this time, several movements that emphasized biblical evangelism emerged before the Reformation.

Peter Waldo ministered in the twelfth century. A wealthy merchant in the city of Lyons, France, Waldo became disheartened with money, and experienced renewal and conversion. He took a vow of poverty and eventually begged alms for the necessities of life. His followers were called the "Poor Men of Lyons," and eventually "the Waldenses." His movement challenged the formalism and authoritarianism of the established church. His followers were looking for a return of the vibrancy of the apostolic era.

Many Waldenses were martyred at the hands of the Catholic church, often because of their conviction concerning the believer's baptism following conversion. They promoted an aggressive evangelism, and their goal was to recapture the dynamic, Bible-centered program of the first-century church. The Waldenses proclaimed the gospel and opposed the established church, as did other groups such as the Henricians, the Arnoldists, the Cathari, the Lollards, and the Petrobrusians. Such groups were the forerunners of the Reformation of the sixteenth century.

Francis of Assisi (1181–1226) ministered in thirteenth-century Italy. His early days of licentiousness and folly ended when he came to Christ. He went from riches to rags to Christ, rejecting any inheritance from his family and devoting his life to the preaching of Christ. Francis's abounding love and joy had a great influence on the people. He organized followers into twos and sent them out to evangelize the multitudes. These followers eventually were called "Franciscans." The Franciscans were particularly effective in preaching to the common people.

Jerome Savonarola (1452–98), a giant of prayer and preaching, sought to propagate the gospel in fifteenth-century Italy. His mental capabilities were great even in his early years, and he faced a promising career in academia. But God had other plans for this brilliant young Italian. In 1475 he enrolled in a monastery in Bologna, where he offered himself as a living sacrifice of service. For the next seven years, he devoted himself to Bible study and prayer.

Savonarola soon was transferred to St. Mark's monastery in Florence, where he failed at first in his preaching. He spent much time praying and fasting over the Scriptures. The Lord eventually led him to Revelation and the message of the apocalypse. This proved to be God's message for the people of that day. Savonarola's preaching from the Revelation brought a powerful awakening and reformation to Florence.

Biographer Misciattelli quoted a contemporary of Savonarola who described his preaching: "Savonarola introduced what might be called a new way of preaching the Word of God; an apostolic way; not dividing his sermons into parts, or embellishing them with high sounding words of elegance, but having as his sole aim the explaining of Scripture, and the return to the simplicity of the primitive church."[27]

Savonarola was eventually promoted to spiritual and political leader in Florence. He declared Florence a theocracy and led a citywide revival. This lasted for about two years until the corrupt leaders began to get a following. Savonarola was eventually martyred for his stand against the immoral practices of the papacy.

Other notable Christian leaders during the years leading up to the Reformation could be cited: Bernard of Clairvaux (1091–1153); John Tauler (1290–1361), the mystic of Germany; John Wycliffe; and Jan Hus—to name only a few. Others who will never be known except in eternity also contributed to the spread of the gospel over these centuries. Still, the ominous influence of the established Catholic church, along with its political might, hindered the followers of Christ from spreading the good news. But a light was dawning on the horizon—the light of the Protestant Reformation.

Evangelism in the Reformation

The sixteenth century stands as a watershed in human history. The influence of the Renaissance, with the rebirth of classical learning, and the Reformation, which paved the way for later spiritual awakenings, can still be felt today. While the Reformation was not primarily an evangelistic movement, it provided the theological basis for the spread of the gospel.

Martin Luther (1486–1546) became convinced of the doctrine of justification by faith. Called the "Apostle of Faith," his emphasis on

[27] P. Misciattelli, *Savonarola* (New York: D. Appleton and Company, 1930), 46.

salvation by faith pointed people to the error of the Catholic Church's salvation-by-works system of merit. His contributions to the field of evangelism and church growth are fourfold. First, Luther helped to bring about a clear and concise gospel. He clarified for the church the message of salvation—salvation by faith, not by works. Second, he emphasized the preaching and teaching of the Word of God. Preaching was central to the public worship service, and the Word of God was to be central to preaching. The Reformation was a call back to the Word of God. Third, Luther emphasized the priesthood of believers, which helped to abolish the spiritual caste system. This also led to an emphasis on personal responsibility for believers to be servants of Christ. Fourth, Luther considered himself an evangelist and preached evangelistically.[28]

John Calvin (1509–64) also made a fourfold contribution to the Reformation and the discipline of evangelism. First, he highlighted the work of God's grace in a person's salvation. Out of this came a focus on the doctrine of salvation based on the principle of divine grace as the only factor in salvation. With his basic premises (sovereignty of God, hopelessness of man, adequacy of Christ, salvation through grace, and grace bestowed through divine election), Calvin renounced salvation by works. Second, he emphasized hymn-singing, insisting on Bible-centered songs. Thus, he linked truths of God to worship. Third, Calvin practiced extemporaneous preaching, emphasizing eloquent speech coupled with an evangelistic accent. Fourth, he practiced personal evangelism through personal appeal and correspondence. He desired that all classes come to Christ.

The most effective group in emphasizing biblical revival during the Reformation was the Anabaptists. This group desired to bring the church back to its New Testament roots. Following the baptism of a group at Felix Manz's home on January 21, 1525, the Anabaptists (rebaptizers) grew. They emphasized the New Testament concept of believer's baptism following conversion. Balthasar Hubmaier (1481–1528) was an Anabaptist theologian and evangelist. He baptized 6,000 people in one year and was burned at the stake in 1528 for his beliefs.[29]

---

[28] Taylor, *Exploring Evangelism*, 154–55.

[29] J. M. Terry, *Evangelism: A Concise History* (Nashville: Broadman & Holman, 1994), 82.

Great Awakenings and Evangelism

In the modern era in the West, effective evangelism was almost always related to spiritual awakening. The greatest evangelistic results, methods, and leaders were born out of revival. In fact, much modern church history in the West may be traced along two central themes: the impact of the Enlightenment and a succession of mighty spiritual awakenings.

In recent centuries, spiritual awakenings have birthed most of the effective advances in evangelism, both in the numbers of converts and in new methods. They have often led to church-planting movements as well. Evangelism does not always lead to revival, but revival always brings the church back to a renewed evangelistic passion. A general overview of evangelism in modern history must emphasize a survey of historical revival movements.

Spiritual awakening or revival is a divine intervention into the church that causes a serious reflection on personal sin and open confession of sin. This results in a renewed awareness of God's presence and fresh power for ministry.[30]

There is much confusion in our day over the terms "revival," "awakening," and "spiritual awakening." Some people use "revival" to refer to the work of God among believers and "awakening" to speak of the conversion of masses to Christ. This is a valid use, seen in the writings of Jonathan Edwards in the eighteenth century. However, I choose to use these terms as synonyms for the following reasons.

First, too many evangelicals think "revival" refers to a four-day meeting with an evangelist, aimed at reaching the lost. This is actually mass evangelism. Such attractional meetings can be useful, but they are not revival. Today, many churches hold such meetings aimed at revival of the saints and conversion of the lost, but it is still a *meeting* unless God moves in a mighty way. Such protracted services might be called "revival meetings" but not "revival." Occasionally, God does send revival in the midst of a meeting! So I use "awakening" and "revival" as synonyms because the word revival has lost its true meaning for many people.

A second reason I use these two terms as synonyms is the biblical terminology associated with them. Several terms in Scripture relate to spiritual awakening. In the Old Testament, key terms include *chayah,* "to live or make alive again," found in Ps 85:6: "Will you not

---

[30] For an elaboration of the material in this section, see M. McDow and A. L. Reid, *Firefall: How God Shaped History through Revivals* (Nashville: B & H, 1997).

revive us again, that your people may rejoice in you?" (NIV). The term is also seen in Hab 3:2 and Hos 6:2. *Chadash* means "to repair or make new," as seen in Ps 51:10: "*Renew* a steadfast spirit within me." David's prayer of repentance following his sin with Bathsheba demonstrates the cry of a saint seeking personal revival. *Chalaph,* "to alter or change," is found in Isa 40:31.

New Testament terms include *anakainō,* translated as "to make new again." The word is found in Rom 12:2: "Be transformed by the *renewing* of your mind." It can also be seen in 2 Cor 4:16; Col 3:10; and Titus 3:5. *Eknephō,* "To be sober, to come to one's senses," is seen in 1 Cor 15:34. Finally, the word *egeirō,* meaning "to awaken from sleep," is the closest biblical expression for "spiritual awakening." Romans 13:11–13, one of the most important texts in the New Testament on genuine revival, uses this term in v. 11: "It is high time to *awake* out of sleep" (NKJV).

So, while some people use "revival" to refer to God's activity among His people and "awakening" to refer to the result of revival on culture, the terms will be used interchangeably in the following overview.

Spiritual awakening is the supernatural work of God. It is divinely initiated. It is the story of God's involvement in history. It is not primarily for our benefit but for God's glory. Spiritual awakening normally comes after a time of spiritual decline in the church and moral decay in the culture. Too many people seek revival simply to help their church grow or to solve problems or to curb a moral slide. These may result from revival, but we should seek revival simply because we want to know and honor God!

An awakening brings the church to a renewed sense of wonder toward God. We have lost the sense of wonder, of holy awe, in our churches. Awakenings renew a sense of amazement at the great God.

Historians are not in agreement as to the number of awakenings in recent centuries. Awakenings can be compared to wars, in that there have only been two world wars, but beyond those many other wars have been fought. The First and Second Great Awakenings were obvious movements of God's Spirit; beyond that, anywhere from one to three more awakenings have been designated by historians. Awakenings differ in depth and extent as do wars, but like wars, when you are in the middle of it, it is quite great in its impact on you! I am convinced that in addition to the First and Second Great Awakenings, at least two more awakenings can be seen in the last four centuries.

The Great Awakening in the eighteenth century occurred on three fronts: Pietism in Europe, the Evangelical Awakening in Britain, and the First Great Awakening in the American colonies.

Pietism

In response to a cold formalism, the movement known as Pietism began in Europe in the late 1600s. One of the early leaders of this awakening was Philip Spener, who wrote the book *Pia Desideria* (Pious Desires), an appeal to spiritual reform in 1675.[31] Spener, called the father of Pietism by many, emphasized the personal nature of the Christian experience. He secured the appointment of A. H. Francke at the University of Halle in 1692. Under Francke's leadership, Halle became "a pietistic center of higher education and revivalism."[32]

Nicholaus Ludwig Von Zinzendorf (1700–60) studied at Halle. Zinzendorf organized prayer groups among the students while at the university. Zinzendorf eventually went to the University of Wittenberg, where he formed the Order of the Grain of Mustard Seed in 1718. In 1722 he acquired an estate that became a safe haven for persecuted members of the Hussite Church. It was from this group that the "Unitas Fratrum" (Unity of the Brethren) or Moravians were born. A particularly powerful movement of the Spirit came at a communion service on August 12, 1727. Following this, a continuous prayer structure developed, and a missionary enterprise began, resulting in one missionary for every 60 Moravians.

Zinzendorf's impact can be traced to his early years at Halle. Key emphases of this awakening included an obvious conversion experience, experimental faith, small-group discipleship, and foreign missions. Pietism ultimately emphasized experiences to the neglect of theology, however—a move that hindered its impact.

The First Great Awakening

The First Great Awakening generally includes the period from the 1720s to the 1740s, although revival embers were lit in later years in the South. Revival fires blazed as early as 1726 through the ministry

---

[31] Fortress Press continues to publish the book, illustrating its status as a classic in Christian spirituality.

[32] E. E. Cairns, *An Endless Line of Splendor: Revivals and Their Leaders from the Great Awakening to the Present* (Wheaton: Tyndale House, 1986), 34.

of Theodore Freylinghuysen in the Dutch Reformed Church in New Jersey. He emphasized four things:

1. *evangelistic* preaching,
2. *zealous* visitation,
3. *church* discipline, and
4. *lay* preachers.

The Tennent family witnessed awakening among their Presbyterian circles in Pennsylvania and the middle colonies. William, the father, began the "log college," a place to train his sons and other young men. This was a prototype for seminaries. Many evangelists, church planters, and revival leaders came from William's influence. Gilbert Tennent was an outspoken leader. He preached a famous sermon, "The Dangers of an Unconverted Ministry," denouncing the unregenerate clergy of his day.

Jonathan Edwards was a catalyst in New England. Edwards was a brilliant student, graduating from Yale as valedictorian at age 16. He read Latin by age six. He pastored a significant Congregationalist church in Northampton, Massachusetts. He witnessed two primary revival movements during the First Great Awakening, including the valley revival of 1734–35. Edwards recorded this revival in his *Narrative of Surprising Conversions.* Keys to the outpouring of God's Spirit, which caught Edwards and his church by surprise, included:

- biblical preaching,
- personal tragedies, and
- youth involvement.

Edwards, one of the greatest theologians, practitioners, and writers in the history of spiritual awakening, wrote his *Narrative* to give an account of the powerful revival that began in 1734–35 in and around Northampton, Massachusetts, where he was pastor. He prefaced this account by noting five powerful revivals during the long tenure of his predecessor and grandfather, Solomon Stoddard. The revival surfaced following a series of messages on justification by faith, and it spread quickly to neighboring towns. Edwards describes the effects of the revival:

> Presently upon this, a great and earnest concern about the great things of religion, and the eternal world, became *universal* in all parts of the town, and among persons of all degrees, and

> all ages . . . all other talk but about spiritual and eternal things, was soon thrown by; all the conversation, in all companies and upon all occasions, was upon these things only, unless so much as was necessary for people carrying on their ordinary secular business.[33]

In 1740–42 came the most powerful season of revival during the First Great Awakening. During this time, Edwards preached his famous sermon, "Sinners in the Hands of an Angry God." In the same period, Edwards wrote a treatise entitled *Some Thoughts Concerning the Present Revival of Religion in New England.*

In 1741 Edwards published *The Distinguishing Marks of a Work of the Spirit of God,* a collection of sermons that included five "marks" that illustrated the Spirit's true activity in revival (see "The Five Marks"). Edwards contributed greatly to the field of spiritual awakening with his writings.

The Five Marks

1. When the operation is such to raise their esteem of Jesus.
2. When the spirit that is at work operates against the interests of Satan's kingdom, which lies in encouraging and establishing sin, and cherishing men's worldly lusts; this is a sure sign that it is a true, and not a false spirit.
3. Men show a greater regard to the Holy Scriptures.
4. If it leads persons to truth, convincing them of those things that are true, we may safely determine that it is a right and true spirit.
5. If the spirit that is at work among a people operates as a spirit of love to God and man, it is a sure sign that is the Spirit of God.

George Whitefield, also involved in the Evangelical Awakening in England with John and Charles Wesley, came to the colonies several times. He preached from north to south, uniting the various movements.

[33] J. Edwards, "Narrative of the Surprising Work of God," in *The Works of Jonathan Edwards,* ed. S. E. Dwight (Edinburgh: The Banner of Truth Trust, 1834), 1: 348.

In the southern colonies, revival spread mainly through Methodists and Baptists. The leaders among Baptists were Shubal Stearns and Daniel Marshall. Most Southern Baptist historians trace their roots to this movement, particularly the ministry of Stearns and the Sandy Creek Church in North Carolina. In 17 years the Sandy Creek Church birthed 42 churches, which in turn produced 125 ministers.[34] In the late 1700s Methodism spread rapidly in the South.

Several truths can be gleaned from the First Great Awakening. God used *different types of people* and *different denominational perspectives*—Gilbert Tennent, Jonathan Edwards, George Whitefield, Theodore Freylinghuysen, and many others. *Effective ministry training* developed from the awakening as many came to Christ and large numbers entered vocational ministry. The log college and the birth of many universities are examples. *Laity* were involved in ministry. *Biblical theology* was emphasized. Genuine revival is more than an experience; it includes a deepened understanding of the truths of God's Word.

The Evangelical Awakening in England

John Wesley (1703–91) and George Whitefield (1714–70) were two key leaders of the Evangelical Awakening in England during the eighteenth century. Some historians have stated that this awakening prevented England from going through an ordeal like the French Revolution. Wesley's experience as a college student at Oxford is probably best remembered by the "Holy Club" that involved both John and his brother Charles, George Whitefield, and a handful of others. Whitefield was converted during those days.[35]

The fact that Wesley was not actually converted until years after his Oxford days does not minimize the impact made on his subsequent ministry by the Holy Club.[36] The Holy Club at Oxford forged relationships between the men who figured prominently in the awakening in England and the American colonies.

Wesley's oft-noted conversion came in 1738. On May 24, 1738, John Wesley attended a society meeting on Aldersgate Street in Lon-

---

[34] McDow and Reid, *Firefall,* 222.

[35] For further information on the life of Whitefield, see A. Dallimore, *George Whitefield,* 2 vols. (Edinburgh: Banner of Truth, 1970).

[36] For further information on the life of John Wesley, see N. Curnock, ed., *The Journal of John Wesley*, 8 vols. (London: The Epworth Press, 1938); J. W. Drakeford, ed., *John Wesley* (Nashville: Broadman Press, 1979); and R. G. Tuttle, *John Wesley: His Life and Theology* (Grand Rapids: Zondervan, 1978).

don. While someone read the prologue to Martin Luther's commentary on Romans, Wesley was converted. Here is the account from his *Journal:* "About a quarter to nine, while he was describing the change which God works in the heart through faith in Christ, I felt my heart strangely warmed. I felt that I did trust in Christ, Christ alone, for salvation."[37] His was a remarkable ministry that, along with Whitefield's influence and Charles Wesley's hymn-writing, affected the spiritual life of the entire nation. Wesley never desired to sever ties with the Church of England, but the Evangelical Awakening resulted in the formation of the Methodist Church.

Under the influence of the Wesleys, the Methodist Church was born. By John Wesley's death in 1791, there were 79,000 Methodists in England and 119,000 around the world.

The "methods" (hence the name "Methodist") that the Wesleys and Whitefield developed included

- societies,
- field preaching,
- hymn-singing,
- disciplined living, and
- publications.

Howell Harris, Daniel Rowland, and others were instrumental in the revival in Wales. Beyond his impact in England, Whitefield made seven trips to the New World. His itinerant ministry spread the gospel across the colonies. What makes this more impressive is that Whitefield was only 26 years old in 1741 when the First Great Awakening was at its peak!

Questions for Consideration

1. How can the history of the church help you see the difference between Christianity as an institution we maintain versus Christianity as a movement we advance?
2. When is the last time you saw God move in mighty power, in such a way that you knew He was at work?
3. Would you agree that in our day we need a God-intervention, a movement that renews the church and leads to passionate witness?

[37] J. Wesley, *The Journal of John Wesley,* N. Curnock, ed., 1: 475–76.

Chapter 8

History II: Nineteenth Century to Our Time

I felt ablaze with a desire to go through the length and breadth of Wales to tell of my Savior; and had that been possible, I was willing to pay God for doing so.[1]

—Evan Roberts

The end of the eighteenth century witnessed a shift that would cause Latourette the historian to call the ensuing nineteenth century the "Great Century" of Christianity. On the heels of the Great Awakening in the 1700s, the birth of modern missions would catapult the vision of the church in the West to the entire globe.

"William Carey may have been the greatest missionary since the time of the apostles," writes Danny Akin, adding, "He rightly deserves the honor of being known as the 'father of the modern missions movement.'"[2] The publication of *An Enquiry into the Obligations of Christians to Use Means for the Conversion of the Heathens* sent a shot across the bow of the church in his day (and should ours

[1] J. E. Orr, *The Flaming Tongue* (Chicago: Moody Press, 1973), 5.

[2] D. L. Akin, *Five Who Changed the World* (Wake Forest: Southeastern Baptist Theological Seminary, 2008), 6.

as well). Through his influence the Baptist Missionary Society was founded in 1792. The London Missionary Society was founded in 1795. Soon many would follow Carey to the ends of the earth.

The Second Great Awakening

The nineteenth century records the sorrowful rise of higher criticism and theological liberalism that would suck the life out of much of the European church in subsequent generations, rendering evangelism almost nonexistent. Higher criticism demonstrated the power of modernist, rational thought when applied to the Bible:

> Higher criticism sought to apply to the Bible the same principles of science and historical method applied to secular works. It was largely dependent upon the study of internal evidence, although available data from linguistics and archaeology were also incorporated. The primary questions concerned the determination of the authenticity and likely chronological order of different sources of a text, as well as the identity and authorial intent of the writers. Higher criticism began most notably with the French scholar Jean Astruc's work (mid-18th cent.) on the sources of the Pentateuch. It was continued by German scholars such as Johann Salomo Semler (1725–91), Johann Gottfried Eichhorn (1752–1827), Ferdinand Christian Baur (1792–1860), and Julius Wellhausen (1844–1918).[3]

The impact of this approach, which won the day among academics and in theological schools, was to diminish the roles of inspiration and revelation and elevate the ability of man to a place over Scripture. In that face of higher criticism, the West saw more seasons of refreshing through spiritual awakenings that spread the gospel and moved the church forward. Following the multiple movements in the great revival of the eighteenth century, the next great season of awakening came at the turn of the nineteenth century with the Second Great Awakening. This revival instilled a fresh passion for God in the emerging American nation.

This movement came soon after the Revolutionary War and is dated from the end of the eighteenth century well into the nineteenth. It was in the milieu of this movement that Carey began his work.

[3] http://www.questia.com/library/encyclopedia/higher_criticism.jsp (accessed October 2, 2008).

Various ideologies affected the church (Deism, skepticism, etc.). In addition, moral deficiencies were rampant in society. Revival touched both the established states on the Atlantic coast and the western frontier beyond the Appalachian Mountains.

Concerts of prayer were called by a group of New England ministers. This appeal was well received across the country.

A major precipitating factor in this movement was the outbreak of revival on college campuses. Skepticism and infidelity characterized the colleges. During this period immediately following the birth of the United States, the colleges in the East were often greatly influenced by European thinkers of the Enlightenment.[4]

Circular Letter of 23 New England Ministers Calling for Concerts of Prayer for Revival

To the ministers and churches of every Christian denomination in the United States, to unite in their endeavors to carry into execution the *humble attempt to promote explicit agreement and visible union of God's people in extraordinary prayer for the revival of religion and the advancement of Christ's Kingdom on earth.* In execution of this plan, it is proposed that the ministers and churches of every Christian denomination should be invited to maintain public prayer and praise, accompanied with such instruction from God's Word, as might be judged proper, on every first Tuesday, of the four quarters of the year, beginning with the first Tuesday of January, 1795, at two o'clock in the afternoon, if the plan of concert should then be ripe for a beginning, and so continuing from quarter to quarter, and from year to year, until the good Providence of God prospering our endeavors, we shall obtain the blessing for which we pray.

The campus of Hampden-Sydney College in Virginia became the first in a series of college revivals. The fertile field of young students played a pivotal role. Four young men—William Hill, Carey Allen,

[4] D. Dorchester, *Christianity in the United States* (New York: Hunt and Eaton, 1895), 316.

James Blythe, and Clement Read—were instrumental in the beginnings of revival at Hampden-Sydney in 1787 and the years following. Because they feared severe antagonism from the other students, the four young men began meeting secretly in the forest to pray and study. When they were discovered, they were greatly ridiculed by fellow students.

President John Blair Smith heard of the situation and was convicted by the infidelity on the campus. He invited the four students and others to pray with him in his parlor. Before long, "half of the students were deeply impressed and under conviction, and the revival spread rapidly through the college and to surrounding counties."[5] Hill later chronicled the revival's impact:

> Persons of all ranks in society, of all ages . . . became subjects of this work, so that there was scarcely a Magistrate on the bench, or a lawyer at the bar but became members of the church. . . . It was now as rare a thing to find one who was not religious, as it was formerly to find one that was. The frivolities and amusements once so prevalent were all abandoned, and gave place to singing, serious conversations, and prayer meetings.[6]

In addition, subsequent revival movements came to the school in 1802, 1814–15, 1822, 1827–28, 1831, 1833, and 1837.[7]

The Yale College revival began under the leadership of President Timothy Dwight, the grandson of Jonathan Edwards. Dwight came to the school when it was filled with infidelity. He began to preach against unbelief in the college chapel. By 1797 a group of students formed to improve moral conditions and pray for revival. A powerful spiritual movement swept through the school in the spring of 1802. A third of the student body was converted. C. A. Goodrich wrote of the change in attitude on campus:

> The salvation of the soul was the great subject of thought, of conversation, of absorbing interest; the convictions of many

[5] B. R. Lacy, *Revival in the Midst of the Years* (Hopewell, VA: Royal Publishers, 1968), 70.

[6] Quoted from Hill's biography in A. D. Thomas Jr., "Reasonable Revivalism: Presbyterian Evangelization of Educated Virginians, 1787–1837," *Journal of Presbyterian History* 61 (Fall 1983): 322.

[7] See Lacy, *Revival,* 68ff.; also Thomas, "Reasonable Revivalism," 322ff.

> were pungent and overwhelming; and "the peace of believing" which succeeded, was not less strongly marked.[8]

The movement spread to Dartmouth and Princeton. At Princeton three-fourths of the students made professions, and one-fourth entered the ministry.

A group of students at Williams College in Massachusetts made a tremendous impact on missions. Samuel Mills entered the college during a time of awakening there between 1804 and 1806. He and four others began to pray regularly for missions. In 1806 at one particular meeting they had to seek refuge from the rain in a haystack. During this "haystack meeting," Mills proposed a mission to Asia. This event was a precipitating factor leading to a major foreign missions enterprise. The first missionaries included Adoniram Judson and Luther Rice. Beyond the colleges, revival began in Northington, Connecticut, with meetings initiated by young people.

After a series of gatherings in 1799, the first real camp meeting was held in June of 1800 at the Red River Church in Kentucky. Crowds gathered in a given community for several days of worship and the observance of communion. Then, in August 1801 at Cain Ridge, Kentucky, 25,000 came together. Leaders included James McGready and Barton Stone, who were Presbyterians. Unusual phenomena were associated with some of the camp meetings. Many leaders, including Methodist circuit rider Peter Cartwright, discouraged such practices.

Charles Finney has been called the "father of American revivalism." A lawyer by training, Finney was powerfully converted in 1821 and embarked on a ministry of revival and evangelism. Finney is perhaps best known for his "new measures," innovative approaches that he incorporated into his ministry. While Finney overemphasized the work of man in spiritual movements, he was yet used of God in the salvation of many. His new measures included protracted meetings and "anxious benches." The "anxious seats" were a forerunner to the modern public invitation, as described by Finney:

> It was at Rochester that I first introduced this measure. . . . I made a call for the first time for persons who were willing to renounce their sins and give themselves to God to come forward to certain seats which I requested to be vacated, and offer themselves up

[8] See C. A. Goodrich, "Narrative of Revivals of Religion in Yale College," *American Quarterly Register* 10 (February 1838): 295–96.

> to God while we made them subjects of prayer. A much larger number came forward than I expected.[9]

The Second Great Awakening stirred a powerful evangelistic movement, with multitudes converted. Further, it introduced significant new methods: the camp meeting and Charles Finney's "new measures," among others. One of the greatest results of this revival came in missions. In 1810 Adoniram Judson and Luther Rice were two of the first missionaries sent overseas by the American Board of Commissioners for Foreign Missions. The missions movement followed a similar time of revival that touched the lives of men such as William Carey in Great Britain.

Many societies were birthed as well. The American Bible Society began in 1816 and the American Tract Society in 1825. Educational impact was seen in the formation of the first seminaries in the United States, including Andover in 1808, Princeton in 1812, and Yale Divinity in 1818. Further, the American Sunday School Union was founded in 1824. Finally, society was changed. The Second Great Awakening began what some have called the "golden age of Christianity."

The Layman's Prayer Revival 1857–58

By the mid–nineteenth century the effects of the Second Great Awakening subsided, due in part to growing prosperity, political turmoil over slavery, and religious extremism (such as the Millerites, who wrongly predicted the return of Jesus in 1843–44). Several simultaneous events occurred at the beginning of this movement, known as the Layman's Prayer Revival. Union prayer meetings, led by Jeremiah Lanphier, began in 1857; they spread quickly to involve over 50,000 within six months across the eastern part of the United States.

Unusual church revivals were reported in Canada, Massachusetts, South Carolina, and other places in 1856–57. Evangelism conferences held by the Presbyterian Church erupted in revival in 1857. Sunday school outreach efforts in the East were also a factor. In New York and Philadelphia, many businesses closed daily to pray.

Multitudes were converted. Seventy-five people were converted in a Brooklyn church revival meeting. A Catskill church saw 115 professions of faith in a few days. In Newark 3,000 people were converted in

[9] *The Autobiography of Charles G. Finney* (Minneapolis: Bethany House, 1977), 159.

two months. In Philadelphia a man began a prayer meeting like those in New York. Soon 6,000 people met daily, and a tent revival was held. It continued for more than four months, with 150,000 attending. Over 10,000 were converted in one year.

God was exalted in this revival. This was the only awakening without a single well-known leader. Also, it came unexpectedly. Further, there was great cooperation among believers. It was part of a worldwide movement, including the revival in Wales in 1859 and the revival in the ministry of Andrew Murray in South Africa. It strongly influenced D. L. Moody during his youth. The Layman's Prayer Revival of 1857–59 was characterized by its wide appeal. Several colleges experienced revival during this time. J. Edwin Orr documented revival movements at Oberlin, Yale, Dartmouth, Middlebury, Williams, Amherst, Princeton, and Baylor.[10]

Global Movements 1900–1910

At the turn of the twentieth century, fresh winds of the Spirit again touched many people. The most visible example of the period was the revival of 1904–08. This included the Welsh Revival and other occurrences as well in the United States and abroad. Some features of the period were controversial, including the birth of modern-day Pentecostalism in 1901 and the subsequent Azusa Street Revival.[11]

The Welsh Revival concerns specifically the movement that began in 1904 in the tiny country of Wales. During one period, 100,000 people were converted in less than six months. A key leader was Evan Roberts. Roberts had four principles for revival:

1. Confess every known sin.
2. Put away every doubtful habit.
3. Obey the Holy Spirit promptly.
4. Confess Jesus publicly.

In the United States many denominations reported record growth. During this time the Home Mission Board of the Southern Baptist Convention began its department of evangelism, and Southwestern Seminary was founded.

[10] J. E. Orr, *Fervent Prayer* (Chicago: Moody Press, 1974), 11–12.

[11] E. E. Cairns, *An Endless Line of Splendor: Revivals and Their Leaders from the Great Awakening to the Present* (Wheaton: Tyndale House, 1986), 177, gives the priority to the Pentecostal movement in characterizing the significance of what he calls a "global awakening" beginning in 1900.

Also, during the last part of the nineteenth century and the early years of the twentieth century, many prominent evangelists began to minister. Following in the line of D. L. Moody, these evangelists saw multitudes converted and many instances of genuine revival. These evangelists included R. A. Torrey, Billy Sunday, Sam Jones, Mordecai Ham, and Wilbur Chapman. This period witnessed as well the rise of music evangelists. Ira Sankey worked with D. L. Moody. Others included Homer Rhodeheaver and Charles Alexander.

Recent Spiritual Movements

While there has been no revival that one could call a "great awakening" in America since at least the turn of the twentieth century and most would argue even longer, several localized or more specialized revivals have occurred since then. The late 1940s and the 1950s was a time of unparalleled church growth and evangelism. The Southern Baptist Convention's greatest years of growth came during this period. J. Edwin Orr, in his final message delivered before his death, noted, "about 1949 there was a wave of revival in colleges throughout the United States."[12]

In the middle of the youth protests surrounding the Vietnam War, the Jesus Movement served to call youths to a radical commitment to Jesus. This was the closest thing to spiritual awakening among youth of the late 1960s and early 1970s. This movement, which did not rival earlier awakenings in impact, generally paralleled the unrest among America's youth during this era. Many people familiar with the Jesus Movement tend to emphasize the countercultural Jesus People (or Jesus "Freaks"), but the renewal among youth was actually much broader. It included powerful church revivals and campus awakenings as well as the more colorful phenomena such as underground newspapers, coffeehouses and communes, and the new music. It was expressed in youth choir tours, youth evangelism conferences, and music festivals. Contemporary Christian music and the rise of praise and worship songs flowed from the stream of this youth revival.

The Southern Baptist Convention (SBC) reported records in baptisms in the early 1970s, propelled mainly by a remarkable increase in youth baptisms. For example, the SBC record for baptisms occurred in 1972 with 445,725. Of that number, 137,667 were youth—the largest number and the highest percentage of youth baptisms during

---

[12] J. E. Orr, *Revival Is Like Judgment Day* (Atlanta: Home Mission Board, 1987), 9.

any year in SBC history. The second highest number of youth baptisms was in 1971. Even more significant than the total baptism figure was the more substantial youth baptism figures. The Jesus Movement reached its peak in 1970–71.

A Fifteen-Year Survey of Youth Baptisms in the Southern Baptist Convention 1971–88[13]

1971	126,127	409,659	30.7	N/A	N/A
1972	137,667	445,725	30.8	24,997,000	0.550
1973	119,844	413,990	28.9	25,287,000	0.473
1974	115,345	410,482	28.1	25,454,000	0.453
1975	116,419	421,809	27.6	25,420,000	0.457
1976	103,981	384,496	27.0	25,305,000	0.410
1977	88,838	345,690	25.6	25,014,000	0.355
1978	97,118	336,050	28.9	24,549,000	0.395
1979	93,142	368,738	25.2	23,919,000	0.389
1980	108,633	429,742	25.2	23,409,576	0.464
1981	101,076	405,608	24.9	23,409,576	0.444
1982	102,259	411,554	24.8	22,358,000	0.457
1983	97,984	394,606	24.8	22,199,000	0.441
1984	91,431	372,028	24.6	21,958,000	0.416
1985	86,499	351,071	24.6	21,632,000	0.399
1986	86,387	363,124	23.8	21,300,000	0.405

In addition, record enrollments and continuous increases characterized all six Southern Baptist seminaries during the decade following the Jesus Movement. Campus Crusade for Christ, a college parachurch ministry, held Explo '72 in Dallas. It resulted in "the most massive gathering of students and Christian laymen to ever descend on one city."[14] Its purpose was to equip and inspire young people in evangelism. Over 80,000 registered for the event, with some 150,000 attending a Saturday music festival concluding the meeting. Evan-

[13] B. Beachem, Student Discipleship Ministries, Fort Worth, Texas, to Alvin L. Reid, Indianapolis, Indiana, January 8, 1990, transcript in the hand of Alvin L. Reid, and *Quarterly Review* (July-August-September 1972): 20–21.

[14] "Baptists among 80,000 Attending Explo '72," *Indiana Baptist* (July 5,1972): 5.

gelist Billy Graham was very favorable toward what he called the "Jesus revolution."[15] Graham noted that during the period an unusually high number of youth attended and professed faith in Christ at his crusades.

A famous revival occurred at Asbury College in 1970, beginning spontaneously during a chapel service. The dean of the college was scheduled to speak, but he felt impressed to have a testimony service. Students began to flood toward the altar to pray. For 185 hours they continuously prayed, sang, and testified. Henry James of the college reported on what happened next:

> Before long, appeals began coming from other campuses for Asbury students to come and tell the story. This intensified the burden of prayer even as it heightened anticipation of what God was going to do. . . . The revival began to take on the dimensions of a national movement. By the summer of 1970 at least 130 colleges, seminaries and Bible schools had been touched by the revival outreach.[16]

Many other recent instances of revival could be named. A stirring example in a local church is Houston's First Baptist. John Bisagno came to First Baptist in 1970, when the church was a declining downtown church. Bisagno watched the Jesus Movement. Unlike many in Southern Baptist circles, Bisagno affirmed the youth of the day, arguing that he would rather see youth yelling for Jesus than sitting barefoot on a park slope taking drugs.

Bisagno led the church to get involved in an effort called SPIRENO (Spiritual Revolution Now), led by evangelist Richard Hogue. As a result the church baptized 1,669 during 1970–71, with the vast majority coming from young people. One reporter stated: "By taking the initiative, they gave their church and hundreds of others in Houston a chance to jump into the flow of this Jesus movement."[17]

Coffeehouse ministries, ocean baptisms, new music, personal evangelism, and many other phenomena characterized the period. There were controversial elements, including the overemphasis on a simplistic approach to the gospel and emotional experiences, the Charismatic movement, and the physical appearance of many of

[15] B. Graham, *The Jesus Revolution* (Grand Rapids: Zondervan, 1971).

[16] H. C. James, "Campus Demonstrations," in *One Divine Moment,* ed. R. Coleman (Old Tappan, N.J.: Fleming H. Revell, 1970), 55.

[17] D. Lee, "The Electric Revival," *Home Missions* (June/July 1971), 32.

the countercultural converts. The benefits certainly outweighed the liabilities, however. Beyond the evangelistic results cited above, the Jesus Movement helped many traditional churches to focus again on the work of the Holy Spirit. Many leaders in evangelism today were converted during the Jesus Movement or radically touched by its impact.[18]

Other 20th-Century Factors

The Rise of the Evangelical Movement

Fundamentalism arose in the latter part of the nineteenth century and the early twentieth as a reaction to higher criticism, theological liberalism, and the growing movement of evolution. Central to its rise was the publication of *The Fundamentals* (1910–1915), a twelve-volume reaction to liberalism.

During the 1920s, fundamentalists waged a war against modernism in three ways: by (unsuccessfully) attempting to regain control of Protestant denominations, mission boards, and seminaries; by supporting (with mixed success) Prohibition, Sunday "blue laws," and other measures defending traditional Protestant morality and sensibilities; and (fairly successfully) by attempting to stop the teaching of evolution in the public schools, a doctrine which they saw as inextricably linked to the development of "German" higher criticism and the source of the Great War.[19] The now infamous "Scopes Trial" of 1925, pitting Clarence Darrow against William Jennings Bryan, served to show fundamentalism as an anti-intellectual movement and led to its disrepute in the eyes of cultural elites.

A movement arose over the past century that sought to avoid the theological errors of liberalism on one hand and the extreme views of fundamentalism on the other. This is what has come to be known as the twentieth-century evangelical movement. The term "evangelical" has at least three broad uses:

---

[18] There are too many to name, but some examples of those who were touched by or provided leadership to the Jesus Movement were evangelist Jay Strack; Ohio evangelism director Mike Landry; HMB evangelism section staffer Jack Smith; Glenn Sheppard, who became the first to lead the Office of Prayer and Spiritual Awakening at the HMB; and many others. This writer, whose dissertation was on the Jesus Movement, was amazed to discover how many people today testify to the enduring positive impact of the Jesus Movement on their lives.

[19] http://www.wheaton.edu/isae/defining_evangelicalism.html (accessed October 2, 2008).

> There are three senses in which the term "evangelical" is used today as we enter the 21st century. The first is to see as "evangelical" all Christians who affirm a few key doctrines and practical emphases. British historian David Bebbington approaches evangelicalism from this direction and notes four specific hallmarks of evangelical religion: *conversionism*, the belief that lives need to be changed; *activism*, the expression of the gospel in effort; *biblicism*, a particular regard for the Bible; and *crucicentrism*, a stress on the sacrifice of Christ on the cross. A second sense is to look at evangelicalism as an organic group of movements and religious tradition. Within this context "evangelical" denotes a style as much as a set of beliefs. As a result, groups as disparate as black Baptists and Dutch Reformed Churches, Mennonites and Pentecostals, Catholic charismatics and Southern Baptists all come under the evangelical umbrella—demonstrating just how diverse the movement really is. A third sense of the term is as the self-ascribed label for a coalition that arose during the Second World War. This group came into being as a reaction against the perceived anti-intellectual, separatist, belligerent nature of the fundamentalist movement in the 1920s and 1930s. Importantly, its core personalities (like Harold John Ockenga and Billy Graham), institutions (for instance, Moody Bible Institute and Wheaton College), and organizations (such as the National Association of Evangelicals and Youth for Christ) have played a pivotal role in giving the wider movement a sense of cohesion that extends beyond these "card-carrying" evangelicals.[20]

I tend to think of the term primarily in the first and third uses above—there is broader evangelicalism, which refers to those who hold to historic evangelical doctrines, and there is the more recent movement noted above. Holding to the central idea that all truth is God's truth, modern evangelicalism argued that instead of fearing the findings of modern science and reason, believers should see that truth discovered through scientific reason does not compete with truth gained via divine revelation.

As a result many modern Christians began to use rational thought and evidentialism to defend their faith. An apologetic developed that

[20] Ibid.

depended heavily upon rational proofs for the existence of God, the reality of the resurrection, and so on.

> Whereas liberal Christians gave up the supernatural elements of their faith in the face of modernity's attacks and fundamentalists gave up the hope of finding anything good via rational and scientific method, conservative evangelicals emphasized rational explanations and defenses, or "a proof oriented Christianity" in which nonbelievers were asked to evaluate "evidence that demands a verdict."[21]

While there is certainly a place for this approach (I would argue particularly in discipling believers in an increasingly post-Christian era), there is also a danger. If not careful we can "attempt to contextualize the gospel message in an overly confident, rationalistic culture that no longer recognizes the possibility of anchoring truth in a transcendent reality."[22] We can unintentionally overuse modernist approaches to turn theology into mathematics, emphasizing our formulas to the neglect of the God of the Bible. Further, it led to too close a relationship between modernism and evangelicalism.

Oliver O'Donovan observed four features of the twentieth century that have led to disillusionment with the promises of modernity and as a result brought a lack of confidence in modernism's validity: (1) the first and second world wars, (2) the reversal of European colonization, (3) the threat of nuclear destruction of the human race, and (4) the evidence of long-term ecological crisis. "The master-narrative that was to have delivered us the crown of civilization has delivered us insuperable dangers," he writes, adding that the result means Western culture "cannot tell where 'straight ahead' lies, let alone whether it ought to keep on going there. The master-narrative has failed."[23]

What does all this mean for the evangelical church and her ability to be effective evangelistically? As our world in the latter twentieth century in the West shifted from modernism to a postmodern posture, more and more people began to question Christianity not on its own merits but because of a perceived (often caused by evangelicals) linkage between Christian truth and modernist claims. In other words, while relying upon empirical methodologies and fact-finding in order

[21] M. Liederbach and A. L. Reid, *The Convergent Church: Missional Worship in an Emerging Culture* (Grand Rapids: Kregel, 2009), 45. The phrase "evidence that demands a verdict" comes from the title of a popular book by apologist Josh McDowell.

[22] Ibid.

[23] O'Donovan, in Liederbach and Reid, *Convergent Church,* 46.

to defend the faith worked in the modern era, reliance upon this methodology may have overreached in two critical ways:

> First, while rightfully claiming we can have a high degree of *certainty* regarding the knowledge about God, there has been a tendency to believe we can have a rather *exhaustive* knowledge of God. In turn, this has led to a loss of respect and wonder at the *mystery* of God's unsearchable wonder. Christians may like to quote C.S. Lewis's famous line about Aslan (Lewis's Christ figure) not being a "tame lion," but when evangelicals take time to honestly evaluate the claims to certainty present in their analytically based systematic theologies, there appears to be very little space given to, or humility about, the mystery and awesome nature of God. It is almost as if we have come to believe that doing theology is the same as solving math equations.[24]

The second area where we can see an erosion of confidence is in how we do discipleship:

> To put it simply, too often discipleship models are relegated to classroom teachings in Sunday school settings . . . with knowledge-based curricula instead of life-on-life, obedience-based discipleship. Thus, while the emphasis on apologetics and systematic theology has been, and will continue to be, a vitally important element of discipleship, there is a growing sense among many that the modern evangelical church has placed so much emphasis on rationalistic defenses and teaching the facts of the faith that it has neglected whole-life ministry and embodiment of the faith. The emphasis on *orthodoxy* has led to the unfortunate neglect of *orthopraxy*.[25]

Evangelistic Innovations

Citywide, Interdenominational Crusades. These crusades began in the nineteenth century and blossomed in the twentieth. D. L. Moody (1837–99) began the march of an army of urban evangelists. Moody teamed with musician Ira Sankey to form the first successful evangelistic team. Their meetings drew thousands in cities from the

[24] Liederbach and Reid, *Convergent Church*, 47.

[25] Ibid.

United States to England. Evangelistic results always occurred; and, at times, deep revival also arose. Moody developed the practice of organizing a steering committee to guide preparations for his crusades. Many have followed his lead, including Billy Graham.

Other evangelists ministering in the cities during the nineteenth and twentieth centuries include:

- Sam Jones (1847–1906), Methodist evangelist who was particularly effective in the southern United States;
- Wilbur Chapman (1859–1918), a Presbyterian evangelist influenced by Moody and who helped Billy Sunday get started;
- Rodney "Gypsy" Smith (1860–1947), a British evangelist who also preached in America; and
- Billy Sunday (1862–1935), the flamboyant former baseball player. He built tabernacles whose floors were covered in sawdust; hence the expression "hitting the sawdust trail."

Of course, the best-known evangelist in history is William Franklin "Billy" Graham. Graham was converted in Charlotte, North Carolina, under the preaching of another prominent evangelist, Mordecai Ham. Graham has preached to more people than any other preacher in history. He has served as a model of a man of integrity and has remained single-minded in his call to be an evangelist.

Denominational Evangelism. This development rose to prominence during the 1900s. At the outset J. Wilbur Chapman, famous for his worldwide crusades, served as evangelism director briefly for Presbyterians in America. In the first decade the Southern Baptist Convention began a division of evangelism for the Board of Domestic Missions (now the evangelization group of the North American Mission Board). At first this consisted of a team of evangelists who preached meetings. The organization developed into a strategy and program-producing arm of the denomination. The Southern Baptist Program of Evangelism in the 1950s was one of its most successful campaigns. In more recent years, simultaneous mass evangelism efforts and evangelistic outreaches in conjunction with the annual Southern Baptist Convention (known as Crossover) serve as examples of the evangelistic leadership of the denomination.

Parachurch Evangelism. This development also came into prominence during this century. The best-known example of this is Campus Crusade for Christ, International, now the largest parachurch organization in the world. Significant contributions include the "Four

Spiritual Laws" witnessing booklet, the "Here's Life" campaign and "Explo '72" in the early 1970s, and the use of the *Jesus* video around the world.

Other parachurch organizations that give some focus to evangelism include Youth for Christ, Youth with a Mission, the Navigators, Young Life, and more recently, Promise Keepers. In the 1990s, parachurch groups and denominations joined hands as a part of AD 2000, a cooperative effort involving scores of evangelical denominations and parachurch ministries, with a goal of sharing Christ with every person on earth by the year 2000.

International Conferences/Congresses on Evangelism. Increased communication and increasing ease of travel globally led to the gathering of Christian leaders on several occasions for the purpose of global evangelization. The World Missionary Conference at Edinburgh, Scotland, in 1910 was the first widely recognized meeting, although it was preceded by five interdenominational meetings with a focus on foreign missions beginning in 1888 and a meeting of 50,000 in New York City in 1900. In 1966 a Congress on Evangelism was held in Berlin, sponsored by the Billy Graham Association and *Christianity Today* magazine. Graham desired to "unite all evangelicals in the common task of the total evangelization of the world."[26] Over 100 nations were represented at this truly global event. Another Congress met in Lausanne, Switzerland, in 1974 with 150 nations represented. There the Lausanne Covenant was adopted in a desire to unite Christians in the common cause of global evangelism. Lausanne II was held in Manila, Philippines, in 1989. The third Lausanne Congress, being held in Capetown, South Africa, in 2010, marks the third continent for the three gatherings, a truly global movement.

International Missions Emphases. The global expansion of Christianity has caused more recent leaders to look at the world through the eyes of the gospel. In 1990 Luis Bush coined the phrase "the 10/40 window" to refer to the region of the world with the largest number of lost people. The term refers to the area in the Eastern Hemisphere between 10 and 40 degrees north of the equator, roughly including northern Africa across southern Asia, with countries such as India, China, Iran and Iraq, Egypt, Algeria, and Libya, to name a few. In this region 95 percent of the 3.2 billion who live there are unevangelized. This reality, and the growth of the concept of unreached people

[26] http://www.lausanne.org/about.html (accessed October 2, 2008).

groups, has motivated missions agencies to focus on sending more missionaries to this region of such great need.

Methodological Evangelism. This catchphrase is used for other key emphases. D. James Kennedy launched his Evangelism Explosion approach to personal evangelism at the Coral Ridge Presbyterian Church in 1970. Churches from various denominations have been trained by this approach. Southern Baptists championed the programmatic approach of training its members in simple methods of personal witness, while Campus Crusade for Christ and other parachurch organizations employed similar tools.

The Church Growth Movement. This movement's impact can hardly be underestimated in the latter part of this century; however, it will be considered in a later chapter.

The Seeker Movement. Megachurch pastor Rick Warren popularized the "seeker-sensitive" movement, while fellow megachurch pastor Bill Hybels emphasized a "seeker-driven" approach. Both approaches grew out of a desire to be more "sensitive" to where lost people are and to become more effective at reaching them. They are not identical, as "seeker sensitive" refers to the goal of removing unnecessary obstacles to the gospel the church often has, and "seeker driven" refers to planning much (or all) of the church—Sunday services, and so on—from the posture of a "seeker." I am personally not comfortable with the latter but believe the former, if not taken too far, can be helpful. Some criticize the tendency to refer to those outside of Christ as "seekers." Willow Creek in fact recently released a book entitled *Reveal: Where Are You?,* in which its leaders admit their approach has not led automatically to spiritual maturity.[27]

The Emerging Church Movement. At the turn of the twenty-first century this movement brought new discussion to the importance of engaging the culture with the gospel. A reaction to the programmatic approaches of the evangelical church and to a heavy emphasis on "attractional" evangelism, this movement has emphasized the importance of engaging the culture. Some in the movement, particularly those deemed "emergent," have forsaken historic biblical convictions in the name of engaging the culture.[28] Those keeping a biblical focus, however, have given helpful insights into engaging the culture and becoming missional in evangelism.

---

[27] http://www.informz.net/pfm/archives/archive_529389.html (accessed October 2, 2008).

[28] For a more thorough treatment of the emerging church movement, see Liederbach and Reid, *The Convergent Church.*

Movements within the larger movement of Christianity come and go. Some are more helpful, some less. We should not fear movements, but neither should we fear holding them to the standard of Scripture. We can be so afraid of wild fire that we miss real fire, but we also must recognize wild fire. I pray that the true fire of God would fall again on the church in our time.

Questions for Consideration

1. Have any of the developments in evangelism in recent history described above affected your understanding of evangelism?
2. What should be retained from the approaches/movements mentioned above? What should be set aside as we move to the future?
3. What lessons from history can help you as a witness today?

Chapter 9

A Theology of Evangelism

The greatest single proof of Christianity for others is not how far a man can logically analyze his reasons for believing, but how far in practice he will stake his life on his belief.[1]

—T. S. Eliot

One of the legends surrounding the Taj Mahal concerns the death of the favorite wife of the Emperor Shah Jahan. Devastated at losing her, the king determined to honor her by constructing a temple as her tomb. The coffin was placed in the middle of the construction site. An expensive, elaborate edifice began to rise around the coffin. As the weeks became months, the Shah's passion for the project surpassed his grief.

One day during the construction, a wooden box was discovered. The emperor ordered the workers to throw the box out; after all, it was only in the way. Shah Jahan had no idea that he had ordered the disposal of his wife's casket, hidden beneath layers of dust and time. The very person for whose honor the temple was built was forgotten.[2]

[1] A. Hirsch, *Forgotten Ways: Reactivating the Missional Church* (Grand Rapids: Brazos Press, 2006), 101.

[2] Adapted from M. Lucado, *The Applause of Heaven* (Waco: Word, 1996), 121.

Tragic? Yes. But the same thing can happen to us. Without maintaining a focus on theology, founded on the Word of God, we can forget why we evangelize in the first place.

Christianity is founded on the conviction that the God of creation has revealed Himself to humanity. The gospel rests not only in the simple statements of faith—God is love; we have sinned; Christ died and rose again for us and will come again; and through repentance and faith we can follow this Christ—but also in the reality of these statements. We must ground our evangelism not only in a verse or two in Romans but also in the whole counsel of God's Word, even as our mission comes from all Scripture, not only the Great Commission passages. The grand drama of redemption—creation, fall, redemption, consummation, and all related to it—must be heralded in a world that decreasingly knows the story.

The record of God's self-revelation is found in the Bible; most specifically and finally, God has revealed Himself through His Son, Jesus. This chapter seeks not to prove this reality but to demonstrate how such a conviction relates to the task of evangelism. The tendency today is to discover a method that works, then find a Bible verse to prove the method is OK. We need evangelism that is grounded in Scripture.

Evangelism and Theology, Not Evangelism or Theology

One cannot adequately practice evangelism apart from a firm biblical base that is rooted in history and founded on a clear theology. At the same time, theology is incomplete without a view toward mission. In a movement, there is no room for practitioners who do not understand the "why" of their driving force. Likewise, in a movement no room exists for a person who speculates on theology without having to live and breathe a life of committed engagement and embodiment of the vision and mission. Paul demonstrated throughout his life and writings of the New Testament, a distinction between theologian and practitioners is a false dichotomy. Thus, *there is a need to keep evangelism and theology together.*

This is true for several reasons:

1. *Evangelism and theology must be kept together to avoid extremism.* Wrongly interpreted and applied, some have used the Bible to lead many people into cults and other heresies. Evangelism

keeps theology tied closely to Scripture. Linking evangelism and theology avoids certain aberrations. Evangelism divorced from theology leads to superficial Christianity. It produces Christians who are ten miles wide and one-half inch deep. Without a doctrinal base, we may eventually forget the very purpose for which we preach! We need to present *truth,* not some watered-down, cheap imitation of the real thing. We need to give people the life-changing, God-inspired gospel without corrupting the message. Theology without evangelism leads to dead orthodoxy. Vance Havner said you can be straight as a gun barrel and just as empty. There are conservative churches across America that are ineffective and spiritually dead. They have the right doctrine, but their practice is far from the biblical standard. In fact, theology without an evangelistic priority means we haven't really understood theology.

2. *Theology and evangelism must remain linked because the Bible always weds theology with practical matters like evangelism.* In the book of Acts, we read sermons filled with doctrinal content. At the same time, the testimony of the believers, their faith in action, played a vital role in their mission. Paul's letters often emphasized doctrine and practice, and we recognize Paul as both a theologian and an evangelist.
3. *People who have been used of God have generally kept theology and evangelism in unity.* Not every great leader in church history was a noted theologian. But at key points in history, when God raised up individuals to play strategic roles in the furtherance of the Christian faith, almost without exception those leaders were adept theologians and active evangelists. Martin Luther, although he was a theologian, called himself an evangelist. John Wesley, so pivotal in British history, was an Oxford man whose sermons were filled with doctrinal content and evangelistic themes. Jonathan Edwards was one of the brightest minds ever produced in America. His writings contain some heady doctrine, but he also played a critical role in the conversion of multitudes in the First Great Awakening.

There has been an unfortunate focus in the Western Church on experiencing faith to the neglect of valuing strong doctrine. "Everyone has warned me not to tell you what I am going to tell you in this last book," C. S. Lewis wrote in *Mere Christianity.* "They all say 'the ordinary reader does not want Theology; give him plain practical religion.'" To such objections he replied: "I have rejected their advice. I do not think the ordinary reader is such a fool. . . . I think any man who wants to think about God at all would like to have the clearest and most accurate ideas about Him which are available."[3]

Evangelism Related to Central Doctrines

While all doctrines relate to evangelism, this chapter will examine crucial subjects related to the evangelistic task. Entire volumes are dedicated specifically to the theology of evangelism.[4] Central issues are considered below.

The Scriptures

Nothing cuts the cord of evangelism faster than a lack of respect for the teaching of the Word of God.[5] I will not argue for the uniqueness and authority of Scripture here; other writings have done that well.[6] I simply note that the uniqueness of Christianity begins with its Holy Book. The Bible makes the bold assertion, without giving any significant defense of its position, that it is the one-of-a-kind self-disclosure of the only true God—the Lord of history. Most significantly, it reveals to us what we must know about Jesus, the Son of God, our Savior. There are enough extrabiblical accounts of the life of Christ to demonstrate that he lived, but a person must come to the Scriptures to find any significant information about God's final self-revelation.

The Bible gives us objective, verifiable information about God and our relationship to Him; however, it is fundamentally a book of faith. The Bible does not tell us everything we *want* to know about reality, but it does tell us what we *need* to know! I do not mean to imply that the Bible's historical or other factual information is irrelevant or inaccurate. But a person must do more than read the Bible and admire its

[3] Cited in M. Liederbach and A. L. Reid, *The Convergent Church: Missional Worship in an Emerging Culture* (Grand Rapids: Kregel, 2009), 172.

[4] In particular, I would note L. Drummond, *The Word of the Cross* (Nashville: Broadman and Holman, 1992).

[5] J. Avant recently displayed the specific relationship between one's view of Scripture and evangelism. See J. Avant, "The Relationship of the Changing Views of the Inspiration and Authority of Scripture to Evangelism and Church Growth: A Study of the United Methodist Church and the Southern Baptist Convention in the United States Since World War II" (PhD dissertation, Southwestern Baptist Theological Seminary, 1990).

[6] See, for example, F. F. Bruce, *The New Testament Documents: Are They Reliable?* (Grand Rapids: Eerdmans, 1943).

majesty. One must encounter its primary Author to truly understand the words of life. One must *live* the Bible.

The Bible is the infallible, inspired, inerrant word of God. It is wholly trustworthy and accurate. Of course, one can hold to a high view of Scripture and not be evangelistic. One can claim a belief in the inerrancy of Scripture but deny its sufficiency. But a person is hard pressed to come to the Bible with a heart of faith and not see the obvious implications and commands of God to proclaim the gospel message.

However, a more insidious affront to scriptural authority has sapped the life of the modern church. This is the invasion of liberalism, which questions the uniqueness of Scripture. Those who have followed this path in modern history have been anything but evangelistic. The findings of modern scholarship, including higher criticism, have to some degree helped our understanding of Scripture. The key is found in the presuppositions one takes to Scripture. In other words, the interpretation of the Bible is as critical as the view of Bible's authority, but the two are not easily separated.

The Doctrine of God

Any discussion of theology must center on the doctrine of God. Drummond said it well when he noted, "evangelism begins in theology, not anthropology."[7] Unfortunately, most modern books on evangelism begin with the need of people—not the sovereignty of God. Most errors related to evangelism are made at this point. While we must understand contemporary culture to communicate the gospel effectively, we must not begin at that point to develop our theology. Starting with the doctrine of man emphasizes *relevance,* which is important; but more critical is starting with the doctrine of God, which emphasizes *significance.*

1. *God is Creator.* God the Creator implies God the Redeemer. God took the initiative to create, to make man in His image, to redeem fallen humanity.
2. *God is One—in three persons.* The God we serve is uniquely one God who has manifested Himself in three persons. The Trinity is the granite from which the monument of evangelism is carved. In God's plan "the Father was to send His Son into the world to redeem it, God the Son was voluntarily to come

[7] Drummond, *Word of the Cross,* 98.

into the world in order to merit salvation by His obedience unto death, God the Holy Spirit was to apply salvation to sinners by the instilling of renewing grace within them."[8]

3. *God is holy.* The attributes of God relate to evangelism; the urgency of evangelism is tied to the character of God! He is holy, and we are not, so we stand condemned. If we could see God face-to-face, our immediate impression would be to stand in awe of the holiness of God. That attribute would transcend all others. Think of Moses' encounter with God in Exodus. He did not jump a pew; he removed his shoes. Think of Isaiah and the cry of the seraphim, "Holy, holy, holy" (see Isaiah 6). Move to the New Testament and John's vision of God in Revelation where the heavenly chorus responded with "Holy, holy, holy" (Rev 4:8). The biblical words for *holy,* both the Hebrew word *qodesh* and the Greek *hagios,* have essentially the same meaning: "to be separate, distinct." God is not the same as us. In fact, there are more references in Scripture to the anger, fury, and wrath of God than to the love of God. Yet God is not only holy, just, and wrathful; He is also love.
4. *God is love.* While God is holy, He offers us a personal relationship with Him that we don't deserve. Drummond is right in noting that *agapē* love is the central motif of the New Testament. However, the *love* of God and the *holiness* of God must be held in balance. We cannot evangelize biblically without both—His holiness and His love. Without God's love, we become mean-spirited. A pastor friend was eating at McDonald's while he watched his six-year-old son play in the playland. He was shocked to see his son putting another little boy in a headlock! He rushed outside to rescue the frightened little lad and sternly reprimanded his son. The son looked at his dad with a confused expression. "But Dad," he replied, "I was trying to tell him about Jesus, but *he just wouldn't listen!*" In contrast, without a view of God's holiness, we refuse to confront people with their need for him. We become soft, even sentimental, toward others. We must keep a balance between conviction and compassion in our evangelism.

[8] R. B. Kuiper, *God-Centered Evangelism* (London: The Banner of Truth Trust, 1966), 13.

Christ and Salvation

We can think of Christ in terms of the *person* of Christ—who He is—and the *work* of Christ—what He has done. He is the God-man, the unique, only begotten Son of God. Historically, two extremes have hindered the understanding of who Jesus is. On one hand, the Docetics emphasized the deity of Jesus, denying He ever became man. He only appeared to be human. On the other hand, the Ebionites said Jesus was *just* a man, denying His deity. Historically, liberalism has typically fallen on the side of the Ebionites, while conservatives at times have minimized the humanity of Christ.

The work of Christ includes His virgin birth, sinless life, death and resurrection, reign in heaven, return, and eternal reign. Most specifically, it concerns the work of Christ on the cross for our salvation. This relates specifically to soteriology, and raises the issue, what is the gospel?

What Is the Gospel?

More than a few today question the validity and veracity of the gospel proclaimed by the words and life of contemporary Christianity. One example:

> So what is this good news? The refined and civilized version goes something like this: Jesus died and rose from the dead so that you can live a life of endless comfort, security, and indulgence. But really this is a bit too developed. Usually it's more like this: if you'll simply confess that you're a sinner and believe in Jesus, you'll be saved from the torment of eternal hellfire, then go to heaven when you die. Either case results in domestication. One holds out for your life to begin in eternity, and the other makes a mockery out of [this] life. The call of Jesus is more barbaric than either of these. It is a call to live in this world as citizens of an entirely different kingdom. In its primitive state the good news could never be separated from the invitation of Jesus to, "come, follow Me." He never lied about the danger or cost associated with becoming a follower.[9]

Another way of looking at how we see the gospel is to examine churches that tend to take an aspect of the gospel and emphasize it to

[9] E. R. McManus, *The Barbarian Way* (Nashville: Thomas Nelson, 2005), 32.

the neglect of other components. One extreme will look familiar to the conventional church:

> In the more modern churches, the triumph of the resurrected Jesus was stressed to emphasize victory, so that being a Christian basically meant you were on the winning team with Jesus and therefore you were a real winner. What they overlooked was the incarnation of Jesus . . . they ignored the fact that Jesus humbly entered into culture to identify with and effectively reach lost people steeped in various kinds of sin. This oversight allowed people to triumphally parade their victory over sin and sinners but failed to call them to humbly incarnate as missionaries in culture to effectively reach lost people. Christians with this mindset can easily come to see themselves as winners and lost people as losers and consequently are often despised by lost people, who find them smug.[10]

On the other hand, newer churches can make a similar mistake:

> Conversely, many other churches are more akin to the so-called postmodern churches focusing almost exclusively on a vegetable-munching hippie Christ's humble incarnation in culture to hang out with sinful lost people, particularly the poor and marginalized. In this mindset, being a Christian means being a nice person who loves people no matter what their lives are like by trying to identify with their cultural experiences and perspectives in a non-judgmental and empathetic manner. What is lacking, however, is the understanding that when we next see Jesus, He will not appear as a humble marginalized Galilean peasant. Rather, we will see the exalted, tattooed King of Kings coming with fire blazing in His eyes and a sword launching from His mouth, with which to make war upon the unrepentant. Until the day of Jesus' second coming we are not merely to relate to people but also to command them to repent of sin and bend their knee to the King before they are grapes crushed under His foot in the winepress of His fury.[11]

Another mistake we must avoid is explaining the gospel in terms of the most simplistic understanding of its message. True, the gospel

[10] M. Driscoll, *Confessions of a Reformission Rev* (Grand Rapids: Zondervan, 2006), 42.

[11] Ibid., 43.

message can be understood by a child, but it encompasses a vastness beyond the understanding of theologians. Keller noted the balance:

> "The gospel" is not just a way to be saved from the penalty of sin, but is the fundamental dynamic for living the whole Christian life—individually and corporately, privately and publicly. In other words, the gospel is not just for non-Christians, but also for Christians. This means the gospel is not just the A-B-C's but the A to Z of the Christian life. It is not accurate to think "the gospel" is what saves non-Christians, and then, what matures Christians is trying hard to live according to Biblical principles. It is more accurate to say that we are saved by believing the gospel, and then we are transformed in every part of our mind, heart, and life by believing the gospel more and more deeply as life goes on.[12]

Keller saw the need to avoid truncating the gospel too much or making the gospel only about initial conversion. The great idea, the wonderful story of the gospel starts in the mind of God, moves through creation, recognizes the fall, sees the providence of God, centers on the work of Christ on the cross and His resurrection, and looks for future consummation of this life and the hope of heaven in eternity. It is indeed more than the A-B-Cs alone.

My colleague and theologian Pete Schemm noted Jesus Himself is the gospel. What does that mean? In summary, he stated:[13]

1. *First, the gospel is not so much an idea or a thing as it is a person.* Note these verses:

- "those who proclaim him" (Acts 15:21)
- "We proclaim Him" (Col 1:28)
- "that you may proclaim the excellencies of Him" (1 Pet 2:9 NASB)
- "we preach Christ crucified" (1 Cor 1:23)
- "that I might preach him among the Gentiles" (Gal 1:16 NIV)
- "to preach . . . the unsearchable riches of Christ" (Eph 3:8 NIV)
- "the gospel of Jesus Christ, the Son of God" (Mark 1:1)

---

[12] http://www.redeemer2.com/themovement/issues/2004/june/postmoderncity_1_p1.html (accessed August 28, 2008).

[13] Notes below come from the class lecture notes of P. Schemm, associate professor of theology at Southeastern Baptist Theological Seminary.

- "the gospel of his Son" (Rom 1:9 NIV)
- "the gospel of Christ" (Rom 15:19; 1 Cor 9:13; Gal 1:7; Phil 1:27; 1 Thess 3:2)
- "the gospel of the glory of Christ" (2 Cor 4:4)
- "the promise in Christ Jesus through the gospel" (Eph 3:6)
- "the gospel of our Lord Jesus" (2 Thess 1:8)
- "believe in Him" (John 6:29; Rom 4:24; 1 Tim 1:16; 1 Pet 1:8 NASB)

So, the gospel is not so much an idea or a thing as it is the announcement of a person. We believe in Jesus Christ, the embodiment of the good news from God to man.

2. *Second, the gospel is the "good news."* "Good news" is *good* because it announces God's intention to rectify what is *bad*.
3. *Third, the "good news" is a canonical theme, not merely a New Testament theme.* Though it is less readily seen in the Old Testament (Hebrew Scriptures), it is still present there.
4. *Fourth, each of these first three observations help to explain what Paul explicitly defines as the gospel in 1 Cor 15:1–4.* Here Paul defines "the gospel" in this way: "For I delivered to you as of first importance what I also received: that Christ died for our sins in accordance with the Scriptures, that he was buried, that he was raised on the third day in accordance with the Scriptures" (1 Cor 15:1,3–4 ESV).

- Gospel as a person (vv. 12ff.)
- Gospel as good news (vv. 1–2; twice)
- Gospel as canonical theme (vv. 3–4; "in accordance with the Scriptures," twice)

Ken Keathley, also a colleague and professor of theology, reminds us that salvation, while individual at one level, is related to the body of Christ as well:[14]

> Think of your salvation testimony as a melody being played on a quiet instrument—a clarinet or oboe, perhaps. You play the tune for the Lord and to anyone and everyone who will listen. Now imagine that one day, while engrossed in the joy of playing

[14] "Contours of a Great Commission Resurgence, Part 5: What Is the Gospel? The Full Orchestra Rendition," August 7, 2008, http://betweenthetimes.com/author/kenkeathley/ (accessed September 23, 2008).

your simple song, you are joined by an enormous, massive orchestra. And not just an orchestra of dozens or even hundreds, but thousands and tens of thousands—and a choir that is even larger. . . . Their sudden appearance is overwhelming. What's more, you realize that they didn't really join you. Rather, it becomes clear that your melody is actually part of a much larger movement of music—a piece marvelous in its intricacy and genius. At that point you realize that your salvation isn't just about you; your redemption is part of a plan that encompasses heaven and earth. . . . The Bible makes much of what the Gospel means for individual Christians and the corporate church, and we should too.

Keathley noted key points of the gospel:

1. The Gospel is "the good news of the Kingdom" (Matt 24:14). The Gospel must be understood within the grand narrative of Creation, Fall, Redemption and Consummation. . . . The Gospel declares that Christ has begun to establish his Kingdom and will return to fully reign over his dominion. All Creation looks forward to that day (Rom 8:22–25).
2. The Gospel is the good news of victory—over Satan and death. Pictures of Times Square packed with thousands celebrating the end of WWII have become iconic of the giddy relief felt when dark days give way to victory. That is nothing compared to the worshipful celebration of the redeemed (Rev 5:11–14). By his death, burial, and resurrection, Christ made an open spectacle of our implacable enemies (Col 2:15). On our behalf he defeated death and the Devil (1 Cor 15:54–57; Heb 2:9–15) and established his supremacy over all things (Col 1:13–23).
3. The Gospel is the good news of forgiveness of sins. In his discussion of the Gospel in 1 Cor 15, Paul emphasizes that Christ died "for our sins." The Gospel is the good news that at Calvary Jesus became our substitute and suffered the wrath of God on our behalf. The blood of Christ is both our propitiation and expiation. It both pleads on the behalf of and cleanses the one who trusts him as Lord and Savior.
4. The Gospel is the good news of reconciliation (Rom 5:6–11; 2 Cor 5:18–21). The Gospel announces that God has

> reconciled himself to us in Jesus Christ. The Gospel is the true "good news of peace" (Rom 5:1; Eph 6:15). In sum, the Gospel is the joyous news that God, by and through his Son, acted to redeem all things—including us—to himself. This is the Gospel of Christ (Rom 15:16; 1 Cor 9:12; 2 Cor 2:12; Gal 1:7; 1 Thess 3:2;).[15]

At the heart of the gospel message is the atonement. The atonement of Christ is the centerpiece of Christianity. Throughout history, a variety of views of the atonement have been debated. While these views help to explain the wonder of the cross, the key word in understanding the atonement is *substitution.* Drummond says it best: "If all the other theories are facets of the jewel of atonement, *substitution* is the core stone from which all the facets are cut."[16] This term is held in contempt by modern liberal scholarship, but the idea of a sin substitute is evident throughout Scripture.

The key question in Christianity is, Why the cross? Why did Jesus die? Erickson offers these five implications of the substitutionary death of Christ:

1. It confirms the biblical teaching of the total depravity of humans.
2. It demonstrates both the love and the justice of God in a perfect unity.
3. Salvation comes from the pure, sovereign grace of God.
4. The believer can be secure in the grace of God.
5. We are motivated not to neglect so great a salvation that came at such a great cost.[17]

While many terms in the New Testament emphasize the work of Christ to save us, Paul gave a clear view of the work of the cross in Romans 3:21–26. He used three terms in this passage that reflect the work of Christ. *Redemption* bears the idea of one who is a slave and whose freedom is purchased. *Justification* is a forensic term, used in the courts. Jesus' death declares us "not guilty." The expression *sacrifice of atonement* looks back to the Old Testament temple service and the idea of shedding blood. Jesus purchased our freedom from

---

[15] Ibid.

[16] Drummond, *Word of the Cross*, 142.

[17] M. J. Erickson, *Christian Theology* (Grand Rapids: Baker, 1998), 822–23.

the slavery of sin, declares us not guilty, and has washed us clean—glory to His name!

The conditions of salvation are very clear in Scripture. These are repentance and faith. If there is a missing word in evangelism today, it is *repent*. One of my students told me he served with a pastor who said he never preached repentance because it made people nervous. Such preaching makes *sinners* nervous! That's like the preacher who said he never preached about tithing because it made people nervous. Yes, it makes *thieves* nervous.

A noble desire to be seeker sensitive may cause some to shy away from repentance. But to minimize repentance is to preach a crossless gospel. Notice the following:

- In Matthew's Gospel, the first word of Jesus' preaching was *repent* (Matt 4:17).
- Our Lord's herald, John the Baptist, preached a message of repentance (Matt 3:2).
- Jesus declared that unless a person repented, he would perish (Luke 13:3).
- At Pentecost, Peter urged the people to repent (Acts 2:38; 3:19; 8:22).
- Paul consistently said a person must repent (Acts 17:30; 20:21; 26:20).

The Greek word *metanoia* translates as "repentance." It means a change of the mind in a deep manner—a change in one's heart, mind, and purpose. This word is often confused with two other New Testament terms, *metamellomai,* which means to have regret or remorse, and *lupeō,* which means to have sorrow.

We have misunderstood the difference between sorrow and repentance. My little girl Hannah says, "I'm sorry, Daddy" every time I catch her doing something wrong. If I say, "Hannah, why did you take that crayon and write on the wall?" she looks up at me with her sad, big blue eyes and says, "I'm sorry, Daddy, I didn't mean to!" Baloney! Of course she meant to. It was not an accident—at least not the fifth or sixth time she did it! What do people think of when they think of repentance? Being sorry? Grieving? Regretting? That's not what the New Testament word means.

Look at 2 Cor 7:8–10. In v. 10, all three of these words are used in the same passage. Verse 8 says, "Even if I caused you sorrow by my letter, I do not regret it. Though I did regret it—I see that my letter hurt you, but only for a little while—yet now I am happy, not because you were made sorry, but because your sorrow led you to repentance. For you became sorrowful as God intended and so were not harmed in any way by us" (NIV). Paul was talking about a time, described in 1 Corinthians, when he had to rebuke the church.

But he went on to remind them about salvation in v. 10: "Godly sorrow brings repentance that leads to salvation and leaves no regret" (NIV). Notice that godly sorrow *leads* to repentance. Godly sorrow is the conviction of the Holy Spirit that leads to repentance unto salvation.

Godly sorrow works repentance unto salvation not to be regretted, but the sorrow of the world brings death. You can be sorry about your sin before God and still spend eternity in hell. You can die in your sin if you don't get beyond "I'm sorry I did wrong." There has to be a desire in our lives that results in this message: "God, I want to change, I want to repent."

What we believe about salvation is crucial because our soteriology will determine our evangelism! For example, the hyper-Calvinist believes God has chosen who is saved and damned, so evangelism doesn't matter. On the other extreme, some emphasize an "easy believism" that stresses human work to the neglect of God's work to save. Many people suffer from a weak soteriology that underestimates the sinfulness of sin and, therefore, minimizes the majesty of God's grace.

We must constantly remind ourselves that God *owes* us one thing—hell. Yet He has lavished His love on us through Christ! Jesus' work on the cross sets us free from the power of sin and death. He did not die just to make *bad* people *good* but to make *dead* people *live* (see Ephesians 2). A conviction about a great salvation leads to a passion for evangelism.

Anthropology and Hamartiology

Both the doctrine of man, *anthropology*, and the doctrine of sin, *hamartiology*, are closely linked. God created man to bring Him glory and pleasure. But it is impossible for a lost person to bring pleasure to God. When Adam and Eve disobeyed, sin entered the human race (see Genesis 3; Rom 5:12–15). We are at enmity with God.

We are born with a sinful nature. Augustine said that it is impossible not to sin. Sometimes this nature is referred to as "the old man" or "the flesh." When we are saved, the old nature, our sinful nature, is not eradicated. Instead, God came into us with His own nature. We were born with a sinful nature; we are born again with the nature of God. The Bible calls this a "new man." Second Peter talks about being partakers of the divine nature (2 Pet 1:4). What happened to the old nature? Romans 6:2 tells us that it is dead. Romans 6:6 says our old nature was crucified with Christ, and yet we still struggle with sin. Positionally the sinful nature is dead, but experientially we still wrestle.

The doctrine of sin, or hamartiology, is greatly neglected in our day. In the Old Testament, the most common word for sin is *chata,* meaning "to miss the mark." The main New Testament term, *hamartia,* has essentially the same meaning. This idea of missing the mark reminds us that the central issue is not the *quantity* of sin but the *reality* of sin. If a person hangs over a great abyss by a chain, only one link must break to bring his death. One need rob a bank only once to be called a bank robber, commit adultery once to be an adulterer, and murder once to be a murderer. All people have sinned. The central issue is not, "Have I sinned less than others?" Instead, we need to ask, "Is sin existent in my life?" The key is sin, not individual sins. We must also remember that it is not simply individual sins that we commit that separate us from God. Rather, it is the sin nature within us—our rebellion that has caused the breach between us and God. Individual sins are symptomatic of a deeper problem.

There are other terms for sin. *Pasha* carries the idea of rebellion (Isa 1:28). *Awah,* "twisting," means intentional perversion. *Rasha* means to act wickedly. In the New Testament, *paraptōma* signifies trespass, *parabasis* means transgression (Rom 4:15), and *asebeia* refers to ungodliness (Rom 1:18). The root of sin is unbelief. Unbelief is a volitional act (see John 3:19).

Eschatology

If you were involved in a church in the 1970s, you probably remember the eschatological fervor associated with the Jesus Movement. The most popular saying at that time was "one way!" The second biggest saying was "Jesus is coming soon—are you ready?" The eschatological chorus, "I Wish We'd All Been Ready" was the signature song of this movement. I know many people who came to Christ during those days out of concern that they would not be ready when the Lord returned.

Eschatology motivates the witness two ways. First, the hope of heaven and the glory to come motivates the believer to invite as many as possible to join in this eternal worship of the creator. The imminent return of Christ was one of the motives for evangelism in the early church, and it should be for us as well. Jesus declared that the gospel must be preached all around the world, and then the end will come (see Matt 24:14). The Lord Jesus tied evangelism to the end of the world and the coming of Christ. In fact, one could make the case historically for a tie between one's eschatological views and one's passion for the gospel. Green argued that a conviction about the imminent return of Christ had no small role in the witness of the early church: "The supreme spur to holy living and dedicated missionary work was this consciousness of the imminence of the end, of the limitations on the opportunities for evangelism, of the ultimate accountability we all have to God."[18] He added, "It is hardly surprising, therefore, that not only in the first and second centuries, but in later periods of the Church, missionary zeal has often flowered most notably in circles which held a strongly realistic hope and likely expectation of the coming kingdom."[19]

A second motivation from eschatology is the reality of hell and judgment. Sadly, many today, including those in the church, either ignore or even deny this essential biblical truth. According to Wells, this relates both to our faith and our practice:

> It is not that the elements of the evangelical creeds have vanished, they have not. The fact that they are professed, however, does not necessarily mean that the structure of the historic Protestant faith is still intact. The reason, quite simply, is that while these items of belief are professed, they are increasingly being removed from the center of evangelical life where they defined what life was, and they are now being relegated to the periphery where their power to define what evangelical life should be is lost. . . . It is evangelical *practice* rather than evangelical profession that reveals the change.[20]

As a result, other views beyond the historic Christian understanding of divine judgment and hell have been offered as more suitable for the modern day. *Universalism* is the belief that ultimately no human

[18] M. Green, *Evangelism in the Early Church* (Grand Rapids: Eerdmans, 1970), 269.

[19] Ibid.

[20] D. F. Wells, *No Place for Truth* (Grand Rapids: Eerdmans, 1993), 53.

being will be lost. Some people are universalists because they believe all humanity is intrinsically good and thus will be "redeemed." Others argue that Christ's death was necessary but that His death was for all humanity—period. What then is the historical, biblical position? Explicit faith in Christ in this life is *necessary for salvation.* American culture is decidedly favorable toward universalism.

Why is this view becoming so popular? Beougher notes several reasons:

- human nature,
- pluralistic culture,
- lack of biblical authority,
- the vastness of the missionary task.[21]

Earlier forms of universalism emphasized the goodness of man and held that he is too good for God to damn; more recent forms affirm that God is too good to damn man. Some people don't espouse these views explicitly but wish they were true. Some universalists actually make their argument from Scripture, emphasizing

- God's desire to save all people (1 Tim 2:4; 2 Pet 3:9);
- Jesus' death for all people (John 12:32); and
- God's promise to save all people (Eph 1:10).

Of course, a plethora of texts illustrate the uniqueness of the gospel and the reality of eternal judgment. More dangerous for evangelism is a practical universalism in churches. We live as if all people are saved. On the other hand, it is just as bad to live as if we don't care whether people are lost.

Pluralism is the view that salvation can come through a variety of religious traditions. That is, devout people, whether Hindus, Buddhists, or Christians, will be saved. John Hick says there is a Copernican revolution in theology, in which we must move from Christocentrism to Theocentrism.[22] Therefore, Hick says, Christian distinctives must end.

The problem with pluralism is that even pluralists, though emphasizing tolerance, are not willing to accept *any* religious system. Some

---

[21] T. Beougher, professor at The Southern Baptist Theological Seminary, shared these thoughts in an unpublished paper at a meeting of evangelism professors in Dallas, Texas, May 10, 1997. I am indebted to Beougher for insights that follow as well.

[22] See J. Hick, *God and the Universe of Faiths*, 2nd ed. (Oxford: OneWorld Publications, 1994).

systems, such as the Peoples' Temple of Jim Jones, fail to be good enough. Ronald Nash notes that "pluralists have not identified a criterion to mark the line between authentic and inauthentic 'responses to the Transcendent' clearly enough to make it work on a broad scale."[23]

Further, pluralism fails to note the obvious contradictions in any serious examination of religious systems. Compare the eightfold path of Buddhism, the five pillars of Islam, and the book of Romans, for example. The most pressing problem for pluralism from the Christian perspective is the obvious and clear declaration that Jesus Christ is the only way to God (John 14:6; Acts 4:12). The problem with these philosophies is that they ignore the claims of Scripture, and they reduce all religions to meaninglessness—all have exclusivistic tendencies.

What does the New Testament say about hell? The Greek term *Gehenna* is used 12 times to refer to hell. The term *eternal* is used 64 times with heaven and seven times with hell. It takes no hermeneutical genius to understand that both are considered eternal. Part of our problem today is that we make God after our personality.

Another view that undermines the biblical conviction of divine retribution is *annihilationism.* All people are resurrected, according to this view, but the impenitent will ultimately cease to exist. Let me offer this counsel on this difficult issue:

- Get your view of eternal punishment from the Bible. Jesus knew more about the love of God than anyone, yet He spoke more on hell than heaven.
- Preach the subject of hell—to the church! Teach sin from the perspective of God. Renew your passion for the lost. Never forget God's grace in redeeming us.

Why is this critical? Because that which is neglected by this generation is rejected by the next.

Perhaps the greatest theological threat to the church today is *inclusivism,* or the belief in a wider hope for those who have not heard of Christ. Evangelicals are increasingly adopting such views. J. D. Hunter in *Evangelicalism: The Coming Generation,* found one of three evangelicals held to a wider-hope view of soteriology—that people who have not heard the gospel can be saved apart from its message.

[23] R. H. Nash, *Is Jesus the Only Savior?* (Grand Rapids: Zondervan, 1994).

"Inclusivists agree with pluralists that God's salvation is not restricted to the relatively few people who hear the gospel and believe in Jesus Christ," Nash wrote. "Inclusivists agree with exclusivists that God's universally accessible salvation is nonetheless grounded on the person of Jesus Christ and his redemptive work."[24] Clark Pinnock and John Sanders are recent advocates of this position.

The so-called "optimistic hermeneutic" of inclusivists makes a distinction between Christ's *ontological* work (what he did, necessity of the atonement) and *epistemological* work (what we need to know about the cross). It gives a salvation role to general revelation.

Consider the following story to illustrate this problem. Two young women from southern California spent the day Christmas shopping in Tijuana, a Mexican border town several miles below San Diego. After a successful day of bargain-hunting, they returned to their car. One of the ladies glanced in the gutter and noticed something moving as if in pain. As they bent down and looked closer, the two women saw what appeared to be a dog—a tiny Chihuahua—struggling for its life. Their hearts went out to the pathetic little animal. Their compassion wouldn't let them leave it there to die.

They decided to take it home with them and do their best to nurse it back to health. Afraid of being stopped and having the dog detected by border patrol officers, they placed it on some papers among their packages in the trunk of their car. Within minutes they were back in California and only a couple of hours from home. One of the women held the sick little Chihuahua the rest of the way home.

As they pulled up in front of the first woman's home, they decided she would be the one to keep and tend the little orphan through the night. She tried feeding it some of her food, but it wouldn't eat. She patted it, talked to it, cuddled it, and finally wrapped it in a blanket and placed it beneath the covers on her bed to sleep beside her through the night. She kept feeling the dog to make sure it was OK.

The next morning the woman decided to take it to an emergency animal clinic nearby. As she handed the weakened animal to the doctor on duty, he quickly interrupted her and asked, "Where did you *get* this animal?"

"We were shopping in Tijuana and found this little Chihuahua in the gutter near our car."

"This is no Chihuahua, young lady. What you brought home is a rabid Mexican river rat!"

---

[24] Ibid., 103.

What appeared to be harmless to these two young women proved to be extremely dangerous.[25] The *ontological* reality that a rabid Mexican rat endangered them made a difference only when they had it shown to them *epistemologically!*

We must never allow culture to dictate to us the character of God. In the kinder, gentler culture in which we live, conviction is touted as a vice, while tolerance is seen as a virtue. God has become so sentimentalized that He has lost His sovereign nature, even in the church. Many scholars, even from within the evangelical camp, are espousing views of the judgment of God that would have been considered heretical in previous generations. We are too easily swayed by our own humanness; we too quickly underestimate the greatness of God.

Questions for Consideration

1. Does theology have a proper place in your Christianity?
2. Does it have the appropriate place in your evangelism?
3. Is your relationship with Jesus, the church, and the world guided by this simple question: What does the Bible say about this?

[25] C. R. Swindoll, *Living Above the Level of Mediocrity* (Waco: Word, 1987), 236–38.

Part II

Spiritual Resources

*M*any books look at the message and the methods of evangelism, but we will never go farther than the power of God will take us. David Livingstone sat at his father's knee and heard stories of great people of faith.[1] As a teenager in Scotland, David began to pray this prayer: "God, send me anywhere, only go with me. Lay any burden on me, only sustain me. And sever any tie in my heart except the tie that binds my heart to yours." He met Mary Moffat, told her of his passion, and together they went to Africa.

Soon after they arrived in Africa, Mary Moffat grew very ill. Having had two children and unable to handle the rigors of life in Africa, she said, "Oh, David, I must go back to England. What are you going to do?" Livingstone replied, "The smoke of the fires of a thousand villages in the African morning sun haunts my soul." And she said, "Then, David, you've got to stay." He said, "I'll join you back in England in a few months." But those few months turned into a year, and that year to two, and then to three and four.

When Livingstone returned to England, the queen of England said when he walked into the royal throne room of Great Britain, it was as though the presence of God had been ushered in. A lion had mauled his arm, and he had lost one eye to the jungle brush. After he had been home only a few months, his wife Mary asked, "David, where are you?" And again he said, "The haunting smoke of a thousand

---

[1] R. Reccord, Southeastern Baptist Theological Seminary chapel service, October 16, 1997.

villages in the African morning sun haunts the soul within me." And she said, "Then let's go back." Not long after they returned, Mary Moffat Livingstone died.

David also died deep in the heart of Africa. The Africans carried his body through the jungles to a ship for its return to England where it now resides. But before they sent the body, they cut out his heart, and it was buried in Africa. The African people said, "His body may go, but his heart must stay, for he brought the heart of the gospel to the heart of our nation."

Our beliefs must be biblically grounded, and our evangelism methods must be effective. But our hearts must be filled with a passion for God. Such a passion flows from the spiritual resources we have as followers of Christ.

Part II deals with the spiritual resources related to evangelism. A spiritual passion for evangelism is essential, as noted by Wesley Duewel: "All other passions build upon . . . your passion for Jesus. A passion for souls grows out of a passion for Christ."[2] John Wesley recognized this and shook a nation. He said, "Give me one hundred preachers who fear nothing but sin and desire nothing but God, and I care not a straw whether they be clergymen or laymen, such alone will shake the gates of hell and set up the kingdom of heaven on earth."[3]

---

[2] W. Duewel, *Ablaze for God* (Grand Rapids: Zondervan, 1989), 103.

[3] Ibid., 107.

Chapter 10

The Work of the Spirit

Evangelism without the Holy Spirit
is like a body without a soul.[1]

—Delos Miles

The early church lacked so many things the Western church has today. They had no completed Bibles, no PowerPoint, no killer worship bands, and no teams of songwriters. Yet they worshipped well. They had no Christian bookstores, Christian schools, or Christian parachurch groups. They did not even have church buildings! Yet they grew disciples. They had no great influence in the culture, no seminaries to train their ministers, and no tax-exempt status to encourage believers to give. They lacked so many things we have. But they seemed to have one thing we lack: much power in the Holy Spirit! In fact, if you take the Holy Spirit out of the book of Acts, it would be hard to imagine them becoming anymore than one more religious sect that arose and then quickly faded away.

Today in so many Christian circles I fear if the Holy Spirit left, most of what we do would continue. We can almost put our faith on autopilot in our day. We need the Spirit! He is the One who illuminates the Word (it is the Sword of the Spirit), the One who guides us

[1] D. Miles, *Introduction to Evangelism* (Nashville: Broadman and Holman, 1981), 199.

into all truth, the One who comforts, the One who gives boldness to witness; the One who does the amazing work of redemption. Those involved in evangelism know the crucial role of the Holy Spirit's power and presence. "No alternative to the Holy Spirit is available for the Christian leader,"[2] stated Duewel, who added, "We are in danger of being better trained and equipped on the human level than we are empowered by the Spirit."[3] Charles Finney exhorted, "I would repeat, with great emphasis, that the difference in the efficiency of ministers does not consist so much in the difference of intellectual attainments as in the measure of the Holy Spirit they enjoy."[4]

As a teenager in the 1970s in a Southern Baptist church, I was a lot like the disciples of John mentioned in Acts 19; I was not sure there was a Holy Spirit! Since the birth of Pentecostalism at the beginning of the twentieth century, in particular the Azusa Street Revival in 1906, there has been an increased interest in pneumatology. One thing is clear: the Holy Spirit's role in evangelism can hardly be overestimated.

The Holy Spirit Is a Person

Why has the Holy Spirit been overlooked in the work of the church? Certainly part of the reason simply comes from the fact that we have learned to do so much in the institutional church in the power of our flesh. But much of the reason as well comes from how we view the Third Person of the Trinity. Some have *neglected* the work of the Spirit. He is intangible, a "spirit," and a little more difficult to picture than the Father or the Son. We tend to confuse corporeality (a physical presence) with reality.

Another reason He is overlooked is *ignorance.* Many churches give very little emphasis to the work of the Spirit. *Extremism* by those who do emphasize the Spirit is another factor in his neglect. Some emphasize certain gifts or attributes to an extreme or they associate certain phenomena with His work.

What do we know about the Spirit of God? First, the Holy Spirit is a *person*, not an "it." In our songs and discussions, we tend to refer to the Spirit almost like the "force" of *Star Wars* movie fame. How do we know He is a person? When speaking of the Spirit, Jesus referred

---

[2] Duewel, *Ablaze for God*, 27.

[3] Ibid., 79.

[4] Ibid., 273.

to Him as a person: "He is the Spirit of truth. The world is unable to receive Him because it doesn't see Him or know Him. But you do know Him, because He remains with you and will be in you" (John 14:17).

Further, the Spirit does personal acts (John 14:26; 15:26; 16:13). He has all the attributes of a person except *a physical body* (Rom 5:5; Acts 1:8; 1 Cor 2:10–13). He can be *treated* like a person (Acts 5:9; 7:51; Eph 4:30).

The Bible teaches there is a seen world and an unseen world. Paul put it like this in Col 1:16: "Because by Him everything was created, in heaven and on earth, the visible and the invisible, whether thrones or dominions or rulers or authorities—all things have been created through Him and for Him." People instinctively are aware of this. How many people do you know who talk about "luck" or "fortune" not because either concept is biblical (they are not), but because they know there is an unseen world. Other cultures see this. There is the concept of the evil eye in Islam, for instance. Many people in their everyday lives do not live out their theology. Many professing followers of Christ check their horoscopes and speak of good luck. Why do they do so? Because we perceive there is an unseen world, yet our anemic teaching on the spiritual realities of our faith in general and of the work of the Spirit in particular do not show believers how His work affects the everyday life they live.

The Work of the Spirit in the Believer

The Spirit Indwells and Seals the Believer at Conversion

Ephesians 1:13–14 refers to the sealing of the Spirit at salvation. Seals were commonly used on documents in the first century. Drummond offers the following ideas to demonstrate the significance of this expression for Christians. First, we wear the stamp of God, as His personal possession. Second, the seal brings the mark of authenticity. It also emphasizes security, for a legal document with a seal in the first century was considered secured. Thus, the term *seal* implies the security of the believer in the new covenant relationship with God. Finally, the seal means service for God is expected. The Holy Spirit who seals us will also guide us.[5]

[5] L. Drummond, *The Word of the Cross* (Nashville: Broadman and Holman, 1992), 188.

The Spirit Fills the Believer for Service

He fills the believer with power and boldness to witness (Acts 1:8; 2:4). Whenever a believer was filled, he or she witnessed as a result. When Jesus declared that His followers would receive power after the Holy Spirit had come upon them and that they would be witnesses, He meant that we could be effective witnesses—but not in our own strength. Effectiveness comes through the power of the Holy Spirit. The key to effective witnessing is not in our technique or our strategy. The key is in the power of the Holy Spirit working within us. The question is, Do we really trust the Holy Spirit? Do we believe He will use someone just like us, and are we walking in that confidence?

Being filled means to be controlled. The question is not so much, How much of the Holy Spirit do you have? but, How much of *you* does the Holy Spirit have? Are we yielded to Him? Being filled is to be normal, consistent, and obvious (Eph 5:18ff.). The word for being "filled" with the Spirit in this passage is *plēroō.* The filling of the Spirit does not refer to a "second blessing" subsequent to salvation. The expression is most often found in Luke and Acts. The term and its derivatives have two main uses. First, being filled with the Spirit refers to the normal, consistent control of the Spirit in the believer's life. This is seen in the Lord Jesus (Luke 4:1), the early deacons (Acts 6), Stephen (Acts 7:55), and Barnabas (Acts 12:24). So the fullness of the Spirit is the expected lifestyle of any believer. After all, Paul reminds us that our bodies are the temple of the Holy Spirit (1 Cor 6:19).

We see this clearly in Eph 5:18. Paul commanded believers *not* to be filled with wine. How can you tell a person is drunk? By his speech, walk, and appearance. Paul also commanded believers to be continuously filled with the Spirit, in a consistent manner. The term is *plēroō,* "to fill." This is the only time Paul refers to being filled with the Spirit.

The verb is passive, emphasizing the role of God in the filling. The present tense notes the continual aspect of the Spirit's control. Further, Paul's emphasis to the church of Ephesus is on the corporate body, not a particular few. Köstenberger summarized this verse in its context. Paul's expression, "in contrast to being drunk with wine enjoins believers to exhibit a wise, maturing lifestyle which is to be expressed in corporate praise and worship as well as in proper Christian relationships."[6]

[6] A. J. Köstenberger, "What Does It Mean to Be Filled with the Spirit? A Biblical Investigation," *Journal of the Evangelical Theological Society* 40, no. 2 (June 1977): 235.

If a pastor entered the pulpit intoxicated, you could tell. It would be obvious. You probably would not listen to him! However, Eph 5:18, which contrasts intoxication with the Spirit-filled life, tells us that it is just as great a sin to preach without the Spirit's control as it is to preach drunk! Lest you think I am picking on preachers, let me say that it is as wrong for a Christian parent to live before their children devoid of the Spirit's control as it is to be a drunkard!

There is another way the term *plēroō* is used. It refers to a "sudden, special filling or anointing."[7] Green said this second use did not refer to "the settled characteristics of a lifetime but to the sudden inspiration of the moment."[8] We see this in Peter (Acts 4:8), the early church (Acts 4:31), and in the life of the apostle Paul (Acts 9:17; 13:9). Believers should live in such a way that the Spirit guides and controls their lives. Still, at times the Holy Spirit gives unusual unction for specific tasks, notably evangelism.

How Can You Know You Are Filled?

The filling of the Spirit does not generally happen through an ecstatic experience or other phenomena. Years ago, I heard pastor James Merritt give this simple test. Produce the *fruit* of the Spirit, as seen in Gal 5:22–23, and perform the *function* of the Spirit, to bear witness to Christ. Jesus tells us the Spirit "will glorify Me, for He will take of what is mine and declare it to you" (John 16:14 NKJV).

Hindrances to the Filling

Scripture tells us we can grieve the Spirit (Eph 4:30) or quench the Spirit (1 Thess 5:19). We grieve by the act of commission, and we quench by omission. My colleague Andreas Köstenberger noted that these passages are not injunctions directly "linking confession of sins to the filling of the Spirit."[9] While this is true, the Spirit is indeed the *Holy* Spirit, and our sins of omission (quenching) and commission (grieving) can hinder the Spirit's control in our lives. We are to confess our sins, said Köstenberger, "in order to enjoy continued fellowship with the Spirit and with other believers."[10]

---

[7] C. Schofield, "Linking Prayer and Bold Proclamation: An Exegetical Study of Acts 4:23–31 and Ephesians 6:18–20 with Implications for Contemporary Church Growth," *Journal of the American Society of Church Growth* 8 (Winter 1997), 68.

[8] Ibid.

[9] Köstenberger, "Filled with the Spirit?" 239.

[10] Ibid.

How Does a Person Receive the Filling?

As noted, there is no set formula that will work, but certain principles do apply. We should yearn for the presence and power of the Spirit who dwells within us. Further, we should never seek the filling; we should seek to be obedient believers (Luke 11:13). Do you desire the Spirit, the *Holy* Spirit, to control your life? Are you willing to yield all you are to Him? Yield yourself to the Spirit and be active sharing the gospel, and believe He will use you to the glory of God.

The Spirit Gives Believers Gifts

There is an increasing emphasis on the role of spiritual gifts in the American church.

- Gifts are not talents. They are Spirit-given abilities for Christian service in the body of Christ.
- Every believer has one or more gifts (1 Cor 12:7; Eph 4:7–8).
- Gifts are varied, and they are given to those in the body of Christ for the good of the body (1 Cor 12:7).
- Believers are to exercise their gifts. Part of God's will is getting to the place where you exercise His gifts.

There are many spiritual gift inventories designed to assist a believer in determining his gifts. However, I believe such tools tend to identify convictions or preferences more than spiritual gifts. They can be helpful, but I would not use them as the primary means of determining the gifts of the Spirit. I find it hard to imagine the apostle Paul encouraging the use of a spiritual gifts inventory in his day! Perhaps such inventories exist because we have failed to teach people thoroughly the Word of God, and how to apply the Word to life.

Here are a few tips to help you determine your spiritual gifts:

- Study the lists in Scripture, asking God to confirm the gifts you have received (Rom 12:3–8; 1 Cor 12:8–10,28–30; Eph 4:11).
- Be a responsible Christian until those gifts are made clear. Don't sit around and do nothing because you haven't found your gift! You find the will of God by doing what you already know to be his will, not by sitting on the sidelines of life. You also discover your gifts by faithful service.

- Listen to the wise counsel of other believers who know you well.
- Exercise those gifts you believe are yours, seeking God's affirmation.

What about the "gift of evangelism"? Much of the literature on evangelism and church growth uses this term. However, the Bible does not say anything about the gift of evangelism. It does speak of the gift of evangelist. Further, some people have argued that in the average church only 10 percent of the people have the gift of evangelist.[11] Others have picked up on this idea. This is a cop-out.

Certainly, some people are more effective than others in witnessing. We need to start where people are. Nevertheless, the New Testament mandate is the total penetration of an area with the total participation of the church members. Jesus never told 10 percent of His followers to win the world to Christ; He commanded all believers to do that—*period.* Every believer must become involved at some level in evangelism.

The New Testament term for *evangelist* in Eph 4:11 might convey the idea of a harvest evangelist where we think of a great evangelist like D. L. Moody or Billy Graham. It could also indicate a person who preached or shared the gospel where it had never been heard, as in the case of Paul. Or one could argue from the New Testament usage that the gift of evangelist, since it refers to equipping the saints for ministry, is a person gifted in teaching and inspiring others to evangelize.

We have to be careful to distinguish between our duty as Christians and our specific gifts. I'm not denying some people are more effective in evangelism than others, even as some men are better preachers than others. But the New Testament does not say some believers are to witness while others are not. The Great Commission is for every believer. Every believer ought to be able at least to administer spiritual CPR. If they meet somebody who wants to be saved, they should be able to tell them how to come to Christ.

Pastor Johnny Hunt of the First Baptist Church of Woodstock, Georgia, discussed the place of spiritual gifts in a message on his philosophy of church growth. He makes a distinction between "servant" gifts and "sign" gifts:

---

[11] See C. P. Wagner, *Your Church Can Grow* (Ventura, CA: Regal, 1980), 86–87, 89–90. Wagner does use the expression *evangelist,* while others use *evangelism,* but his usage still does not match the usage of the term in Scripture.

> God has given us servant gifts. Let me tell you churches that are filling them up today: Churches . . . that are dealing with sign gifts. "Ah, I want to be there where somebody speaks in tongues. I want to be there where there is interpretation of that. Oh, I want to be in a service where there's prophecy." You want to get into that mystical movement of the Spirit of God. Friend, if you want to get down where the rubber hits the road, you leave those sign gifts and get into the serving gifts. They are laid out for us clearly in the word of God in Romans 12:3–8. Let me just mention them to you: Wisdom, teaching, helps, hospitality, giving, government, mercy, faith . . . Those are gifts that God has given the church, and He's given them to us.

During this message, Hunt then went into the congregation to note individuals with particular gifts:

- a Sunday school teacher with an uncanny ability to prepare others to teach;
- an usher who serves others;
- a man with the gift of faith, who challenges the church to build bigger buildings and dream greater dreams; and
- an individual with obvious organizational giftedness, who organizes the many international mission trips taken by the church.

The Holy Spirit in the Believer's Witness

We never witness alone. We always have the Spirit with us. How does He aid us?

- He empowers us to witness (Acts 1:8).
- He gives us wisdom (Luke 12:12).
- He gives us boldness (Acts 4:31).
- He helps us in our praying (Rom 8:16).
- He gives us the burning desire to see people saved (Acts 4:29–31).

It was a rough day—four hours of driving—and I was late to a meeting. After I arrived, the meeting yawned on for five hours. Finally, I got to bed. I was staying at a military base. I had just drifted off to sleep when someone knocked at my door. The lady at the door said, "There's a bomb threat. We need to evacuate the building immediately."

A bomb threat? On a military base? I got dressed and headed out the door. I asked her, "Does this sort of thing happen all the time?"

"No. There's a package underneath a car in the parking lot and we don't know what it is. You need to get out to the field quickly." We went out to the field, and I could see armed military personnel along the perimeter. Security vehicles, a fire truck, and other vehicles arrived. Lights were flashing everywhere, and soldiers walked around talking on walkie-talkies. There was a sense of urgency.

Fortunately, there was no bomb. And we were able to go back to our beds. But I thought about that—urgency. There is a ticking going on. It's not the ticking of a bomb. It's the beat, beat, beat of hearts—hearts of people one heartbeat away from eternity without Christ. Do we sense that urgency? The Spirit of God gives us the urgency to share Christ.

The Holy Spirit teaches believers truth. The Holy Spirit, Jesus said, would bear witness to Jesus—not to Himself, not to others—to be witnesses to the truth of the gospel, the truth of the Christian faith. John's Gospel tells us that we will know the truth and the truth will set us free. Jesus also said that the Holy Spirit would guide us in the truth. The Holy Spirit helps us to gain victory over sin: "So I say, live by the Spirit, and you will not gratify the desires of the sinful nature" (Gal 5:16 NIV).

Temptation is not sin; temptation is an enticement to sin. The thought that comes across our mind—the attitude that we think about—is not sin. The Holy Spirit helps keep us from fulfilling that temptation to the point where it becomes sin in our lives. The Holy Spirit works to bring into our lives the risen life of Christ.

Some passages in the New Testament talk about the work of the Holy Spirit in us, and other passages talk about Christ in us, the hope of glory. There's no contradiction in the Godhead. The Holy Spirit works in us to bring alive the resurrected Christ in our lives.

The Work of the Spirit in the Unbeliever

The Spirit Precedes the Witness (Acts 10:1–15)

We read of the Holy Spirit's work ahead of the witness in the account of Cornelius in Acts 10. Before leading Peter to share Christ with Cornelius the Spirit had already been at work in his life. On a summer day in Evansville, Indiana, my witnessing team was ready to call it a day. We decided to knock on just one more door. A thirty-one-year-old man answered the door and listened politely with little obvious interest. Sensing our fatigue, he invited us into his mobile home. He still seemed totally uninterested, but I continued to share Christ with him. When I came to the point of inviting him to respond to the gospel, he suddenly burst into tears. "I am a paramedic," he said. "Over the last two weeks I have thought about death every day." He opened his heart in repentance and faith. The Spirit had been preparing him for our visit. I have seen this happen many times when sharing Christ.

The Spirit Convicts the Unbeliever

> Nevertheless, I am telling you the truth. It is for your benefit that I go away, because if I don't go away the Counselor will not come to you. If I go, I will send Him to you. When He comes, He will convict the world about sin, righteousness, and judgment: about sin, because they do not believe in Me; about righteousness, because I am going to the Father and you will no longer see Me; and about judgment, because the ruler of this world has been judged. (John 16:7–11)

The term *elegchō* is translated "convict" or "convince." The Spirit of God, our Comforter *(paraklētos)* of the converted, becomes the prosecutor of the unconverted, convicting the lost of three things:

1. *Sin.* Spurgeon, commenting on the conviction of the Spirit in his life, said, "When the Holy Ghost made sin to appear sin, then I was overwhelmed with the sight. . . . A naked sin stripped of all excuse, and set in the light of truth, is a worse sight to see than the devil himself."[12] It is the work of the Spirit, not our argumentation, that convinces a lost person of his sin.
2. *Righteousness.* The Holy Spirit convicts the world that righteousness before God comes not by human effort. Only God can impute righteousness to a sinful creature.
3. *Judgment.* The world, as well as Satan, will be judged (see John 16:11; 1 Cor 1:18). Those individuals not convinced of

[12] C. H. Spurgeon, *Twelve Sermons on the Holy Spirit* (Grand Rapids: Baker, 1973), 137.

the truth of the gospel will see it as a stumbling block or foolishness (1 Cor 1:18). But for those who respond to the Spirit's conviction, the response is like that of my favorite contemporary hymn:

O mighty cross, my soul's release!
The stripes He bore have brought me peace
His sacrifice on Calvary
Has made the mighty cross a tree of life to me.[13]

The Spirit Does the Work of Regeneration (John 3:5–6)

"He saved us not by works of righteousness that we had done, but according to His mercy, through the washing of regeneration and renewal by the Holy Spirit" (Titus 3:5). On a busy day at an airport, one man was particularly rude. He had more bags than allowed, they were overstuffed, and the skycap mentioned this to him. He demanded that his bags be checked. The skycap went about his business, and the man didn't give him a tip. A couple standing next in line said to the skycap, "You certainly seemed cool. That man was so rude to you, it's hard to believe you didn't retaliate." The skycap smiled and said, "No big deal. That man's going to New York, and his bags are going to Brazil." The skycap had total control over the bags. The Holy Spirit—not you or me—changes the eternal destiny of people.

The Holy Spirit in the Witnessing Encounter

The Holy Spirit takes a willing witness and a seeking sinner and brings them together to make a new believer. Philip and the eunuch are biblical examples (see Acts 8).

The Holy Spirit will lead us to divine appointments if we are sensitive to him. Pastor Ronnie was on an errand. A man approached Ronnie and noticed the name of the church on the van. After learning Ronnie was the pastor, he said he was going through some serious problems in his life and had several major decisions to make.

Ronnie was in a big hurry, but he agreed to take time to talk with the man. The stranger shared his heart and the decisions he faced. Ronnie shared the gospel with the man. When he asked the man if he desired to turn from his sin and place his faith in Christ alone as Lord,

[13] D. Baroni and J. Chisum, "O Mighty Cross," in *Firm Foundation* (Mobile: Integrity Music, 1994).

the man said yes. Many times I have seen this or heard of it being repeated in similar fashion, as the Spirit creates divine appointments for faithful witnesses.

How This Works

The work of the Spirit through people to lead to salvation can be described as a "net." Imagine a young man named *Joe* who grew up in a totally irreligious home. When Joe went to college, his assigned *roommate* turned out to be a "Jesus Freak." He was extremely excited about being a Christian. He would do Jesus yells in the shower and have a devotional time at six o'clock in the morning, even on Saturdays. He constantly prayed about everything from tests to world peace. Joe had never known anyone who took religion so seriously. They had some interesting conversations from time to time, but Joe never made any kind of response to the gospel. For the first time in his life, however, he did begin to ask himself what he believed about God. They only roomed together a semester.

After college graduation, Joe got a corporate job. He had a *secretary* who was a Christian. She kept a small sign on her desk that read "Prayer Helps," and every Monday morning she came to the office and talked about the Sunday worship music, the sermon, or a special event at church. From time to time she would invite Joe to bring his family to her church, but he always made an excuse not to come.

What Joe noticed most about his secretary was her disposition. She always seemed happy, and she never talked about people in the office. She did her best with every responsibility, and her uplifting spirit was contagious. Occasionally, Joe would say something about wishing he could bottle and sell her optimism, and she would respond by saying that "Jesus likes to give my kind of joy away to any person who really wants it." Joe didn't agree with her religious beliefs, but he did like the impact they made on her and his office.

Joe eventually joined a health club. One day he was looking for a racquetball partner, and the club teamed him up with another member. His opponent was very competitive, and they made a good match. When they were visiting casually in the locker room afterward, Joe was shocked to learn that this guy was a *youth minister* from a local church. He had always thought that ministers were religious professionals who spent all their time in church. They began playing together and became friends. Joe became interested in what the youth minister did at the church, and occasionally they got into theological discussions. The youth minister answered some of Joe's questions about God, but Joe still had little interest in church or thinking seriously about a personal faith.

After a few years, Joe was transferred to another office on the West Coast. His *boss*, one of the top producers in the company, turned out to be a committed Christian. Once or twice he would invite the office to his home. Without fail, the boss would say something to the group about the role Jesus played in his life. Often he invited Joe and his family to church and occasionally Joe would go. It was not as stuffy and formal as he thought it would be.

For the first time, Joe was with a superior who was a committed Christian. Joe always thought of religion in terms of your private beliefs about God, but this man was deeply affected by his faith at many levels of his life. Joe greatly respected this man's work habits and abilities, and he began to understand that religious convictions were a major factor in defining his boss's character.

One spring Joe was flying across the country to a national convention. The *lady* next to him was going to the same convention. They began chatting, and suddenly Joe found himself opening up and telling her about some serious problems. His marriage was about to fall apart, and he was feeling like a rat trapped in a maze with no place to go.

The woman listened for a time and then told him that he sounded just like she and her husband did three years ago. They were going opposite directions in their careers and were about to file for divorce when a friend shared what Jesus could do for her. The lady said she became a Christian, and slowly Jesus began putting the pieces of her life in order. Now she was happier than ever before because she knew that God loved her and that He had the power to help her.

Joe was deeply moved. He had never thought of God as one who would get involved in the personal lives of people. He began to realize that what he believed about God could affect far more than his theological opinions. It could impact his daily life.

A few weeks later, Joe was home alone when his doorbell rang. *Two people* from an area church had come to ask him if they could tell him about Jesus. Joe invited them in, and 45 minutes later he gave his life to Christ. Although the witness team led Joe to Christ, they were only the final strands in a net of witnesses that the Holy Spirit used.

God Himself is the great harvester. He takes the various witness efforts of His children, weaving them into a great net guided by the Divine Fisherman, the Holy Spirit. And the awesome thing is, when a new believer is born into the Kingdom, he gets to be a part of the net as well as he goes about sharing the good news.

Questions for Consideration

1. Do you think often of the work of the Spirit in your life and witness?
2. Thinking again of Eph 5:18, do you focus more on avoiding evil (like becoming drunk) but fail to focus enough on being filled with the Spirit?
3. What difference would it make in your witness if you lived daily a life that looked for the Spirit's work around you, seeking opportunities to partner with Him in sharing the good news?

Chapter 11

The Power of Prayer

That Satan trembles when he sees the weakest saint upon his knees, why not make him tremble? Why not storm the very gates of hell? Nothing could please God more. In the conflict that is upon us, certainly we can ill afford to neglect one weapon Satan does not have in his arsenal and the one he fears the most—prayer.[1]

—Ralph Herring

A young pastor of a rural congregation stood to preach. Unknown to him, his son had made a paper airplane during Sunday school (probably due to a deacon's kid). The preacher had no sooner given his first point than the little boy swung the plane through the air with a loud "vrooom!" A few people chuckled, but his dad was embarrassed. "Son," the pastor exclaimed, "don't do that again."

The young preacher returned to his message, while his son returned to his imagination. Sure enough, the boy let his thoughts get away from him and went "vroom!" even louder. A second time his father corrected him, obviously flustered. After regaining his composure, he began to preach again. Then the boy did the same thing again, this time letting the plane go. It made a perfect circle, landing

[1] R. Herring, *The Cycle of Prayer* (Nashville: Broadman Press, 1966), 62–63.

in Sister Hazel's hair! All the people laughed, except the pastor and Sister Hazel. The preacher snatched up his son and headed out the back door. The entire congregation saw the little boy's face peering over his dad's shoulders screaming, "Pray! Pray! It's gonna be *bad!* It's gonna be *bad!"* This little boy learned the urgency of prayer.

Mature believers should demonstrate an urgency in prayer for far more vital reasons, not the least of which is the lostness of people all around us. So many churches focus on praying for temporal matters, giving little focus to more weighty matters of eternity. As a young pastor I led our church on Wednesdays to focus as much or more time to praying for eternal needs as for temporal needs. In a matter of time God began blessing us with newborns in the Kingdom.

The Importance of Prayer

Consider what these famous Christians have said about prayer:

- *Charles Spurgeon:* "Of course the preacher is above all distinguished as a man of prayer. He prays as an ordinary Christian, else he were a hypocrite. He prays more than ordinary Christians, else he were disqualified for the office he has undertaken."[2]
- *William Carey:* "Prayer—secret, fervent, believing prayer—lies at the root of all personal godliness."[3]
- *Martin Luther:* "I have so much business I cannot get on without spending three hours daily in prayer." "He that has prayed well has studied well."[4]
- *William Penn,* describing George Fox: "Above all he excelled in prayer. . . . The most awful, living, reverent frame I ever felt or beheld, I must say was in his prayer."[5]

What is prayer? The most common word for prayer in the Old Testament is *palal,* which means "to fall" or "to prostrate before" someone. It often signifies intercessory prayer. In the New Testament, the most common words are *euchomai* and *deomai. Euchomai* and its cognate *proseuchomai* are more general terms for prayer, while *deomai* has a more specific idea of seeking for a particular need.

---

[2] W. Duewel, *Ablaze for God* (Grand Rapids: Zondervan, 1989), 212.

[3] R. Foster, *Celebration of Discipline* (New York: HarperCollins, 1988), 33.

[4] Ibid., 34.

[5] Ibid.

Prayer is more than talking to God. It is *intimacy* with God. It is a reflection of our desire to know God. Prayer draws us closer to God, and it leads us away from the world, the flesh, and the devil. I like the definition of prayer used by my first doctoral student, Chris Schofield, who now serves in the area of prayer and evangelism at the North American Mission Board. Schofield defines prayer as "communion and dialogue with the triune God through a personal, love relationship with Jesus Christ."[6] This definition emphasizes both the *love* relationship and the *doctrinal* aspect of prayer by emphasizing the Trinity. I use this definition of prayer: "intimacy with God that leads to the fulfillment of His purposes."

A few years ago, a survey showed that over 90 percent of Americans pray. If 90 percent of Americans *really* prayed, our country would be different morally! In the 1980s a survey of over 17,000 members of a major evangelical denomination who attended seminars on prayer for spiritual awakening gave frightening results. These believers, obviously interested in prayer, communicated that the laity spent less than five minutes a day in prayer; worse still, the pastors said they prayed no more than seven minutes a day on average![7]

Let me take this one step further. While at Houston Baptist University, I had the privilege of meeting several members of the Houston Rockets, in the period when they won back-to-back NBA titles. One was a devout Muslim. After winning their second championship, this player delayed a victory parade because it was his time of prayer. He fasts during the daylight hours for the entire month of Ramadan, one of the pillars of Islam.

A devout Muslim will wash his hands and face three times, kneel toward Mecca, and say his prayers five times each day. Imagine such devotion—talking to a god who does not exist! Part of the reason for the devotion is the salvation-by-works system in Islam. Still, should we as believers not be ashamed when we fail to spend time talking to the God of the universe?

Prayer: intimacy with God that leads to the fulfillment of His purposes.

Prayerlessness is one of the greatest sins of American Christians. One of the greatest hindrances to evangelism in our day is a lack of

[6] C. Schofield, "Biblical Links Between Prayer and Evangelism" (ThM thesis, Southeastern Baptist Theological Seminary, May 1995), 11.

[7] D. S. Whitney, *Spiritual Disciplines for the Christian Life* (Colorado Springs: NavPress, 1991), 62.

biblical prayer for evangelistic purposes. Consider the average church, and notice how much time is spent praying for physical needs. This is biblical and right (see James 5). But too many prayer meetings are like organ recitals: we pray for hearts, livers, and other organs. Very little praying is done for spiritual needs. How much times does your church spend praying specifically for lost people, for laborers, and for God to honor your evangelistic efforts?

Prayer is vital because it is at the heart of Christianity. Prayer is intimate communication with God and is possible only because Jesus' death on the cross provided the means for our relationship with God. R. A. Torrey summarized the significance of prayer:

> Our whole life should be a life of prayer. We should walk in constant communion with God. There should be a constant looking upward to God. We should walk so habitually in His presence that even when we awake in the night it would be the most rational thing for us to speak to Him in thanksgiving or petition.[8]

There are other reasons to pray. Jesus set the example (Mark 1:35). God commands that we pray (Luke 18:1). Through prayer we receive from God: "Ask, and it will be given to you; seek, and you will find; knock, and it will be opened to you" (Matt 7:7 ESV). This verse carries the idea of a child looking for a parent.

Our house was one of many in our area to be affected by Hurricane Fran in September 1996. We had a hole in our roof from a huge limb, my car was crushed, Michelle's car was dented, we lost many trees, and the storm frightened our kids. When the hurricane came, we spent an entire night in the hall listening to our house being bombarded by missiles created from falling tree limbs.

One night some time later a thunderstorm came. Our daughter Hannah began to cry out to us. We didn't immediately answer, since we were asleep. Then she got up and began to look for us. We didn't tell her to go back to her bed. We didn't tell her she was being disobedient. We saw a frightened child in need of a dad and a mom. We let her crawl up in the bed with us, and we gave her comfort.

In the same way, God expects us to serve Him out of obedience and to fulfill daily acts of obedience. But there are times when we need Him in a desperate way, and we cry out to Him, and we don't

[8] R. A. Torrey, *How to Pray* (Pittsburgh: Whitaker House, 1983), 81.

give up until we find Him. During those times, God is more than willing to meet our needs like a good parent.

Prayer also brings relief from anxiety. Paul exhorted believers to replace worry with prayer (see Phil 4:6–7). Prayer provides deep joy to the Christian as well: "Until now you have asked nothing in My name. Ask, and you will receive, that your joy may be full" (John 16:24 NKJV). Through prayer, we have power in overcoming Satan (see Eph 6).

Prayer unlocks the door into a growing relationship with God. Intimacy in prayer builds this relationship. Read the prayers of Abraham, Moses, David, and Paul, and see the intimacy they experienced. Finally, prayer is effective in the work of evangelism. We should pray for harvesters for evangelism work (see Matt 9:36–38).

It is one thing to say we believe in prayer; it is another to pray in faith. S. D. Gordon said, "You can do more than pray after you have prayed, but you cannot do more than pray until you have prayed." Prayer is foundational to the Christian life.

Jesus, Our Example in Prayer

The best way to learn to pray is by studying how Jesus prayed. The Gospel writers recorded a request from the Lord to teach them. They did not ask, "Lord, teach us *how* to pray," but "Lord, teach us *to* pray" (Luke 11:1). We learn best from His example. How did Jesus pray?

- He modeled prayer (John 17).
- He spent time in personal prayer (Mark 1:35).
- He prayed at important events (Matt 26:36–44; Luke 6:12).
- He taught the importance of prayer (Matt 6).

Prayer and Spiritual Warfare

The New Testament teaches the reality of spiritual warfare. Chuck Lawless is an authority on spiritual warfare and its relationship to evangelism. Here are his thoughts.

The Spiritual Warfare of Evangelism: Reaching People through Taking on the Enemy

Chuck Lawless[1]

It seemed to me that Greg was completely closed to the good news of Jesus. No matter how much I shared the gospel, he had no interest in following Christ. The Bible meant little to him. The arguments about Christ carried no weight for him. He was, as one church member put it, "just living in the dark."

Have you ever found personal evangelism to be difficult like that? Maybe you are facing the reality of spiritual warfare in your attempts to be an effective personal evangelist. Our goal in this article is to examine what the Bible says about the warfare we face as we try to reach unbelievers.

Lost People Are Blinded to the Gospel

The apostle Paul told the Corinthians that unbelievers are blinded by the god of this age (2 Cor 4:3–4). The "god of this age" is Satan, who is also called the "prince of this world" (John 16:11 NIV) and the "ruler of the kingdom of the air" (Eph 2:2 NIV).

He operates in the "domain of darkness" (Col 1:13; see also Acts 26:18).

The persons we seek to reach—like Greg in the opening illustration—are in spiritual bondage, and our task is to proclaim a message of liberation and freedom. The enemy counters, striving to hold his captives in chains. Though God has already defeated Satan and secured salvation for His own through the cross (Col 2:15), the battle is nevertheless a real one.

Satan's strategies for keeping unbelievers blinded are several. The enemy provides the lies to which unbelievers cling, such as "I'm good enough," and "I can always wait until tomorrow to follow God." He makes sin attractive and alluring, convincing the unbeliever that following God will mean a loss of pleasure. He snatches away the Word of God before it takes root in an unbeliever's heart (see Matt

---

[1] Used by permission of C. Lawless. Lawless serves as the Dean of the Billy Graham School of Missions, Evangelism and Church at The Southern Baptist Theological Seminary in Louisville, Kentucky. A PhD graduate of Southern, he also served as a senior pastor for 14 years prior to joining the Graham School. He is the author of seven books, including *Discipled Warriors: Growing Healthy Churches That Are Equipped for Spiritual Warfare* (Kregel). He is also president of the Lawless Group, a church consultation firm (www.thelawlessgroup.com).

13:3–9,18–23). More specifically, Satan blinds unbelievers to the gospel by promoting distorted views of the gospel itself.

For this reason, evangelism must be accompanied with *prayer.* Evangelism is the task, but prayer is the power behind the task. If only God can open blinded minds, does it not make sense to seek His guidance and intervention as we evangelize lost people?

Undiscipled Believers Are Targets for the Enemy

Scripture affirms that Satan continues to attack persons who become believers. Jesus warned Peter that Satan demanded permission to "sift you like wheat" (Luke 22:31). Peter himself later warned believers, "Be of sober *spirit*, be on the alert. Your adversary, the devil, prowls around like a roaring lion, seeking someone to devour" (1 Pet 5:8). The apostle Paul likewise admonished believers to "put on the full armor of God, so that you will be able to stand firm against the schemes of the devil" (Eph 6:11). James, too, called believers to resist the devil, presupposing that the enemy would attack (Jas 4:7). If Satan does not attack believers, such recurrent warnings would seem irrelevant and unnecessary.

The enemy especially aims his arrows at young believers who have not been discipled. He strikes them with doubt and discouragement. Sometimes he hits them with loneliness, as they move away from their non-Christian friends and try to fit into a church that is unfamiliar to them. At other times, he lures them with the same temptations they faced as non-believers. Whatever his strategy may be, he wants to strike at new believers before they get solidly planted in the church.

Our response to Satan's strategy is simple: intentionally teach new believers to put on the armor of God. That is, the church's task is not complete when non-believers come to Christ. The essence of "putting on the armor" (Eph 6:10–17) is not about magical prayer that applies the weaponry to believers' lives; rather, it is about discipleship and spiritual growth that affect all of one's life. Wearing the armor is about daily living in truth, righteousness, faith, and hope, while always being ready to proclaim the gospel of peace found in the Word.

But, will a new believer understand how to live as a Christian if we do not teach him? An effective evangelism strategy simply must include an uncompromising commitment to discipleship for both the evangelist and the new convert. In the spiritual battles we face, discipleship means the difference between victory and defeat.

Proclaiming the Word Is Spiritual Warfare

In my work as dean of the Billy Graham School of Missions, Evangelism and Church Growth, our research teams have studied thousands of evangelistically growing churches. Each of our studies has shown that proclaiming the Word has been a primary factor in the churches' effectiveness in evangelism and assimilation.

That finding should not surprise us, though. The Word is alive and powerful (Heb 4:12), converting the soul (Ps 19:7), and protecting us from sin (Ps 119:11). The Word is the "sword of the Spirit" (Eph 6:17). It is the weapon to which Jesus Himself turned when He faced temptation (Matt 4:1–11).

Three times, the devil tempted Jesus in the wilderness, and three times the Son of God responded by quoting God's Word (Matt 4:1–11). The simple phrase, "It is written" was enough to cause Satan ultimately to back down from the battle. The enemy is no match for the Word.

To illustrate this truth with regard to evangelism, it is clear that the enemy seeks to undermine the biblical truth that personal faith in Jesus Christ is the only way to God. Exclusivity of salvation in Christ alone is largely rejected, with a growing number of American adults believing that "all good persons" will go to heaven whether or not they know Jesus Christ as Savior. While the church buys the lies of pluralism and inclusivism, Satan "disguises himself as an angel of light" (2 Cor 11:14) and lulls unbelievers into a false sense of spiritual security. We must prepare for, and counter, this strategy by passionately proclaiming the biblical truth that personal, explicit faith in Jesus is necessary for salvation (John 14:6; Rom 10:9–10).

Personal Prayer

Where you are as a Christian five years from now will depend on your praying more than any other factor. There is no time more valuable than time spent with God. I learned this in a course during my first semester in seminary, through a valuable resource called the 2959 Plan developed by Peter Lord.[9] This approach emphasized certain practical considerations related to personal prayer.

Let your gaze be on God, your glance on your requests. Calvin Miller reminds the believer to "never start praying before you've stopped to look at God."[10]

---

[9] P. Lord, *The 2959 Plan*, rev. ed. (Grand Rapids: Baker, 1989).

[10] C. Miller, "Praying without Ceasing," in *Evangelism for a Changing World*, ed. T. Beougher and A. Reid (Wheaton, IL: Harold Shaw, 1995), 40.

Let prayer be your first choice, not your last. One of the worst statements uttered in the church is, "There is nothing we can do but pray." Can we do any better than pray? We can do more but not better. Yes, there are occasional times when the followers of God are told to stop praying and get moving (as in the crossing of the Red Sea; Exodus 14), but in most cases too little praying is the greater problem.

Pray retail, not wholesale. In other words, pray for specific needs. We don't live in generalities; we live in a specific place with specific needs. A prayer list helps in this regard.

Pray more from conviction than from crisis. Daniel is a great example in prayer. When Daniel received the news that he would be thrown into the den of lions, notice how he responded. He faced Jerusalem and prayed morning, noon, and night just as he had done previously (Dan 6:10). What consistency! Daniel could respond like this because he was accustomed to talking to God out of conviction—not just when he faced a crisis. Crises are not times to get acquainted with God! We should walk with God before the crises.

The reason for personal devotional time is to develop intimacy with God. Billy Graham said the minister who does not have a daily quiet time will fall away in 10 years.

A warning: Devotion time is not a spiritual rabbit's foot. Calvin Miller issues a threefold warning of an unrealistic focus on God:

1. Loving the time to meet God more than loving God Himself. This breeds a sort of inner addiction: "I've always wondered if many of these who go off with the rhetoric of holiness but never took the time to minister."
2. Developing an otherworldly aloofness: "When someone translates as hyper-godly, most of us become hyper-nervous around them."
3. Succumbing to the "sweet-little-Jesus" syndrome with "the saccharine Christ of gooey pietism."[11]

In your devotional time, certain tools help in keeping a fresh, intimate walk with God:

- Daily Bible reading keeps our focus on God.
- Keeping a journal has been practiced for centuries by saints from John Wesley and George Whitefield to countless believers today.

[11] Ibid., 147.

- Include names, specific concerns, and answers in a prayer list.
- A devotional book can be helpful as well.

Features of Prayer

As we pray, certain features can guide our time to enhance our intimacy with God.

Praise

This is our response to the person of God. We praise Him for who He is. A little girl attended a prayer service with her mother. She sat on the back pew while her mom and a few others knelt at the altar to pray. She listened closely while the adults cried out to God, some weeping. Finally she could sit still no longer. She stood on the pew, looked up into heaven, and cried, "Dear God! A, B, C, D, E, F, G, H, I, J, K, L, M, N, O, P, Q, R, S, T, U, V, W, X, Y, Z. Amen!" Then she sat down.

The mother, a bit embarrassed, asked her, "Honey, why did you say that?"

"Because you were all praying such beautiful prayers, and I wanted to talk to God. I didn't know the words, so I thought if I gave God the letters, he could make the words come out right."

This might not work for a forty-year-old believer, but I believe there is something about a sincere child's prayer, just with the letters, that brings praise to God. When we do not know the words to pray, God still hears the cries of our heart. Let us never become so sophisticated in our spirituality that we are afraid to offer God praise.

Praise is not noise, just as reverence is not silence. It is the acknowledgment of God's greatness. It is recognizing He is "hallowed," or "holy," as the Model Prayer tells us (see Matt 6:9).

Thanksgiving

This is our response to the goodness of God. Thank Him for what He has done. "Enter His gates with thanksgiving" (Ps 100:4). "Give thanks in everything" (1 Thess 5:18). An attitude of gratitude should permeate our lives.

Confession

Confession is our response to the holiness of God. Our sins will hinder our praying (see Ps 66:18). As we pray, we can ask the Holy Spirit to reveal each sin in our lives. Then we can confess the sin (see

1 John 1:9). When broken relationships are involved, we should seek to make them right as well.

Intercession

This is our response to the love of God. When we ask of God, Foster reminds us, we are not "trying to manipulate God and tell Him what to do. Quite the opposite. We are asking God to tell us what to do. God is the ground of our beseeching. . . . Our prayer is to be like a reflex action to God's prior initiative on the heart."[12]

Petition

Petition is our response to the love of God for us. It is appropriate and necessary for us to ask God to meet our needs. However, in our consumer-driven culture, we can learn from this prayer of petition from an anonymous soldier:

> I asked God for strength that I might achieve;
> I was made weak that I might learn humbly to obey.
> I asked God for health that I might do greater things;
> I was given infirmity that I might do better things.
> I asked for riches that I might be happy;
> I was given poverty that I might be wise.
> I asked for power that I might have the praise of men;
> I was given weakness that I might feel the need of God.
> I asked for all things that I might enjoy life;
> I was given life that I might enjoy all things.
> I got nothing that I asked for—
> but everything I had hoped for.
> Almost despite myself, my unspoken prayers were answered.
> I am among all men most richly blessed.[13]

Listening

There is another aspect about prayer that must not be missed: listening to God. You may not be aware of it, but wherever you are as you read this book, noises are all around you. Rock-and-roll music is all around you. Rap tunes are playing. People are discussing various topics from sports to finance. The only thing you need to hear these voices is the proper receiver. A radio will suddenly usher into your presence a bevy of sounds.

[12] Foster, *Celebration of Discipline*, 42.

[13] C. R. Swindoll, *Living Above the Level of Mediocrity* (Waco: Word Books, 1987), 113.

Prayer operates the same way. God is constantly speaking to us, teaching us, leading us. The question is not whether God is speaking but if we are listening. God consistently speaks to us through His Word, but do we hear Him? He occasionally speaks to us through circumstances and other people. He also speaks at times through the still, small voice of His Spirit. Are we listening? If you walk with God, you will be prompted by Him to witness. This cannot be taught as much as it is learned through the school of prayer taught by the Holy Spirit.

Consecration

Consecration is a prayer of commitment to God. Often in Scripture believers made specific, fresh acts of consecration: Jonah in the whale's stomach (Jonah 2:1–10), David following his sin with Bathsheba (Ps 51), Paul, our Lord, and others. In our times of prayer, we are often confronted with the need to make a fresh, new commitment to God.

Daily Personal Worship: Practical Tips

Establish in your heart and mind the importance of the devotional time. One of the most liberating lessons I learned from the school of prayer is that we must disciple ourselves to pray in all circumstances. I once thought great men and women of prayer loved to pray so much that it was a constant joy to be in the presence of God. But then I read Foster's comments: "We must never wait until we *feel* like praying before we pray."[14] Prayer is a discipline. Many times we pray out of a desire to be with God. Other times we pray out of a sense of holy desperation. But at other times we pray not because it is convenient or comfortable but because it is *right.* Sometimes I am not in the "mood" to pray in the morning. But I have discovered that if I don't take time to pray, my mood gets worse as the day goes by!

1. *Designate a time and place for your time with God.* Guard the time.
2. *Do whatever is necessary to be spiritually prepared.*
3. *Adjust your time occasionally to avoid monotony.*

As you pray, make the Scriptures a part of your time. Praying Psalm 51, the prayer of David after his sin with Bathsheba, should help us understand the seriousness of our sin and the greatness of our God.

[14] Foster, *Celebration of Discipline*, 44.

Other tips on prayer:

- Change your prayer time, mix it up; begin with Scripture sometimes, with prayer other times.
- Read a book on prayer annually.
- Talk to other Christian friends.
- Read the journals and biographies of great Christians.

Linking Prayer and Evangelism

The great man of prayer, E. M. Bounds, said, "Prayer does not stand alone. . . . It lives in fellowship with other Christian duties."[15] This is particularly true about evangelism. You cannot evangelize effectively on a consistent basis without prayer. In his research of growing churches, Thom Rainer discovered prayer ranked with biblical preaching and teaching as one of the major reasons churches in the survey reached lost people.[16]

Features to Remember

Pray for Boldness to Witness

Notice this prayer of the early church that links prayer and evangelism:

> "And now, Lord, consider their threats, and grant that Your slaves may speak Your message with complete boldness, while You stretch out Your hand for healing, signs, and wonders to be performed through the name of Your holy Servant Jesus." When they had prayed, the place where they were assembled was shaken, and they were all filled with the Holy Spirit and began to speak God's message with boldness. (Acts 4:29–31)

Chris Schofield made a vital point about this passage. "The prayer for 'boldness' (from *parrēsia),* which has already been associated with the apostolic witness in 4:13, is significant in at least two ways. First, notice that the apostles are not seeking revenge or the end of the opposition but rather courage and freedom of speech. Second, they

[15] E. M. Bounds, *The Necessity of Prayer* (Springdale: Whitaker House, 1984), 31.

[16] T. S. Rainer, *Effective Evangelistic Churches* (Nashville: Broadman & Holman, 1997), 11–17.

were seeking this boldness that they might proclaim the gospel. . . . Their motive was centered on God's redemptive work."[17]

Pray in the Spirit's Power

Another key passage is Eph 6:18–20. Paul followed his discussion of the armor of God with a request for believers to pray for bold proclamation of the gospel. Prayer is seen as an indispensable part of the armor of God. Praying "in the Spirit" is not a reference to praying in tongues but to prayer "in the presence, control, help, influence, and power of God's Spirit."[18] Paul exhorted the Ephesians to pray for "utterance," or *parrēsia,* an openness to preach the gospel. This is the expression translated "boldness" in Acts 4:29,31. Paul was in prison as he wrote these words, asking for courage to share Christ. Certain truths emerge from these two chapters, Acts 4 and Ephesians 6: boldness to proclaim the gospel is a legitimate request to bring before God. Such boldness comes only from God. It cannot be "worked up." Such boldness comes through the prayers of God's people.

Pray for Harvesters

In Matt 9:38 Jesus, seeing the multitude wandering about like sheep with no shepherd, encouraged prayer for the Lord of the harvest to send laborers. We should pray that God would awaken believers to the need of the world for the gospel. We must pray for God to call out those who would go to the ends of the earth proclaiming Christ. We should pray for God to raise up more ministers of the gospel who would lead churches to have a gospel passion.

Praying Specifically for the Unsaved

Robert Speer, a Presbyterian missionary leader, said, "The evangelization of the world . . . depends first of all upon a revival of prayer. Deeper than the need for men; deeper, far, than the need for money; deep down at the bottom of our spiritless lives, is the need for the forgotten secret of prevailing, worldwide prayer."[19]

Korea is a great example of the impact of prayer. In 1966 about 11 percent of the Korean population was Christian. By 1978, it was 19

---

[17] C. Schofield, "Linking Prayer and Bold Proclamation: An Exegetical Study of Acts 4:23–31 and Ephesians 6:18–20 with Implications for Contemporary Church Growth," *Journal of the American Society of Church Growth* 8 (Winter 1997): 67.

[18] Ibid., 71.

[19] W. S. Monneyham, "Getting More Hooks in the Water Is Not Enough," *Christianity Today,* 25, no. 16 (September 18, 1981): 20.

percent; 1981, 22 percent; in the 1990s over one-third of the people in Korea were believers. Korea also has the largest Presbyterian, Methodist, and Assemblies of God churches in the world.

The secret to this Korean explosion is prayer. Many Koreans pray early every day. Some pray all night on Friday nights. I once heard a Korean pastor say that the average Korean Christian prays an hour a day. One reason the Korean church prays so much is the threat of North Korea. Our problem today is we don't see the threats of worldliness, carnality, culture, ungodliness, and apathy that should motivate our prayers.

Charles Sullivan tells of a time when he gave the invitation and a man in his seventies came forward to give his life to Christ. His wife came down the aisle behind him with the glow of God on her face. After Sullivan counseled the man and prayed with him, he reached for a membership card to fill out, as we Baptists do, but the wife stopped him. She told Sullivan that he wouldn't need a card. She reached in her Bible and pulled out an old, yellow, tattered card.

"Forty years ago, I made a commitment to pray for my husband's salvation daily," she explained. "As a sign of my commitment, I filled out a membership card with my husband's name, and checked 'profession of faith' and 'baptism.' The only thing we need to complete is the date." God had answered her prayer.

A bedridden woman in London, England, had been able to cultivate the life of prayer. She had read in the papers about evangelist D. L. Moody's work in Chicago. She didn't know Moody or anyone associated with him. Placing that paper under her pillow, she began to pray, "Lord, send this man to our church." Moody did go to London in 1872 when his church building was in ashes back in Chicago.

While Moody was speaking to the YMCA, a pastor invited him to preach to his congregation. Nothing happened the Sunday morning Moody preached. After the service, the sister of that invalid woman had informed her that a Mr. Moody of Chicago had preached and that he was to speak again that evening. The invalid woman declared, "Oh, if I had known, I would have eaten no breakfast, I would have spent all the time in prayer. Send me no dinner, leave me alone, lock the door. I'm going to spend the whole afternoon and evening in prayer."

That evening the building was packed to hear Moody. The atmosphere was different, and the power of God fell on that place. Five hundred people gave their lives to Christ. Great revival began, and Moody's career as an evangelist multiplied because of that sick lady's prayer.[20]

Here are specific items for which you can pray for those who need Christ:

- Ask God to open their spiritual eyes (2 Cor 4:4).
- Ask God to set them free from spiritual captivity (2 Tim 2:25–26).
- Ask God to give them ears to hear (Matt 13:15), faith to believe (Acts 20:21), and will to respond (Rom 10:9).
- Ask God to send people into their lives to witness to them (Matt 9:38).
- Ask God for ways to build caring relationships (1 Cor 9:22).
- Ask God for opportunities to witness (Col 4:3).
- Ask God for boldness to witness (Acts 4:29).
- Ask God for an opportunity to invite them to a harvest event (Luke 14:23).[21]

Prayer can give us a yearning to share the gospel with others. A seminary student was taking his son to preschool one morning when he noticed a man walking along the side of the road. The student, named Joel, was prompted to pray for that man. He promised that he would share Jesus with this man if he were still on this road on his return. However, after leaving the preschool complex, he thought nothing of the man.

After a stop at the grocery store, Joel headed home. As he neared home, he saw the young man again. As he pulled into his driveway, Joel realized all the seminary in the world didn't matter if his faith was silent. "I returned to the young man," Joel recalled, "and gave him a ride."

As Joel drove the stranger home, he remarked that "the man upstairs" had looked out for him. Joel began to share with him the good news of Jesus. The conversation flowed freely as God opened the man's heart to the gospel truth. They stopped along the road, and he repented of his sin and asked Jesus to save him. God will use us in witnessing for Him *if* we walk with Him in communion through prayer.

[20] J. G. Hallimond, *The Miracle of Answered Prayer* (New York: The Christian Herald, 1916), 69–71.

[21] *Praying Your Friends to Christ* (Alpharetta, GA.: North American Mission Board, 1998).

Corporate Prayer

Martin and Ginter, in *Power House,* made a distinction between prayer ministries and the church as a house of prayer. "A prayer ministry involves a portion of the congregation in ministry, as with a youth ministry. . . . Such a ministry may take the form of missionary prayer circles; times of prayer open to the whole church such as a Wednesday night prayer meeting; or men's/women's/youth's prayer meetings; a prayer room; an intercessory team; prayer ministry before/during/after the church service; or a prayer chain."[22]

In contrast, a house of prayer "will have prayer saturating every aspect of its individual and corporate life. Having significant prayer will be seen as the first thing to do when planning, when meeting, etc. There will be teaching on prayer from the pulpit, in Sunday school classes, and in small-group settings. People will think of prayer as a major factor to be used at first to solve any problem."[23]

In other words, the goal is to have a church where prayer permeates its fabric—and where lost people receive a high priority in its praying. Not every church is a house of prayer, but every church can have an effective prayer ministry.

I recently heard of a church who set aside 90 days to pray for 80 unchurched families. After the 90 days of prayer, teams from the church went to visit these homes. At least 69 families welcomed the visit. The church also visited another 80 homes for whom they had not prayed. Guess how many homes welcomed them? One. Can you see the difference?

Questions for Consideration

1. How important is prayer to you?
2. Do people who know you think of you as a person of prayer?
3. Would you try this simple experiment: for a period of time, perhaps the next month, would you pray this simple prayer daily to see what God does in your life? "God, give me (1) an opportunity to witness today, (2) the wisdom to see it, (3) and boldness to take it."

---

[22] D. Ginter and G. Martin, *Power House* (Nashville: Broadman & Holman, 1994), 16.

[23] Ibid., 17. This book offers many resources on specific prayer ministries.

Chapter 12

Testimony

For we are unable to stop speaking
about what we have seen and heard.

—Peter and John in Acts 4:20

"*What you do speaks so loudly that I cannot hear what you say.*" These familiar words of Ralph Waldo Emerson ring true in our day. The testimony of the believer, both in word and deed, is crucial to sharing Christ. How can we tell others with confidence, as did Peter, "about what we have seen and heard"? Believers excited and grateful for the change in their lives by the gospel can be powerful tools in the hand of God.

Assurance of Salvation

Following my freshman year of college, I spent a summer selling books door to door. Most of the time I sold a reference book for schoolchildren. It was a good product overall; however, I soon learned that I was best at convincing people with limited resources to buy the product. As the weeks passed, I became convicted that the value of this product was not worth what some people were willing to pay, and the fact that I could convince someone to buy my product did not necessarily mean they should.

Confidence in one's product matters in sales. It is even more important in sharing the gospel. Please note, the gospel is not about selling a product—we are offering a gift! But one hindrance to a confident Christian life is a lack of certainty about our own salvation. The apostle Paul was certain of his (see Phil 1:6). John talked as well of the confidence of knowing Christ: "I have written these things to you who believe in the name of the Son of God, so that you may know that you have eternal life" (1 John 5:13).

I remember the first time I visited the First Baptist Church of Woodstock, Georgia, a perennial leader in evangelism. I stayed with a family of church members. The wife's love for Christ glowed. When I asked her about her joy in the Lord, she said, "It is amazing how much joy you can have when you are really saved." She had been an active church member for many years but had never been converted. After meeting Christ, the change in her life was obvious to her and to others.

Billy Graham has said that the greatest field of evangelism in America is the church pew. I am convinced that we who lead churches must exhort our people consistently to be sure they are in the faith. Confidence in one's conversion brings enthusiasm in evangelism! Here are eight keys to assurance of salvation.

1. *Memory of one's conversion.* While some believers may not remember the exact date of their conversion, most can remember the time they met Christ. We ought to cherish that day when we passed from death unto life.
2. *Promises of Scripture.* Passages from the Bible on the certainty of salvation include Acts 16:31; John 3:16,18; and Rom 5:9–10.
3. *The Spirit's presence.* Romans 8:9,16, speak of the fact that the presence of the Spirit is indicative of a genuine Christian.
4. *Answered prayers.* First John 5:14–15 gives evidence.
5. *Discipline by God.* Hebrews 12:8 tells us God disciplines His children.

   Of these eight keys, 1 John gives three evidences in a series of cycles throughout the book:
6. *Righteous living.* First John tells us we are not to continue in sin if we are Christians. This does not refer to sinless perfection but to a state of life not characterized by habitual sin.

We will still sin even as Christians, but the pleasure of sin is not enduring.

7. *Sound doctrine.* A true Christian will be convinced of the truth of Scripture. A young Christian may not understand much about doctrine, but a believer cannot consistently deny the truth of the revealed Word of God. I was a child when I came to Christ. I did not know what a virgin was, let alone the virginal conception of Jesus. But I am fully confident in this biblical truth now. Can a believer be deluded by false teaching? Certainly. But the mark of a believer is his or her recognition of the truth.
8. *Love for other Christians.* First John 3:14 tells us believers will love one another. In fact, the assurance of salvation is the theme of the First Epistle of John.

Sharing Your Conversion Testimony

Biblical Examples

The Bible gives several examples of personal testimony. For example, we read of the man born blind (see John 9). After the remarkable physical and spiritual changes in his life, the man was confronted by the Pharisees. He replied, "I was blind but now I see!" (John 9:25 NIV). He told his story. The Samaritan woman went into her community saying, "Come, see a man" (John 4:29).

On two occasions in the Acts, the apostle Paul gave his testimony (see Acts 22; 26). Peter and John also declared, "We cannot but speak the things which we have seen and heard" (Acts 4:20 KJV). Obviously, the early believers communicated their salvation to others.

Its Importance

Every Christian has a testimony. A personal testimony is something every Christian can share. I once thought my testimony was insignificant because it was not dramatic. If you feel that way, remember the fact of conversion is more vital than the circumstances surrounding it. In today's culture with its emphasis on personal experience (witness the infomercials with testimonials, Facebook and MySpace pages with biographical info, and other means of personal storytelling), the testimony can be an effective tool in one's witness.

At this point I want to make one thing very clear: the greatest reality of one's conversion testimony is just that—you have been converted! The focus should be to exalt our great God and Savior Jesus Christ. I have often been at youth camps or other events in which the only testimonies given consisted of a dramatic conversion from drug abuse, promiscuity, or some other grossly sinful lifestyle. Don't get me wrong, those are amazing testimonies to God's grace. But so is the story of a child raised in a godly home who as a youngster yields his life to Christ and follows Him for a lifetime.

I encourage you to use today's technology to make much of the testimonies of believers. Record and post testimonies regularly on your church Web site; teach your youth how to write their testimony succinctly on their Facebook or personal blog; encourage the use of the testimony, both the more dramatic and the more consistent.

It Is Relevant

A testimony is not ancient history; it is something that happened in our lifetime. People are looking for living, real, spiritual experiences. Johnny Hunt, pastor of First Baptist Church, Woodstock, Georgia, came to Christ in a powerful way. His best friend was an agnostic. Some time after Johnny's conversion, his friend said to him, "I have a problem. I am an agnostic. I'm not sure there is a God or if you can know there is a God. So here's my problem—what happened to my friend?" Johnny's friend was saved and is now in the ministry.

It Is Unique

You are an authority on your testimony. You may not be on anything else, but you are an authority on what God has done in your life. You may not know the answer to every question, but you know what happened to you.

TV talk shows, talk radio, the World Wide Web, the Internet, and chat rooms demonstrate the hunger that people have to communicate with one another. I spend a little time every week or so on the Internet, chatting with people and seeking opportunities to witness. One of the things I've discovered is that people are interested in learning about other people.

It Holds Up a Mirror to the Person with Whom You Share

Your testimony gives people something to which they can compare their lives. The focus is on Christ and the change he has made in your life, but it still is a mirror for that person. When my former professor, James Eaves, was pastor at the First Baptist Church, Albuquerque, New Mexico, years ago, a waitress was converted. She sent out invitations to her friends to attend her baptism, followed by a party at a friend's home. She also invited her pastor to the party and gave him an opportunity to say a few words. More than 17 of her friends were converted as a result of her conversion and witness.[1]

Guidelines for Sharing One's Conversion Testimony

1. Write out your testimony, seeking the Spirit's guidance.
2. Give adequate but precise details showing how Christ became your Lord and Savior and how Christ meets your daily needs. Make sure you exalt the Christ of your experience more than your experiences.
3. Use language the nonbeliever can understand.
4. Relive your testimony as you tell it. This will enable you to present it with loving enthusiasm.
5. Relate your testimony to the Scriptures, using pertinent verses as they are needed.
6. Speak distinctly and in a natural tone, avoiding any mannerisms that might detract from the presentation.
7. Be brief (two or three minutes). People are interested in your testimony but not your life story!
8. Ask the Holy Spirit to help you present Christ so the unbeliever will want to know Him and will come to know Him personally.
9. Share your Christian testimony regularly with other Christian members of your family, then with Christian friends, until it becomes a natural part of your daily conversation. Then share it with your lost friends and others.
10. After sharing your testimony, ask, "Has anything like this ever happened to you?" This question is a simple way to move into the gospel presentation.

Jesus said that if we are ashamed of Him, He will be ashamed of us. Let us never be ashamed of telling others what God has done through Christ for us. The more you share your testimony, the more comfortable you will become. You will learn to adapt it to the audience to whom you are speaking. For example, when speaking to a teenager, I emphasize the changed lives of youth from my past and the impact

[1] D. Miles, *Introduction to Evangelism* (Nashville: Broadman and Holman, 1981), 194–95.

they had on me. To a person reared in church, I will emphasize the fact that I grew up in church but realized church involvement was not my primary need. Adapting is *not* embellishing. Avoid the temptation to add details that did not actually happen. Have confidence that God can use your story just as it happened.

Here in a nutshell is my testimony. Mine would not be of the dramatic variety, but my conversion is as amazing as the apostle Paul's, for Jesus Christ changed my life and I have never recovered!

> I grew up in the south, where the tea is sweet and the summers are hot. My parents began taking my older brother and me to a small, young church when I was pretty young. I was a pretty good kid, not particularly rebellious, not given to more gross sins. At age 11, something amazing happened there (this was 1970). In a short period of time, a number of hippie-freak types (genuine weirdos) came into our church and were radically changed. I saw God work among these young adults, many of whom had been doing really bad things—drug abuse, sexual promiscuity, etc. I began to look into my own heart and realized it was not pure, either. I saw those young people so altered in their attention, so hungry to know God, so passionate about their relationship with Jesus that I realized I had nothing like that—only a collection of Bible stories in my head. That August, I gave my life to Jesus Christ to use as He saw fit. I asked for forgiveness for all my sin, and surrendered my life to Him. I have never been the same. For me the journey of following Christ started slowly but accelerated in my high school years. I began to love the Bible and saw God answer so many prayers. Since then He has given me a wonderful family and a place to serve. Believe me, the journey is awesome! My story may not be too dramatic, but the change I have seen Jesus make in my life has been nothing short of amazing. It is not always easy to follow Jesus, but it is never boring. Has anything like that ever happened to you?

A Recovery Testimony

The reason the organization known as Mothers Against Drunk Driving makes such an impact is that the founder lost her son to a drunk driver. Chuck Colson's passion for prison ministry is fueled in large measure by his own time spent in prison. The difficulty my wife and I experienced before we had kids, coupled with the severe illnesses both our children faced in childhood, has given us a special burden for infertile couples and those who have lost children. It is amazing how many people have common struggles. A recovery testimony is the story of how God has helped you through a difficulty since coming to Christ. It gives praise to God for His work in bringing us through a crisis.

The Spiritual Autobiography

Another way your story can have an evangelistic impact is through your spiritual autobiography. The spiritual autobiography includes the following features:

1. The autobiography should exalt God above all else.
2. The autobiography for evangelism should include intimate knowledge of God and personal religious experience.
3. The spiritual autobiography is easily communicated through different media. Some of my students have begun to print copies of their personal testimonies in more detail—something like an autobiography that I'm describing here. As they go door-to-door, meet people, or write people to whom they are witnessing, they include copies of their autobiographies. A personal experience of a changed life will gain a hearing with some people when a sermon in a church building would not.
4. The information in a spiritual autobiography will be more effective when you share it with people in your own cultural context. The spiritual autobiography is effectively used in a public church setting or a public gathering where you have time to give more than your testimony. The testimony is brief and to the point, demonstrating the change brought by the gospel when you were first converted. The spiritual autobiography goes through much more detail, looking at the different aspects of your life before and after you came to Christ. Include both high and low spiritual marks, giving an honest, personal description of your life in Christ.

Here is an example of a remarkable autobiography of a young lady named Darcy.[2]

> Recently someone asked me about my tattoos. I always start chronologically. My first tattoo rests on my left shoulder blade; she is a yellow and purple fish that looks similar to an angelfish. She has a bright blue flirtatious cartoon eye. She has remained nameless for 17 years. I started drawing her in high school. She was my doodle, my daydreams. "How wonderful it would be to jump in the ocean and swim away" . . . and "Oh, how I feel like a fish out of water. I am suffocating and I wish this pain would end."
>
> My father left and divorced my mother when I was five or six. My mother told me that on the day he moved out, I invited my dad into my room for a tea party. After pouring the airy tea into my favorite blue-flowered plastic china cups situated in front of two of my stuffed friends and my father, I poured my cup full and sat down. I then picked up my cup for a sip, looked my dad in the eye and said, "I just want you to know that you are the one who is going to be lonely; not us." I finished my tea in one gulp and left my Dad sitting in my room with lifeless friends, which is where he continues to dwell to this very day.
>
> My dad thought he found life in the arms of women. These women became my competition: "How is it that I can get my father's attention?" My father remarried quickly and soon I was in competition with two younger women: my stepsisters. I cannot say enough about my stepmother; she was a second mother to me, she gave and gave and I loved her. I developed close relationships with my two sisters also. But my father always remained aloof. To me he was this person I longed to have a relationship with; I longed for him to tell me he loved me, I longed for his praise, I longed for any interaction. I never could figure out a way to hold my father's attention.
>
> And as it was, neither could my stepmother. I do not know why I remember their divorce the way I do; it could not have possibly happened the way I remember the events unfolding. But it seems like one day my eldest stepsister came to pick me up from my mom's house to take me back to their house to have dinner. When I got to the house my stepmother was already

[2] Darcy's story is used by permission.

crying and I was informed that my father had left, they were getting a divorce, and she and the girls were moving to Colorado Springs at the end of the month. I felt completely abandoned.

I did not realize how severely this affected me until I saw my (ex)stepmother for the first time following their leaving. I think it was in '96 or '97, so I was in my mid-twenties. I saw her at my aunt's house. I remember just sitting there not saying a word, but just staring at her and hanging on her every word. I found myself even following her around their house. I felt like I was small child. The feeling I get just thinking about this encounter is so surreal. Never have I seen a more wounded soul, except perhaps my own. We shared a common wound, and all I wanted to do was to embrace her and cry for her as much as for me.

So, she and the girls were gone, my dad was out chasing women, and my brother Kip, who incidentally is one of my most favorite people, graduated from high school and left for Georgia Tech. It was just my mother and myself. My mother began hitting her stride at this point in her life. She had just finished college, had worked her way up through the ranks at Naples Community Hospital and was the Human Resources Director, and had spiritually begun to grow. We always enjoyed a close relationship. It was not perfect, but it was the one relationship I could count on.

I, on the other hand, was hitting the streets of rebellion; smoking, drinking, and sexual experimentation. I was mentally mature for my age, I was headstrong, and I started receiving unwanted attention from older men. One event in particular happened at a camp I used to attend every year. I never told anyone what happened and buried it deep. But years later I went back to this camp for a ladies retreat with my mom and some of her friends, and he was still there. I then dealt with the crushing blow of guilt knowing that because I never said anything more, girls were probably molested.

My father married a woman named Tara the fall of my eighth grade year. I moved in with them for my first three years of high school. Tara and I developed a great relationship over time. I give her all the credit; I was not an easy teenager to be around. From this marriage I received the blessing of two half brothers,

Hunter and Cody. Hunter was born while I was in my junior year of high school and Cody my freshman year at FSU. Hunter quickly became the apple of my eye. This was a good thing because I was the built-in babysitter due to the fact that I spent most of my time grounded for drinking or smoking pot or flexing my independence in one way or another.

Caring for Hunter aroused my desire to get married and have babies. As far back as I can remember, all I have ever wanted to be was a stay-at-home mom. I used to envy my friends who had mothers who were home waiting with hugs and snacks when they arrived home from school. I longed for my own family and I longed to be married. The problem was I could never figure out how to keep a boyfriend. At 16, I gave in and slept with my boyfriend. I remember thinking, "I guess I might as well get it over with." Triumph for him, but for me it was a promise of marriage and love. A couple of months later school was out and he moved. He did not move out of town, just across town, but he never called after that. It was a long tumultuous summer. I seriously thought I was going to die of a broken heart. I simply could not understand where I went wrong: "Didn't I do everything he wanted? Why do men leave?" As it happened, I did not die of a broken heart, and we ended up re-establishing a solid friendship.

I lived out the next couple of years angry and frustrated. I decided to take control of my heart by deciding that I would keep emotion out of sexual relationships. Sex was used to show a dominance of power; it was mine to give or take away. And then, from out of the past came the boy who had broken my heart in high school, the one who had first held my heart, but had left it in shards. My roommate and I had decided we needed a break from college. Our idea was to sell everything we owned and then move to the Caribbean, wait tables, and just live. I shared my wanderlust with the old boyfriend and he said, "Why don't you move to Hawaii. I have always wanted to live with you before we got married." With the potential of marriage on the table, I jumped. I sold everything I owned and moved to Hawaii, which is where I sat for my second tattoo.

I have a sun tattooed on my right ankle. Its detail has faded over the years, but the effects of my move to Hawaii are about to be shared. I lived in Hawaii for six months in the town of

Kailua. I made a home on Koolau Street. I enjoyed the domestic life of cooking, cleaning, ironing, etc, serving my not-yet-husband. For work I was a short-order cook at a bar and grill called "The Shack" (it is still open and I have never found a better burger to date!). It was a local hangout, and I was given a local name, "Ka-la-pume-a-hanh-a," which means "warmth of the sun." I got the tattoo to memorialize my Hawaiian name, but today it serves as a reminder of how the sun feels good but leaves you burnt, while the Son provides true warmth.

Environmentally, Hawaii was where the idea of being with a woman began to take root. During my time there, my relationship with the guy I was living with was not great—I was raped (not by my boyfriend), and I had become friends with a lesbian couple and been introduced into the gay lifestyle. I left Hawaii not just broken hearted, but spiritually and mentally broken. Whatever ideas I had about God had been replaced with the picture of this mean old man sitting in heaven giving me a taste of what I desired and then shooting me down with lightning bolts of rejection and pain. About a week before I left the man I felt sure I was supposed to have married in Hawaii, he was going out with his friends and, commenting on his shirt, I said, "Well you are not going to meet the girl of your dreams in that shirt," to which he replied, "Darcy, I have met the girl of my dreams; I just can't live with her." I began to hate God. "Where did I go wrong?" "What is wrong with me?" "What do men want?" When I got back to college I studied harder because it was obvious I was going to have to take care of myself, and I played harder because it was the only time I felt good. I began to dabble in same-sex affairs and considered myself bisexual until I realized that being with women was probably the safer bet. By the time I went to chiropractic school, I was a full-fledged lesbian with a cool tattoo to prove that I was serious.

My third tattoo started out as two scientific female symbols linked together and colored in with a rainbow-colored camouflage. I designed it myself and it made it into the artist's book. For the next 10 years I searched for relationships with women that were safe. I was an activist; I marched in parades and worked to promote same-sex marriage. I helped raise money for the same groups that today are millions of dollars strong. I knew how to defend homosexuality with the Bible, and I led people away from Christ. I led friends into the homosexual lifestyle. I felt free and in control. I was gay and proud to be so. But as the years wore on and wore me down, I found nothing that I was looking for. I did not find marital bliss. I did not find emotional safety. I did not find happiness. Rather, I found death and dying, depression, and dysfunctional relationships to extremes. I was living in Boston when I hit bottom. In the depths of my depression, my first thought in the morning was "I hate my life." I had been burnt by the sun and was drowning in the sea of my life. I bore the classic markings of a God-hating, totally depraved human being. It is no wonder that Paul uses homosexuality as THE picture of depravity. Homosexuality is the ultimate in self-love; this idolatry screams, "I love myself more than anyone else, so I want to be with someone just like me because they will then have to love me as much as I love me."

During this time I began to be wooed by God. I began talking to Him (well, more yelling at Him), airing out my frustrations. It is funny, because I spent time telling people God did not exist and convincing myself of the idea. My life was bad, and therefore God could not exist. But then when it came down to it, I knew He did exist. He was a mean man who would not give me what I wanted. I knew He had the power to give me what I wanted. I knew He could make my life better, but I would scream at Him one night at the ocean's edge in a wild thunder storm, "What do you want from me? I am a good person, what else do you want from me? Why don't you ever give me what I want?" But, the fact is, I was not a good person, I was a self-loving God-hater, I did not give God obedience, so in fact He did give me what I wanted, which was not Him. I believe this was the beginning of my salvation process. I began to see my life differently; I began to detest everything in my life.

A couple of months later my mother came up for a visit. My mother is not the savior in this story, Christ is. But because she never stopped praying for me, God allowed her to be the Gospel carrier for me. The Lord laid upon her heart a message to just shine forth the light of Christ, rather than His contempt for my lifestyle. He loved me through her, and I was drawn into a night of Q&A about a relationship with Christ. A week or so later, I found my childhood Bible, began reading, and was saved in my apartment. I had reached rock bottom, and I found Christ is the Rock at rock bottom. My moment of salvation was not sweet and pretty, but rather it was ugly, yet completely sufficient. I surrendered my life to Him. I shook my fist in the air and told Him if He wanted my life, he could have it because I certainly could not manage it. I spoke to him with an air of "Good luck; let's see how you do with this mess." In my head I did not believe that he could fix me, but in my heart I knew that all I had to do was follow Him wherever He wanted me to go and things would get better. I moved from Boston five days later.

Three months later the Holy Spirit brought about conviction and repentance over my homosexual lifestyle. This event was preceded by a non-combative conversation with a strong Christian that confronted my false beliefs about homosexuality. Weeks later, I lay prostrate before the Lord, confessing that I knew what the Bible said about homosexuality, but that I had heard so many interpretations about what it all meant that I needed Him to speak. I cried out to Him in conviction, "Lord if being gay is okay, then give me peace, but if it is not right in Your eyes, deliver me, because I do not want anything to come between us." I was granted repentance and I cried, "Forgive me Lord—I do not want this," and He delivered me! I was free from homosexuality from that moment on. I have never stumbled back into or even longed for that lifestyle ever again.

Most people scoff at such a miraculous turn, but to them I say, "I guess I am just too dumb not to believe that the power of the cross would not completely deliver me." Oh, there was work that I can put a theological point on now: put off/put on, MAKING every thought captive to the obedience of Christ, etc., but the work is that of the Holy Spirit. Environmental work included completely abandoning the lifestyle, which included losing every friend I had, and living as my newly created self, a child of God, sister to Christ, and in-dwelt by the Holy Spirit. Getting ready for my first date with a man after being saved by Christ was interesting because it was hot and I had to figure out a way to cover up the tattoo on the inside of my left ankle. I eventually wrapped it with an Ace bandage and said I hurt it running. For weeks I worked on a redesign. For weeks I cried out to God for help. For weeks, I felt like I was too broken in my past to ever be able to be truly loved or blessed by God. I had the mark of a wretched past. And then, I had the idea to surround the symbols with a butterfly and to add one more symbol. My thought was that the symbols would represent the Godhead, the blessed Trinity. And as for the butterfly—well it symbolized my transformation. This tattoo, my butterfly, forever reminds me of the work of grace in my life.

I end this story with the encouraging words of God to us as penned by his servant Paul in his letter to the Ephesians (2:1–10):

> And you were dead in your trespasses and sins in which you previously walked according to this worldly age, according to the ruler of the atmospheric domain, the spirit now working in the disobedient. We too all previously lived among them in our fleshly desires, carrying out the inclinations of our flesh and thoughts, and by nature we were children under wrath, as the others were also. But God, who is abundant in mercy, because of His great love that He had for us, made us alive with the Messiah even though we were dead in trespasses. By grace you are saved! He also raised us up with Him and seated us with Him in the heavens, in Christ Jesus, so that in the coming ages He might display the immeasurable riches of His grace in [His] kindness to us in Christ Jesus. For by grace you are saved through faith, and this is not from yourselves; it is God's gift—not from works, so that no one can boast. For we are His creation—created in Christ Jesus for good works, which God prepared ahead of time so that we should walk in them.

Again, your conversion may not be as dramatic. But I used Darcy's story not only to give an example of the autobiography but also as a reminder of the deep need so many have for Christ. The autobiography takes 15 to 25 minutes to share, a testimony, 90 seconds or so. The autobiography is probably 10 pages, double-spaced.

It would be appropriate for you as a church leader to share your autobiography occasionally with those you lead. Pastor, tell it to your church annually or at special times. Sunday school teacher, tell your story to your class. It may encourage them to do the same. Even if you never have the opportunity to give your spiritual autobiography in a public place, just writing it out can be a great spiritual exercise. When my wife and I were going through the missionary approval process for the Home Mission Board, we had to write our autobiography.

What a wonderful experience it was for me to reflect over my entire life and remember how good God has been.

In the witness training that I lead, I require each participant to write his or her personal testimony. On more than one occasion, individuals in the training have discovered they had no testimony and were converted! A simple exercise you can do in a Sunday school class or an evening service, for example, is to provide paper and pencils and ask participants to write their conversion testimony. You might use Paul's testimony in Acts 26 as a biblical guide, followed by the sharing of your own testimony. Then challenge the participants to share their testimony with someone during the next week.

Questions for Consideration

1. Have you ever written out your conversion testimony? If not, please do so.
2. How often do you tell your testimony to others, both believers and unbelievers?
3. Have you ever taken the time to write out your spiritual autobiography?

Chapter 13

The Potency of Consistency: Character

The transformed character of Christian men and women is the key to world evangelization at the end of the twentieth century and beyond.[1]

—Leighton Ford

In the first century, the changed lives of believers played a vital role in their witness. Their fearlessness in the face of persecution, conviction before skeptics, integrity in a culture of ungodliness, and boldness to proclaim the gospel grew from their character. One striking characteristic of the first Christians was their reflection of Christ. The truth of the gospel proclaimed by a person devoid of character is the epitome of hypocrisy.

While in Houston, we lived only 30 minutes from Six Flags. So when my son Josh turned six, I took him to the theme park. My zeal in taking my firstborn to his first theme park clouded my judgment. I took Josh up the Skyscreamer, a ride that lifts you up several stories and then drops you like a rock. About one millisecond into the drop,

[1] L. Ford, *The Power of Story: Rediscovering the Oldest, Most Natural Way to Reach People for Christ* (Colorado Springs: NavPress, 1994), 10.

I knew it was a mistake. Josh was screaming and crying, scared to death. I promised him we would never take that ride again. That was not a Father of the Year moment for me.

I love adventure, but we all can push our limits. Christianity is the greatest adventure you could ever live but one fraught with challenges. Satan lurks nearby always and will wait 20 years for one chance to wreck your testimony. Only the most disciplined person can traverse the path to godliness and be all that God has called him to be, and that only with the Spirit's help. Let's face it: living the Christian life is not hard—it is impossible! It is if we do so in our power. We dare not follow Christ frivolously as if the choices we make have no consequence for our faith and our witness.

What are the marks of those who live the Christian life to the fullest? This chapter examines the very practical matters that make a big difference in evangelism. Skills, methods, and experience in evangelism are good; doctrine is essential. But the gospel presented by a believer whose life exemplifies the character of Christ is best.

The apostle Paul models the character required of the witness. You cannot separate the preaching of Paul from the character of his life. In fact, Paul consistently referred to his character as a demonstration of the reality of his message. You see this clearly when he addressed the leaders of the church at Ephesus (see Acts 20). I like to call this the first seminary class, or at least the first pastor's conference. OK, that is a bit of a stretch, but at this point Paul gives training to ministers of the church at Ephesus, and character lies at the heart of what he says. This passage offers a glimpse into the role of the relationship between a person's lifestyle and his or her witness.

If there is one word that summarizes how we must reach this culture—from the Millennials, to the Generation Xers, to the aging Boomers, to the retiring Builders, it is this word: *real.* Be real. Believers must be real. Our culture is sick of phonies. The outing of ministers guilty of everything from immorality to greed has become commonplace. The world is not looking for Christians who are perfect; they are looking for Christians who are real, who demonstrate a changed life, whose lives give honor to Christ.

Some believers fail to witness because they know there are issues in their lives that bring reproach to the name of Christ. While some mistakenly think they have to be on some higher spiritual plane before they can witness, there are issues of obedience we must face to be effective in personal evangelism.

In a post-Christian world, people need a demonstration of the gospel that accompanies an explanation of its truth. Some people don't attend our churches because they are afraid they may become like us! They are still without excuse, but we are also accountable for our behavior. I agree with those who say the chief mark of character is self-control. Great saints in history have been marked by an awareness of the role of Christian character.

The Life of the Witness

- *Robert Murray McCheyne:* "Lord, make me as holy as a saved sinner can be."[2]
- *R. A. Torrey:* "Power is lost through self-indulgence. The one who would have God's power must lead a life of self-denial."[3]
- *Spurgeon:* "Whatever 'call' a man may pretend to have, if he has not been called to holiness, he certainly has not been called to the ministry."[4]

Integrity

What are the building blocks of Christian character? Paul's counsel in Acts 20 guides us. He told the Ephesian Christians: "You know, from the first day I set foot in Asia, how I was with you the whole time" (Acts 20:18). He was not bragging; he was stating reality. They had watched him three years. Paul went on to say, "I have not coveted anyone's silver or gold or clothing" (Acts 20:33). One of my best friends in the ministry made this statement to one of my classes: "You will spend half your life in ministry just staying out of trouble."

We should be aware of those areas that specifically pull at our integrity. My wife cannot watch violent movies because of issues from her childhood. I grew up in a very stable, loving home, so violence in film does not affect me the same way (no, I do not watch slasher movies). Satan knows your areas of weakness, so you and I should be on guard. This is especially true of evangelism. The first thing an individual, a church, or a denomination loses is commitment to evangelism. Only a life demonstrating the character of Christ

---

[2] W. Duewel, *Ablaze for God* (Grand Rapids: Zondervan, 1989), 68.

[3] Ibid., 88.

[4] C. H. Spurgeon, *Lectures to My Students* (Grand Rapids: Baker, 1977), 9.

will keep evangelism as a priority. D. L. Moody, the great evangelist, knew this. He once said that "character is what you are in the dark."[5] If our motives are impure, they will eventually be discovered. Paul's evangelism was consistent with his life.

G. Campbell Morgan told of that great English actor Macready. An eminent preacher once said to the actor: "What is the reason for the difference between you and me? You are appearing before crowds night after night with fiction, and the crowds come wherever you go. I am preaching the essential and unchangeable truth, and I am not getting any crowd at all."

Macready replied: "This is quite simple. I present my *fiction* as though it were *truth;* you present your *truth* as though it were *fiction.*"[6]

A more positive picture of the impact of integrity is told by Duewel:

> A British nobleman was passing through a village in Cornwall, England, and after searching in vain for a place to purchase alcoholic beverages, asked a villager, "How is it that I cannot get a glass of liquor in this wretched village of yours?" The old man, recognizing the rank of the stranger, respectfully took off his cap and bowed. . . . "My lord, something over a hundred years ago a man named John Wesley came to these parts." The peasant then turned and walked away.[7]

Humility

Paul said to the Ephesians that he served the Lord with great humility (Acts 20:19). In ministry, the greatest temptation is the desire for status. That is one of the major hindrances to evangelism in the church. Many churches today are hindered in their evangelism because key laypersons as well as ministry staff are more concerned with their personal standing than the evangelistic growth of the Lord's church. Pride hinders evangelism.

When we are young and opportunities come our way, we typically say, "Why me, Lord?" surprised that God would save and use people like us. But as we become experienced, educated, and inflated, we are

---

[5] Attributed to Moody; source unknown.

[6] G. C. Morgan, *Preaching* (London: Revell, 1937), 36, italics added.

[7] Duewel, *Ablaze for God*, 56.

more tempted to say, "Why *not* me, Lord?" wondering why we were overlooked for this or that position.

I was brought to tears by a student in my spiritual awakening course. A big, strong, handsome guy who had been radically saved for only three years, Brad was a bona fide "Jesus freak." In our prayer time, Brad shared with the class that the church he attended had called him to be a youth intern. Most in that class were pastors or were serving the Lord in a variety of staff positions beyond "intern." But this was Brad's first position. With a gleam in his eye, and child-like wonder, he told the class, "I feel like a lottery pick in the NBA draft. I can't believe a church would ask me to serve on its staff." Brad's humility and awe at the call of God is a glowing example of a humble life.

My heroes are men like Roy Fish, my major professor at Southwestern Seminary, a man of God; Robert Coleman, who wrote *The Master Plan of Evangelism*; the late Bill Bright of Campus Crusade for Christ; and Billy Graham. Why have these men served Christ so well for an entire lifetime? Because they have humility. Humility helps us finish well.

On the other hand, I have too often seen young ministers with a great deal of ability crash and burn because they lacked humility. Once a young student came to me, announcing boldly how the little church he had served as interim thought he was such a great preacher that they declared he would be the next Billy Graham. He lasted one semester in seminary and soon was out of the ministry. If you find yourself constantly talking about your achievements more than your need for Jesus, you live in great danger. Humility recognizes we cannot live without Christ.

Passion

Paul served the Lord *with tears* (Acts 20:19). He told the Ephesians, "Therefore be on the alert, remembering that night and day for three years I did not stop warning each one of you with tears" (Acts 20:31). See the passion of Paul as he prepared to go to Jerusalem, knowing chains were waiting (Acts 20:22–24). For what are you passionate? What drives you? What causes you great joy? Is it a passion for God? You will never overcome the rejection that comes with evangelism apart from a passion for God.

We have been wired with passion. Passion is not a reflection of personality. I am a type A and pretty hyper. My wife is very quiet and meek. But her passion for Jesus is every bit as strong as mine. Jonathan Edwards wrote an entire treatise about the vital role of our affections. We are all passionate; the question is for what are we most passionate? Are we driven by those things that would honor God? How do I find my passion? How can I use that for the gospel? What do you talk about in and think about in your spare time? What consumes your thoughts? That is your passion. Another way to think about your passion comes from looking at extremes. What brings you the greatest joy? I get great delight when a student or believer suddenly "gets it" about the gospel, someone who suddenly realizes God can use them for His glory. My passion is for teaching.

On the other hand, what brings you great anger? I do not mean when you do not get your way (which is why we usually get mad). I mean what gives you righteous indignation, like the time Jesus cleared the temple? It drives me crazy to see believers caught up in the machinery of the institutional church, lives set on spiritual autopilot, with no yearning for God. It bugs me that so many believers miss the great thrill of taking risks for the gospel. So, my passion has driven me to teach evangelism.

People who have been used of God, particularly in times of great revival, came from different backgrounds, traditions, and educational experiences. Yet they had in common a deep passion for God. One thing I try to do at least once a year is read a biography of a great saint—someone like Jonathan Edwards, George Whitefield, or D. L. Moody. I look for the reason God used them so effectively.

One thing I've discovered about these people is that they all had a passion for God. They were very zealous toward their heavenly Father. Consider what Whitefield, that great preacher in the First Great Awakening, wrote in his journal: "I was honored today with having a few stones, dirt, rotten eggs, and pieces of dead cats thrown at me."[8]

What about Paul? He had a passion for evangelism: "I did not shrink back from proclaiming to you anything that was profitable, or from teaching it to you in public and from house to house." (Acts 20:20). Again, let's compare this passion to Whitefield. Whitefield said, "God forbid that I should travel with anyone a quarter of an hour without speaking to them about Christ."[9] What about passion

---

[8] *Christian History,* vol. 13, no. 2: 3.

[9] Ibid.

for the gospel? Paul said, "I testified to both Jews and Greeks about repentance toward God and faith in our Lord Jesus." (Acts 20:21). Consider that monk, Martin Luther. See Luther standing before the Diet of Worms and listen to what he said: "My conscience is captive to the word of God. I cannot and will not recant anything, for to go against conscience is neither right nor safe. Here I stand. I cannot do otherwise. God help me. Amen."[10]

I'm convinced that the main reason many Christians never witness is that we have *gotten over Jesus.* It's just that simple.

Consider what Jonathan Edwards, that brilliant Puritan, said: "Two things exceedingly needful in ministers as they would go about any great matters to advance the kingdom of Christ are zeal and resolution. . . . A man of but ordinary capacity will do more with zeal and resolution than one of ten times the parts in learning without them. More may be done in a few days or at least weeks than can be done without them in many years. Those fewer possessed of them carry the day in almost all affairs."[11]

*We do not need wildfire; wildfire does not glorify our holy Christ. It is holy fire, the fire with which the Holy Spirit baptizes us. We need the fire and zeal of the early church when almost every Christian was ready, if need be, to be a martyr for Christ.**

*Duewel, *Ablaze for God*, 108.

People may listen to the preacher's preaching, but they will follow his passion. Puritan pastor Richard Baxter wrote: "That will be most in their ears, which is most in your hearts."[12] Duewel wrote: "A passionless Christianity will not put out the fires of hell. The best way to fight a raging forest fire is with fire."[13] He recorded the passion of others as well: "When William Booth . . . was asked by the king of England what the ruling force of his life was, he replied, 'Sir, some men's passion is for gold, other men's passion is for fame, but my passion is for souls.' "[14]

---

[10] R. H. Bainton, *Here I Stand: A Life of Martin Luther* (Nashville: Abingdon Press, 1950), 144.

[11] J. Edwards, "Thoughts on the Revival," in *The Works of Jonathan Edwards,* ed. S. E. Dwight (Edinburgh: Banner of Truth, 1834, reprint, 1987), 1:424.

[12] M. McDow and A. L. Reid, *Firefall: How God Shaped History through Revivals* (Nashville: B & H, 1997)172.

[13] Duewel, *Ablaze for God*, 28.

[14] Ibid.

Purity

Paul's testimony to the Ephesian elders (see Acts 20:26–34) is a model of purity. A life of personal holiness and purity is essential for effective soul winning.

We all must keep ourselves in an environment where we are open to correction, from accountability on the Internet to accountability in our daily lives. I had the privilege of hosting a Paul–Timothy conference in Houston during 1995. Thirty handpicked young leaders sat at the feet of three effective ministers: John Morgan of Sagemont Church in Houston, John Bisagno of Houston's First Baptist, and Fenton Moorhead of the Sugar Creek Baptist Church in Sugar Land, Texas. Heed the words of John Bisagno: "My father-in-law, with three earned doctorates, a Baptist preacher, said only 1 out of 10 men who started in ministry at 21 is in it at 65. I didn't believe it. I wrote the names of 25 men I knew in college. Today only 5 survived, and we're not 65 yet."

My anecdotal observations have confirmed these numbers. Each semester I ask 10 percent of my students in a given class to stand. I tell the seated students to look around and to note that, statistically speaking, those standing represent the number from the class who will be in ministry in their sixties. Students are stunned by the realization.

Bisagno added the four pitfalls believers should diligently avoid:

- Sex—we must never be alone with a person of the opposite sex if we are married (unless it is our mother, wife, sister, or daughter).
- Money—if you are in ministry vocationally for the money, you will leave it for greener pastures!
- Discouragement—we all get discouraged, which is why we need brothers to encourage us.
- Ambition—vision to change the world is one thing, but ambition has destroyed many a gifted young man.

An evangelist friend with a great burden for an awakening in our day traveled to study in Edinburgh, Scotland. He visited the tiny principality of Wales, which has been visited with mighty revival several times in the modern era. He discovered a lady who had been converted in the Welsh Revival of 1904–1905 as a little girl, and who knew Evan Roberts personally. Roberts was a principal human agent in the Welsh Revival.

My friend sat in the little cottage of the elderly woman. "What was the secret of Evan Robert's power?" he asked. She simply looked into her fireplace, and in her thick Welsh accent, replied, "Mr. Roberts was a very godly man."

"Yes, I know that, but tell me more. Why did God use him?"

The lady continued to look into the fire. "God used Mr. Roberts because he was a godly man," she said.

My friend was frustrated. Pressing further, he said, "Yes, I know, but tell me specifics. How did he pray? What did he do?"

The elderly lady turned and faced my friend. "Young man," she said sternly, "the reason God used Mr. Evan Roberts was that he was a very, very godly man." Finally he got the point. You can be gifted as a preacher, an organizer, a leader, but there is no substitute for godliness.

Conviction

Paul told the Ephesian elders he held back nothing from them (Acts 20:27). He made his convictions clear. We live in a day when too few preachers teach doctrine while so many believers hunger for truth. Paul warned the leaders of the church of his day to be wary of wolves in sheep's clothing (Acts 20:19–21). If you are a pastor, you will protect the flock from such. One of the ways you can tell a pastor is truly a shepherd is by how he responds when the wolves show up!

This is true for Christian parents as well. I constantly challenge parents as I speak in churches not to let their children finish high school without going to a Third-World country on a mission trip. Why? Because it helps young people develop convictions about a lost world and the need of the gospel, and to see that their God does not only dwell in a church building in the U.S. Our son went to Latin America in high school, and I recently took our teenaged daughter to Asia. I fear too many in the church have a disconnect between stated convictions and their actual lives. Almost every semester I will have a student in my office heartbroken because he or she has been called to the nations as a missionary, but their parents, active in church (sometimes even pastors!) are unhappy that their child wants to leave the country. Do we really have conviction?

When I was a teenager, my high school class was the first in Alabama to begin mandatory driver's education. One of our assignments was watching a gruesome film that consisted of photographs of automobile accidents involving young people who were drinking and driving. It showed tremendous carnage, burned bodies, decapitations. It was horrible.

When we left that film, we were convinced we would never drive that way and end up like that. But, in the months to come, we got our licenses, and not everyone drove the way we said we would. This is a familiar scenario—repeated in many settings. Some people live by conviction, while others live by intention.

How do we live a life of conviction? Here are four simple principles.

1. *Live by principle, not by feelings.* We pray because it is important, not because we feel "spiritual" all the time. We should witness out of obedience, not because we are comfortable doing it. Our character must grow out of convictions hammered on the anvil of the Word of God.
2. *Listen to God, not to popular opinion.* Even in the church, popular opinion can be wrong. We live in a culture driven by popular opinion polls. Our political leaders make decisions by these polls. Further, with the proliferation of talk shows on television, call-in shows, radio talk shows, and Internet chat rooms, individual opinions have displaced the Word of God for many people. But it doesn't matter in the final analysis what Oprah Winfrey or Rush Limbaugh or even the president of the United States believes. What really matters is what God says.
3. *Prioritize sacrifice rather than comfort.* Again, our culture leads us astray at this point. The path of least resistance is the rule, not the exception. The typical approach is, "How much do I have to do to get by at the job?" "Just let me pass the course; I don't care how much I learn."

   A man and his wife went to the doctor. The man had a serious illness. Finally, the doctor found the problem, diagnosed it as very serious, and brought the wife in first to talk to her. "Your husband has a rare condition," he said, "and he will die unless you do certain things. First of all, you have to sterilize everything in your home, and you'll have to do that on a regular basis. Second, you will have to prepare special meals. These meals are not easy to prepare, and it's going to take some time. Third, you must wash everything in the house every week in a special solution that's very expensive. Finally, you're going to have to wait on his every need and take care of him in every way. If you don't do this, he has only a few weeks to live."

While they were driving home the husband asked, "What did the doctor say?" "Honey," she replied, "he said you only have a few weeks to live." Human nature takes the easiest path.

4. *Consider the long-term consequence of your decisions.* Compromise is birthed in the maternity ward of immediacy. I tell my students that it is not where they are but where they are headed that matters. We must keep our eyes on the long haul of ministry.

   If evangelism is important to you, your conviction will stand in the face of anything that seeks to lead you astray. Billy Graham passed through a serious time of spiritual testing shortly before his Los Angeles crusade. His friend Charles Templeton had rejected the authority of Scripture and ridiculed Graham's convictions. After a time of struggle, Graham experienced personal revival and a deep time of consecration to the Word of God. Following a talk with a Christian leader, Graham placed his Bible on a stump, declaring, "I accept this book by faith as the Word of God."[15] From that point on Graham was ready for God to use him in an uncommon manner. His convictions have guided his life.

Priorities

Paul indicated his priority in his address to the Ephesian elders: "So that I may finish my race with joy, and the ministry which I received from the Lord Jesus" (Acts 20:24 NKJV). We have almost made busyness a spiritual gift. Calendar planners are like the Bible to most people in our culture. The truth is that if you don't control your time, someone else will. You do have time to do what is important; sometimes you will not have time for much else. And if you don't live by your priorities, you will die at the hand of circumstances.

I had a doctoral student conduct a study of pastors and priorities. He discovered every pastor he surveyed would say his priorities were God, then family, then ministry. But he found that when he drilled deeper into how they lived their lives, their families typically got the leftovers of his time. There was a time when ministers were actually taught that a pastor's priorities should be God, then ministry. "If you

[15] J. Pollock, *To All the Nations* (San Francisco: Harper and Row, 1985), 41.

take care of your ministry," they were advised, "God will take care of your family." Years of teaching many preacher's kids has demonstrated how that line of thinking has not turned out very well at all. I am grateful for the president at my seminary, Danny Akin, who, as great a theologian, leader, and president as he is, he is an even better father. Your family is your ministry, and Paul told Timothy that if you cannot manage your home, you are not likely to be effective to manage the people of God.

John Morgan of Sagemont Church in Houston illustrated the many forces tugging at our time. "I remember a personnel committee meeting. One person said, 'Be careful about overextending yourself.' Another said, 'Your ministry comes first.' Another said, 'Your family is your ministry.'"

Morgan's dad, a pastor, took him deer hunting the day the season began every year since he was six years old. He spent time with his son. After decades of pastoring, John determined one of the greatest things his church did was to set aside each Thursday for family night. "We have designed our churches to destroy our families," he told a group of young ministers. "I went 18 years before I took a vacation. It was the most foolish thing I ever did."[16]

Those of us in ministry must avoid the temptation of seeing ourselves as more significant than our spouses due to our calling. In our driven culture, failing to live by our priorities can sap our evangelistic effectiveness.

If you are biblical and godly in the way you treat your family, you will treat the things of God, especially the gospel, in a godly manner as well. John Bisagno once told me that his sons recalled the greatest day of their lives was when he bought a new boat and took them out of school two hours early to go fishing. Howard Hendricks once asked his adult children to name the most significant memory of him from their childhood. Their reply was not some deep theological truth he taught them; it was those times he got on the floor and wrestled with them!

Bisagno advises: "Every day, do something in your spouse's world. Wash dishes, go buy gas, something that touches her world." Paige Patterson gave me excellent counsel about time with my kids. He said to find out what they really like, then do it with them. I have done everything from coaching soccer and basketball to going to UNC games, the mall (a lot), and more to enjoy what my children

[16] From the Paul–Timothy conference mentioned earlier.

enjoy. And now, as they are young adults, they actually love to go with Michelle and me places where I minister. Josh drums in the worship band, Hannah helps in a variety of ways from photography to set up, and Michelle is the ultimate traveling mom. I did not plan on having such a great time ministering with my family like I so enjoy now, but it is no doubt a culmination of many years of investment in what matters. If your life is not guided by priorities, you will never keep evangelism in its rightful place in your life.

The True Test of Character—Attitude

Notice Paul's attitude regardless of what he faced. Knowing persecution awaited him, he said his desire was to "finish my race with joy" (Acts 20:24 NIV). The greatest hindrance to our personal evangelism is our attitude. On the other hand, the greatest aid to our witness is an attitude that honors Christ. Further, sour attitudes do much to disrupt the fellowship of the body of Christ. We are responsible for our attitudes. In the New Testament one can often read of joy coupled with affliction (see 1 Thess 1:6). That does not fit the practical theology of many in the West.

An attitude of entitlement plagues the American church. I fight it all the time. Recently I arose *really* early to catch a plane to Atlanta. Monday morning early is not the time to be in an airport. The whole planet seems to be flying somewhere then, and that morning the whole state of North Carolina appeared to be at RDU International. I flew to my meeting, an annual gathering of SBC evangelism leaders with the North American Mission Board. I would be sitting in meetings for two days. As I am the poster child for Attention Deficit Disorder (ADD), sitting in meetings has never been my forte. Add to the fact that I had been away most of the summer doing youth camps and missed my wife, and you can see perhaps why I went to the meeting in a less than jovial mood.

Then it hit me: my sour disposition had nothing to do with the meeting or my personality. It even had little to do with the fact that I missed my family. I was after all going to an important meeting with some of the most godly, passionate people I know. Why was I so whiny?

I had succumbed to the cultural Christian disease I call "entitlementism." Entitlementism refers to a person who feels entitled to something regardless of whether they did anything to earn it. From something as broad as universal healthcare to feeling justified for stiffing the waiter if we didn't like the meal we selected, entitlementism marks our age.

Let me be theological for a moment. We are entitled to something. We are entitled to hell and judgment. We are wicked sinners whose best righteousness is filthy rags. So let's not be too hasty in demanding that for which we are entitled. Resist entitlementism. Embrace gratitude.

Recently our dog we have had since we first moved to Wake Forest over 14 years ago, a golden retriever named Precious, had to be put down. She had come to the place where she could hardly walk. She was miserable. Yet in the last few months when Michelle and I sat on the back deck and watched the birds (we love to do that although our children think we are hopelessly middle aged), when we came outside she always got up and came to see us, wagging her tail. If we motioned her away, she simply went away. She never acted as though she were entitled to be petted because she protected our home or because she had been so loyal for so many years. No, she simply loved to be around us. No entitlement mentality. Sometimes I really miss that dog.

So I repented of my attitude in Atlanta and enjoyed the meeting and even learned some things. Amazingly, I did not even get bent out of shape when my flight home was delayed. I enjoyed watching a man older than me act like a child because apparently the airlines did not understand he was entitled to an on-time departure even when the weather made such a departure extremely dangerous. Why did I avoid the attitude on my return when I had so embraced it on my departure? Because I replaced entitlementism with gratitude, and that made all the difference. Attitude matters. In fact, our attitudes, if not checked, can destroy our witness more quickly than anything else.

We should never ignore significant hardships or times of pain. There is a time to hurt, to have sorrow, to be provoked because of ungodliness. But how many times do things of little consequence fuel our disposition and cause negative reactions?

Here are some principles concerning our attitude.

1. *I am responsible for my attitude.* Our culture teaches us to blame others for our mistakes. I cannot always control my circumstances, but I can control my attitude.

2. *My attitude is either my friend or my enemy.* A man moved with his family to a new town. He asked a resident, "What are people around here like?"

   "What are they like where you come from?"

   "Really nice."

   "That's the way they are here."

   Another man moved in the next week and spoke to the same resident.

   "What are people like here?" the new citizen asked.

   "What are they like where you come from?"

   "Not friendly at all."

   "That's the way they are here." The resident knew attitude makes the difference.
3. *I must constantly correct my attitude.* Paul faced times of discouragement. Your commitment to evangelism must overcome seasons of lean harvests and disappointments. Otherwise, despair and even bitterness can sap the life from us. Bitterness can ruin the witness of any Christian.
4. *My attitude is contagious.* While teaching at Houston Baptist University, I was privileged to have a young lady from Africa attend my required classes in Old Testament, New Testament, and Christian doctrine. She was a devout Muslim when we met. I shared Christ with her. While she seemed uninterested, I sought to live a contagious Christian life before her.

   On the bottom of her final exam in Christian doctrine, she left me a note that thrills me to this day. "Dr. Reid, thank you for how you have spoken to me in your life. I now know that Jesus Christ is God's Son, and have given my life to Him. I have never been so happy!" The key to reaching this young lady, more than my arguments, was a contagious Christian attitude.
5. *My attitude reflects my walk with God.* A person's relationship with God is not determined by church attendance or position, as important as they are. What really matters is the attitude we convey toward the things that matter to God, toward circumstances, toward the gospel. Therefore, our attitude affects our witness.

Mike Landry was evangelism director for the Ohio Baptist Convention for many years before serving as pastor of the Sarasota Baptist Church in Florida. Mike was an atheist in the late sixties and early seventies, but he came to Christ through the Jesus Movement. Mike told me that the only difference between his life and those Christians he went to high school with was that he didn't have to get up early on Sunday morning. He got to sleep in—that was the only difference. But then after going off to college a year, he came back and he saw a change in some students' lives. The Jesus Movement had occurred, and some of the young people he knew had been radically changed. This led to a series of events that ultimately resulted in his conversion. Mike's story demonstrates how a person's lifestyle can affect his or her witness among lost people.

Questions for Consideration

1. Which of the marks of character above would you consider your strongest? Which is your weakest?
2. How important is it to you that you make changes in your life so that your character reflects your witness?
3. Here is a practical exercise that can help you analyze your current lifestyle. Perhaps this will lead you to measure whether the character of Christ transcends your own agenda. Using the following grid, record how you spend your time during the next three weeks.

	Sun.	Mon.	Tues.	Wed.	Thurs.	Fri.	Sat.
6:00 A.M.							
7:00 A.M.							
8:00 A.M.							
9:00 A.M.							
10:00 A.M.							
11:00 A.M.							
12:00 P.M.							
1:00 P.M.							
2:00 P.M.							
3:00 P.M.							
4:00 P.M.							
5:00 P.M.							
6:00 P.M.							
7:00 P.M.							
8:00 P.M.							
9:00 P.M.							
10:00 P.M.							
11:00 P.M.							

Chapter 14

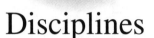

Disciplines

> *I'm taken by this, because there is nothing I want more than for my life to matter. I want to be used profoundly by God, to be seized by his great and mighty hand and thrust onto the stage of history in order to do something significant. With as pure of a heart as I can muster, this isn't about fame or prestige. It's about wanting my life to count where it is needed most. There is a great movement of God that has been set loose in this world, and I want to be on the front lines. And I have felt this way for a long time.*[1]
>
> —James Emory White

I lived in Indiana serving the state Baptist convention as I finished the writing of my doctoral dissertation. Another young man also pursuing a PhD served as a pastor in southern Indiana. He is the man I quoted above. James White has continued to push me to think through his writings as he did in personal conversations almost 20 years ago. I can relate to the quote above. I long for my life to matter, to be all God made me to be. I believe in the heart of every Christ-follower there is a hunger for their life to matter, to be con-

[1] J. E. White, *Serious Times: Making Your Life Matter in an Urgent Day* (Downers Grove: InterVarsity Press, 2004), 10.

sumed with serving the Most High God. But most never get there. "Sadly," he continued, "for most it ends there. The feeling comes and then fades." He added:

> We allow the movement of God on the surface of our spirits to become lost amid the stones the world tosses thoughtlessly into our lives. As a result, we lose the vision God can give us of our world and our place in it. Too quickly, and often without struggle, we trade making history with making money, substitute building a life with building a career and sacrifice living for God with living for the weekend. We forego significance for the sake of success and pursue the superficiality of title and degree, house and car, rank and portfolio over a life lived large. We become saved, but not seized; delivered, but not driven.[2]

For us to find effectiveness in ministry, whether in evangelism, in family life, or anywhere we seek to make an impact, it will take more than passion. It will also require discipline. White discovered the secret to turning the passion for God into a living, vibrant walk—discipline was required. Our experience-driven church culture often underplays the powerful place of discipline.

Spiritual Formation

Growth as a follower of Christ includes being increasingly formed into the likeness of Christ. "The spiritual disciplines," Whitney wrote, "Are the God-ordained means by which we bring ourselves before God, experience Him, and are changed into Christlikeness."[3] We can no more grow into Christlikeness without spiritual disciplines than we can grow into excellent physical stature without food and exercise.

Speaking on the cost required for true discipleship, Dallas Willard is right in noting that "we would do far better to lay a clear, constant emphasis on the cost of *non*-discipleship as well."[4] I may not know you, the reader, personally, but I know this about you—to this point, your life has not turned out exactly the way you thought it would. So many things happen in life over which you have no control, but you

---

[2] Ibid.

[3] D. Whitney, *Ten Questions to Diagnose Your Spiritual Health* (Colorado Springs: NavPress, 2001), 92–93.

[4] Ibid.

can control how you respond to them. You and I absolutely can and must control our disciplines.

The subject of spiritual disciplines has become one of the topics of great interest in recent years. Richard Foster's *Celebration of Discipline* and Dallas Willard's *The Spirit of the Disciplines* have helped to bring a renewed interest in disciplined Christian living in an undisciplined culture. Don Whitney's *Spiritual Disciplines for the Christian Life,* which includes evangelism as a discipline, is my favorite. Such emphases have helped to shift the focus for many believers away from a what's-in-it-for-me? attitude to a more biblical concept of living focused on honoring God.

Spiritual disciplines refer to the New Testament reality that, while we are saved by God's grace, we are called to live lives worthy of our calling. Discipline in our day is considered a vice more than a virtue. Many people think of discipline in negative terms—with images of monks cloistered in seclusion, stern-jawed Olympic hopefuls who have given up a "normal" life for their goals, and so on. We may admire such people to some extent; we just don't want to pay the price to be *like* them. Give us an infomercial-style holiness—five minutes a day to become like Jesus—that is the Christianity too many of us crave.

Foster noted that the key to the disciplines is not sternness but joy: "The purpose of the Disciplines is *liberation* from the stifling slavery to self-interest and fear. . . . Singing, dancing, even shouting characterize the disciplines of the spiritual life."[5] Disciplines give focus and structure to the heart of what Christianity is: a personal, intimate relationship with our Creator. The disciplines give focus to the larger view of Christianity. Rather than focusing on specific details that look "Christian," such as turning the other cheek or going the second mile, the disciplines produce that "sort of life from which behavior such as loving one's enemy will seem like the only sensible and happy thing to do."[6] As Whitney put it, "Discipline without direction is drudgery."[7]

Discipline for the sake of discipline leads to bondage and legalism. However, a lack of discipline leads to an unproductive life at best and a shipwrecked life at worst. Discipline is never an end in itself; it is a means to a greater good. An athlete is disciplined to win

---

[5] R. Foster, *Celebration of Discipline* (New York: HarperCollins, 1988), 2.

[6] D. Willard, *The Spirit of the Disciplines* (San Francisco: HarperSanFrancisco, 1988), 9.

[7] D. S. Whitney, *Spiritual Disciplines for the Christian Life* (Colorado Springs: NavPress, 1991), 13.

the race; a student is disciplined to learn important truths; a couple is disciplined to enjoy a long and joyful life together. And a Christian is disciplined because such a life leads to true intimacy with God.

Our Lord Jesus knew something of a disciplined life. Read the Gospel of Matthew, and see how Jesus responded to people. He had great compassion for the multitudes, always making Himself available to them. He had little positive to say to the Pharisees and other religious hypocrites; note His scathing attack of them in Matthew 23. But there is another group: those who are committed to follow Jesus. Read the Sermon on the Mount and see the standard He expected of His disciples. Read His words in Luke 9:23: "Then He said to [them] all, "If anyone wants to come with Me, he must deny himself, take up his cross daily, and follow Me." There is a cost, as Dietrich Bonhoeffer has written, to discipleship.[8]

The examples of great believers in Scripture also give witness to the importance of discipline. Behold Joseph, who was victimized over and over again, yet he never saw himself as a victim. How could this be? Joseph had great faith coupled with a disciplined life. Look at Moses, Daniel, and Paul. As you read about Whitefield, Edwards, Bunyan, and others, you find people who lived lives of great sacrifice and discipline.

> *"Christianity has not so much been tried and found wanting, as it has been found difficult and left untried."**
> *G. K. Chesterton*
>
> * Willard, *Spirit of the Disciplines*, 1.

What Are the Key Disciplines?

Writers on the subject identify numerous disciplines, although they are categorized in varying ways. Disciplines include the following, although the lists are not exhaustive. Note the slight differences among these three authors:

[8] See Bonhoeffer's book, *The Cost of Discipleship*.

FOSTER:	**WHITNEY:**	**WILLARD:**
INWARD DISCIPLINES:	Bible Intake Prayer	**DISCIPLINES OF ABSTINENCE**
Meditation Prayer Fasting Study	Worship Evangelism Serving Stewardship	Solitude Silence Fasting Frugality Chastity Secrecy Sacrifice
OUTWARD DISCIPLINES:	Fasting Silence and	
Simplicity Solitude Submission Service	Solitude Journaling Learning	
CORPORATE DISCIPLINES:	**DISCIPLINES OF ENGAGEMENT**	
Confession Worship Guidance Celebration Service Prayer Fellowship Submission	Study Worship	

Notice the disciplines are the same in some categories and quite different in others. Whitney, for example, includes evangelism as a discipline. I agree with him, and I will say more about this later. Disciplines have to do with those areas of spiritual growth in which we are to grow, through God's grace, into mature children of God.

LIVING THE DISCIPLINES

Disciplines can be abused and become legalistic, binding, and even addictive. This is where corporate fellowship and worship with the body of Christ help us to maintain a balance. The disciplines are best attained in the context of personal accountability to a small group or a fellow believer. Legalism tears us down, emphasizing the times we miss our goal of godliness; accountability builds us up, focusing on our successes more than our failures.

How do we discipline ourselves to serve God? Whitney offers these motivations.[9]

- We are motivated by *obedience* (see Deut 13:4).
- *Gratitude* motivates us (see 1 Sam 12:24). Recognition of the great salvation God has given us makes us cry with the psalmist, "I would rather be a doorkeeper in the house of my God than dwell in the tents of wickedness" (Ps 84:10 NKJV).
- *Gladness* spurs us to service: "serve the LORD with gladness" (Ps 100:2).
- God's *forgiveness* is another encouragement.
- *Humility* and *love* provide two final reasons we can discipline ourselves to serve the Lord.

Discipline composes an important part of all facets of life. What is true in education and in relationships is even more true in our walk with Christ. Paul told Timothy to discipline himself for the purpose of godliness (1 Tim 4:7). The word for discipline in this verse is the Greek verb form of the word from which we get the English word "gymnasium." The same discipline required for a healthy body is that necessary for a healthy Christian life. But, as important as a healthy body is, our spiritual health matters more, for it relates to eternal issues.

We are not alone in our discipline. At my house, I have had exercise bikes, a treadmill, dumbbells, ankle weights, and various forms of exercise equipment. They do me little good. Why? Because I must be disciplined to use them. Don't you hate those infomercials with people ripped like a professional athlete telling you to buy their product, when you *know* they are in such fabulous shape because they have a personal trainer? The greatest exercise help is another person to encourage us, to push us, to believe in us. I was in great shape in high school because my coach pushed me. Time in the weight room was not optional!

You may not have a personal trainer for your physical life, but you *do* have one for your spiritual life—the Holy Spirit! What did Jesus say? "When He comes, He will guide you into all truth." Solomon exhorted: "Apply your heart to instruction" (Prov 23:12 NKJV). The Holy Spirit of God will guide the serious believer who truly desires to "discipline himself for the purpose of godliness."

The greatest privilege we will experience is knowing Christ, being a child of God, having eternity in our hearts. And the greatest joy we

[9] Whitney, *Spiritual Disciples,* 112–17.

can experience beyond conversion is seeing another person come to Christ. As late evangelist J. Harold Smith said in our seminary chapel, leading someone to Christ is almost like getting saved all over again!

Still, the motivation of gratitude and the sense of privilege for being a herald of our great God are not the only reasons we share Christ with others. Evangelism should be a disciplined part of our Christian life. When we are in school, we are held accountable. We take tests! We are required to be disciplined. I love to study, so I have stayed disciplined as a reader since finishing school. But it is easier to be disciplined when you have a teacher holding you accountable.

It is the same way in relationships. Many couples are disciplined in the way they treat one another while they are dating. But let them be married a few years, and see how they take each other for granted. Lack of discipline is often the problem.

Selected Disciplines Related to Evangelism

In this chapter we will examine several disciplines that play a significant role in personal evangelism.

Study

"The purpose of the spiritual disciplines is the total transformation of the person," wrote Foster. "They aim at replacing old destructive habits of thought with new life-giving habits. Nowhere is this purpose more clearly seen than in the discipline of study."[10] The believer is to be transformed (cf. Rom 12:2). How? By the renewing of the mind (cf. Rom 12:2; Phil 4:8). In my own experience, the reading and study of the New Testament played a key role in my early commitment to evangelism. Too many believers are involved in the *trappings* of faith (church attendance, etc.) but live *defeated* lives. The battle is lost with the mind.

The foundation of study for the Christian is the Word of God. Studying alone is not the issue. What you study is crucial. Some people are "Gideon Christians," those who are always looking for signs. Others are "Mystical Christians," who live by "instinct" or feeling. Then there are "Guru Christians," who find a preacher they like, treat him like a spiritual guru, following him in print, sermons, and so

[10] Foster, *Celebration of Discipline*, 62.

on, as if his words are gospel. The need of the hour is for "biblical Christians," who use Scripture as their guide. Study the Scriptures continually can help you to stay focused on the gospel and its power to change the world.

At times I have students complain about taking tests. They grow weary of studying. This is what I tell them: Imagine you have a child with a brain tumor. You take him to see a brain surgeon. The doctor says, "Yeah, I can fix this. I've been to class. I've studied it. I've never been tested as to whether I can do brain surgery. But I am sure I can do it." You wouldn't want that person to perform brain surgery on your child, would you? Our faith will be tested and our growth challenged; we must give attention to study.

Foster cites four steps for study: repetition, concentration, comprehension, and reflection.[11]

Repetition

Be repetitious in studying God's Word. Here are examples.

1. *Read the Bible through annually.* As a seminarian, I taught a group of retired persons a Bible study weekly for one year. One lady, a godly woman in her eighties, told me she had read the Bible through more than 20 times. I became ashamed. I could name books I had read several times, and I had read parts of the Bible over and over, but I had read the Bible through only once in my life, and I was a minister!

Since that time, I have read the Bible through almost every year. Many years I used the *One Year Bible* (Tyndale). I cannot overestimate the treasure of wisdom I have gained from an annual, panoramic view of God's Word.

2. *Read the same Bible book* seven times (one time daily for a week), or thirty-one times (one time daily for a month).

3. *Memorize Scripture.* Memorizing Scripture can play a vital role in witnessing. We partner with the indwelling Spirit of God as we share. The Spirit helps us to know what to say, but we can certainly help by giving him material with which to work! Scripture memory certainly allows the Spirit more freedom to work.

Don't exhaust yourself in this memory work. If memorizing comes easily, then memorize portions: Psalm 1, Romans 8, and so forth. If you are a mere mortal like most of us, work on certain key verses consistently. My son had learned more Bible verses by memory by

[11] Ibid., 64–66.

the first grade than I had learned by the time I finished high school. Why? Our church used the AWANAs program, which emphasizes Scripture memory.

While I was in high school, our minister of music had everyone who planned to go on choir tour memorize certain Bible verses. I still remember the first verse we learned: "Call to Me and I will answer you and tell you great and wondrous things you do not know" (Jer 33:3). The verse still guides my life in a meaningful way. In college I was in a small accountability group. Each week we learned a new verse, using material from the Navigators. Become accountable to someone; hide God's Word in your heart. It will aid your witnessing by causing you to think more on the Lord, which will give you a spiritual sensitivity to lost people.

Concentration

Find time daily or at least weekly to study, to concentrate on what you have been reading. Let's be honest: laziness is a great sin in the contemporary church. R. C. Sproul put it like this: "Here, then, is the real problem of our negligence. We fail in our duty to study God's Word not so much because it is difficult to understand, not because it is dull and boring, but because it is work. . . . Our problem is that we are lazy."[12]

Comprehension

Comprehension focuses on *knowing* the truth we study. This leads to "Aha!" moments of fresh discovery. George Whitefield read many books before and after his conversion. But he said he gained more from studying the Bible than all other books combined.

Reflection

Reflection reveals the significance of what we are studying. One of my professors once gave this formula: Knowledge – application = frustration. Reflection makes the truths we learn become personal. Use God's teachings to change your life and the lives of others. Hide the Word of God in your heart, and see how it helps your witness.

Fasting

Whitney gave an excellent definition of *fasting:* "A biblical definition of fasting is a Christian's voluntary abstinence from food for

[12] Whitney, *Spiritual Disciplines*, 32.

spiritual purposes. It is *Christian,* for fasting by a non-Christian obtains no eternal value because the Discipline's motives and purposes are to be God-centered. It is *voluntary* in that fasting is not to be coerced. Fasting is more than just the ultimate crash diet for the body; it is abstinence from food for *spiritual* purposes."[13] Fasting in a broader sense deals with more than food. It is the denial of any normal activity for the purpose of serious spiritual activity.

I almost never heard anyone speak of fasting in my younger days. Through the influence of leaders such as Bill Bright, fasting is being practiced by more and more believers. I often preach in churches where believers are involved in fasting and prayer for revival. This can only help the cause of evangelism!

The Bible is filled with examples of people who fasted: Moses, David, Elijah, Esther, Daniel, our Lord Jesus, and Paul. Corporate fasts are recorded as well, both in the Old Testament (Judah in 2 Chronicles 20) and the New Testament (early church in Acts 13). Jesus spoke of the importance of fasting (see Matt 9:15).

In the second century, Polycarp, bishop of Smyrna, exhorted the Philippians to "return to the word which was handed down to us from the beginning, 'watching unto prayer,' and persevering in fasting."[14] Obviously, fasting was still a significant practice in the church beyond the New Testament era.

Scripture indicates different types of fasts:[15]

- normal fast (abstaining from food) (Matt 4:2; Luke 4:2),
- partial fast (Dan 1:12),
- absolute fast (no food or drink) (Ezra 10:6),
- supernatural fast (Deut 9:9),
- private fast (Matt 6:16–18),
- congregational fast (Joel 2:15–16),
- national fast (2 Chr 20:3), and
- regular fast (Lev 16:29–31).

The purpose of fasting is to move our attention from our appetites to God Himself. John Wesley, who led the Methodists to fast two days each week, said, "First, let [fasting] be done unto the Lord with our eye singly fixed on Him. Let our attention be this, and this alone,

[13] Ibid., 152.

[14] Polycarp, "Epistle to the Philippians," *Apostolic Fathers,* vol. 1 of Ante-Nicene Fathers (Grand Rapids: Eerdmans, 1988), 77.

[15] Whitney, *Spiritual Disciplines*, 153–54.

to glorify our Father which is in heaven."[16] Such a focus will give us insight into the heart of God for a lost world.

A young man came to me who felt a call to go overseas as a missionary, yet had never personally led anyone to Christ. "How can I go overseas to do that which I have not done here?" he asked. He called me for advice. I gave him some practical tips on sharing Christ and some places to go in our area. Then I told him the best advice I had: "When I feel ineffective in my personal witness," I told him, "I take a day to fast and pray for God's hand on my life and witness. I seek to see God afresh, as He truly is. And then I spend hours simply crying out to God for effectiveness, for unction, for the power of the Spirit."

A day or so later he e-mailed me. He too had spent a day fasting and praying. And that very day he led someone to Christ for the first time! What price are we willing to pray to know God so well that we can be used by Him for His great purposes?

Meditation, Silence, Solitude

The disciplines of meditation, silence, and solitude are not the same, but they are similar in that all involve quietness and disengagement from the busyness of our lives. Meditation in the Christian sense emphasizes obedience. As we meditate, we fill up our minds. This is different from emptying them, as in Eastern thought.

"Christian meditation, very simply, is the ability to hear God's voice and obey His word."[17] How can we know God in an intimate way unless we learn to listen to Him? The psalmist declared, "I am awake through each watch of the night to meditate on Your promise" (Ps. 119:148). This is no syrupy sort of buddy-buddy relationship that dishonors the transcendence of God; on the contrary, we meditate upon Him and His words in awe of the fact that He has condescended to us and desires intimacy with us.

In America we have a mountain called Rushmore. Consider the microwave, the Internet, fast food, e-mail, HOV lanes, wi-fi, podcasts, iTunes, and smartphones. How did we survive before Google? All of these things encourage us to speed up the pace. I love music, but music is beautiful only when it has rests to help you appreciate the melody. At times we need replenishment—physical, spiritual, and emotional replenishment.

[16] Ibid., 17.

[17] Foster, *Celebration of Discipline*, 17.

Christian meditation involves focusing on God—specifically on obedience and faithfulness. Our culture's frenzied pace has infected the church. I confess this is one of my greatest struggles. I am a hyperactive, type A, driven person. Meditation is not the easiest thing for me. I often succumb to the theory that the person who is busiest is most important and, therefore, most spiritual. In our fast-paced culture, an emphasis on meditation is needed.

James Emory White's writings again help me at this point. He writes about how he discovered the value of getting away regularly to reflect, meditate, and be rejuvenated. In a time of great frenzy in his life, a mentor confronted White:

> "If you could do one thing that would rejuvenate you spiritually and emotionally, what would it be?'
>
> "I didn't have to pause. I knew the answer. 'I would go to the mountains and be alone . . .'
>
> "Good, you should do that once a month."
>
> "I laughed. 'You've got to be kidding. Once a month? The mountains? I don't have the time! My life is too busy, too full, to put something like that into my schedule."[18]

His mentor responded with words that changed the trajectory of White's life: "If you don't, you will end up in a ditch. You will burn out, lose your ministry, perhaps even your family, and become a casualty of the cause.'"[19] White knew he was right. So he began to go to the mountains regularly.

I encourage you to find a place of solitude, of refuge, from the busy world in which you live. Further, I challenge you to take a personal retreat, a day spent alone with God, at least annually, and better, several times a year. Take your Bible, a notebook and pen, and a bottle of water. If you have health issues take what you need medically. But do not take the needless things we tend to think we need. Leave your music, and discover the melody of God in silence. Leave your commentaries and devotional books, and meet Christ in the Scriptures. Leave your e-mails and texting, and simply write in a notebook your thoughts to God.

I had a class of church planters who were required to take a spiritual retreat for a day. One said that day saved his ministry. More than one said they had never spent so much time with God at once in their

---

[18] White, *Serious Times,* 87.

[19] Ibid., 87.

life, and it totally changed their perspective. Get off the ferris wheel of a busy life and meet with God. It just might change your life. And it may save it.

Service

About a year following the fall of Communism in Romania, I was privileged to travel there to teach and preach. I had never seen such poverty—people standing in line half a day for a tiny can of ham—and yet such a spirit of servanthood. The believers in Romania were so grateful to be free to worship and so happy that Christians from America came to help them learn the Word of God that they would literally give me anything.

One woman in her eighties wore a pair of men's boots, one with a hole in it—probably the only shoes she had. Yet she cooked us the best red peppers from her tiny garden. I don't like red peppers, but these peppers tasted like honey because I was overwhelmed by her servant heart.

Jesus said, "For even the Son of Man did not come to be served, but to serve, and to give His life a ransom for many" (Mark 10:45). We must discipline ourselves to serve. Such a focus makes evangelism more practical, for we are serving people with the greatest news imaginable. Servant evangelism, one of the most exciting approaches to sharing Christ in our day, will be considered in a later chapter. If we are to reach a culture that is increasingly negative or even hostile toward our faith, we must take the posture of service, not entitlement.

The Discipline of Evangelism

One of my most fulfilling experiences as a professor is taking a group of students, youth, or laypeople to share Christ with others. There is something exhilarating about setting aside time to share Christ. Evangelism is not easy work; it requires discipline.

It is true that evangelism is a natural result of a passionate life transformed by the gospel. But we must not witness only when opportunities jump into our laps. We must look for times and places to share the gospel. The average church member can fill his calendar with religious activities and push evangelism to the periphery. This is easy to do because evangelism is so intimidating. Pastors can stay busy visiting the sick, counseling, preparing sermons, and going to meetings and never get around to evangelism. It takes discipline to do evangelism.

Whitney wrote that witnessing is comparable to the postal service. Our success is not gauged by the response of the person to whom we deliver the message. Instead, "success is measured by the careful and accurate delivery of the message."[20] We can *discipline* ourselves to faithfulness, and such faithfulness leads to godliness.

This could mean establishing scheduled times to witness. When I served as evangelism director in Indiana, most of my time was spent with pastors and church leaders. I dealt with my need to witness in three primary ways. Whenever I was in town on the night our church had weekly visitation, I went. I taught witness training a great deal and took those I taught out to share our faith. I also joined a local health spa to be around people who needed a Christian witness. It was the only way I could consistently meet lost people.

In Houston it was much easier for me to witness. Houston Baptist University, though a Baptist school, drew many unchurched people, particularly to its pre-med and nursing programs. I set aside time weekly to talk to students specifically about Christ. Many met the Lord; years later some still write me. Now I travel so much I have ample opportunities to share Christ in airplanes and restaurants. Each semester I take my classes out to witness, and I still witness when in town through our local church's ministry.

Obviously, my schedule is not typical. I share it to show that I have to make a constant, disciplined effort to share Christ regularly. And I don't do this because I teach evangelism; I do it because of my love for Christ.

When I was 11 years old, I was a skinny kid. In fact, I had to run around in the shower to get wet! I had the physique of Olive Oyl. My mom had to take up my pants, and when she did, I only had one back pocket! Maybe it wasn't *that* bad, but I was extremely thin and insecure. During my eleventh summer, I met Jesus in a life-changing way. I have never gotten over it! I was so grateful that God would save a skinny little hick like me. But I soon learned that my relationship with Christ required discipline.

In fact, that is the way God made us in every aspect of our lives. We need discipline. Children beg for discipline because they need limits; it gives them security. Our bodies need discipline in our eating

---

[20] Whitney, *Spiritual Disciplines*, 97.

and exercise. Unfortunately, the older and more "successful" we become, the less disciplined we tend to be.

I require students to attempt to share Christ with a person each week during the semester. I say "attempt" because on the one hand I do not want to be a legalist and cause a student to force the gospel on someone, but on the other I have learned the more you attempt to speak about Christ, the more you have opportunities to share Him with others! I cannot number how many students have thanked me for that assignment. I have even had a few write me later and repent for their attitude about the assignment, realizing later what a great impact it made on their life.

Although I was thin as a youngster, I started playing football in the ninth grade and began lifting weights. By the end of my junior year, I could bench press 300 pounds and was the strongest guy on my team—except for a teammate who played for Bear Bryant's national championship teams in 1978 and 1979. I can't lift that much now. I was much more disciplined as an athlete then. One reason I was disciplined was that I had a coach who encouraged me. What if all believers had a group of believers who held them to a high standard in the arena of personal evangelism? Who is holding you accountable to speak to others about the best news ever known?

You cannot win until you begin. So start where you are, disciplined for the glory of God. It is not where you are but where you are headed that matters.

> *If you were to describe your discipline spiritually, would you be comparable to an Olympic athlete in training, a weekly gym rat, or a couch potato?**
>
> * Willard, *Spirit of the Disciplines*, 1.

Questions for Consideration

Donald Whitney's writings in my opinion are must reading on this subject. His excellent little book *Ten Questions to Diagnose Your Spiritual Health* can help you to examine where you are in your own spiritual formation:

1. Do you thirst for God?
2. Are you governed increasingly by God's Word?

3. Are you more loving? Whitney describes the importance of loving other believers, the lost, and your family.
4. Are you more sensitive to God's presence?
5. Do you have a growing concern for the spiritual and temporal needs of others?
6. Do you delight in the Bride of Christ?
7. Are the spiritual disciplines increasingly important to you?
8. Do you still grieve over sin?
9. Are you a quick forgiver?
10. Do you yearn for heaven and to be with Jesus?

PART III

Intentional

Love All, Serve All.

—Slogan of the Hard Rock Café

Ernest Shackleton led an unsuccessful attempt to reach the South Pole. In 1900 he published the following advertisement in a London newspaper: "Men Wanted for Hazardous Journey: Small wages, bitter cold, long months of complete darkness, constant danger, safe return doubtful. Honor and recognition in case of success." So many people responded to the ad that Shackleton later declared, "It seemed as though all the men in Great Britain were determined to accompany me, the response was so overwhelming."[1]

Evangelism is not exactly like conquering Antarctica, though some may fear the task in the same way! But evangelism can motivate us to make the impact for which we were created. Any believer who takes seriously the command to share Christ will do so with some level of fear. This book recognizes that fear. Many of us have knocked on a door while witnessing, only to pray, "God, please don't let them be at home!"

Knowing how to go about the practice of evangelism brings great confidence. We must be biblical in our witness. We must share Christ out of the depth of the spiritual resources available. But we must also be intentional. Think about the things that happen if you are not intentional. If you are not intentional in your diet, at some point in life you will get fat. If you are not intentional in watering houseplants, they will die. So much in life requires intentionality. This section examines areas where intentionality matters.

---

[1] W. J. Bennet, *The Book of Virtues* (New York: Simon & Schuster, 1996), 493.

Chapter 15

The Need of the Hour: Leadership

Good is the enemy of great. And that is one of the key reasons why we have so little that becomes great. . . . Few people attain great lives, in large part because it is just so easy to settle for a good life."[1]

—Jim Collins

From the time Michael Jordan hit the game winner in the 1982 national championship until now, I have been a huge UNC basketball fan. Living near the campus and attending games there over the past decade and a half have only made being a fan sweeter. After Dean Smith retired in 1998 and Bill Guthridge coached the team effectively for three years, Matt Doherty became head coach in 2000. Doherty played with Jordan in that '82 championship. His second season was the worst in decades at Carolina, posting an 8–20 record—ending a thirty-one-year streak of 20 or more wins. After a 17–15 season the next year, Doherty was replaced by Roy Williams. In two years Williams led the team to the national championship and

[1] J. Collins: *Good to Great: Why Some Companies Make the Leap . . . and Others Don't* (New York: HarperCollins, 2001), 1.

back to the national prowess they had known. My point? Leadership matters, whether in sports, business, or in a local church.

I have argued in this book that the world has been and will be changed more by movements than institutions. The movement of God we call the church has experienced an ebb and flow from effectiveness and great impact to mediocrity and ineffectiveness throughout her history. When we think of those times when the church moved to greatness evangelistically, theologically, or culturally, we think of men of God who were great leaders: Peter, John, and Paul; Augustine and Chrysostom; Luther and Calvin; Grebel and Manz; Wesley and Whitefield; Edwards and Tennent; Spurgeon and Moody; the list could go on at great length. By greatness I do not mean the simplistic way we measure greatness in the church today, by the three B's: Buildings, Bodies, and Budgets (or in my context as a Baptist: Buildings, Baptisms, and Budgets). Such an institutional measuring stick fails to see the greater impact of movements. No, when the church has moved forward for the glory of God and the sake of the gospel, she has influenced entire cultures to change. Her influence has gone far beyond the confines of church buildings or church parishes.

The Western church has a great need for leaders who will advance the church from the malaise of mediocrity to great impact once again. We have some excellent leaders; we certainly need more. Leadership has become a topic of great interest among evangelicals. Multitudes of books, seminars, and lectures have been prepared on the subject. Entire cottage industries have sprung up to approach the subject. Leadership gurus have emerged in the church and the corporate world (sadly, often the two have no distinctions from each other). I began this chapter with a quote from a book dealing with businesses because it actually goes against the grain of conventional wisdom on leadership and has discovered principles consistent with Scripture. More about that in what follows.

God has hardwired humanity to need leaders. You see this in every sphere of human life. How many times have we seen a terrible sports team suddenly turn things around or a business move into profitability or a church go from stagnation to vibrancy because of one simple factor: a change in leadership. If you are a leader, whether in a staff position at a church or as a layleader, parachurch leader, or any other position where you have influence over others, learning to be a better leader matters.

Those who intentionally lead them to both a burden for unbelievers and effectiveness in telling the good news lead evangelistic churches. Churches that will move from conventional to missional and become increasingly effective in reaching the unchurched around them will do so in no small part because of leadership.

Evangelistic Leadership

This book has been written for students, ministers, and laity—in fact, any believer who seeks to learn more about evangelism. Let me say a specific word to the reader who is a pastor: unless the pastor leads the church in its evangelistic fervor, the church's commitment will soon wane.

Philips Brooks was right when he said, "If God called you to preach, don't stop to be a king." On the other hand, Spurgeon was correct in admonishing if you can do anything besides preach, by all means do it. The call to be a pastor of a local church is indeed a high calling. The need of our day is for pastors who lead their churches in evangelism.

Paul used three words interchangeably to refer to the office of pastor. *Poimēn,* or "pastor," denotes shepherding a flock. Hence, pastors are to feed, protect, and nurture a congregation. The word translated "bishop" or "overseer" is *episkopos.* The pastor is the leader of the church. Jesus is the sovereign head, but the pastor is the human leader. Finally, a pastor is a *presbuteros,* an "elder," or a mature example to the flock.

Unfortunately, some people have unrealistic expectations of pastors, thinking they should have a big "S" on their shirts. Note the following description of a "perfect" pastor:

> He preaches exactly 20 minutes and then sits down. He condemns sin but never hurts anyone's feelings. He works from 8 A.M. to 10 P.M. in every type of work from preaching to custodial service. He makes $60 per week, wears good clothes, buys good books regularly, has a nice family, drives a good car and gives $30 per week to the church. He also stands ready to contribute to every good work that comes along. He is 26 years old and has been preaching for 30 years. He is tall and short, thin and heavy-set, handsome. He has one brown eye and one blue; hair parted in the middle, left side dark and straight; the

> right, brown and wavy. He has a burning desire to work with teenagers and spends all his time with older folks. He spends all his time with a straight face because he has a sense of humor that keeps him seriously dedicated to his work. He makes 15 calls a day on church members, spends all his time evangelizing the unchurched, and is never out of the office.[2]

If I have learned anything about ministry and evangelism over the years, it is this: almost *everything* rises or falls with leadership. In the Bible, when God began to do a work, he set aside someone as the anointed leader—a person who understood humility and submission to God but was also bold and courageous.

The writer of Hebrews admonished, "Remember your leaders who have spoken God's word to you. As you carefully observe the outcome of their lives, imitate their faith. Jesus Christ is the same yesterday, today, and forever. . . . Obey your leaders and submit to them, for they keep watch over your souls as those who will give an account, so that they can do this with joy and not with grief, for that would be unprofitable for you" (Heb 13:7,17). Paul told the Ephesian church that God gifted leaders to equip the church for ministry (Eph 4:11–16).

Paul on Leadership

In his last letter, Paul gave Timothy sound advice concerning leadership. In 2 Tim 2:1–15 we can glean principles for leading in evangelism. Following a word of exhortation in verse 1, Paul outlined to Timothy how to multiply leadership and thus the ministry. He followed the exhortation with three analogies for sound leaders, concluding with a testimony concerning his own example and recognition of the faithfulness of God. The inspired words of Paul provide the perfect framework for developing principles of effective leadership.

Lead with Confidence in God's Call

Paul exhorted Timothy to "be strong in the grace that is in Christ Jesus" (2 Tim 2:1). Timothy faced an awesome task, but one the Lord himself had ordained. Timothy was probably insecure about the

---

[2] R. G. Puckett, "The Perfect Pastor," *Biblical Recorder,* February 1, 1997.

task before him. He was neither the first nor the last church leader to struggle with such emotions. If God has called you, He will sustain you. It is far less about your ability and far more about His call.

One of the attributes of effective pastors whom I have admired is their ability to rest in the call of God on their lives. Adrian Rogers tells the story about when he was first called to ministry. He began to think, *God, you can't call somebody like me. I'll never be of any use to you. Why would you call someone like me?* He genuinely struggled with his call.

One night he went out into a football field to spend time with God. And he said, "God, unless you fill me with your Spirit and your power, you'll never use me; I'll never be of any use to you." He got on his knees before God. He felt he could not get low enough, so he laid down on the ground to humble himself before God, begging God to use him, to fill him, to empower him. He still didn't feel low enough, so he dug a hole and put his nose in it, getting as low as he could to the ground. God will never use us unless we realize that we are nothing apart from Him.

As a leader, you must recognize that you will take abuse by virtue of your position. In his first pastorate, John Morgan was berated weekly by a lady in his church. After one occasion when she ripped the young pastor unmercifully, John and his wife retreated to their seminary housing. John's dad, himself a pastor, called that evening. John poured out his broken heart. The elder pastor gave sage advice to his son: "John, when you hang up, get a quiet place to pray. Then thank the Lord for the opportunity to preach. Thank God that you made it home tonight. Then thank God that you are not married to that woman!"

If God has called you to be a leader, you should be yourself. Don't copy others. Be strong in the grace of God. While in Houston, I observed closely the ministries of John Bisagno, pastor of First Baptist Church, Houston, and Ed Young, pastor of Second Baptist Church in that great city. These men led two of the strongest churches in America, and they are only a few miles apart. But their leadership styles are dramatically different. Be yourself.

The church that John MacArthur serves grew through verse-by-verse preaching. Chuck Swindoll did the same with warmth and humor. Ed Young has grown a church reaching upwardly mobile Houstonians. Get to know *who* you are in Christ, *like* who you are, and *be* who you are.

Lead by Equipping Other Leaders

"Great men lead people," Bill Bright of Campus Crusade for Christ said, "but greater men train leaders." Paul sounded this advice to Timothy when he declared, "And what you have heard from me in the presence of many witnesses, commit to faithful men who will be able to teach others also" (2 Tim 2:2). While serving in Indiana, I saw firsthand the reality that the greatest barrier to overcome in church growth is the 200 mark in attendance. A primary reason for this is that, when a church grows to this size, a pastor must train leaders or employ more staff to facilitate further growth. The training of leaders has received too little attention. Paul mentored Timothy, and Timothy mentored others.

How did Jesus lead others? He taught the multitudes. He sent out 70 to preach. But He called 12 to walk with Him, live with Him, learn from Him. Then He especially poured His life into three—Peter, James and John. Did the church erupt and spread through the multitude He taught? No, some of those He taught yelled "crucify!" before His death. He poured His life into a few. And today you read this book because of their impact.

Mentoring is very popular today, and that is good. Two kinds of mentoring develop leaders: formal and informal. The formal style generally follows the example of Jesus and His disciples. A pastor or leader will gather regularly with a small group for teaching and accountability. When I was in college, a man took two other students and me through intensive discipleship, Scripture memory, and witnessing. This was an invaluable experience to me. I know pastors who effectively mentor key laymen; others mentor young men who have surrendered to vocational ministry. I spend specific, consistent time with certain students, particularly doctoral students, in a mentoring relationship.

Informal mentoring looks for opportunities to mentor on a more short-term or casual basis. We should not underestimate the teachable moments that arise spontaneously. Taking laity or students with you to conferences can be life changing. I hardly ever go anywhere by myself. I love to take students (I love to make them drive!) and talk about ministry as we travel. Such informal mentoring has proven to be a great augment to my classroom teaching.

Let me say a word to young ministers and in particular seminarians who may be reading this book. If you would long to be mentored or discipled by a more mature believer or be in a small group, be *teachable*. Most young ministers are; most are like sponges hungering to learn. But some, especially those who are obviously gifted and/or have had success early in ministry, fall into the trap of thinking they are God's gift to the ministry. I have seen a few so arrogant in their views they will not listen to instruction or corrections. And rarely do those last an entire life of ministry. Of all the traits you can cultivate, being teachable may be the best.

There is also great value in peer mentoring. The greatest thing that ever happened to me in my seminary experience was the development of a mentoring friendship with four other men during our doctoral work. The five of us and our wives get together annually each summer, and we keep up through phone calls and letters during the year. These men, though my age, are my heroes, and they provoke me to good works.

Mentoring in evangelism is vital. As evangelism director in Indiana, I worked with a young man who was attempting to plant a church. He felt unprepared to witness and had become discouraged. I began to spend time with him and put him in contact with others who could encourage him. He attended an evangelism conference in Atlanta, where he stayed in the home of a soul-winning layperson, a member of the First Baptist Church of Woodstock, Georgia. He also received special evangelism training in Indiana. As a result, he began winning people to Christ. After a year of effective witnessing, his mission church led the state in baptisms by ratio! I often take my students with me to share Christ as well.

The philosopher Aristotle, in his *Nichomachean Ethics,* described three kinds of friendships: (1) friendship of utility, based on usefulness derived from your association; (2) friendship of pleasure, based on pleasure in each other's company; and (3) friendship of virtue, derived from mutual admiration. Perhaps mentoring is best done when all three of these elements exist and when it is founded on biblical teaching.

Lead with Humility

Paul also told Timothy to be like a soldier (2 Tim 2:3–4). A soldier understands the importance of serving others, both his commander and his country. Rather than leading in an autocratic matter, the servant-leader is the biblical model. Jesus said we are to be ministers or servants. He declared, "For even the Son of Man did not come to be served, but to serve, and to give His life—a ransom for many" (Mark 10:45). The word "serve" means "to heal broken bones." It also means to "furnish a house."

Hear the sage wisdom of pastor John Morgan, who planted the Sagemont Church in Houston from a handful of people and watched it grow to a megachurch over 40 years: "I lead by example. If we need satellite parking, I park the farthest away. When we eat, I never go first. Be low key. People call me 'Brother John.' If you have to tell people you are the pastor, that you answer only to God, and that God speaks to you, you are headed for trouble."

To demonstrate a servant heart, Morgan did the following: "We have Wednesday night suppers. I began bussing the tables, then some staff helped me. I didn't tell the deacons. After a year, the deacons joined in. Some members have tears in their eyes; they don't want me to do it!"

Being a servant means being human, being transparent. There is a difference between *vision* and *ambition.* Ambition's goal leans toward self-fulfillment, self-recognition, and self-gratification. Vision regards something we receive from God, not what we dream on our own. I often ask my students to identify the vision God has given them. Billy Graham has never strayed from God's vision for his life. Neither should we.

Fenton Moorhead, my former pastor, said, "We must admit our mistakes. If you make a mistake in public, apologize in public." He adds: "The little things are important. A nine-year-old wrote me, telling me she enjoyed the sermon, and made comments. I called her and gave her guidance. Her mom was thrilled that I called."

A principle of leadership: the leader must be able to handle power well. Lord Acton's dictum was, "Power corrupts and absolute power corrupts absolutely." Heed his warning. John Bisagno says, "You should never use all the power and the authority you have as a leader. As a leader, take more blame than you deserve and give more praise than is deserved—not in a manipulative kind of way but in a spirit of humility."

Demonstrate a servant attitude in the way you talk about God and other people. Rick Warren says there is nothing spectacular about a pastor who says, "I love to preach." What is much more significant, Warren argues, is the pastor who says, "I love my *people.*" Your respect, your awe, your wonder that God has called you will say much to those who follow you. John Bisagno says, "Leadership must be granted by the people and earned by you."

In Jim Collins' book *Good to Great* he studied companies that featured a dramatic and sustained turnaround. He found principles consistent with Scripture. For instance, he described what he called a Level Five (L5) leader as the most effective. What are the primary traits of a L5 leader? One trait is an unwavering commitment to the company. The other, which was surprising to his research team, was the remarkable modesty and humility of the leaders of great companies compared to those whose companies exhibited mediocrity, as these quotes demonstrate:

> In contrast to the very *I*-centric leaders of the comparison leaders, we were struck by how the good-to-great leaders *didn't* talk about themselves. . . . When pressed to talk about themselves, they'd say things like, "I hope I'm not sounding like a big shot." . . . Those who worked or wrote about the good-to-great leaders continually used words like *quiet, humble, modest, reserved, shy, gracious, mild-mannered, self-effacing, understated, did not believe his own clippings;* and so forth. . . . The good-to-great leaders never wanted to become larger-than-life heroes. They never aspired to be put on a pedestal or become unreachable icons. They were seemingly normal people quietly producing extraordinary results.[3]

Sounds like a pretty good description of the leadership style of Moses or David or Paul, or for that matter our Lord Himself. In a day when CEO-driven, self-promoting pastoral models that imply one must be a Type A, ADHD, overly aggressive type who has mastered all the leadership principles of the gurus of our time, we need more men of God who walk and lead in humility.

Too many leaders in ministry have become so accustomed to the "profession" of ministry that they have forgotten the purpose of the ministry they lead. Humility helps us to avoid such an attitude. A notorious British criminal stood condemned to die. The morning of his execution the prisoner observed the minister as he walked beside him to the gallows, reading Bible verses without emotion. Stunned the chaplain seemed so unmoved by the circumstances of the day, he said to the preacher, "Sir, if I believed what you and the church say you believe, even if England was covered with glass from coast to

[3] Ibid., 27, 28.

coast, . . . I would walk over it—if need be on my hands and knees—and think it worthwhile, just to save one soul from an eternal hell like that."[4]

Lead Others to Greatness for God

Paul's second analogy is that of an athlete competing for a crown (see 2 Tim 2:5). Observe the commitment of Olympic gold medalists—the sacrifices they endure for a temporal crown. Why the years of training for a few moments of glory? They have a passion, a vision for the prize. No coach has ever told his team, "Our goal is to lose every game by an embarrassing margin." We play sports to win. We compete in athletics to do our best. While ministry should not be a competition, we ought to have the drive of an Olympic athlete in our passion to honor Christ!

Inside the heart of every person is a desire to make an impact. God has given each Christian a vision that he or she must fulfill. Your role as a leader is to help others catch the vision that God has for their lives. No one is less motivated than a person who is called upon to fulfill the goals of another person. But a visionary leader sees the potential in others that they do not see in themselves. Goethe said, "Treat a man as he appears to be, and you make him worse. But treat a man as if he already were what he potentially could be, and you make him what he should be."

Who knows but that you may have a missionary under your influence. A great pastor. A businessman whose success will mean millions of dollars contributed to the cause of Christ. Many are not involved in evangelism because they have no idea of the impact they can make. Leaders need to provide vision and hope to the people of God.

Athletes push themselves and often take risks. Leaders must constantly push those they lead to avoid complacency. Pastor Mark Driscoll observed, "I've learned that sometimes the most important thing a leader can do is to create strategic chaos that forces people to pull together and forces on an urgent need, therefore subtly getting rid of . . . complaints in a subversive way."[5] Keeping people focused on the mission helps to lower the impact of those who hinder the mission.

---

[4] W. Duewel, *Ablaze for God* (Grand Rapids: Zondervan, 1989), 121.

[5] M. Driscoll, *Confessions of a Reformission Rev* (Grand Rapids: Zondervan, 2006), 82–83.

People instinctively want a challenge, to be a part of something bigger than they are. The institutional church typically does this by mammoth building projects requiring some level of sacrificial giving, and much more rarely by pushing people to sacrifice their time and energy to reach people unlike themselves.

Lead by Faith

Notice Paul's analogy of a faithful farmer (see 2 Tim. 2:6). A farmer works the ground, believing the harvest will come. The doubting farmer will give up on the harvest at the first sign of drought.

I love these words of Aristotle: "That which we learn with delight we never forget." Expectant, excited, encouraging leadership is found in most evangelistic churches. Take a moment and think of the one person who most influenced you in your walk with Christ. It was probably his or her *encouragement* that made the greatest impact. Faith is contagious. If you are an encourager, those whom you lead will grow in their own sense of expectancy. An optimistic leader, driven by faith in God, moves forward in confidence in God's desire to bless a church that pleases him. Such a leader does not jump on the bandwagon of every fad that comes along. An expectant leader's faith is in God, not his own ability, so he is not tossed to and fro by the latest craze.

We can have confidence in the gospel. We can *expect* God to honor a faithful church. Paul said that we should know the times, which means literally an intimate understanding of the society in which we minister (Rom 13:11). Cultures change, demanding innovative, contextualized approaches to reach lost people. But our understanding of culture should lead us to address societal needs with a Christ-centered solution, not a culture-driven approach (Rom 13:12–13).

Lead by Defining Reality

Paul offered himself as an example (see 2 Tim 2:7–14). In verse 14, Paul summarized the previous verses by commanding Timothy to remind those whom he led of such vital truths. One of the most significant things a leader can do is to define what is real, what is truth, to those whom he leads. People with Type-A, extroverted, charismatic personalities lead more easily as a rule, but leadership must be founded on the timeless principles of Scripture, not the force of one's personality.

Leadership is defining reality. Our understanding of reality comes from God's Word. Defining reality means confronting people who refuse to follow. It means standing firm in the face of the skeptical, the apathetic, or the indifferent. It means recognizing that wolves will come into your church in sheep's clothing, and you as the leader must constantly focus on the mission at hand. The epitaph on a hypochondriac's tombstone read, "I told you I was sick." You will constantly have to choose the hill on which you are willing to die. Some leaders lose their authority to lead by becoming involved in secondary decisions in the church. A great leader does not become a micromanager but instead keeps his attention on the core values that matter, not unlike the apostles who kept their attention on "the ministry of the Word and prayer."

For what reason would you surrender your ministry? If a church's actions mitigate against evangelism, will you give in or defend the gospel? While many pastors lose their ministries for bad reasons, some things are worse than losing your job. One is losing your convictions. We need leaders who will declare boldly the unsearchable treasures of Christ from a heart of love and without fear of the consequences.

Lead by the Strength of Your Character

Leadership is influence. Throughout his epistles the apostle Paul held himself up as an example. You must have integrity, conviction, and character. Without this, those whom you lead will recognize the emergence of the "Barney Fife" syndrome in your life. Remember Barney from the *Andy Griffith Show*? He carried a gun, but it had no bullets. Having a badge without bullets is like being in a leadership position with no respect. If you have to tell people you are the leader, you are not the leader!

If your present ministry is just a stepping-stone for your ambition for the future, people will figure that out. More importantly, God has already figured it out. But if you demonstrate a genuine love for God and a love for the people to whom you minister, more than a few will follow you. Love *everyone,* but move with the *movers.* Over time, they will follow. Your burden for lost people will become their burden.

I learned this in Indiana. When I went there—first as associate, then as evangelism director—I knew I was getting in over my head. So I asked two people for advice: Carlos McLeod, evangelism director for the Baptist General Convention of Texas; and Malcolm McDow, my professor at seminary.

Both gave me great advice. They told me that I should not go to the churches in Indiana promoting my programs or plans. They advised me to preach the Word of God and let the people sense my passion for Christ and the gospel. When the people sensed my love for God and a desire to help the churches rather than convincing them to use my programs, they would follow my leadership.

These leaders were exactly right. I knew little about Indiana and less about denominational leadership. But the Lord gave me a great burden for the lost people and the churches in Indiana, and he honored my ministry there more than I could have asked or dreamed.

Pastors often complain about the seven words that kill churches: "We've never done it that way before." It is difficult to get people to change. But if we are to lead people to be open to change, we must demonstrate that we are open to change. Model the truth that change is normal, not the enemy. If you love contemporary worship but are in a traditional church, you will have to change as much as the people at first, meeting them where they are. Are you as excited about changing yourself as you are about changing others?

As a church grows, leadership styles change. Leading a church of 100 people is different from leading a congregation of 300, 500, or 1,000. Many pastors never lead a church beyond 200 people in attendance, not because there are no more people to reach, but because the pastor must change his style of leadership. He must relinquish responsibilities (read "power") to laypeople and eventually to other staff. He must move from being a shepherd to serving as a rancher.

"No Christian leader is the person of God that our Lord wants him to be unless day after day the consuming desire of his heart is that people come to Christ."[6] These words from Wesley Duewel demonstrate the importance of linking leadership in ministry to evangelism. As a leader, ask yourself: Are those I am leading more excited about evangelism because of my leadership? Are they more effective in sharing their faith? A person who thinks he is leading when no one is following is only taking a walk.

The central issue of getting people involved in witnessing is leadership. Let me give you a sad example of this. I participated in a witnessing effort in a church in the Southwest. The young pastor was obviously nervous about door-to-door evangelism. He read the

[6] Duewel, *Ablaze for God,* 105.

passage about Jesus sending out the 70 where Jesus said, "I watched Satan fall from heaven like a lightning flash" (Luke 10:18). Commenting on this statement, he said, "Some people interpret this to mean that the witness was so powerful that it caused Satan to fall." (By the way, that's the way most interpret it.) He went on to say, "That's not how I interpret it." He spent about five minutes explaining that Satan was going to give everyone a hard time, people would not be interested, and so on. That's the most blatant example of defeatism I've ever experienced. By the time he finished his explanation, I was so discouraged I almost didn't want to go out witnessing.

This young man didn't like to go out and witness. It was uncomfortable for him. Pastors can hold their people back. Soul-winning pastors beget soul-winning churches. Here are some ways you can encourage your people to get into the fields.

- Talk about your witnessing. If you would simply share an example of witnessing to someone once a week, those you lead would understand your passion for evangelism.
- Let your people know that success is as much in the witnessing effort as it is in actually winning people to Christ. Get them to love fishing as much as catching.
- *Do not* tell only your favorite few stories from days gone by. Instead, tell current, live accounts: "Just yesterday, I shared Christ with the paperboy."
- Tell these stories in a way that emphasizes the work of God over your ability.

Try this in your church or class: Ask how many people have ever had a Mormon or Jehovah's Witness knock on their door. Usually, it is 90 percent or more. Then ask how many have ever had anyone approach them to share Christ. Usually the number is more like 10 percent. This is a striking reminder that we have been too reluctant to lead people to share Christ with others.

Questions for Consideration

1. Which of the leadership traits above would be your strongest?
2. Which need most improvement?
3. How can your leadership become more focused on encouraging others to share Christ?

Chapter 16

Personal Evangelism: The What

Evangelism is not a task that God does Himself. Rather, He sovereignly chooses to accomplish this work through His children. If God saw fit, He could use the stones to bear witness to the truth of the gospel (Matthew 3:9); He could use animals (Numbers 22:28) or angels (Luke 2:8–15). But He has chosen to use us, weak and sinful as we are, for this eternally significant work.[1]

—Mark McCloskey

Did you hear about the three pastors who met in an accountability group? One day they told one another their greatest hidden sins. The first said, "Don't tell my congregation, but I'm an alcoholic." The next confessed, "If my people knew I'm a compulsive gambler, they would fire me." The third said, "I hate to admit it, but I'm addicted to gossip, and I can't wait to get out of here!"

It seems more Christians are better at talking about other things or people than about the gospel. And more talk about evangelism than actually do it. In this chapter, we will focus on some specific ways to

[1] M. McCloskey, *Tell It Often, Tell It Well* (San Bernardino, CA: Here's Life, 1986), 75.

witness to others. But first, let us address the problem of fear. How do we get people in our churches to overcome their fears?

Facing Our Fears

Paul told young Timothy, "God has not given us a spirit of fearfulness" (2 Tim. 1:7). In my witness training through the years, two primary fears surface again and again: the fear of failure and the fear of rejection. After all, no one wants to fail, and no one enjoys being rejected by others.

Failure

If you have attempted to witness, you know about this fear: "I don't know what to say. What if they ask a question I can't answer?" The fear of failure is real. How do we cope with it?

This fear may exist because we *misunderstand our task.* We are called to faithfulness. Faithfulness to share is our measure of success. Our Lord Jesus did not win every person with whom He shared. We are ambassadors. Ambassadors do not speak on their authority but for another. We must remember that God holds us accountable for obedience, not perfection. Remember Jesus called us to follow Him, and if we did so He would make us fishers of men (Matt 4:19). If we enjoy *fishing* as much as *catching*, we will experience a lessening of this fear as we focus more on the joy of telling good news and less on our "success."

Michael Jordan is arguably the best basketball player in history. Yet he missed many shots. During the 1997 NBA playoffs, a Nike commercial featured Jordan musing over his career. "I've missed nine thousand shots . . . I've lost almost three hundred games," he pondered. "Twenty-six times I have been trusted to take the winning shot and missed." Then he concluded: "I've failed over and over in my life—and that is why I succeed!"

We do not remember Michael Jordan as an all-time great because he is perfect but because he is *tenacious.* He won't quit. He won't let the fear of failure defeat him. The same season the commercial aired, in game one of the 1997 NBA finals against Utah, Michael Jordan was again trusted to take the game-winning shot, and he made it. He later hit the key shot in a game when he was sick with the flu. You can make it, too, as a witness—and what you are doing is far more important than a basketball game!

Where do we get the false notion that we should be able to answer any question a person raises? Nowhere in Scripture are we told that an effective witness must be a Bible know-it-all. I see this attitude in seminary students. *I am getting a Master of Divinity,* they think, *so I must know all the answers.* We don't have to know everything; we must know what *matters.* Our focus should be on the essential gospel, not the trivial chatter of society.

Personal evangelism is caught more than taught.

This leads me to the best practical solution for this fear: *witness training.* What a joy it is to show people how simple it is to use a tract to present Christ. "I can do *that!*" they say. Believers who earnestly desire to serve Christ will find such training helpful. Witness training that allows people to learn through classroom experience, role playing, and field experience helps them to see that they can do it. The best training comes from going with another believer who shares his faith regularly to watch and learn.

Rejection

Rejection is an inevitable part of witnessing. The most winsome person on earth will not convince everyone the truth of the gospel. I have yet to meet any person who loves rejection. *Facing* rejection rather than *avoiding* rejection is crucial. We must understand the reasons for rejection in order to face it to the glory of God.

The Principle of Transference

Transference states that positive and negative feelings occur as a result of prior experiences. It is always present in new relationships; it is unconscious; and it can be positive, negative, or both. For example, you as a pastor might introduce yourself to a hospital patient. Before he even gets your name, he starts cursing you! Perhaps he didn't like something about some preacher somewhere—and he's taking it out on you. A lot of times you are the lightning rod for things that have nothing to do with you. When we share the gospel with people, they may not appreciate what we say, but we shouldn't take this personally.

While serving as evangelism director, I provided leadership in a witnessing conference. As part of the training, we went out in threes to visit. The chairman of deacons at the church took my team to the "meanest guy in town." His name was Mike. We sat in his living room, talking about sports. I transitioned to the gospel by asking, "Mike, do you know for certain you have eternal life and that you will go to heaven when you die?"

Immediately, Mike's hands went up as if to form an invisible wall. "I don't talk about religion in my house," he said. I could sense his hostility, so I said, "Mike, I understand that I am a guest in your house. But, several years ago, Jesus Christ radically changed my life, and I have never gotten over it. As passionate as I am about sports, my love for God is deeper."

For the next 20 or 30 minutes, we discussed spiritual things. Mike did not receive Christ, but he did listen. As we left, he told me I was the first preacher who treated him as a person, with respect. He had been negative toward me because of his past experiences. I am happy to say that he was eventually reached for Christ. We must not take it personally if a person rejects us.

The Engel Scale (see a simplified version in Figure 11.1) illustrates the reality that not every unsaved person will receive Christ on their first encounter with his truth.[2] They may be atheists, but your witness could cause them to begin to think of spiritual things. Another person may be having questions; your witness can give answers. While we want to win everyone with whom we share, the truth is we will not. But we can help each person to consider more clearly the claims of the gospel.

The Role of Rejection

We desperately need a paradigm shift in the American church. We must revisit the biblical teaching that *we are never more like the prophets or Jesus than when we are rejected.* How could you identify a true prophet in Old Testament times? What they said came true, and they led people toward faithfulness to God. The obsession with a consumer-Christianity focused on comfort and blessing will not push a believer into discipleship that values sacrifice for the gospel. A characteristic of a true prophet was that people often didn't like what he said.

---

[2] J. F. Engel and H. W. Norton, *What's Gone Wrong with the Harvest? A Communication Strategy for the Church and World Evangelism* (Grand Rapids: Zondervan, 1975), 45.

Figure 11.1

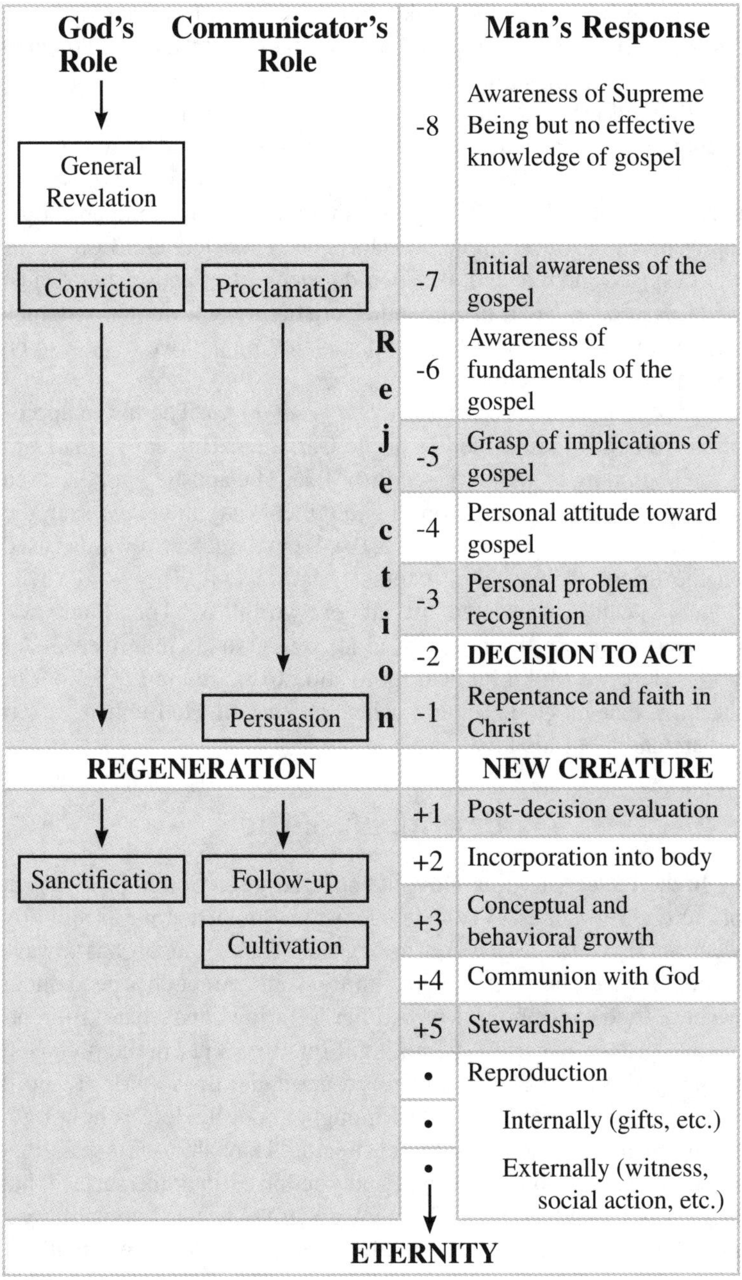
God's Role
Communicator's Role
Man's Response
General Revelation
-8
Awareness of Supreme Being but no effective knowledge of gospel
Conviction
Proclamation
-7
Initial awareness of the gospel
Rejection
-6
Awareness of fundamentals of the gospel
-5
Grasp of implications of gospel
-4
Personal attitude toward gospel
-3
Personal problem recognition
-2
DECISION TO ACT
Persuasion
-1
Repentance and faith in Christ
REGENERATION
NEW CREATURE
+1
Post-decision evaluation
Sanctification
Follow-up
+2
Incorporation into body
Cultivation
+3
Conceptual and behavioral growth
+4
Communion with God
+5
Stewardship
Reproduction
Internally (gifts, etc.)
Externally (witness, social action, etc.)
ETERNITY

How do you know Micaiah was a true prophet? Because Ahab didn't like what he had to say! You know Amos was a true prophet because he was told, "Go back where you came from, buddy" (see Amos 7:12). They were rejected because they said the truth. So when we speak the truth, some people are going to reject us.

What did Jesus say in the Beatitudes? "Blessed are you when they insult you and persecute you and falsely say every kind of evil against you because of Me. Be glad and rejoice, because your reward is great in heaven" (Matt 5:11–12). If you want to be in grand company spiritually, take note of how much you have been rejected. Our Lord Jesus was despised and rejected. We should never seek rejection, but it must be understood as a part of authentic Christianity. The quota for wimps has been met in the church. We must be loving, but we must also be bold, in spite of rejection.

We need to replace our fear with a greater fear. There's an appropriate place for fear in the life of the Christian. The fear of the Lord is the beginning of wisdom (see Prov 1:7). The apostle Paul declared that we must all appear before the judgment seat, the *bēma* seat, the rewards seat of Christ (see 2 Cor 5:10). We will receive rewards based on the things we've done, whether good or evil. The word "evil" (*phaulos*) can be translated "trivial" or "worthless." Then Paul says, knowing therefore the *terror* of God, we persuade men (see 2 Cor 5:11). Here we find a biblical motivation to share the gospel out of the holy fear of God. Having a healthy fear of God enhances our understanding of his love.

Let God Push You

In the matter of witnessing, it's necessary for God to push us out of our comfort zones. When Hannah was a youngster, we as a family went annually for a vacation to Myrtle Beach. Hannah has always loved the water, but at that point simply would not put her head under water. I tried everything. I bribed her, offering candy bars. I threatened to ground her from swimming. I finally got her in the pool next to me, grabbed her neck, and shoved her under the water! OK, no, I did not do all those things, but I thought about it. Here is how I got her to do it—I reasoned with her. I said, "Hannah, look across that big pool. There is a lot of water, and you have fun at the surface, but there is so much more you can enjoy under the water if you will trust me." Reluctantly at first, she finally went under. And from that day until now she is easily the best swimmer in our family. She found so much more to life once she pushed herself.

Witnessing can be like that. So many believers miss so much of the joy of trusting Christ because they skim the surface of the faith, never going deep, never taking risks. We're nervous, we're afraid, but when we step out and do something that honors God, it is exhilarating and rewarding beyond description.

How sad it would be for a person to grow up in a church, attend faithfully, become a devoted follower of Christ—but never learn to share his faith. Could it be that there are many Christians, even key church leaders, who have never consistently witnessed? Is it possible that there are many longtime believers who have *never* shared with a single lost person their testimony of how Christ changed their life? Are we as leaders not robbing saints of great joy by failing to show them the pleasure of witnessing?

A former student and effective evangelistic pastor named Jerry has taught me a couple of techniques to help people overcome their fear of witnessing. First, when Jerry witnesses to people for the first time, he asks how many times anyone else has shared Christ with them. Most people to whom he witnesses have never had anyone witness to them. This gives Jerry—and it should give each of us—a greater sense of urgency. The reason many people have not given their lives to Christ is that no one has told them how!

A second thing Jerry has done is sobering as well. One year when his church led the local association in baptisms, he checked with a funeral director in his town to determine how many people had died the year before. He discovered more people died that year than the entire association baptized. That served as a powerful motivation for both Jerry and his church to tell others—in spite of the fears that go along with witnessing.

The Approach to a Witnessing Encounter

When witnessing, many people have a difficult time guiding the conversation from the secular to the sacred. A good approach is helpful in doing this. By the "approach" I mean *the initial contact with a lost person, through words and actions, which establishes enough relationship to allow a witness for Christ.*

While teaching a required Old Testament course at Houston Baptist University in 1994, I noticed one young lady asked several questions about the course the first day. Most students just hoped to get through the syllabus so class would be over, but Allison continued to probe. Finally, she said, "I am a practicing Jew, in the nursing program, and I am very nervous about studying the Hebrew Bible at a Baptist school."

I assured her that she would be treated with respect. Speaking with her after class, I learned the reason for her anxiety. While a student at another institution, she was approached by Christian witnesses. When Allison replied she was Jewish and not interested, they replied, "Oh well, we know you aren't. After all, you Jews killed Jesus." This was *not* the best approach. I told Allison that not every Christian was like that and encouraged her to share her thoughts with the class.

Approach: the initial contact with a lost person, through words and actions, establishes enough relationship to allow a witness for Christ.

As we moved into Exodus, I asked Allison to explain a Jewish Seder (Passover) service to us. She went crazy with excitement! She demonstrated the whole service, complete with leg of lamb, the candy, and the trimmings. The students were wowed, the professor was impressed, and Allison felt a part of the class and the school.

As the class continued, I shared openly with Allison due to our friendship. By the end of the course, Allison said, "You know, I think Jesus may be the Messiah after all." She even went to hear me preach. Although I moved and lost touch with Allison, the approach I took helped her become more open to the gospel. While this encounter occurred over a period of time, the same can be said about a one-time witnessing encounter.

I have met many believers who know how to share their faith but who struggle mightily in moving a conversation toward the gospel. While practical material follows including examples of how to go about this, remember your goal is more than to get the presentation out to a person. You want to help this person understand the gospel in his or her context. When possible you should so share that if the person does not trust Christ, you can continue to speak with them in future conversations. Too often we share once and then leave the person alone. We should be seeking to make friends, not just contact that person once.

Your life screams to others. Some people's lives scream depression, others fear, others anger. But some people's lives shout out a passion for God and great joy! Imagine you are sitting in a circle surrounded by six chairs. If the half dozen people who know you best sat around you and were asked to say what your life said by your words and actions, what would they say?

The gospel is the power of God for salvation, so helping a person to hear the gospel in a context he understands matters. A good approach eases tensions of the person with whom you share. It is more winsome if you build rapport prior to moving into the gospel. A good approach also helps you to be able to share Christ more with this person later. Often we talk to an individual once, and if she is uninterested, we give up. We should continue to seek opportunities to live and speak the gospel to those we know. It eases the fears of the witness. One definition of soul-winning is "a conversation between two people, both of whom are nervous."

How to Approach a Person to Follow Christ

The most significant practical detail related to personal evangelism is this: In order to win lost people to Christ, we must talk to lost people! You can build rapport by finding something in common with another person in only a couple of minutes. A great start is to ask, "Where are you from originally?"

Approach People with a Heart of Love

People are not stupid; they can tell if you care! You may stumble in the presentation. You may not answer every question they have. But your ability to look them in the eye and to lead them to sense that something important has happened in your life will overcome a world of mistakes. A concern for people will overcome other factors.

I have known people who stumbled through the presentation, even breaking into tears—partly because they were nervous, partly because they knew they were messing up—and still they led somebody to

Christ. People can tell three things about you and me in a fifteen-minute conversation. They can tell if:

1. We care about them. People really do not care how much you know about God unless they can tell you also care about them!
2. We believe what we are talking about.
3. We have the hand of God on our lives.

Paul commended the Thessalonian believers for the impact their lives made with the gospel. They truly "lived loudly" the changed life they experienced in Christ. In fact, 1 Thess 1:8 says their lives so heralded the gospel that the apostles did not have to say anything. Imagine being in a community where the believers there share the gospel so consistently that the pastor did not need to do so! I am still looking for that community in our day.

Herschel Hobbs tells the story of a hardened criminal awaiting execution. Several pastors and ministers tried to reach him for Christ. Typically, they focused on what a sinner he was and how he needed salvation. This only hardened his heart. Then a layman came to see him. He sat with him and said, "You and I are in a terrible fix, aren't we?" The humble layman's identification with the hardened criminal led him to weep, and soon he repented of his sins and trusted the Savior. How should we approach people?

Approach in a Spirit of Prayer

Prayer opens the door for the wisdom of God. "For the Holy Spirit will teach you at that very hour what must be said" (Luke 12:12). Our efforts are in partnership with the work of the Holy Spirit.

Approach with an Attitude of Expectancy

Believe he or she will be interested. A student in Houston visited my office to ask about her grade. I asked Sabrina if she ever thought about spiritual things, to which she replied, "Yes." I shared Christ with her, and in a short while, we were on our knees in my office, as she gave her life to Christ!

Be Sensitive to the Spirit

The more you witness, the more you will learn to listen to the Holy Spirit. Even if you give a terrible approach, God can still use you. Bill Bright said we fail in witnessing only if we fail to witness.

We learn to witness by doing it. And I will say it again—evangelism is *caught* more than *taught.*

In Claremont, New Hampshire, I met Eileen, an apartment finder for the town. I asked her, "You know the area well; what is the greatest need?" Immediately, she said, "There is a lot of hopelessness here." I handed her a tract that said "Here's Hope" on the cover (*that* got her attention!). I told her, "We are here to tell others of the hope of Jesus." She was a recovering alcoholic and said she did more counseling than apartment finding.

I shared my testimony, and she replied with a nebulous belief in a nebulous God. She had never heard a clear presentation of the gospel. After sharing with her, I said to her, "Jesus Christ radically changed my life." She replied, "I can tell he has!" I did not lead her to Christ, but it was another example that many people will talk about spiritual matters.

Models of a Good Approach

Learning some basic models can give confidence. The approach one takes can be *formal,* as with Jesus and Nicodemus. Don't be afraid to be direct. I have told students to take gospel tracts and simply say, "I have this crazy professor who says I have to read this booklet to someone. Can I read it to you?" One student did that, and then came to class in tears. This direct approach opened the door for him to lead a person to Christ. Or we can be *informal* as Jesus was with the Samaritan woman (see John 4) and with Zacchaeus (see Luke 19). Here are three simple ideas for approaching people to witness.

Explore, Stimulate, Share[3]

Explore
Get to know the other person. Ask questions, listen, and be alert.

Stimulate
Raise their interest. Simple questions are effective:

- If you ever want to talk about the difference between religion and Christianity, let me know.
- When you attend church, where do you attend?

---

[3] I am indebted to T. Beougher, evangelism professor at Southern Baptist Theological Seminary, for this concept.

- Have you thought more lately about spiritual things?
- Would you say you have a personal relationship with Jesus Christ, or are you still in the process? This question has been very effective!
- In your opinion, what is a real Christian?
- What do you think of ______? (God, Jesus, the Bible)
- Who do you think Jesus Christ was?
- We've been friends for a while. Could I share with you a very important part of my life?

The last question is good for somebody you've known for years but to whom you've never witnessed. I had a businessman in Tennessee who said to me, "I've been on the job for several years, and people know that I'm a Christian, but I've got friends to whom I've never witnessed. How do I go about witnessing to them?" I sensed he really wanted to know. He had one person in particular in mind. I will call him Bob.

"Let me tell you what you need to do for Bob," I replied. "First of all, you need to go to church tomorrow. Go forward to recommit your life to Christ and say that you've not been the witness you need to be. Tell the entire church that. Monday morning find Bob and ask him if you can speak to him for a minute. Then tell him, 'Bob, I need to apologize to you because of something I haven't done. Yesterday I told my church that I've not been right, and I'm sorry. I want you to know the greatest thing that ever happened to me.' Then go right into your testimony."

Share

Respond to their needs. Apply the gospel to where they are.

Personal Testimony

The personal testimony is a great way to move into a gospel presentation. You might ask, "Where are you from originally?" After their answer, say "That's interesting. I am from. . . ." Move into your testimony, followed by, "Has anything like this ever happened to you?" If they cannot give a clear testimony, move into the gospel.

Acrostic

An acrostic gives you a mnemonic tool to help you remember what to say, especially if you are a novice at witnessing. One example is the acrostic FIRE.

***F**amily*—simply ask the person about his family, where he grew up, if married, kids, etc.

***I**nterests*—ask about work, hobbies, sports teams, etc. You will likely find some things you have in common.

***R**eligious background*—Do not ask if they go to church. Ask, "When you attend church, where do you attend?" Such a question requires more than a yes or no answer (a sure conversation stopper) and assumes the best, not the worst of the person. Or you could ask about their spiritual interests, etc.

***E**xploratory questions*—Questions can help you transition to speak about the gospel, such as: "Have you come to a place in your life that you know for certain that you have eternal life and that you will go to heaven when you die?" "Suppose you were standing before God right now and he asked you, 'Why should I let you into my heaven?' What do you think you would say?"

Servant Evangelism

A simple act of kindness provides a marvelous way of introducing the gospel. This particular approach is explained in detail in the following chapters. A simple example I use often is to ask a server in the restaurant if I can pray for them before our meal (always accompanied by a good tip!).

Tools for Sharing Your Faith

Your goal should be to learn how to talk about the things of God as you would talk about anything. In our family we have always attempted to avoid compartmentalizing God-talk from the rest of life, so that speaking of Jesus comes naturally, not in a contrived way. Still, as a learner there are some tools that can assist you in learning to share Christ better.

Marked New Testament

The first way I trained anyone to witness was by showing him how to mark a New Testament. One of the most used approaches to share Christ in history is the Roman Road, incorporating verses from Romans (1:16; 3:23; 6:23; 5:8; 10:9–10). There are many excellent Bibles already marked to assist the witness in sharing Christ. The approach *Share Jesus Without Fear* involves the use of the Bible. A positive feature of this is obvious: it gets people into the Word of God to see what Scripture says. A negative would be that if this were the only method you use, you would not be able to share anytime you did not have a New Testament with you.

Gospel Tracts

I confess to being a big fan of tracts, having led more people to Christ that way than any other. The first person I ever led to Christ, I used the *Four Spiritual Laws* booklet produced by Campus Crusade for Christ. Spurgeon said more people are in heaven because of tracts than any other means. Here are six useful principles for using tracts in witnessing.

1. Never use a tract you haven't read. (Some are weak theologically.)
2. Brevity is desirable.
3. Use tracts that are attractive.
4. Be enthusiastic about the contents.
5. Be sure the tract sets forth the facts of the gospel.
6. The tract should explain the process by which a person becomes a Christian, particularly emphasizing repentance and faith.

Tracts are valuable for several reasons. They keep the witness on track with the gospel, and you can leave them with people for later reading and reflection. They typically have helpful information both in leading a person to Christ and for immediate follow-up. Negatively, tracts can take the place of a more personal, involved witness by developing a "tract bomb" attitude that causes you to leave a tract without much more involvement. And of course, there are some really bad tracts out there, so choose them carefully.

Memorized Presentations

The best examples of memorized presentations are from Evangelism Explosion (EE) and FAITH Evangelism, which uses this word as an acrostic to assist in sharing Christ. The NET is another memorized approach.[4]

Some people criticize memorized presentations because they are "canned." In my experience, *any* presentation of the gospel—a marked New Testament, tract, or testimony—is canned, if the person sharing Christ doesn't care about the person hearing the message. In fact, sermons and Bible lessons are canned if you focus on the delivery more than the discipleship. But the discipline of witnessing such an approach offers has aided many believers in their growth in personal evangelism.

Regardless of whether you use EE, FAITH, Billy Graham's materials, The Way of the Master,[5] or any other approach, make sure the presentation you use emphasizes the need of the lost person, as well as the work of Christ, and the biblical response (repentance and faith). A person cannot be saved unless he realizes he is lost and in need of saving. The law of God has a purpose—to show us our need for salvation and our insufficiency to save ourselves. We are not trying to get someone to "pray the prayer." We are attempting to help individuals meet the God who created them.

Role-Playing

Let me encourage you to train others to witness. A helpful way to teach believers to witness is through role-playing. I wish someone had taught me as a teenager how to witness and to role-play sharing the gospel. I wish seminary students would take more time to stop debating Calvinism or eschatology and help each other to become more effective in witness by role-playing. I believe I could have won 20 or 30 of my friends to Christ in high school because I was a leader, I was well liked on the campus, and I was a Christian. I had many friends, both Christians and non-Christians, but I didn't know how to communicate the gospel clearly one-on-one. I could get people to come to church, and I saw some of my friends come to Christ, but how I wish someone had trained me. When I was a freshman in college, somebody taught me how, and it changed my life.

My students tell me that of all the things I teach in class, nothing helps them more than when I take a few minutes to role-play a given witnessing situation. If you are a pastor, you might be surprised at the impact you would have in helping your people learn to witness

[4] See eeinternational.org; lifeway.com/faith; namb.net/thenet.

[5] See www.wayofthemaster.com.

by simply taking time in a service annually to role-play sharing your faith. It is caught more than taught!

When I served at a local church, at times I would use a service for practical training. I would give everyone a tract, then have them spend some time role-playing with one another. I do this in class. In fact, for a few semesters I somehow got away from role-playing in class, and it made a negative impact on the effectiveness of my teaching.

I had been a pastor and was on staff at a church before I had ever watched anyone witness. I am convinced of the importance of watching somebody else. Sometimes I'll go out witnessing with a pastor and say, "Let me watch you one time. I still have a lot to learn. Then you watch me and let's talk about it." The best way to teach someone to witness is to take them with you to witness. This leads to effective learning and effective witnessing.

Practical Examples

Many tools/witness training programs help in sharing one's faith. Some were mentioned, but recent examples include The Way of the Master, Share Jesus Without Fear, FAITH Evangelism, the NET, and Evangelism Explosion. Pastor Tim Keller of Redeemer Presbyterian Church in New York City talks about using "gospel summaries" to share Christ. Here are two examples:[6]

Do-Done summary (see example in Bill Hybels, *Becoming a Contagious Christian*).

> **"Do."** *All forms of religion (formal or informal), are spelled D-O because they tell us we have to perform good works and obey moral and religious laws in order to find God, to achieve forgiveness, nirvana, or peace. But you can never be sure you have done enough.*
> **"Done."** *But Christianity is spelled D-O-N-E because God sent his son to earth to live the life we should live, and die on the cross to pay the debt we should pay for wrongs we've done. Buddha said, "Strive w/out ceasing"; Jesus said, "It is finished"* (John 19:30).

[6] T. Keller, *Evangelism: Studies in the Book of Acts Participant's Guide* (Redeemer Presbyterian Church, 2005), 26–27.

To become a Christian is to turn from "do" to "done" by asking God to accept you for Jesus' sake and commit to live for him.

Sin-Salvation summary (based on a paragraph in John Stott's *The Cross of Christ*):

Sin *is us substituting ourselves for God, putting ourselves where only God deserves to be—in charge of our lives.*

Salvation *is God substituting himself for us, putting himself where only we deserve to be—dying on the cross.* Read 2 Cor 5:21.

To become a Christian is first to admit the **problem**: *that you have been substituting yourself for God either by religion (trying to be your own* **savior** *by obedience to moral standards) or by irreligion (trying to be your own* **lord** *by disobedience to moral standards). And second to accept the* **solution**: *asking God to accept you for Jesus' sake and know that you are loved and accepted because of his record, not yours.*

Calling for a Decision

We are obligated to God and the other person to ask for a decision whenever possible. At times this can't be done because of time factors or interruptions. But the gospel presentation is incomplete without a call to decision. Intellectual awareness of the gospel does not mean salvation has occurred. We need to look for opportunities to draw the net. Paul reminded the Corinthians in 2 Cor 5:11 that because we as Christ followers will stand before the Judgment Seat, that fear should motivate us to persuade men. Not to manipulate but to be persuasive. We cannot make a person respond to the gospel nor should we, but we should challenge them to do so.

In assisting people in their commitment to Christ, we must remember we cannot always determine what is happening in their hearts. We must explain the message, pray for them, and trust the leadership of the Spirit.

Leading to a Commitment

Asking questions of the person with whom you have shared the gospel can help. Examples:

1. *Transition Question:* "Does what we have been discussing make sense to you?"
2. *Willingness Question:* "Is there any reason why you would not be willing to receive God's gift of eternal life?"
3. *Commitment Question:* "Are you willing to turn from your sin and place your faith in Jesus right now?"

Explain the commitment the person is to make. When using a tract, read the prayer to the person, asking if it expresses their desire to know God. Remind the other person that Christianity is a relationship, not a ritual. They are to talk to God personally.

You can pray with the person, having them repeat after you. You can have them pray in their own words. You can invite them to pray silently. Note: the Scripture does not give a prescribed "sinner's prayer," so a formula is not required. However, the Bible does teach a lost person to cry out to God in prayer for salvation (Rom 10:9,13), so a sinner's prayer can be deduced from Scripture. The danger is in emphasizing the reciting of words more than the attitude of the will.

Further, I would avoid such terminology as "accepting Jesus into your heart," a concept that is not found in Scripture. Repentance and faith are the conditions; further, receiving the gift of salvation is a biblically valid expression. The question is not, do I accept Jesus, but does Jesus accept me? Thankfully, the response is *yes*, when we come in repentance and faith.

When I have shared Christ with a person who wants to repent and believe, I typically follow a simple process. First, I pray *for* the other person, thanking God for bringing us together, for the wonder of salvation, and the work of the Spirit. Second, I pray *with* the person, helping them as needed to cry out to God for salvation. Finally, I ask the other person to thank God for what He has done through Christ, and I thank God as well. I have heard some wonderful prayers of gratitude on occasions like this.

Practical Ideas for Personal Witness

David Mills complied a list of ideas to help you to use in your witness or to think about further practical ways to share your faith.

62 Ideas for Sharing Christ's Love[1]

David Mills

1. List all the lost people you know and pray for them daily. Ask God for His power and compassion. Ask God to keep the lost people you know alive until you or someone can get the gospel to them.
2. Make a commitment to witness everyday. Few things happen without a prior commitment.
3. List all the persons in your concentric circles (family, friends, neighbors, marketplace contacts, church) and make a commitment to witness to them.
4. Do not forget to share your testimony and the gospel with the children or grandchildren in your family. This is witnessing, too, and of the most urgent kind.
5. When at a restaurant, leave a generous tip (15% or 20%) and a tract. Write your contact information on it, too.
6. Before your meal, ask your server, "We are about to ask God to bless our meal. Is there anything we can pray for you about when we do?" Usually, most servers are burdened for family and health.
7. When you attend church with a lost friend, be sure your friend sits in the seat next to the aisle and you sit next to him or her. This will help your friend to walk the aisle to profess faith in Christ. Your friend will not climb over people to profess faith in Christ if he or she is sitting in the middle of the pew. All aisle seats in churches must be reserved for lost people.
8. Gently approach people who are sitting by themselves and appear to be alone. Start a conversation and share the gospel.
9. Invite a friend to a concert, revival, or special worship service at your church. Following the service, go out for dessert and talk about the message presented in the service.
10. Send a birthday card to a friend. Enclose a personal note sharing about your own spiritual birthday.
11. Clip a special article from a daily devotional guide or newspaper religion column and mail it to a friend who needs to know Jesus. Include a personal note conveying love and compassion.
12. Subscribe to a favorite devotional guide or Christian periodical for a friend.

---

[1] The following ideas were inspired by M. Hollifield's *60 Ways to Share Christ and His Love* (Cary, NC: Baptist State Convention of North Carolina, 1995). The author has incorporated some of Hollifield's ideas here.

13. Write a letter or note of thanks to one who serves in the military services in our country. Include a Scripture reference of 2 Tim 2:1–4.
14. Design your own business card to introduce yourself. Include a gospel presentation on the back of the card.
15. Take contemporary Christian CDs to a juvenile detention center, youth-receiving home, or shelter. Attach a note to each item sharing John 3:16.
16. Take copies of a Christian magazine and leave them in laundromats. Write the name of your church on each copy and a note saying you hope an article in the magazine will be particularly helpful to the reader.
17. Leave a sealed candy bar or snack near the electric meter attached to your home. Attach a tract or note of "good news" to the candy bar and state that you would like to share both.
18. Leave a refreshing drink of cold water for the person who picks up your garbage. Attach a note including John 4:14.
19. Ask your pastor to make a 10–15 minute video presenting the plan of salvation and explaining believer's baptism. Share the video with a lost friend.
20. Go down to the local "hang out" where young boys play basketball. Ask to join the game. Share your testimony before you leave.
21. Visit a lonely senior adult living at home, in a retirement center, or in a nursing facility. Share John 14:1–6 and present the gospel.
22. When in a drive through, give the "Here's Hope" tract, saying, "This is a tract about Christ and how He gives hope. Will you take this and read it sometime?" Then ask, "Has anyone ever taken time to share with you the message of Christ's hope?"
23. Fill up with gas, go to the grocery store, or frequent convenience stores when no other patrons are there. Give away the "Here's Hope" tract as in #22.
24. Write out your personal testimony. Practice giving it by sharing it with a friend. Do this twice a day for seven days.
25. Write a note of congratulations when a friend, neighbor, or family member is recognized for success. Share how every good and perfect gift is from above.
26. Develop several one-liners that communicate the essence of the gospel. When you see someone treated rudely, say to the person next to you, "I sure am glad Jesus is more gracious than that."
27. Develop a personal tutoring ministry for children of single parents or students who need to learn English as a second language. Use the ministry for opportunities to share Christ. Drive these children and families to church.

28. Get the Jesus Video and invite a group of internationals to view the film with you. Explain to them how they can receive Christ as Savior.
29. Make a personal phone call to one who has received discouraging news recently. Share your personal testimony of how God sustained you in your hour of need. Pray with them over the phone.
30. When you notice a stranger reading a newspaper, offer him/her a gospel booklet, and say, "Excuse me, when you get an opportunity, you might like to read some good news that you might not find in there."
31. Cross-stitch attractive book marks with a gospel message. Share them with friends who enjoy reading.
32. Share a Christian book with a friend. Tell them after they read it you would like to hear their opinion of it. Billy Graham's biography is a hit!
33. Share a tape of one of your pastor's special sermons with a friend or neighbor. Use this as an opportunity to share the plan of salvation.
34. Include a gospel tract and note of appreciation along with a brief personal testimony when you mail your monthly utility payments.
35. Compose an e-mail signature that includes a Scripture reference explaining Christ's salvation and worth.
36. Make a visit to new parents. Take a copy of *Parent Life* to share with the new mom and dad. Share how Christ's salvation helps you parent.
37. Wear a "Power Band." Share the meaning of each colored bead with a lost friend. Materials are easily available at most department stores.
38. Send a Valentine card with a gospel tract sharing about God's love.
39. During family devotional times, help family members to pray for the salvation of their lost friends. Encourage family members to tell their friends about Christ.
40. When your children invite friends for a sleepover, use your family devotional time to share John 3:16.
41. Host a baptism party for family members when they follow Christ in baptism. Invite their friends and have the new convert share a testimony of salvation.
42. Take a plate of home-baked cookies or a pie to a new neighbor. Include a note of welcome to the neighborhood, a New Testament, and church info.

43. Host a dinner party or picnic for neighbors. Include conversation about relationships and conclude with an account of your most important relationship in life.
44. Write a letter to your personal physician thanking him for his care. Include an acknowledgment of the Great Physician.
45. Host a Christmas, Easter, or other Christian holiday celebration in your home, and invite neighbors and community public servants. Share a brief devotional and tell how Christ has made this holiday season special to you and your family.
46. Write a letter of thanks to your local elected officials. Tell them that you will pray for them as they seek to be of service to the community. Include a reference to your faith.
47. Demonstrate the love of Christ with the giving of a gift. Share fresh produce or fruit from your garden. Tell the receiver you enjoy sharing the love of Christ with others.
48. Offer your yard for a backyard Vacation Bible School or Backyard Bible Club.
49. Plan a wild game dinner inviting hunters in your community to bring a "dish." Ask a popular Christian sportsman to tell stories of interest, share his personal testimony, and present the gospel.
50. Conduct a Health Fair in a low-income housing area. Use Christian professionals to screen cholesterol and blood pressure levels. Conclude the screening with a Christian doctor or nurse sharing a gospel presentation.
51. Host a financial planning seminar. Advertise in the community. During a refreshment time, ask a Christian in the financial community to share a brief testimony including the parable of the "rich young ruler."
52. Sponsor a Marriage and Family class or seminar for engaged couples in your community. Enlist a qualified Christian Counselor to teach and share a Christian witness.
53. Host a seminar on "Writing Your Will," led by a Christian lawyer. Ask him to conclude with his personal testimony on spiritual preparation for death.
54. Go through the Sunday school roles of your church and list the names of Sunday school members from grade four through senior adult who are not church members. Witness to those on this list each week until finished. These are the most cultivated persons in your community.
55. Offer a "Teen's Basic Car Care and Simple Mechanics" course to the teenagers in your community. Ask a respected layman to give a brief devotional, sharing how he came to accept Christ. (Eccl 12:1)

56. Host a pizza party for a local high school ball team and guests. Show a Christian video that relates to youth.
57. Challenge your local high school athletic team (any sport) to play your deacons, church staff, or other ministry group. After the game, provide a pizza dinner. Give a devotional or other Christian book of interest to the team. Thank them for participating.
58. As a church group, set up a booth at community festivals or fairs. Give away cold water, drinks, and small gifts. Offer free copies of Scripture and gospel materials.
59. When a church group does any event, be sure to register all attendees for door prizes. Use these cards as a prospect list.
60. As a church group, conduct a block party. Have several trained witnesses to do personal witnessing.
61. Encourage your church or Sunday school department to host an appreciation banquet for local law enforcement officers or other community servants. Use a layman to share a personal testimony.
62. Teach your members to sit in the middle of the pew or row of chairs during worship. Leave the aisle seats for lost people so they can get out into the aisle quickly and without having to step over everyone.56. Host a pizza party for a local high school ball team and guests. Show a Christian video that relates to youth.

Follow-up and Assimilation

When a person becomes a believer, he or she is birthed into the kingdom of God. But he is a baby spiritually and in need of nurture. Immediate follow-up can help a new believer in her or his time of spiritual infancy. Churches have neglected follow-up. We have left a generation of baby Christians stranded, unsure of how to grow.

In his book on this subject, Waylon Moore makes the following point concerning follow-up.

> Follow-up is the conservation, maturation, and multiplication of the fruit of evangelism. Winning and building are inseparably linked together in the scriptures. There is no continuing New Testament evangelism without follow-up. They are God's "two-edged sword" for reaching men and making them effective disciples for Christ.[7]

[7] W. Moore, *New Testament Follow-up* (Grand Rapids: William B. Eerdmans, 1963), 17.

There are two extremes we must recognize in dealing with the subject of follow-up. First, there is the extreme that emphasizes follow-up so strongly that witnessing occurs only in the most ideal settings—settings in which the growth of the new Christian is virtually ensured. We must remember that Philip shared Christ with the eunuch (Acts 8), although he was not able to stay with the Ethiopian to assist his growth. On the other hand, there are those who are extremely evangelistic but who give little regard for the nurture of new Christians. This extreme emphasizes *decisions,* not *disciples* as Jesus did.

Practical Steps

Be as urgent about follow-up as you were about sharing Christ. When a person trusts Christ, do not wait a week or two to help him to grow.

Help the new believer with assurance. Immediately after a person repents, pray a prayer of thanksgiving, then ask the other person to thank God in his or her own words. I have heard wonderful, simple, earnest prayers uttered by baby Christians. Then go over their commitment with them briefly. Encourage them by reminding them that heaven rejoices in their commitment.

Give specific guidance in the Christian life. Many tracts do this well. Help the new believer discover the best time for Bible study and prayer, the name of persons who would rejoice in this person's salvation, and the names of those who need to hear the gospel.

Biblical Model

Waylon B. Moore lists four ingredients in New Testament follow-up:[8]

1. Personal Contact
2. Personal Prayer
3. Personal Representatives
4. Personal Correspondence

Follow-up begins with a proper understanding of evangelism. A church functioning with a definition of evangelism that focuses on decisions rather than disciples will not emphasize follow-up.

[8] Ibid., 29–36.

Follow-up is helped by building a gregarious fellowship. A program alone is not the cure. Build a spirit of friendliness in the congregation. Statistics indicate that if a new believer doesn't make seven friends during the first year in the church, he or she likely will not stay there. New Christians need good role models.

Be the type of person with whom new converts want to be. A joyous, aggressive church provides a great atmosphere for follow-up. In addition, take new believers out witnessing. This is great follow-up. Also look for ways to enhance current structure for effective follow-up: the Sunday school, more ministry, and so on.

Provide tools for the new converts, such as *Beginning Steps,*[9] a booklet with instructions in the Christian life. The following points are covered in this resource:

- Assurance
- Baptism/church membership
- Bible study
- Prayer
- Corporate worship/fellowship
- Witness
- Discipleship

Jesus called His followers to make disciples, not decisions. Assimilating new believers into a local church is part of the evangelistic task. What are factors today that help to assimilate new believers?

In his excellent book *Membership Matters,* Chuck Lawless found churches that do a better job of assimilation make use of new member classes. A novelty in many churches only a few years ago, such classes are not only growing in use; they are growing in acceptance by church members.[10] Church leaders feel the main reason for such classes is to teach the core values of the church to new people. The new believers agree but overwhelmingly see their benefit as providing a means to meet others in the church and develop relationships as well.

I heard a speaker tell a story about the late entertainer Jimmy Durante, who often entertained troops during wartime. On one occasion, he was visiting a military hospital. The administrator asked him to stay for a short show in the auditorium. Durante said he had to

[9] To order a copy go to http://www.namb.net/site/c.9qKILUOzEpH/b.4145595/.

[10] C. E. Lawless, *Membership Matters: Insights from Effective Churches on New Member Classes and Assimilation* (Grand Rapids: Zondervan, 2005), 22.

leave for appointments, but the administrator insisted. "Five minutes," Durante agreed, "but then I must go."

The sick and wounded were brought into the auditorium. Durante did a brief routine, and the crowd clapped and cheered profusely. Instead of leaving, the comedian continued—for a full hour. The elated administrator asked him why he stayed so long.

"When I did the first routine," Durante replied, "I noticed two men in the front row. The one on the left had lost his right arm. The one on the right had lost his left arm. When they clapped, they clapped as one. I was so moved, I couldn't leave."

When we learn that what we give in evangelism as we share Christ, lead people to Him, and help them to grow does not compare to what we will receive, we will share the gospel.

Questions for Consideration

1. What fear most likely hinders your witness?
2. Is presenting the gospel a part of your lifestyle?
3. Suppose for a moment that you are the only Christian in your world. No one you know is saved—neighbors, work associates, family, or friends. What are the odds of any of these coming to Christ if you continue to witness at your current level?

Chapter 17

Personal Evangelism: The How

Some wish to live within the sound of a chapel bell; I wish to run a rescue mission within a yard of hell.[1]

—C. T. Studd

How can a church move believers forward in their witnessing knowledge and action? How can they engage and equip believers to share Christ both missionally and intentionally to those around them? How do we get the prepared laborers off the front porch and into the harvest field? How do we not only teach personal witnessing but also actually get believers to put their knowledge into practice?

Ways to Engage Believers in Witnessing

Personal evangelists have traditionally been released into the lost world in three different ways:[2]

[1] http://www.evangelismcoach.org/2008/01/evangelism-quotes-and-quotations (accessed October 27, 2008).

[2] I am indebted to D. Mills for his thoughts on these three terms. The latter term in each category is the term he uses, while I use the former. The concepts are virtually identical, however.

1. *Assignment visitation/planned evangelism.* This approach consists of regular, reoccurring, and scheduled evangelism opportunities. Jesus commanded this intentional approach to evangelism, saying, "Go and make disciples of all nations" (Matt 28:19). Weekly visitation and follow-up of guests to church provides one opportunity. Weekly door-to-door surveys of neighborhoods offer another.
2. *Lifestyle/spontaneous evangelism.* This approach consists of witnesses sharing the gospel as they go through their lives. Jesus said, "As you go, preach" (Matt 10:7 NKJV). In this approach, witnesses start conversations with a friend, a stranger, and an acquaintance with the intention of sharing the gospel. This may happen at a convenience store, a grocery store, a hair salon, a laundry mat, or when a delivery person delivers a package or a pizza. Jesus often practiced this approach to personal evangelism.
3. *Missional/relational witness.* This approach consists of witnesses sharing the gospel intentionally with family, friends, and neighbors. Because they have the opportunity to see these persons often, witnesses can demonstrate a holy and resurrected life in front of these persons. They must guard themselves against allowing the relationship to hinder personal witnessing, and they must guard themselves against delaying the sharing of the gospel for weeks, months, and years for fear of ruining the relationship. Andrew demonstrated this approach early in Jesus' ministry. Immediately after meeting Christ, Andrew found his brother Peter and brought him to Jesus (John 1:39–42). The latter approach takes more of a posture of a missionary and is needed to a greater extent in an increasingly unreached culture.

While training and modeling of all three should take place in a local church, and while different believers may be more effective at one than another, there is a simple way to learn all three approaches. This can happen through the concept of s*ervant evangelism.* It is the simplest, most transferable, and most enjoyable approach for moving believers closer to a biblical lifestyle marked by consistent witnessing. My friend David Wheeler, who describes it in detail, introduced me to the concept:

Understanding Servant Evangelism[1]

David Wheeler

The Biblical Example . . .

When Jesus met His first disciples along the shores of the Sea of Galilee, He called them to do more than simply leave their nets behind. His call was an invitation to be involved in both evangelism and discipleship. Ultimately, this same call would become an entreaty to live a radical new life. This life demanded total commitment to the servant example of Christ.

Thus, the disciples' spiritual rebirth was so profound and joyful that they could not possibly keep it to themselves. As new creations, their faith overflowed into every aspect of their lives. Both their relationship with the Heavenly Father and the way they viewed the unredeemed around them were forever transformed.

The disciples spent three years walking with Jesus learning what it meant to be channels of His love, grace, and servanthood. In His role as both evangelist and mentor, He modeled for them, and for us, what it meant to be His agents of hope in a misguided, sinful, and hurting world.

Through His witness, Jesus demonstrated that every dimension of life was included in the Father's redemptive concern. While He was primarily concerned with the salvation of one's eternal spiritual souls, He forbade us to ignore physical and emotional needs.

Think about it, Jesus' model of evangelism combines both a ministry of compassionate servanthood with a strong verbal witness. This is why Jesus is most commonly recorded in the Gospels proclaiming the good news of salvation and forgiveness, then moving into the crowds to touch and to heal (see Matt 4:23–25).

Probably His greatest verbal expression of this concept is found in Mark 10:42–45. In response to the entitlement mentality of James and John, who desired to sit at the "right" and "left" of Jesus when He came into His glory, He responds, "You know that those who are regarded as rulers of the Gentiles lord it over them, and their high officials exercise authority over them. Not so with you. Instead, whoever wants to become great among you must be your servant, and whoever wants to be first must be slave of all. For even the Son of Man did not come to be served, but to serve, and to give his life as a ransom for many" (NIV).

Every Christ follower should be deeply convicted by the instruction to become a "servant" and "slave of all." Just as Jesus washed the feet of the disciples, Christians are to do the same for a hurting world that is dying

[1] Used by permission of D. Wheeler.

to see authentic examples of a loving Savior! In the end, Christians must understand that an unbelieving world will not believe what we say about Christ and faith until they first see the truth manifested through His followers. In a sense, we are implored by the biblical example to wrap our faith in the flesh of daily living.

What Is Servant Evangelism . . .

Servant evangelism is a combination of simple acts of kindness and intentional personal evangelism . . . it involves intentionally sharing Christ by consistently modeling biblical servanthood.

The concept is as old as the New Testament. Like many profound truths, this one is so simple it is easily missed: Get a group of believers, say for instance at a local church, and begin practicing simple acts of kindness with an intentional aim toward evangelism. In many cases, such acts of kindness open the door for the greatest act of kindness a Christian can give: the gospel.

Understand what kindness means. It does not mean telling people what they want to hear so they will feel good about themselves. Servant Evangelism involves more than mere acts of kindness. There are valuable ministries, such as taking a loaf of bread to newcomers and others, which are helpful, but they are not explicitly evangelistic. Servant Evangelism is intentionally evangelistic, though by no means does it seek to coerce in a negative sense. When doing an act of kindness, the witness says, "I am doing this to show the love of Jesus in a practical way." Then, as the Holy Spirit opens the door, usually through the individual responding, "Why are you doing this or that?" the one performing the act of servanthood has a captive audience and proceeds to share their conversion testimony coupled with the gospel presentation. If the other person is not open for discussion, the witness goes no further, except to offer a gospel tract, literature, or prayer. However, experience reveals that Servant Evangelism allows a presentation of Christ more than twice as often as simply presenting Christ to a stranger. Think about it, wouldn't it be a cruel gesture to offer to wash someone's car and fail to tell him about the Water of life? To give a lightbulb without telling of the Light of the world? To clean a toilet without telling about the only One who can cleanse a person's heart from sin?

Both Liberty Baptist Theological Seminary in Lynchburg, Virginia, and Southeastern Baptist Theological Seminary in Wake Forest, North Carolina, use this approach in its personal evangelism classes. Part of class is used as a laboratory with the students venturing out in small groups to evangelize. Some students have chosen to purchase sodas and give them to passersby in the town's business district or using umbrellas to escort people into the mall on rainy days. Others go door-to-door in older communities with nine-volt batteries to check residents' smoke detectors. One student doing this was able to lead a person to Christ for the first time in his life—was he ever excited! Another group may have a free car wash (FREE—no money accepted) at a local church, mall, grocery store, or the parking lot of a department store such as Wal-Mart or K-Mart. Patrons will usually try to give money, but the students refuse. Their response is always, "We're simply showing the love of Christ in a practical way." At one of the car washes, a man from a Hindu background was saved.

Keep in mind, *Servant Evangelism means intentionally sharing Christ by modeling biblical servanthood*.

Some believers have gone door-to-door, giving away free lightbulbs: "You'll probably have a lightbulb go out sometime, so here's one," they say. "By the way, did you know that Jesus said He is the light of the world? It is amazing to see how responsive people become as the result of a simple gift or act of servanthood.

The same testimonies can be multiplied one-hundredfold across America and the world by congregations, student ministries, denominational agencies, youth groups, and many others who have adopted Servant Evangelism as a mode of intentionally sowing and reaping the gospel seed. Whether feeding quarters into a washing machine at a Laundromat to share the gospel, washing car windshields at the mall, giving away coffee or sodas at local stores, going door-to-door with packages of microwave popcorn with the note attached "Pop in and see us sometime," or providing free gift wrapping for a local store at Christmas, Servant Evangelism provides an effective, if not essential, approach to intentionally share one's faith in today's contemporary culture. As mentioned earlier, it is "the biblical example to wrap our faith in the flesh of daily living."

Three Servant Evangelism Projects that Work . . .

Gas-buy-down. Secure a local gas station and buy-down every gallon of gas that is sold from 11 AM to 1 PM by 25 cents per gallon up to 20 gallons. If the gas is $3.00 per gallon, it would be sold for $2.75 per gallon and the church will make up the difference. Church member will pump the gas and wash windshields.

Adopt Local Public Schools. Take fresh donuts to the teacher's lounge each week. Volunteer to take up tickets for sporting events, or feed the teachers for free on in-service days.

Use Intentional Connection Cards. The connection cards can say something as simple as, "We just wanted you to know that we care." On the back is a small map to the church and any pertinent information. The cards are good for any servant evangelism activity; however, when utilized by Christians in cases like anonymously paying someone's bill in a restaurant, or being in the drive-through line at a fast food restaurant and paying for the car behind you, it is an effective way to plant seeds. This also works in Starbucks, Sonic, or any number of other opportunities.[2]

[2] Go to www.innovatechurch.us under "outreach" for more information and ideas on SE. Also go to www.servantevangelism.com for numerous ideas; or go to www.namb.net and secure the *Servanthood Evangelism Manual* by A. Reid and D. Wheeler. See also J. Falwell, *Innovate Church* (Nashville: Broadman & Holman, 2008), 139–40.

Assignment Visitation/Planned Evangelism

Servant evangelism is an exciting and effective way to mobilize believers to witness, but it is only one way. Servant evangelism can be used with other effective methods.

The early believers went "house to house" (see Acts 5:42; 20:20). This approach is biblical, and it is also effective. Kirk Hadaway discovered that 76 percent of Southern Baptist churches *that are growing* conduct weekly visitation.[3] This approach is conducted in two primary ways. First, it occurs through local churches that develop a list of prospects, systematically sending witnessing teams to see these persons. Churches that conduct ongoing evangelism training are effective with this method. Second, it occurs when individuals plan out times of witness to those they know who are without Christ.

Jesus, in a general way, assigned the church to witness, beginning in Jerusalem (see Acts 1:8). He was also more specific (see Matthew 10). The angel assigned Philip to witness to the eunuch (Acts 8:26). Ananias was "assigned" to talk to Saul (Acts 9:10). Although Philip had been in Caesarea (Acts 8:40), the Lord planned instead to send Peter to Caesarea to share Christ with Cornelius (Acts 10).

Assigning believers to witness to individuals in a planned manner is systematic in its effect. An up-to-date prospect file, easily maintained

[3] C. K. Hadaway, *Church Growth Principles* (Nashville: Broadman & Holman, 1991), 21–22.

on computer, is essential for an effective assignment-based evangelistic ministry. Such an approach helps to evaluate whether or not the gospel has been shared in a given area. The first rule of cultivating prospects is to be among unsaved people. Following are six proven ways to discover prospects.

1. *Annual church survey.* Use a FRAN card (friend, relative, associate, or neighbor).[4] Distribute these cards once a year in the worship service. Encourage members to note unchurched people whom they know.
2. *Door-to-door prospecting.* Some churches go door-to-door annually, primarily to discover prospects. Some churches actually pay college students during the summer to do this work. First Baptist Church, Jacksonville, Florida, takes their young people by busloads during the summer through the community to discover prospects.
3. *Register guests at all services.* Some churches have effective events that may not win many people to Christ, but they are an excellent way to discover prospects. Many people will attend a Christmas presentation or an Easter music special. Register *everyone,* and then note the guests.
4. *Telephone survey.* This is similar to a door-to-door survey. Some churches call every home in their church field periodically to discover prospects.
5. *Sunday school or church roll.* You can sometimes find unchurched prospects on the Sunday school or church roll, particularly by discovering relatives of those already enrolled.
6. *Newcomer or utility lists.* These lists can be purchased in most communities.

One way to conduct assignment visitation is by sending witnesses to visit specific people. While the goal of a church should be to bring believers to the point of discipleship where they are living missionally in the culture like the early church, you can still focus on specific people in your community through planned personal witnessing. Door-to-door evangelism serves as an example. Jesus sent His disciples to homes (see Matthew 10). He stipulated they were to visit the houses inhabited by Jews (Matt 10:5–6). He also warned them of the difficulties they would face. The early Christians preached Christ

[4] elmertowns.com/books/resourcePkts/FRANtastic/FrantasticDays%5BETOWNS%5D.pdf - (accessed April 23, 2009).

"in every house" (Acts 5:42 NKJV). Paul testified that he witnessed house to house (Acts 20:20).

Perhaps no evangelistic approach has been attacked more than this one. I would simply like to introduce the "experts" who say door-to-door evangelism is dead to people whom I have led to Christ "cold turkey" by using this method. Many churches have been started this way. The reason this method doesn't work for many is because they don't try it!

That being said, going door-to-door is not the only way to reach a community, nor is it necessarily the best way. Some who do practice door-to-door witnessing often do very little to build relationships or be incarnational in their community. Further, some gated communities won't allow such an approach. But too many have given up on it too quickly. It remains a biblical, effective method. Why has this method fallen on such hard times? One reason is the false assumption that people are turned off by anonymous visits.

I led a Mormon to Christ once simply because I had been more consistent going door-to-door than the Mormons in that area had. The woman was impressed by our efforts.

The older I get, the more sophisticated I want to be. Too many of us want to avoid the grunt work of ministry. But many people won't hear about Christ unless we knock on their door. Let me state this positively: *Everyone, sooner or later, thinks about God.* When they do, you want them to think of you. By consistently saturating your community, through door-to-door witnessing, servant evangelism, incarnationally living out the faith, and a variety of other ways, you can increase people's God-consciousness.

A final reason many people have overlooked this approach is that it is not the latest thing going. It is old news. We want the latest, most effective, most helpful approach that will get the gospel to people.

Sharing Christ, impacting eternity, can become a joyful experience for many. In 1989 I worked with several other people to assist a church in Oklahoma City on a door-to-door campaign. I was teamed with two women in their seventies who were lifelong members of that church. They were nervous, telling me they had never done this before. But did we have fun! The women were so encouraged by this experience that they made a commitment to do the same thing once a week from then on. Imagine, they were almost octogenarians and were lifelong church members, but they had never done that. God help us to teach people the *joy* of serving Christ through evangelism!

We never know whom we might meet behind the next door. In 1992 I was responsible for helping lead the Crossover Indianapolis effort prior to the SBC. Prior to the major door-to-door emphasis just before the convention, during the spring we had teams come from all over the country to this pioneer area to go door-to-door witnessing with our churches.

One church in Indianapolis had a team go out door-to-door. They met a lady who was open to the gospel and came to Christ. The next day the team went by to see her on a follow-up visit. She told them that the very afternoon they came to visit her, she was considering suicide. She had already made plans for her kids, she was going to purchase the gun, everything was in order—and then the group came by to lead her to Christ. "My circumstances haven't changed," she told them, "but my attitude has." This illustrates the urgency of getting out and telling people about Christ.

Here are seven ways to increase your success at door-to-door witnessing or other times of assigned visitation.

1. *Smile, smile, smile, always smile.* A pleasant face begets a pleasant response.
2. *Be polite, regardless of the response.* You cannot tell how the Holy Spirit will honor your efforts.
3. U*se an effective survey tool.* Here are some examples.

   Personal Opinion Poll
   - Are you currently active in a church? YES NO
   - What do you feel is the greatest need in this area?
   - Why do you think people go to church?
   - If you were looking for a church, what would you look for?
   - What advice would you give me or a pastor of a new church?
   - Can I share with you how Jesus Christ has changed my life?

If answer is no, say thank you. If answer is yes, share your testimony, and then ask, **"Has anything like this ever happened to you?"**

If answer is yes, say, "Great!" and ask them to tell you about their testimony.

If answer is no, or if they give an unclear testimony, say, **"God loves you." Then go into a presentation of the gospel.**

How Saddleback Began: "A PERSONAL Opinion Poll"[5] (Five Questions to Ask)

- Are you currently *active* in a local church?
- What do you feel is the greatest need in this area?
- Why do you think most people don't attend church?
- If you were looking for a church, what kind of things would you look for?
- What advice would you give me? How can I help you?

4. *Offer a gift, as in servant evangelism*—free lightbulbs, carnations at Mother's Day, a Christmas ornament, and so on.
5. *Have clearly designated areas, good maps, and instructions to avoid overlap and confusion.* The folks going out are nervous enough; so don't add to their anxiety.
6. *Train the surveyors to take good, clear information.* I wish I had a nickel for every survey form filled out in such a way that no one could use it. The surveyors should ask themselves, *if a total stranger picked this up in a month, would it help him or confuse him?*
7. *Cover an area well.* It is better to survey half of your church field well than to cover the entire area poorly.

There are significant strengths of door-to-door evangelism.

- It is biblical.
- It saturates the community.
- It requires little training and therefore allows greater involvement.
- It will win some people to Christ.
- It will uncover excellent prospects.
- It recognizes that some people are ready to receive Christ.
- It will honor God and be blessed by Him.

Many pastors have told me about door-to-door witnessing efforts that seemed to bear no fruit, but it planted a seed that eventually led to a rich harvest. God is looking for people who are anxious to tell others his good news!

---

[5] Taken from Rick Warren, "The Purpose Driven Church Conference," notes, May 15–17, 1997, at Saddleback Community Church, Lake Forest, California.

We must admit that door-to-door witnessing also has certain weaknesses.

- It allows little time to build rapport.
- Follow-up is much more difficult.
- Not every community can be reached this way.

Missional/Relational Witness

We were created to worship. Out of that context we proclaim the good news of the One we worship so that others can join that movement. Ultimately the goal of growth in Christ in this life is to become a daily, moment-by-moment Christ-follower who shares His gospel not out of compulsion or from an assignment but because it is our very nature. If every believer in a nation lived that way, many nations would be different in a few years.

Missional witness means we witness in the context of our lifestyle with people we know and have a relationship. It is more holistic—unlike knocking on a door of a stranger, being missional means there may be times when you will not talk about Christ explicitly with the other person but are always seeking to demonstrate a changed life. I have neighbors I want to see saved. I do not share Christ every time we have a conversation. In some cases they would never talk to me. I try hard to be a good neighbor and a good friend. The remarkable thing is that by doing this, most of the time the neighbor brings up spiritual matters! My goal is to see all my neighbors saved. In the meantime, I want to be their friend. But friends do not let friends go to hell.

When Paul described how the gospel came to the Thessalonians in 1 Thess 1:5, he said it came through words, power, the Holy Spirit, and assurance. But then he added, "You know how we lived among you for your sake" (NIV). The lifestyle of the apostle helped his witness. Read 1 Thessalonians 1–2 and see the missional life of Paul. Read Acts 20:17–24 and see how Paul got to know the Ephesians and shared the good news in the context of living it out before them. We must be intentional, but we must also be missional.

Missional witness means we will build relationships with others who do not know Christ to love them to Him. It means we will appreciate (though sometimes not embrace) their interests and cultural distinctives. I was part of a research team who surveyed pastors in a western state about their personal witness. We asked a couple of questions that nailed several of those surveyed. First, we asked how many meals they had shared with an unbeliever in the past year. Second, we asked how many times they had an unsaved person in their home. Pastors began to realize they had given little time to building relationships with others outside the church. The institutional church has devoted so much effort to getting people into the building that it fails to value missional living adequately. If it means reducing the number of events at the church building in order to give believers time to build relationships with neighbors, so be it.

Relational evangelism consists of ongoing witnessing encounters with people we know—family members, coworkers, and friends. Relational evangelism allows repeated opportunities to witness. Andrew shared Christ with Philip (John 1:40–41), and Philip shared with Nathaniel (John 1:45). Many people will be won to Christ only after a significant relationship is built up over a period of time.

Lifestyle/Spontaneous Evangelism

Spontaneous evangelism is sharing Christ with people whom you may never see again: a waitress in a restaurant, a passenger on an airplane, a plumber repairing your sink. Jesus often encountered people in this manner, as did Paul. Sharing Christ with waiters and waitresses, especially when the restaurant is not too crowded, can be very effective. Sometimes, after building a little rapport, I will ask the waitress, "Has anyone told you today that God loves you?" Generally, nobody has! I have been able to share Christ this way on many occasions.

I will never forget an occasion during a national witness-training seminar in southern Indiana. Three participants in the seminar were having lunch, laughing, and having a good time. Their sweet spirit made an impression on the waitress. She enjoyed serving them so much she offered them dessert on the house. One of the pastors said to her, "The reason we are having such a good time is because of Jesus." They began to share Christ. When he neared the place of offering her a chance to respond, she was called to another table. After serving them, she came back, pulled up a chair, and sat down! One member of the group began to serve tea to the other tables, and they led her to Christ!

R. A. Torrey gave two important rules to remember when witnessing in public:

1. *Obey the Holy Spirit.* If you feel led to witness, it is more likely the Holy Spirit is leading you than the world, the flesh, or the devil.
2. *Never embarrass the person to whom you are witnessing.* Don't get him in trouble with the employer, for example, when you share.

Every person saved by the power of God has a commission to invite others to join that movement, to become worshippers of the one true God. William Booth, founder of the Salvation Army, reminds us of the call to tell others of the Savior's love:

> "Not called!" did you say? "Not heard the call," I think you should say. Put your ear down to the Bible, and hear Him bid you go and pull sinners out of the fire of sin. Put your ear down to the burdened, agonized heart of humanity, and listen to its pitiful wail for help. Go stand by the gates of hell, and hear the damned entreat you to go to their father's house and bid their brothers and sisters and servants and masters not to come there. Then look Christ in the face—whose mercy you have professed to obey—and tell Him whether you will join heart and soul and body and circumstances in the march to publish His mercy to the world.[6]

Questions for Consideration

1. Have you ever attempted to witness through the means of servant evangelism?
2. Can you name at least two people with whom you have developed a relationship who do not know Christ? What are you doing to share Christ intentionally with them?
3. Have you thought about how you can be missional in reaching your neighbors or coworkers?

[6] http://www.tentmaker.org/Quotes/evangelismquotes.htm (accessed October 27, 2008).

Chapter 18

Church Evangelism

My goal is to help the people of God fulfill the mission of God.[1]

—Pastor David Platt

Both an institution and a movement, the local church has been and will continue to be God's primary plan of ministry until Jesus comes. She is an institution, one of three God gave us (home, church, state), and as such she can keep the people of God focused on truth and purposeful in mission. As a movement she can be the chief agent for the gospel's spread and cultural change in a given area. The body of Christ, the people of God, the fellowship of the saints, the local church at her best provides a place of instruction, corporate worship, encouragement, and serves as light and salt in the culture. At her worst, a local church given over to institutionalism, legalism, or license, can actually be the chief enemy of the gospel in a community. We have tended to make discipleship increasingly simplistic while making church life more bureaucratic and complex. Neil Cole of Church Multiplication Associates recognizes the need to reverse

[1] From a personal conversation with the author.

this trend: "We want to lower the bar of how church is done and raise the bar of what it means to be a disciple."[2]

We must teach people that the primary place of ministry for the church of the Lord Jesus Christ is outside the church building. The most evangelized, the most reached area in your community is the building in which your church meets on Sunday. There's only one problem: this is also the place where the fewest number of lost people are likely to be.

Church growth has become a popular topic in Evangelicalism in recent years. This is not a bad thing; however, I fear that sometimes we so focus on church growth, in particular techniques and methods, that we forget that God Himself is the one who grows the church. We will not succeed in reaching unbelievers if we fail to BE the church God intended us to be. The church is more than an outreach center, yet if the church seeks not to reach people, she can hardly be called a church.

This chapter will focus specifically on evangelistic growth—true church growth in the biblical sense. The church in Jerusalem added 3,000 people in one day at Pentecost; then converts were added daily. Soon the number of men stood above 5,000; then priests came to the faith, and eventually the numbers were so great that Luke couldn't report them.

Some people complain about an emphasis on numerical growth in the church. I like to remind them that one book of the Bible is called Numbers! Seriously, one can be too zealous for numbers, but those who criticize an emphasis on numbers usually do so because their numbers are few. I agree that one cannot measure church growth by numbers alone. Let's assume that a church in a rapidly growing area is growing at the same rate as a church in a declining population area. Is it as effective as the second church? What about retaining members? Is a growing church effective if it baptizes 100 people annually but grows in attendance by only a dozen per year?

The Western Church in the 21st Century

Each semester I ask my students a very telling question. First, I ask them to raise their hand if they were actively involved in a local church through their childhood. Almost 90 percent indicate they

[2] N. Cole, *The Organic Church: Growing Faith Where Life Happens* (San Francisco: Josey-Bass, 2005), 50.

were. Then, I ask how many want to go back to serve a church just like the one in which they were raised. Out of over a thousand students surveyed in recent years, only three raised their hand. What do I make of that? These students overwhelmingly wish to serve God in churches of their tradition, but they realize something is not right about the DNA in most churches they know. They recognize that if we are to become effective once again in reaching our communities, things must change.

What Is A Church?

Evangelism is essential to the church because the church will cease to exist without evangelism. Further, God's plan to reach the world is through local congregations. The New Testament word for "church" is *ekklēsia.* In the Greek world, it usually described an assembly of people. This word occurs 115 times in the New Testament. It refers to a local congregation 95 times; the other references are to the general church.

The church is a congregation of baptized believers who join together to honor God and to fulfill his mission in the world. In a larger sense, the church includes all believers of all time. Implications for the doctrine of ecclesiology on evangelism are many. Some emphases today hinder evangelism because they grow out of a faulty view of the church.

God's Plan to Reach the World

First, some people have forgotten that the local church is God's plan to reach the world. I have a great love for parachurch organizations. I led the first person to Christ in my own personal evangelism through the *Four Spiritual Laws* booklet produced by Campus Crusade for Christ. I was discipled in college with materials produced by the Navigators. I have participated in rallies with such organizations as Young Life and Promise Keepers. Such groups have played a wonderful and significant role in the furtherance of the gospel. But the base for reaching the world, according to the New Testament, is the local church.

The apostle Paul planted churches wherever he went. His letters are to churches or leaders of churches to give guidance to those leading local churches. Mark Driscoll noted how three areas must be balanced to be an effective church, and what happens when a balance is not there:[3]

1. *Church + Culture – Gospel = Liberalism.* These are churches that have forgotten the unchanging gospel, focusing on today, leading to compromise.
2. *Church + Gospel – Culture = Fundamentalism.* These are churches that isolate themselves from culture. The unintended consequence of their desire to protect the gospel is that they separate themselves from the very people they are called to reach.
3. *Gospel + Culture - Church = Parachurch.* Some today love lost people and love the gospel but have given up on the church. Some even go so far as to argue the church is no longer needed. Such a naïve and unbiblical view must be rejected. The local church has been and will continue to be God's chosen way to grow believers and reach the unchurched. Parachurch ministries exist because local churches have failed to be what God called them to be.

Second, some people see the church as irrelevant. Many today are down on the church, and it is true that some churches are irrelevant. I have seen some whose favorite hymns must be "I Shall Not Be Moved" because they won't do anything for God! But the church is God's idea, and we dare not run ahead of Him! When a local church is the church as God intended—not perfect, but functioning as the body of Christ—nothing is more powerful for reaching a community for Christ. Even as I am finishing this chapter, I am on a plane returning from a strong, vibrant, evangelistic church. There is nothing on earth that can substitute for it! What an awesome tool it is in the hand of God!

Jesus is the head of the church. The pastor is not; the deacons are not; the charter members are not. The church is the visible manifestation of the kingdom of God in this age. A person cannot love Jesus and despise His church.

Third, some people today are victims of the "edifice complex." This is institutionalism at its worst. They see the church as a building—not people. The church is *not* at Fourth and Vine or on Main Street. The *building* is there. On Sunday morning, the church is

[3] M. Driscoll, *Confessions of a Reformission Rev* (Grand Rapids: Zondervan, 2006), 15–16.

gathered in that geographical location where the church facilities are. On Monday, the same church is *scattered*—on the job, at the store, at school, in the neighborhood. We must recapture this biblical ideal. It is hypocritical to sing praises to God with all our hearts on Sunday as the church gathered and say nothing about His goodness throughout the week as the church scattered. If the body of Christ acted throughout the week as we do in Sunday worship, what a difference it would make!

Fourth, some people make a sharp clergy-laity distinction that is not scriptural. Yes, God has set apart ministers to lead churches, but they are to *lead* the work—not *do* all the work. Ministers are to equip the saints to do the work of the ministry (see Eph 4:11–12). If anything, we would be more accurate to say every believer is clergy! Now, ministers are also saints, so we are to do the work also. Many ministers never share Christ with others. We must lead by example. I share my faith because I am a Christian; I preach and teach because I am a minister.

We don't go to church, we are the church. We go to corporate worship, but the church is a people, not a place.

Fifth, there is sometimes an unhealthy and unbiblical emphasis on fellowship. This is particularly true in rural churches in the South where the most significant time in the church year is homecoming with dinner on the grounds! My aunt, a member of a rural Alabama Baptist church, once quipped that Baptists won't get to heaven without a paper plate in their hands! The New Testament does speak of fellowship meals, but these meals were held around the observance of the Lord's Supper—not in honor of Granny Smith's banana pudding.

Fellowship, as in biblical *koinōnia,* is crucial. But fellowship is not built on food or by avoiding conflict, as in the sentiment, "Let's not hurt anybody's feelings." How do you build a great team? I grew up in Alabama, where Bear Bryant's football coaching was legendary. Alabama's teams never seemed to have the number of all-Americans that Notre Dame or Southern Cal did. Bryant's genius was in convincing good players to play like all-Americans. He could build a team with a clear focus. Their focus was on winning, and they were single-minded.

Fellowship misunderstood undergirds an institutionalism that hinders the work of the gospel. Focus becomes centralized toward matters of church business over gospel witness. Joel Rainey described the conventional church's problem with excessive institutionalism in a congregational polity:

> Though I continue to have a great appreciation for the church where I grew up, I noticed that little to nothing could be substantially accomplished in this church without numerous committee meetings, motions, amendments, and secret ballots. I remember wondering how many more might be won to Christ if business was simply turned over to trusted leaders and missions became the primary concern of all of those who showed up to cast their votes.[4]

Do you want to build fellowship in your church? Then get a single-minded focus in the church—a focus on reaching people for Christ. The early church shared Christ in one accord at Pentecost. When they faced persecution, they united in prayer for boldness to speak the Word of God (see Acts 4:29–31).

In his unique way, Driscoll describes his introduction to a bizarre collection of "churches" as a young believer in Seattle. It struck him that all the places he visited claimed to be churches but had very different missions:

Example One (Gay Agenda "Church")

"One church [was] particularly confusing. They promoted homosexuality but made me take off my ball cap upon entering the church. It seemed odd that a male greeter who had likely had sex with a man before church chastised me for wearing a hat in church because I was disrespecting God."[5]

Example Two (Social Activist "Church")

"Down the street, another woman pastor and her gay male associate pastor with the lovely rainbow on his eloquently sassy robe both spoke passionately about the need to get rid of our nuclear weapons. Their message did not connect with me."[6]

Example Three (Prosperity Gospel Church)

"From the printed material and the sermon, it was readily apparent that this church was into the bling-Christ, who will make you rich and

[4] J. Rainey, *Planting Churches in the Real World* (Missional Press, 2008), 41.

[5] Driscoll, *Confessions , 48.*

[6] Ibid., 49.

cure all your diseases, except for epidemics of consumerism and '80s charismullet hair, of course. They even taught that Jesus was a rich man and that only people who lack faith get sick, presumably like the junior varsity Job and Paul."[7]

Example Four (Legalistic Church)

"One fundamentalist church I visited was doing a series on Revelation, and the pastor's face was so red that I thought he was going to blow a gasket. He yelled about the end of the world at the battle of Armageddon, which was going to happen in ten or fifteen minutes, from what I could surmise. . . . His mission seemed to be simply to get off the planet as soon as possible, which didn't sound very incarnational to me."[8]

His conclusion from visiting these and many other examples: "No matter what the tradition or theological perspective, the one common thread that wove all the churches together was that they were each on their own mission instead of on Jesus' mission to transform people and cultures by the power of the Holy Spirit through the work of the gospel."[9]

> *"How sad that we've settled for a growing campus instead of striving for a transformed community."**
> Bob Roberts
>
> *B. Roberts, *The Multiplying Church* (Grand Rapids: Zondervan, 2008), 109.

Approaches to Growing Churches

Suffice it to say that under normal circumstances a church ought to grow. Rick Warren has it right when he says the critical issue is not church *growth* but church *health*.[10] A healthy, Christ-honoring church is more likely to grow than a divided or spiritually dead congregation. A brief summary of more recent attempts to help churches become effective for the gospel follows.

---

7 Ibid.

8 Ibid.

9 Ibid.

10 http://legacy.pastors.com/RWMT/article.asp?ID=200&ArtID=1726 (accessed April 23, 2009).

TYPES OF EVANGELISM ACCORDING TO THE CGM [1]

E-0 evangelism: Evangelizing unsaved persons within the congregation.

E-1 evangelism: Evangelism that crosses barriers related to the church building or the perception of the church in the mind-set of the unsaved.

E-2 evangelism: Evangelism that crosses ethnic, cultural, and class barriers.

E-3 evangelism: Evangelism that crosses linguistic barriers.

[1] See E. Towns, ed., *Evangelism and Church Growth* (Ventura: Regal Books, 1995), 206.

The Church Growth Movement

We can't discuss growing churches without considering the impact of the Church Growth Movement over the past generation. Churches have been growing since the first century. But the Church Growth *Movement* refers to the specific phenomenon arising out of the influence of Donald McGavran and continuing through the ministry of such men as Peter Wagner, Win Arn, Elmer Towns, and many others. It became an influential force in the evangelical world for a generation, although in recent years it has lost much steam as other movements have arisen.

Church growth began in the book of Acts, but the Church Growth Movement began in 1955 with the publication of Donald McGavran's *The Bridges of God.*[11] This movement began overseas and was imported to the United States. McGavran (1897–1991) is the founder of the movement. His parents and grandparents were missionaries. He was ordained by the Disciples of Christ in 1923 and received his PhD from Columbia University in 1936. He served as a missionary in India. McGavran asked, "Why do some churches grow while others don't?" His book was published to address this and other important questions. C. Peter Wagner (b. 1930) served as a foreign missionary in Bolivia, South America, for 16 years. In 1971 he began teaching at Fuller Seminary. He has written numerous books and articles: *Church*

[11] D. A. McGavran, *The Bridges of God* (New York: Friendship Press, 1955).

Growth and the Whole Gospel, Leading Your Church to Growth, and others.[12]

Other leaders of church growth and church growth advocates include Ralph Winter, Arthur Glasser, Charles Kraft, Win Arn, John Wimber, Kert Hunter, George Hunter, Elmer Towns, John Vaughn, Rick Warren, C. Kirk Hadaway, Thom Rainer, and Gary McIntosh.

Thom Rainer has become increasingly significant as a leader, particularly among Southern Baptists, but among evangelicals as well. Rainer has been particularly influential in balancing all the interest in innovative approaches with more conventional churches that also grow churches. Further, Rainer has reminded church growth leaders that we should measure growth by evangelistic impact above anything else.

The Church Growth Movement has offered many helpful contributions to evangelistic church growth. For example, this movement has noted there are different levels of evangelism.

Wagner summarized the Church Growth Movement in six presuppositions:[13]

1. Nongrowth displeases God.
2. Numerical growth of a church is a priority with God and focuses on new disciples rather than decisions.
3. Disciples are tangible, identifiable, countable people who increase the church numerically.
4. Limited time, money, and resources demand that the church develop a strategy based on results.
5. Social and behavioral sciences are valuable tools in measuring and encouraging church growth.
6. Research is essential for maximum growth.

The findings of the Church Growth Movement have been helpful in assisting churches to grow. Some of the findings or emphases have proven controversial. For example, its emphasis on pragmatism (emphasizing results to an extreme) may lead to lack of attention to biblical truth.

Few aspects of the Church Growth Movement provoke more controversy than the homogeneous unit principle. The principle states that people typically come to Christ "without crossing racial, linguistic, or

[12] C. P. Wagner, *Church Growth and the Whole Gospel* (New York: Harper and Row, 1981); *Leading Your Church to Growth* (Regal Books, 1984).

[13] Ibid., 78.

class barriers."[14] Wagner says, "The rationale upon which a homogenous unit is determined is a group which can 'feel at home.'"[15]

The problem with the homogeneous unit principle is in its application. Used as a description, it can be helpful. We will reach people who are most like us. One need not be a rocket scientist to see this. But this is far different from being *prescriptive,* or saying we should *only* reach people like us.

Models for Evangelistic Church Growth

One of the significant shifts in church growth at the dawn of a new century is the movement from specialists who analyze trends as the leaders of church growth to effective pastors who model such growth. This is true in denominational leadership as well. The old paradigm emphasized the development of new tools, methods, and strategies coming from denominational leaders and think tanks. In the future, effective tools and strategies for church growth will be birthed on the field. Denominational leaders will shift to the position of discovering and announcing proven methods in churches rather than discovering or creating them. Growing churches, not professors or specialists, will set the pace for effective church growth.

Purpose-Driven Church

An example of a model church approach is the Purpose-Driven Church model of Rick Warren, lived out in the Saddleback Community Church in southern California. Saddleback represents Christianity as a movement in a specific location. Warren's strategy focuses on moving from secondary issues, such as programs, finances, buildings, events, or seekers, to the primary issue: a biblical, purpose-driven focus. "Absolutely nothing will revitalize a discouraged church faster than rediscovering its purpose,"[16] he contends. He cites a familiar survey in which church members were asked, "Why does the church exist?" Some 89 percent responded: "The church's purpose is to take care of my needs and my family's needs." Only 11 percent said winning the world to Christ is the church's purpose. Ninety percent of pastors who were asked the same question said the church exists to

[14] D. McGavran, *Understanding Church Growth* (Grand Rapids: Eerdmans, 1980), 223.

[15] C. P. Wagner, *Our Kind of People* (Atlanta: John Knox Press, 1979), 75.

[16] R. Warren, *The Purpose-Driven Church* (Grand Rapids: Zondervan, 1995), 82.

win the world to Christ, and 10 percent said it exists to care for members.[17]

The slogan for Saddleback comes directly from the New Testament: "A Great Commitment to the Great Commandment [Matt 22:37–39] as the Great Commission [Matt 28:19–20] will grow a Great Church."[18] Five key words are used to summarize the five purposes of the church in the Purpose-Driven Church model:

1. *Worship.* "Love the Lord your God with all your heart" (*magnification*).
2. *Ministry.* "Love your neighbor as yourself" (*ministry*).
3. *Evangelism.* "Go and make disciples" (*mission*).
4. *Fellowship.* "Baptize them" (*membership*).
5. *Discipleship.* "Teach them to obey" (*maturity*).

Warren also describes the fivefold purpose of the church with the words *edify, encourage, exalt, equip*, and *evangelize*. Certain principles are timeless and unchanging! Saddleback is not a church with a nice purpose statement that is never displayed in the life of the church. The entire organizational structure is built around the five purposes.

The goal of the church, using the analogy of a baseball diamond diagram, is not to get them on first base but to get them around the bases into active ministry and evangelism. Warren argues that *everything* in the church should be done on purpose: assimilating new members, programming, education, small groups, staffing, structuring, preaching, budgeting, calendaring, and evaluating progress. Some have criticized Warren's approach for its simplicity and its focus on seekers. Others have foolishly tried to clone his model in other settings with poor results. Effective leaders know how to learn from other leaders like Warren and to adapt. When I eat a watermelon, I know how to chew up the fruit and spit out the seeds.

Other examples could be given of pastors of large churches who have set forth principles for growth and who host conferences on effectiveness, including Bill Hybels at Willow Creek in Chicago, Ed Young of Fellowship Church near Dallas, Andy Stanley of Northpointe Church in Atlanta, all of which are young churches led by their founding pastors. Established churches such as First Baptist,

[17] Ibid.

[18] Ibid., 102.

Woodstock, Georgia, and First Baptist, Jacksonville, Florida, also merit study for their growth.

Emerging Church

More recently the "emerging" or "emergent" church movement has given much attention to effective ministry in a postmodern culture. Because this movement is still "emerging" it is hard to consider in a brief amount of space. However, at least two clear groups have evolved since its beginning. The "emergent" side has tended to be less likely to uphold the unchanging truth as has the conventional church. It has also been excessively critical of the modern church. Brian McLaren and Doug Pagitt would be recognized leaders in the "emergent" side of the movement.

The "emerging" side of the movement includes those who compare more theologically with evangelicals, preach the gospel, and have been effective in reaching very unchurched people. Many would be more open on social issues such as alcohol while affirming traditionally conservative views such as complementarianism regarding gender roles. An example of the latter would be Mark Driscoll and the Mars Hill Church in Seattle. More detailed taxonomies of this new movement include Scott McKnight's five "streams" and Ed Stetzer's three broad categories: relevants, reconstructionists, and revisionists.[19]

Stetzer's simple taxonomy of the emerging church movement evaluates its approach to contextualization.[20] He cites three groups:

Relevants. "There are a good number of young (and not so young) leaders who some classify as 'emerging' that really are just trying to make their worship, music and outreach more contextual to emerging culture. Ironically, while some may consider them liberal, they are often deeply committed to biblical preaching, male pastoral leadership and other values common in conservative evangelical churches. They are simply trying to explain the message of Christ in a way their generation can understand."

Reconstructionists. "The reconstructionists think that the current form of church is frequently irrelevant and the structure is unhelpful.

[19] For more detailed analyses see M. Liederbach and A. L. Reid, *The Convergent Church: Missional Worship in an Emerging Culture* (Grand Rapids: Kregel, 2009); S. McKnight, "Five Streams of the Emerging Church," http://www.christianitytoday.com/ct/2007/february/11.35.html (accessed October 27, 2008); E. Stetzer, "First Person: Understanding the Emerging Church," *Baptist Press,* January 6, 2006.

[20] Taken from http://www.sbcbaptistpress.org/bpnews.asp?ID=22406 (accessed October 9, 2008).

Yet, they typically hold to a more orthodox view of the gospel and Scripture. Therefore, we see an increase in models of church that reject certain organizational models, embracing what are often called 'incarnational' or 'house' models. They are responding to the fact that after decades of trying fresh ideas in innovative churches, North America is less churched, and those who are churched are less committed."

Revisionists. "Revisionists are questioning (and in some cases denying) issues like the nature of the substitutionary atonement, the reality of hell, the complementarian nature of gender, and the nature of the gospel itself. This is not new—some mainline theologians quietly abandoned these doctrines a generation ago. The revisionist emerging church leaders should be treated, appreciated and read as we read mainline theologians—they often have good descriptions, but their prescriptions fail to take into account the full teaching of the Word of God."

Suffice it to say that the emerging/emergent movement even in its varying forms has already become a significant force in the Western church and brings with it the need both to affirm the contributions it brings and jettison the error it encourages. One would be unwise to generalize this movement as a newer form of liberalism on the one hand, although some adherents would fit that characterization, or the only way to be effective in our time on the other.

Revitalizing a Stagnant Church

Because church life in the West has been recognized as being in trouble particularly in terms of evangelistic effectiveness, one of the greatest needs for our time is for leaders to move churches toward effectiveness from stagnation. A recent study of over 300 churches from a variety of denominations that had moved from decline to revitalization offers encouraging help for church leaders who long to see their churches grow again. These churches declined for at least five years followed by two to five years of evangelistic growth. Published as a book entitled *Comeback Churches* by Ed Stetzer and Mike Dodson, the findings can encourage any leader that hope exists for any church. I would add, however, that two indispensable ingredients exist for any stagnant church to begin growing: you must *want* to grow (most say they do), and you must be willing *to pay the price* to grow (sadly, many do not). In *Comeback Churches* Stetzer and

Dodson discovered 10 areas of change that most affected the churches to become effective again:[21]

1. Prayer
2. Children's Ministry
3. Evangelism
4. Youth ministry
5. Leadership
6. Missions
7. Assimilation
8. Worship
9. Sunday school/small groups
10. Organizational structure

Look at the list carefully. Most of these you would expect, although at this point I would remind you that we often need ruthless attention to familiar truth. It is one thing to say "of course a church should pray" and another to become a praying church. As a young pastor I watched a church move from a decade of decline to remarkable growth and would agree that deep, earnest, consistent prayer was most vital. And, the vast majority noted that a shift in worship style to celebrative and more contemporary helped. But look closer. Two factors that most leaders I meet completely overlook are children and youth. It is no surprise that I have a chapter in this book dedicated to each of these. Yet this is so often overlooked. I would submit that a healthy and biblical focus on reaching children and their families and youth holds the key to renewed growth in most churches.

Beyond these essentials for helping a church toward revitalization, a few other practical features can help.

Know Your Church Field

To help your church become more effective in its witness will take nothing less than a movement of the Holy Spirit bathed in prayer. But it will also take some common sense. We are to be spiritual and shrewd. I have met earnest, passionate ministers who simply could not translate their zeal into effective ministry. Knowing your church field and the people who live there can help you to lead your church

[21] E. Stetzer and M. Dodson, *Comeback Churches* (Nashville: Broadman and Holman, 2007), 192–97.

effectively. Discover all you can about your area. In our day, finding this information on the Internet is quite easy.

You should be aware of basic *demographic* information: population, economic status, social characteristics (how many singles? How many families with youth?). *Psychographic* research can show you the basic attitudes and lifestyles of residents. *Ethnographic* studies help you know the ethnic makeup of your community. These and others can help. Of course there is no substitute for you living among the people you seek to reach and personal observation. We are often better at complaining about lost people than at getting to know them to share the gospel. The Internet offers tools and Web sites to help churches become more aware of the community around them.

Change the Culture

If most churches are not growing, how do we get them to grow again? Books have been written on this subject. Suffice it to say that the most critical element is the presence of God in the midst of a renewing church. Jesus said, "*I* will build *My* church" (Matt 16:18). Stagnant churches must redirect their purpose. Critical to this is leadership, which is addressed in another chapter. Here are a couple of ways to help revitalize a church. One has to do with getting your people away from the church field to another place immersed in missionary work. The other has to do with getting people out of the church building into small groups in your church field.

Note that for a church to change it will take a change not in programs or other cosmetic work; it will take a change in culture, in the DNA of the church. That takes time. A local church is not a jet ski; it is an aircraft carrier! The wise pastor will take much time and give much space to lead a church to move from a monument to a missional movement. The reason I wrote this book is to help churches with this very process. He will also tie as much of the future to the best of the church's past. Change should come without unnecessarily alienating people. However, there will be hills on which to die, and the pastor must have the conviction to stand boldly and lovingly when necessary. My colleague George Robinson is the most effective person I know at leading effective short-term mission trips to "strike the match" of evangelistic passion.

Utilize Short-Term Mission Trips (see sidebar next page)

Striking the Match of Strategic Short-Term Evangelistic Missions[1]

George Robinson

Much harsh criticism has been dealt toward short-term missions (STM) recently, some justified and some not. Field missionaries have grown frustrated with "tour groups" coming in and snapping a few photos, doing a little work, and reinforcing the stereotype of the "ugly American." Stan Guthrie noted in his book *Missions in the Third Millennium*, "The long-term people at first ignored this trend. Then they dismissed it. Now they are trying to work with it. Some are even trying to learn from it."[2] The missiological struggle with this imminent paradigm shift has only intensified as the estimated number of participants has risen into the millions annually.[3] It seems that the move to incorporating STM into long-term missions strategy is just beginning to be taken seriously. After more than a decade of working with and researching STM, I have become convinced that when used properly, these volunteers can serve as a catalytic force that ignites evangelistic fervor and makes a lasting impact through the establishment of reproducing churches.[4]

Starting a Wildfire

A metaphor for church multiplication is a *wildfire*—something that has a small beginning but soon rages and spreads to affect everything around it. So the goal of any missionary, short or long term, should be to start a spiritual wildfire. But most of the time wildfires do not just happen. There must be a source. One way to start a fire is with a match. A match, like a STM team, has a limited time with which to accomplish its purpose before it burns out. Most matches will burn for about 5–10 seconds, and if it fails to ignite a fire on some other

---

[1] This article is based on G. Robinson, *Striking the Match: How God Is Using Ordinary People to Change the World through Strategic Short-Term Missions* (e3 Resources, 2008). Available at www.e3resources.org or www.amazon.com.

[2] S. Guthrie, *Missions in the Third Millennium: 21 Key Trends for the 21st Century* (Waynesboro, GA: Paternoster Press, 2000), 105ff.

[3] R. Peterson, G. Aeshliman, and R. W. Sneed, *Maximum Impact Short-Term Mission* (Minneapolis: STEM Press, 2003), 253.

[4] In the mid-90s George Robinson went on his first STM with a ministry that is now known as e3 Partners. e3 Partners uses short-term mission teams as a catalytic part of an indigenous-based, long-term church planting strategy. Since that time Robinson served as a field-based missionary in South Asia, hosting STM teams and utilizing them to evangelize an unreached people, and eventually joined e3 Partners serving there for six years as South Asia Strategy Coordinator and Church Planting Training Director.

object that can serve as fuel, it is no longer useful. It is crucial that STM teams be equipped for and motivated toward appropriate cross-cultural evangelistic encounters. By taking the time to train the team members to share their personal testimony and a simple biblical gospel presentation, you are in effect performing quality control on your matches.

The Kindling

Occasionally if you take a match and throw it onto the ground it might start a fire, but that is not the best way to ignite a wildfire. The best way is to make the conditions right for burning by preparing a small, strategically organized gathering of kindling. For the sake of the metaphor we will say that the kindling is made up of national leaders in whatever location one works. There is a precise way of organizing that kindling to maximize the potential for starting a raging fire. STM organizers need to prioritize the equipping of indigenous national leadership by going to the target area in advance of the volunteer team in order to establish a mutually agreed upon long-term strategy. It may be that the nationals you plan to work with may not yet have an understanding of how to strategically use the STM team. By equipping those leaders in the biblical principles of evangelism that leads to the establishment of new churches, the trip organizer is in effect arranging the kindling and making the conditions right for a spiritual wildfire.[5] There is nothing more frustrating than trying to start a fire with either wet matches or wood. Therefore, it is imperative to make sure that all who will be involved in the STM trip are prepared in advance.

Ignition

When both sides in this potential partnership have been prepared through equipping, then it is time to strike the match by introducing the STM team to the prepared kindling of indigenous national leadership. The volunteer team must go into the journey with the understanding that their role is a temporal one and that their goal is to partner with the nationals in such a way as to empower them, so that by the time the journey comes to an end, the nationals are ablaze with vision, training, and encouragement. The purpose of the strategic STM should

[5] The book of Acts is replete with examples of how the apostle Paul modeled and reproduced these values. Along with e3 Partners I helped to develop a free resource called *First Steps: Mobilizing Your Church to Multiply.* This manual can be used to equip your STM teams and national leadership alike. See www.e3partners.org.

be partnering to share the simple transcultural message of the gospel in such a way that disciples are made and brought into new home groups that are located in the target area. The most effective tool that I am aware of to facilitate this is the *Evangecube*.[6] This tool uses unfolding pictures that demonstrate the problem of sin, God's solution in Christ Jesus, and the need to surrender through repentance and faith. It also includes a pictorial guide to basic discipleship and church planting principles. By equipping both the volunteer team and the nationals hosting them with a simple tool like the *Evangecube*, STM trips can become catalytic events that ignite something that lasts long beyond the presence of the team.

Fanning the Flame

Following the catalytic event of striking the match during the STM trip, it is crucial to add fuel to the fire by establishing interdependent partnerships with the indigenous leadership through helping them to develop and achieve ever-expanding church reproduction strategies. Individual STM ventures can result in localized fires. National-led strategies can potentially spread that blaze throughout the region. I have personally witnessed these spiritual fires spread across cultural barriers and even into other surrounding countries as nationals send teams out from their newly established churches to repeat the process—without the help of North Americans altogether.

Conclusion

What God started with a match that has long-since been consumed, He can turn into a wildfire that spreads a passion for His glory through evangelism that leads to church multiplication. As you pray about how to be involved in the fulfillment of the Great Commission, it is my prayer that you will become a fire-starter and that God will use you and all your influence to set the nations ablaze with the gospel of Jesus Christ.

[6] Available at www.e3resources.org.

Small Groups

Small groups provide the intimacy people need to connect and to grow. From traditional Sunday school to the growth recently of small groups in homes, small groups can be a vehicle to help move a church to a missions focus. Small groups can be an entry point for the unchurched who may not be comfortable walking into our worship services. They provide a means for missional believers to engage with lost friends in a more personal manner.

Sunday School

In the conventional church the Sunday school has been central to small group discipleship. It can continue to be an effective part of both discipleship and evangelism. I believe in the Sunday school. I thank God that when I was in seminary, I learned about Sunday school principles and the Growth Spiral.[22] I learned about the importance of Sunday school enrollment, tracking enrollment, and starting new classes. One of the stats I heard was that if you start a new Sunday school class and focus on outreach, within a year it will enroll an average of 26 new people. When I tracked that in two churches as a pastor and as a minister of education, we averaged exactly 26 people for every adult class we started! These two churches, both of which grew dramatically, one doubling in a year, grew organizationally through the Sunday school.

We took the Growth Spiral concept, which focuses on such issues as Sunday school enrollment, outreach, and new units, and adapted it to our church by scaling it down and simplifying it. Our people had no clue about Sunday school enrollment. They thought that if you didn't attend three weeks in a row, you ought to be dropped from the roll. It was a major struggle to get them to see you should keep people on the roll!

Sunday school is about reaching people as well as teaching. In the churches where I have served, we had to reorient our people to the true purpose of Sunday school. Most people think that Sunday school exists to teach the Bible. When the Sunday school movement began in Southern Baptist life, the Sunday school had a threefold purpose: (1) to teach the Bible, (2) to reach people with the gospel, and (3) to minister to the body of Christ. We had worker meetings, and we elevated evangelism through the Sunday school. We even drew up a

[22] See A. Anderson, *The Growth Spiral* (Nashville: Broadman Press, 1993).

covenant and had our Sunday school teachers sign it. It included a commitment to make weekly contacts and to set the pace for others. The teachers did not have to come to visitation every week, but they committed themselves to make contacts. In the past, as many as 80 percent of converts came through the Sunday school. This is changing because the front door, the worship service, is becoming a more significant factor in reaching unreached people.[23]

How do we get Sunday school teachers involved in outreach? Weekly worker meetings are essential. The next step is to secure a layperson who is teachable to be Sunday school director. A teachable spirit is absolutely critical. I enlisted a director like this and took him and two or three other leaders to a Sunday school conference. They got such a vision for Sunday school outreach that I had to calm them down a bit! I didn't want them to run ahead too fast because they would get beat up by the other laypeople. Gradually, over a year's time, we began to implement some of those changes. If your Sunday school is not evangelistic, it may take a year or two to change it. Find those teachers who are open to outreach and work with them. Encourage everybody. As you change, love everyone, but move with the movers.

You must also close the back door in Sunday school. Having observed numerous churches with strong Sunday schools, I'm convinced this is crucial. We had excellent retention of new Christians in the last churches I served, and it was because we were a Sunday school-based church.

Off-Campus Small Groups

Thom Rainer discovered the important role of small groups in reaching the unchurched, as many church leaders described small groups as "indispensible in reaching the unchurched."[24] Small groups can be formed around common interests to build a bridge to share Christ. These "affinity groups" can help to attract those with a common interest and develop community among the members, whether believers or not. In his excellent resource *Seeker Small Groups,* author Gary Poole encourages the concept of the "open chair" in groups, or the idea that there is always a seat to be filled. Poole argues that filling

---

[23] See J. E. White, *Opening the Front Door* (Nashville: Convention Press, 1992).

[24] T. Rainer, *Surprising Insights from the Unchurched* (Grand Rapids: Zondervan, 2001), 168.

the open chair is one of the most effective ways to keep a small group focused outward toward those who need Christ.[25]

Small groups are effective for several reasons, including: (1) they can be used by any sized church and require few resources; (2) they can work alongside existing Sunday school structure to further evangelism; (3) the most evangelistic small groups keep the Bible at the forefront of their focus; (4) small groups meeting in homes are more effective in reaching the lost than groups meeting on the church campus.[26]

The Key to Evangelistic Effectiveness: Contextualization

We have the greatest message, the most wonderful news in history. Yet we often fail to communicate the news in a way that those outside our church walls can understand. Duane Elmer illustrates the need to contextualize the gospel in a given culture with a story:

> A typhoon had temporarily stranded a monkey on an island. In a secure, protected place, while waiting for the raging waters to recede, he spotted a fish swimming against the current. It seemed obvious to the monkey that the fish was struggling and in need of assistance. Being of kind heart, the monkey resolved to help the fish. A tree precariously dangled over the very spot where the fish seemed to be struggling. At considerable risk to himself, the monkey moved far out on a limb, reached down and snatched the fish from the threatening waters. Immediately scurrying back to the safety of his shelter, he carefully laid the fish on the ground. For a few moments the fish showed excitement, but soon settled into a peaceful rest. Joy and satisfaction swelled inside the monkey. He had successfully helped another creature.[27]

We must have a passion for the lost and a concern for their souls. But we also need a little sense about how to go about our task. Missionaries in foreign lands have long understood the need to contextualize

[25] G. Poole, *Seeker Small Groups* (Grand Rapids: Zondervan, 2003), 240.

[26] Adapted from W. Moore, "Small Group Evangelism" (DMin project, Southeastern Baptist Theological Seminary, 2008), 219. See also M. Rice, "Equipping Leaders to Reach the Unchurched Through Small Groups Using Gary Poole's *Seeker Small Groups* (DMin project, Southeastern Baptist Theological Seminary, 2005).

[27] D. Elmer, *Cross-Cultural Connections* (Downers Grove: InterVarsity Press), 14.

the gospel in a given culture. Now, the church in the West must do so more than ever at a time when even many believers want to distance themselves from the perspective so many have of Christianity. I have found it interesting to scan the Facebook profiles of many of my younger Christian friends at the line for "Religious Views." My younger friends who are overwhelmingly believers rarely put "Christian" or "Baptist;" they are far more likely to put things like "God hates religion," "I have a relationship not a religion," or "religion is for people who do not have a cause." These young believers instinctively want to distance themselves among their friends from anything that smacks of "organized religion."

Many churches are not wired to contextualize the gospel. I heard Steve Sjogren, pastor and missional thinker, give a summary of how the church today relates to culture. I think his tripartite view helps us to analyze where churches are today.[28] First, some churches *evade* the culture. The Bible certainly exhorts believers to be separate from the world (1 Pet 2:9–10). Some more liberal churches illustrate what happens when biblical separation is ignored, leading to a denial of truth in the name of relevance. Whether it is homosexuality or other issues, their desire to engage culture leads to an attempt to remove "outdated" biblical customs, but too often this moves beyond customs to theology. The result is a church that looks just like the world but has lost any power to change it. More conservative churches should look in the mirror as well, for our emphasis on consumerism, prosperity, and the "abundant Christian life" is too often a cover for buying into the world's system of materialism and self-gratification. This can lead churches that claim to believe the Word to ignore biblical ideals of sacrifice and the cost of discipleship.

Separation from worldliness does not contradict our Lord's command to impact culture with the gospel. Some churches just don't want to have anything to do with the world, including people for whom Jesus died. Churches that seek to evade the culture basically do it out of one or two reasons; some evade the culture out of fear—fear that worldliness will creep into the church, fear our children will not grow up following Christ, and so on. The circle-the-wagons form of the faith rarely leads to effective ministry.

The other group who seek to evade the world quite honestly just don't care about the world. They tend to focus on "important" issues

---

[28] While I heard Sjogren share this understanding at a conference, you can see it worked out in S. Sjogren, *Conspiracy of Kindness* (Ann Arbor: Servant, 1993).

such as whether people should clap or not in church or whether guitars violate Scripture, or whether the carpet should be green or brown. Such believers have confused *preferences* with biblical *convictions* and become derailed on the way to obeying God. And many of the parents of that ilk are sacrificing the future of their children on the altar of their preferences. We should remain unstained from the world; however, we must not be removed from the people for whom Christ died.

Other churches seek to *pervade* the world, or to use their strength in numbers and influence to change culture. These are folks who seek to overpower the culture by might, be it political, social, or economic. They draw the line between the good guys and the bad guys; the problem is their line is between the church and the unchurched, not between the Lord and the forces of principalities and powers in high places. Lost people are not our enemy; they are captive to the enemy. Churches with this view resemble political rallies more than the body of Christ. Incidentally, these churches can be on the far left, typically being liberal Democrats, or to the right, typically Republican. This group overemphasizes the role of political involvement over the gospel. This is not to criticize those who are involved in politics; for we have a biblical responsibility to be involved in civil affairs; it is a plea that churches and groups maintain a focus on the gospel and the need to give priority to the power of the gospel over political persuasion. Remember that most believers in history have been in the minority with little power in their culture. These are not neutral churches—these churches hinder the work of God. Sometimes we think just because someone or a group is unfamiliar to us, they must be wrong.

It is time for the church to get out of the sanctuary and into reality.

The biblical church *invades* the world. Certainly the other two have some merit. We should separate ourselves from sin, and we should use our influence in the political realm. A biblical Christian is distinct from society and yet is a good citizen in it. We are, as Augustine put it, to be a city within the city. Our distinctiveness should be less about our clothing or outward matters, and more a distinction in our character and our love. *Jesus invaded the world through His incarnation!* Such a church will be in the culture among the people making an impact for the gospel. It is the church that emulates the life of Jesus, who left His home in glory to come and live among us to give us the opportunity to be a part of His kingdom. We invade the culture not to become like it, but so that more and more will become worshippers of the Most High God.

> *I simply argue that the cross should be raised at the center of the marketplace as well as on the steeple of the church. I am recovering the claim that Jesus was not crucified in a cathedral between two candles; but on a cross between two thieves—on the town's garbage heap; at a crossroad so cosmopolitan they had to write His title in Hebrew and Latin and Greek... at the kind of place where cynics talk smut and thieves curse, and soldiers gamble. Because that is where He died and that is what He died about. That is where the churchmen ought to be and what churchmen ought to be about.*[1]
>
> [1] G. G. Hunter III, *Church for the Unchurched* (Nashville: Abingdon, 1996), 98.

Let us remember the penetrating words of George McLeod (see sidebar).

We do run the risk of error on two sides of the pendulum when we seek to contextualize. Newbigin recognized this: "Everyone with the experience of cross-cultural missions knows that there are always two opposite dangers, the Scylla and Charybdis, between which one must steer. On the one side there is the danger that one finds no point of contact for the message as the missionary preaches it, to the people of the local culture the message appears irrelevant and meaningless. On the other side is the danger that the point of contact determines entirely the way that the message is received, and the result is syncretism. Every missionary path has to find the way between these two dangers: irrelevance and syncretism. And if one is more afraid of one danger than the other, one will certainly fall into the opposite."[29]

[29] L. Newbigin, *A Word in Season* (Grand Rapids: Eerdmans, 1994), 67.

We cannot sit idly by in a sea of lostness. We cannot go forward to contextualize the gospel fearful of either extreme. There was a time when missions meant sending American Christians into foreign lands to live among the people there and to bring the gospel to them. In those times we could push off the task of contextualization to them. The time has come to help Christians and their churches become effective missionaries to their own communities. We must call churches (including their leaders!) to transform the traditional view of missions as something carried out only in foreign nations and to apply that urgency to our cities and our neighborhoods. "Jesus has called us to one, love the gospel (loving our Lord), two, the culture (loving our neighbor), and three, the church (loving our brother)," Driscoll writes. "One of the causes of our failure to fulfill our mission in the American church is that the various Christian traditions are faithful on only one or two of these counts."[30]

Part of our problem is we have missions committees and evangelism committees in the church. Such a compartmentalization from our institutionalism has not produced either a greater practice or passion for the gospel. We must avoid the opposite extremes of traditionalism on the one hand, which is resistant to change for all the wrong reasons, often confusing theology with preference, and technique-driven ministry on the other, which overemphasizes relevance and innovation to the neglect of theology. That brings us to the vital issue related to becoming missional: contextualization.

The International Mission Board of the Southern Baptist Convention adopted the following five principles of contextualization.[31]

Principles of Contextualization

1. We affirm that the Bible is the only infallible text that exists. It is appropriate to evaluate all other books by the Bible. We encourage our personnel to search the Scriptures daily to see whether the principles presented by any text or teacher are true (Acts 17:11). Content that is in accord with biblical truth should be embraced. What is contrary to sound doctrine should be rejected.

[30] M. Driscoll, *The Radical Reformission* (Grand Rapids: Zondervan, 2004), 20.

[31] http://imb.org/main/news/details.asp?StoryID=6197 (accessed October 9, 2008).

2. We affirm that there is a biblical precedent for using "bridges" to reach out to others with the gospel (Acts 17:22–23). The fact that Paul mentioned an aspect of the Athenians' idolatrous worship was not a tacit approval of their entire religious system. He was merely utilizing a religious element of their setting (an altar to an unknown god) to connect with his hearers and bridge to the truth. Similarly, our personnel may use elements of their host culture's worldview to bridge to the gospel. This need not be construed as an embracing of that worldview. It should be noted that Paul not only used their system to connect, he also contrasted elements of it with the truth. Our evangelism must go beyond bridges to present the whole unvarnished truth of the gospel (1 Cor 15:1–4).
3. We affirm an incarnational approach to missions that is bound by biblical parameters. Following the example of Him who became flesh (John 1:14), it is appropriate that our personnel continue to tailor their ministry to their setting. The apostle Paul likewise embraced this approach, "I am made all things to all men, that I might by all means save some" (1 Cor 9:22b KJV). We advocate the learning and appropriate utilization of language and culture. Constant vigilance is required lest contextualization degenerate into syncretism. Where linguistic categories and cultural mores are deficient, these must be challenged and corrected with biblical truth.
4. We affirm both the sufficiency and unique nature of biblical revelation (2 Tim 3:14–17). We deny that any other purported sacred writing is on a par with the Bible. While reference to a target people group's religious writings can be made as a part of bridge-building, care should be exercised not to imply a wholesale acceptance of such.
5. We affirm the need to be ethically sound in our evangelistic methodology (2 Cor 4:2). Becoming all things to all men in an incarnational approach does not necessitate an ethical breach. Jesus instructed His disciples to be as "wise as serpents, and harmless as doves" (Matt 10:16 KJV). We are to be wise in our bridge-building. We are to be harmless in our integrity as we hold forth the truth.

In their book *Comeback Churches,* Stetzer and Dodson use the analogy of a ball team making a great comeback. As a parent of two athletic children, few things thrill me like watching one of my own help their team to a comeback victory. I am finishing this chapter on the heels of Hannah's volleyball team making an unlikely run to the finals in the state championship game, losing to the eventual national champion as well. In the process they came from behind to defeat their archnemesis, the only team to sweep them in the regular season. I will never forget that night when they rallied to win in five games, propelling her young school to the title game in their first year of eligibility. How much more joy will it bring to the Lord Himself when a church turns from being a stagnant monument to a vibrant, missional fellowship. Remember the Alamo? It began as a mission, became a battlefield, and became a museum. Sounds like more than a few churches I have seen. But when the mission is recaptured, there is the sound of victory!

Questions for Consideration

1. Would you describe your current church's evangelistic effectiveness as (a) missional, contextual, and thriving; (b) fairly effective; (c) not very effective; (d) on life support?
2. Does your church or ministry have a good grasp on the community it seeks to reach?
3. What are you doing to be effective in contextualizing the gospel in your area?

Chapter 19

Worship Evangelism: Linking the Glory of God to the Gospel

Nothing is more difficult to carry out, nor more doubtful of success, nor more dangerous to handle, than achieving a new order of things.[1]

—Niccolo Machiavelli, *The Prince*

I love corporate worship. I love being with the people of God to meet with God through songs and hymns, through prayers and offering, and the preached Word. I minored in music and have been a minister of music (we were not called "worship leaders" back then) in several churches. I take a worship band with me because I love vibrant worship. For several years I played bass in the band. Corporate worship with the people of God will endure as a mark of the Christian movement.

When a church gathers on Sunday for corporate worship, the main focus should be on God. Too many believers act as though worship

[1] Cited in A. Hirsch, *Forgotten Ways: Reactivating the Missional Church* (Grand Rapids: Brazos Press, 2006), 49.

is about them, focusing on preferences more than becoming living sacrifices. Our time of corporate worship should focus on exalting a great God and celebrating a risen Lord. But that does not have to exclude the lost. Worship can be a wild card that trumps our differences and our prejudices. People whose lives are focused on worshiping God overcome all sorts of barriers.

A hillbilly from West Virginia found himself serving the Lord at Armitage Baptist Church in Chicago. He began to go into the neighborhood inviting children to church. Betty Cherry was the mother of some of the children—an African-American lady who spent her life in the city, who had nothing in common with a West Virginia hillbilly. But through his influence, this former prostitute, who lived in drunkenness for 18 years, came to a time of worship at Armitage on New Year's Eve, 1982. She was eventually saved through the witness of a lady named Dawn who had been a prostitute as well before coming to Jesus. Later, Betty led the ARMS (Armitage Reaching Many Souls) evangelism ministry.[2]

Her story: "Right away I was discipled. The church became a second home and a second family—at times my first family." Through her ministry at ARMS Betty has reached hundreds with the gospel. One lady was from Puerto Rico—she came to Christ, then moved to Milwaukee, where she began an ARMS ministry to the Hmong people group. Imagine that—a hillbilly touched a black, drunken prostitute who reached a Puerto Rican who reached Hmongs. How? Because truth and love trump our differences. And that is why true worship is so vital. Genuine worship will trump the differences in any congregation.

People should have freedom to encounter the living God. In the cultural context of the Middle Ages, freedom meant stained-glass windows for an illiterate population to assist in communicating biblical stories. In the twenty-first century, stained glass is lovely but not integral to the worship experience. Fifty years ago a vast pipe organ enhanced worship for many, whereas a keyboard and drums does the same for lots of young adults today. A plexiglass lectern or a table and stool have replaced a big, elaborate pulpit from one generation for many in another.

Corporate Worship

A woman from a free congregational tradition visited a liturgical service. She continually punctuated the message of the pastor with

[2] "Changed Lives at Armitage Baptist Church," *SBC Life*, June/July 1999, 5.

"Praise the Lord!" Finally, a member of the church turned around and said to the guest, "Excuse me, but we don't praise the Lord in the Lutheran church." A man down the pew corrected the member: "Yes, we do," he said. "It's on page 19."[3]

The revolution in worship services in contemporary evangelicalism is obvious. More than 25,000 congregations use overhead projectors as an aid to singing contemporary choruses each Sunday. The church where I attend regularly incorporates drama in its services. Thousands of other congregations sing only the old hymns of the faith. Many use some sort of "blended" style to meet the needs of their members and to make the services palatable for the unchurched. Radical changes in corporate worship have led to "worship wars"[4] in more than a few congregations.

R. W. Dale said, "Let me write the hymns and the music of the church, and I care very little who writes the theology."[5] He understood the powerful impact that worship has on the church. The corporate worship of a local church also affects its evangelistic growth.

Martin Luther understood the power of music in worship. "I really believe, nor am I shamed to assert," said the Reformer, "that next to theology there is no art equal to music."[6] Luther further recognized, "Experience proves that next to the Word of God music deserves to be extolled as the mistress and governess of the feelings of the human heart."[7]

Most questions about worship deal with style rather than substance. But more about that later. Let us begin with a theology of worship from the pages of Scripture.

Worship in Scripture

Worship for the Hebrew meant to come before the Lord in humility. Hebrew worship focused on giving offerings to the Lord. A number of terms in the New Testament denote worship. *Latreuō* is one of many that emphasize veneration of God. The familiar word *proskuneō* ("to worship") focuses on one's allegiance to the Lord.

[3] P. Anderson, "Balancing Form and Freedom," *Leadership,* Spring 1986, 24.

[4] E. Towns, *Putting an End to Worship Wars* (Nashville: Broadman & Holman, 1997), considers this issue in detail.

[5] R. W. Dale, *Nine Lectures on Preaching Delivered at Yale, New Haven, Connecticut* (London: Hodder and Stoughton, 1952), 271.

[6] P. Smith, *The Life and Letters of Martin Luther* (New York: Barnes and Noble, 1968), 346.

[7] R. Bainton, *Here I Stand* (Nashville, Abingdon, 1947), 267.

To state it simply, worship is to be God centered. Much of what we do in church is a means to a greater end. Worship is an end in itself. Worship relates directly to the emotions; however, true worship goes deeper.

True worship of the ancient Hebrews was predicated on the activity of God in history[8]—in particular on the initiative taken by God to reveal Himself to His people. Thus, Abraham was called by God (see Genesis 12). In response, Abraham built altars of worship. God revealed to Noah the coming judgment on humanity. Noah responded in obedience by building the ark, and he worshiped God by building an altar after the flood. Ultimately, an elaborate process of worship developed through the tabernacle and the temple. Too often the people of God missed the genuine relationship with God in their ritual, so prophets like Amos exhorted the people to true worship. The Psalms provided songs for worship, while national festivals reminded the people to seek the Lord. Eventually, the synagogue service became the heart of Jewish worship.

The New Testament worship services patterned themselves after the synagogue. However, Phifer noted key differences in the worship services of the early Christians.[9] The New Testament writings, particularly Paul's letters and the Gospels, soon became a prominent part of the services. To the Psalms were added Christian hymns, some of which are probably included in Paul's epistles (Phil 2:5–11). Paul encouraged the singing of "psalms and hymns and spiritual songs" (Eph 5:18–19 NKJV). Baptism and communion were added features of Christian worship. Zeal characterized the services. The resurrection emphasis led to a celebrative spirit. Christian worship moved from the Jewish Sabbath to the Lord's Day, commemorating the resurrection of Jesus.

Ralph Martin reminds us that, although we can gain a general knowledge about worship in the early church, "there is, of course, no place in the New Testament which clearly states that the church had any set order of service, and very little information is supplied to us about the outward forms which were in use."[10] By the early second

---

[8] For further study, see H. W. Bateman, ed., *Authentic Worship: Hearing Scripture's Voice, Applying Its Truths* (Grand Rapids: Kregel, 2002); R. P. Martin, *Worship in the Early Church* (Grand Rapids: Eerdmans, 1974); D. R. Hustad, *Jubilate! Church Music in the Evangelical Tradition* (Carol Stream, IL: Hope Publishing Co., 1981); R. E. Webber, *Worship Old and New* (Grand Rapids: Zondervan, 1994).

[9] K. G. Phifer, *A Protestant Case for Liturgical Renewal* (Philadelphia: Westminster, 1965), 23.

[10] Martin, *Worship in the Early Church*, 134.

century, the *Didache* gave evidence of a greater sense of structure in worship.[11]

This means that the *style* of worship is not prescribed in the New Testament but the *substance* of worship is—in particular, the celebration of the risen Lord. Just as evangelism must keep a proper tension between the changeless message and changing methods, worship must give attention to a biblical focus while avoiding the temptation to prescribe one form of worship. This tension is borne out in history.

Christian Worship in History

The ritualism of the Middle Ages mitigated against true worship. Even more foreboding was the theological shift away from an emphasis on a regenerate church, leading to multitudes that observed the liturgy without a personal knowledge of the One whom they worshipped. Only a dramatic theological restructuring could rescue worship.[12]

The Reformation brought such a restructuring. Martin Luther returned the Bible and the hymnal to the people. Luther introduced hymns with more familiar tunes that were theologically rich and written in the language of the common man. Donald R. Hustad commented, "Worthy lyrics sanctify the secular melody."[13] Jesuit Adam Conzenius complained that "Luther's hymns have destroyed more souls than his writings."[14] If only the contemporary church could grasp as Luther did the dynamic of biblical lyrics and a winsome melody! Calvin emphasized the singing of the Psalms in his services.

The Pietists of the late seventeenth and early eighteenth centuries began writing subjective hymns, reflecting their emphasis on religion of the heart. At this same time, British pastor Isaac Watts began composing hymns. Such hymns as "When I Survey the Wondrous Cross" and "We're Marching to Zion" set a new standard for English church songs, thus his title "the father of English hymnody." By the turn of the nineteenth century, over 130 hymn collections had been printed.

---

[11] Webber, *Worship Old and New*, 52–53.

[12] The historical material is adapted from A. L. Reid, "Evangelistic Music," in *Evangelism and Church Growth,* ed. E. L. Towns (Ventura, CA: Regal, 1995).

[13] Hustad, *Jubilate!,* 127.

[14] S. Miller, *The Contemporary Christian Music Debate: Worldly Compromise or Agent of Renewal?* (Wheaton: Tyndale, 1993), 115.

Franklin Segler wrote that "a religious awakening has always been accompanied by a revision of the liturgy."[15] More recent centuries have witnessed the increasing role of music in the evangelistic mission of the church. One can trace the roots of music used for evangelistic purposes to the Evangelical Awakening and the ministry of John and Charles Wesley. Charles Wesley wrote more than 6,000 hymns. These were crucial to the theology of early Methodism. His brother John preached biblical sermons that emphasized the application of the text to life. To these Charles wed hymns utilizing secular tunes.

The impact of the songs of the Wesleys is hard to overestimate. To a largely illiterate population the hymns taught doctrine and supported Christian experience, combining "the revivalist's fervor with the cooling elements of disciplined poetry and biblical theology."[16] Further, early in the Evangelical Awakening the wide use of singing, particularly the singing of groups of young people along the cities and roads of the countryside, had a profound impact. Thousands of nominal Christians were caught up in evangelistic fervor that shattered old forms and traditions and opened new channels of spiritual growth for entire congregations.

The camp meetings of the Second Great Awakening were characterized by simple, emotional hymns, many with evangelistic appeals. The camp meeting songs developed into the gospel hymn, marked by a verse and chorus. *The Southern Harmony,* a collection of camp meeting songs published in 1835, sold 600,000 copies over 25 years.

Charles Finney worked closely with local churches in urban centers, so a different type of revival song was needed to reach the people in the cities. The church hymnals set too high a standard for some tastes, but the typical camp meeting songbook's standards were too low. Thus, he utilized Thomas Hastings, who published an early hymnbook, as a musician in the urban setting.

The first true music evangelist to be widely recognized was Ira D. Sankey (1837–99), who teamed with evangelist D. L. Moody. Sankey led congregational songs and sang solos. Sankey served as an emerging model for music evangelists. "The Ninety and Nine," "Jesus of Nazareth Passes By," and others made a great impact on believers

---

[15] F. M. Segler, *Christian Worship: Its Theology and Practice* (Nashville: Broadman, 1967), 46.

[16] H. McElrath, "Music in the History of the Church," *Review and Expositor* 69 (Spring 1972): 156.

and unbelievers alike. Lord Shaftersburg did not exaggerate when he said, "If Moody and Sankey had done nothing else but teach us 'Hold the Fort,' their visit would have been worthwhile."[17] He and Philip P. Bliss published *Gospel Hymns and Sacred Songs* in 1875. This collection included hymns which they, Fanny Crosby (1823–1915), and others had penned. Between 50,000 to 80,000 copies were sold by 1900.

Sankey was followed by scores of other musicians who teamed with evangelists. These included Charles Alexander, partner with J. Wilbur Chapman and R. A. Torrey; Homer Rodeheaver, who teamed with Billy Sunday; and more recently Cliff Barrows, with the Billy Graham team.

In the twentieth century, music on the radio, Stamps-Baxter gospel quartet music, and revivalistic southern hymns have added to evangelistic music. With the rise of evangelistic music, a tension developed between music designed to worship God and music primarily aimed at reaching the lost.

The Jesus Movement during the late 1960s and early 1970s laid the groundwork for a significant shift in the corporate worship of the American church. The charismatic movement added to the growing awareness of a need for freedom in worship.

Charles E. Fromm noted that for several decades the church resisted change in worship, leading up to the revolution that occurred in the 1960s and beyond:

> By the mid-sixties, it was generally acknowledged that if God had ever spoken at all through music, it had only been in the cherished hymns and psalms of the forefathers; that all things musically modern were, at best, tainted and unprofitable; and that spiritual song was best left safely locked up in the sanctity of ceremony.[18]

The changes in musical forms were influenced by young people who came to Christ in the Jesus Movement. The innovations served to present a new freshness in worship *and* were useful in reaching others as a result. In fact, the primary focus of much of the new music was evangelistic. Donald Hustad stated that "it should be obvious

---

[17] M. Taylor, *Exploring Evangelism (*Kansas City: Nazarene Publishing House, 1984), 326.

[18] Cited in A. L. Reid, "Impact of the Jesus Movement on Evangelism Among Southern Baptists" (PhD diss., Southwestern Baptist Theological Seminary, 1991), 99.

that the motivation behind all the pop-gospel phenomena of our day is evangelism."[19]

The rise of contemporary Christian music and the accompanying explosion of Christian radio stations after 1970 laid the groundwork for dramatic changes in worship services. Two streams merged to create the genre known today as contemporary Christian music. Folk music, especially as it was expressed in the youth musical, eventually merged with the rock sound of the Jesus Movement coffeehouses to form what is easily recognized today as contemporary Christian music.

The youth musical became a powerful medium for attracting young people to the gospel message in the late 1960s and early 1970s. Such musicals came out of the sixties and the increasing popularity of the folk song and such personalities as Bob Dylan, Joan Baez, and Peter, Paul, and Mary. "Do Lord," "Give Me Oil in My Lamp," and "I've Got the Joy, Joy, Joy, Joy Down in My Heart" became part of church youth fellowships.

The first widely used youth musical was *Good News.* The evangelistic focus of the musical is evident in its title. Ralph Carmichael and Kurt Kaiser then wrote *Tell It Like It Is.* Others included *Celebrate Life* by Buryl Redd and Jimmy and Carol Owens' *Come Together.* Soon youth choirs became the heart of many youth groups, while youth choir tours covered North America.

Contemporary Christian music began in the coffeehouses and youth fellowships of the period and mushroomed into a five-hundred-million-dollar industry annually by 1990. John Styll, president of the Gospel Music Association in 1993 and publisher of *Contemporary Christian Music* magazine, summarized the advent of the genre:

> Contemporary Christian Music was born out of the counterculture movement of the 60s. Disillusioned hippies who found the answer in Christ used their most natural means of expression—music—to proclaim the joy of their salvation and to share Christ with others. It wasn't organ music either. It was the music they understood.[20]

[19] D. R. Hustad, "Music in the Outreach of the Church," Southern Baptist Church Music Conference (June 9–10, 1969), 48.

[20] J. W. Styll, "Sound and Vision: 15 Years of Music and Ministry," *Contemporary Christian Music* (July 1993), 42. By 1981 contemporary Christian music was the fifth leading category of music, ahead of jazz or classical. In 1983, five percent of all record sales were gospel music, the majority of which was contemporary Christian music. Also, by the early 1980s, there were over 300 exclusively Christian music radio stations. See C. Flake,

Dozens of "Jesus rock groups" had begun playing in southern California. Larry Norman, called the "poet laureate" of the Jesus Movement by some, was one of the best known leaders. His simple ballad about the second coming of Christ, "I Wish We'd All Been Ready," was a signature song of the movement. Chuck Girard and Love Song were referred to as the "Beatles of the Christian music world" by some. Nancy Honeytree, Don Francisco, the Second Chapter of Acts, Barry McGuire, Keith Green, Eddie DeGarmo, Dana Key, Petra, Amy Grant, Brown Bannister, and Dogwood sprang from coffeehouse and similar ministries in the early 1970s. Jesus music festivals provided another forum for musicians to share their songs.

Contemporary Christian music was effective in evangelism through mass rallies, high school assembly programs, and festivals. Richard Hogue stated that the voice that young people listened to in the early seventies was not the athlete, but "the musician and the intellectual."[21]

The music of the Jesus Movement endured because of its close relationship with a major reason the movement began in the first place. Positively, the Jesus Movement was experiential and evangelistic, emphasizing a relationship with Christ. Negatively, it was a protest movement against the institutional church. The music gave a spiritual compass to a generation that felt disenfranchised due to the "generation gap."

Morgenthaler observed, "In the 1970s and 80s, much of the evangelical church experienced a *worship revolution:* an upheaval of traditional worship forms brought on by a belated, yet significant, 'cultural awakening.'"[22] The new musical styles among the youth gradually gained favor in many churches. But favor was not universal, as Carol Flake observed:

> Not all evangelicals were cheered by the success of CCM [contemporary Christian music]. The rock of ages they clung to did not roll with the times. Not surprisingly, Ralph Carmichael's first concert at the National Religious Broadcasters convention stirred few amens. The growth of contemporary Christian music and the opening of the gates between sacred and secular genres

---

Redemptorama: Culture, Politics, and the New Evangelicalism (Garden City: Anchor Press, 1984), 175–76.

[21] Reid, "Impact of the Jesus Movement," 119.

[22] S. Morgenthaler, *Worship Evangelism: Inviting Unbelievers into the Presence of God* (Grand Rapids: Zondervan, 1995), 282.

> stirred up a long-simmering controversy over the devil's role in rock and roll.[23]

Instruments associated with pop music, such as guitars, electric keyboards, and drums, stormed into many churches with the new songs. Such instruments became more acceptable in some churches because of their use in youth gatherings. The idea of an electric guitar in a worship service caused a virtual apoplexy to many, as illustrated by one pastor's observation: "I'll never forget the first Sunday they had all those guitars in there. [Some members] just went nuts."[24]

Bob Burroughs, a worship leader and composer, linked the Jesus Movement with revivalism of the past by stating that contemporary music, with guitars, amplifiers, and so on, was "the biggest thing to hit Christian music since Ira Sankey joined D. L. Moody!"[25] Added to the rise of contemporary Christian music was the advent of praise and worship choruses, developing out of the Jesus Movement but receiving significant impetus from the charismatic movement. Publishing houses such as Maranatha! Music and Sparrow Records emerged during this period.

Choruses became the inroad into the mainstream of worship services. Such songs gave a new and needed sense of freedom, emphasizing the experiential side of the faith. However, the Jesus Movement was also characterized by a simplistic and even self-centered theology, which also crept into worship. Unfortunately, this focus added to the shift in our consumer-driven culture to receiving a blessing from God rather than giving an offering to God.

More recently, movements such as Passion in the United States and the worship music of Hillsong in Australia among others has led to a greater desire for corporate worship that is participatory rather than passive in nature.[26] I mention I travel with a contemporary worship band of excellent young musicians (my son Josh being the drummer!). While extremely gifted, they never do "special music," a conventional staple in corporate worship where the congregation

---

[23] Flake, *Redemptorama*, 178.

[24] Reid, "Impact of the Jesus Movement," 124. Also E. C. Raymer, "From Serendipity to Shindig!" *Church Recreation,* July/August/September 1968, 22.

[25] B. Burroughs, "What Did You Say?" Southern Baptist Church Music Conference, June 4–5, 1971), 43; F. H. Heeren, "Church Music and Changing Worship Patterns," *Review and Expositor* 69 (Spring 1972): 190.

[26] Passion refers to a mostly collegiate worship movement in recent years. For more information go to 268generation.com. Hillsong refers to the worship movement coming from Australia and the Hillsong Church. See hillsong.com.

sits passively for a song performed by a soloist, choir, or ensemble. Instead, in the style of recent worship leaders, they only do songs in which the entire congregation participates. The congregation becomes the choir, and the entire band the prompters. I was reminded how great this shift is by our daughter Hannah. Raised in a contemporary church, Hannah came to chapel with me one day while in middle school. The leader that day led the singing by moving his hand as a conductor, the way I knew all my years in church services. She had not seen this, so when she watched him waving his hand wildly from the stage, she looked at me with big eyes, asking, "What is he doing?" Times indeed are changing.

To summarize, worship in the Bible focused on the character of God. Throughout history, music and worship styles have changed with the growth and expansion of the church. In the modern era, musical changes often paralleled times of spiritual awakening and renewal. Over the past century, a distinction has developed between music focused on worship and music designed for evangelistic services. Added to this are the experience-oriented choruses of the Jesus Movement and the charismatic movement, resulting in services that focus on meeting contemporary needs without demonstrating a true understanding of worship. How can we keep the best of contemporary worship without abandoning the biblical focus?

Our chapel services at Southeastern Seminary are the greatest on earth. God receives great honor as the seminary community gathers for a time of worship every Tuesday and Thursday. Still, I marvel at the difference in the spirit of the services when we move from singing a couple of hymns to a combination of hymns and choruses with more of a flow and more contemporary instrumentation. The warmth, the richness is apparent when the latter takes place. On the negative side, more contemporary songs tend to be softer in doctrine, and tend to emphasize personal blessing over the greatness of God. Fortunately there is a growing trend of contemporary hymns with greater depth on the horizon. The second most likely place to get theology is our singing. In a given service, what do the songs you sing say about God? In six months in your church, can a person have a significant understanding of the nature of the faith? Or do they leave just knowing they "feel good" when they sing their songs?

Implications for Evangelism from Scripture and History for Corporate Worship Today

Theological Base

We must affirm the *vital role of theology* in all we do. Music and worship are inherently experiential, so one must constantly assess worship services from a theological perspective. Theology matters, but too often we don't emphasize its role. Our focus on modern methods to help churches grow has opened the evangelical church to criticism on theological grounds. Sally Morgenthaler made the point: "In the 90s we are getting quite good at target practice—honing in on the lifestyles, habits, wants, and needs of particular people. Yet in our zeal to hit the bull's-eye, we have forgotten that *God grows the church through spiritual power*."[27]

Morgenthaler cited Barna who discovered that the key thing unchurched people are looking for in a church is not a certain worship style but specific doctrinal beliefs. She added, "To replace doctrine with style is to totally misinterpret the message our culture is sending." Barna also said, "We have 325,000 Protestant churches, 1,200 Christian radio stations, 300 Christian television stations, and 300 Christian colleges. . . . During the last eight years, we in the Christian community have spent in excess of $250 billion in domestic ministry and have seen a 0 percent increase in the proportion of born-again adult Christians of this country. Are we concerned about this? Do we feel any accountability for this picture?"[28]

Most churches are so introverted that they are not concerned about honoring God through the worship experience or about bearing fruit through new believers. The sad truth is, we born-again Christians are an insulated, narcissistic subculture, involving ourselves with very few people outside our own churches. How can we witness to the lost if we do not know anybody who fits that description? "Some churches have perfected the art of draining other churches."[29]

We must remind ourselves that our primary object in life is to glorify God. Our adoration of God must transcend any other object of ministry, including our desire to see churches grow. There is no better way to glorify God than to bring a lost sheep to the Shepherd (Luke 15).

---

[27] Morgenthaler, *Worship Evangelism*, 36, italics added.

[28] G. Barna, "How Can Today's Churches Minister More Faithfully?" *Growing Churches* (January–March 1992), 18.

[29] Morgenthaler, *Worship Evangelism,* 27–28.

Morgenthaler gave a PASS formula to test songs for worship. "Personal—they related someway to people's everyday lives and involved their whole being, including their emotions. Attractive—they hold people's attention. Straightforward—both Seeker Bob and Saintly Bill can understand and latch onto them quickly. Substantive—give a thoroughly biblical message that is faithful to the whole counsel of scripture."[30]

Distinguish between Evangelistic Services and Worship Services

An evangelistic service, ranging from contemporary seeker services to traditional mass evangelism, can include elements of worship, but its purposes are different. Many church leaders fail to distinguish between a seeker service, which is evangelistic by design, and a seeker-sensitive worship service, which welcomes the unsaved. Evangelistic services are needed but not to the neglect of worship services. Os Guinness put it well: It is "perfectly legitimate" to "convey the gospel in cartoons to a nonliterary generation incapable of rising above MTV. . . . But five years later, if the new disciples are truly won to Christ, they will be reading and understanding Paul's letter to the Romans."[31]

Weekly services dedicated to the worship of God *can* have an evangelistic impact. George Hunter and others have stated that our culture is becoming more like the apostolic era. Our postmodern, post-Christian era demands genuine worship by radically changed believers who honor God with their lives. Such worship not only glorifies God but also draws the attention of unbelievers (Psalm 126; Acts 2:47; 16:25ff; Rom 15:9–11; 1 Cor 14:23–25).

Worship leader Tommy Coomes came to Christ because of the genuine, dynamic worship at Calvary Chapel, Costa Mesa, California, the mother church of the Jesus Movement. It was the worship that drew him to Christ. He later observed, "There is a spiritual dynamic going on in authentic worship that can't be reasoned away."[32] Don McMinn said it well:

> Music is not the power of God for salvation, and neither is the media of writing, speaking, or sign language. The gospel is the

[30] Ibid., 213. See also M. Dawn, *Reaching Out Without Dumbing Down* (Grand Rapids: Eerdmans, 1995), 202.

[31] O. Guinness, *Dining with the Devil* (Grand Rapids: Baker, 1993), 28–29.

[32] Morgenthaler, *Worship Evangelism,* 92.

power of God to salvation, and when it is presented, regardless of *how* it is presented, lives will be changed.[33]

Celebration

We should give proper attention to *celebration* in our worship services—not celebrating our experience but the resurrected Lord. Hustad has warned that "the 'new enjoyment' may lead to a worship hedonism which is another form of idolatry—worshiping the experience instead of worshiping God."[34] Confession and brokenness are necessary for honest worship to occur; still, celebrating the resurrection of Jesus Christ should be the focus of our worship. When He is our focus, we are reminded that Christianity is not primarily fun; it is *essential.*

Resist False Dichotomies

Generalities like "sing great old hymns only," or "sing only newer songs," should be resisted. Such dichotomies lead to a reductionism that fails to distinguish between the timeless and the trendy, the contemporary and the faddish. Some people sing choruses because this is the music they like, with little thought given to the issue of worshiping God. Others hold to a more historic, traditional approach because in their minds, it demonstrates authentic worship. Perhaps the truth is that they just don't like change!

Style and substance are both vital, but substance must guide stylistic concerns. We must never make "either-or" that which is actually "both-and." There is no one all-encompassing worship style that will reach the multitudes or exalt our great God.

Understand the Difference between Personal Preference and Biblical Truth

I participated in a recent evangelism conference that featured music quite popular about 20 years ago. The keynote speaker commented that the recent changes in worship style hindered evangelism. More than a few people older than me have repeated his perspective to me. The problem is that such opinions are not verified by research.

[33] D. McMinn, *The Practice of Praise* (Waco: Word Music, 1992), 129.

[34] Hustad, *Jubilate!*, 164.

One recent study found that a primary factor in growing congregations was actually moving to more of a contemporary worship style.[35] Thom Rainer's study of effective evangelistic churches found the following about style:

1. *Various worship styles are effective.* In this survey, the *quality* of worship was seen as more important than the particular style.
2. *The atmosphere of the service is critical for reaching people.*
3. *The attitude of those leading the service played a bigger factor than the style:* "Leaders describe their worship services with such words as *warm, exciting, loving, vibrant, hopeful,* and *worshipful.*"[36]

We must keep a healthy balance between *new music* and *lasting songs.* Bob Burroughs, while affirming and writing many contemporary scores, feels that an overemphasis on singing choruses instead of hymns could become detrimental:

> The praise chorus music itself in some churches has taken the place of the hymnal, and the music is so shallow . . . that the great hymnody of the church, which is a teaching aid also for theology, and for doctrine . . . is lost. When you sing "Alleluia, alleluia" over against "A Mighty Fortress" or "Savior, Like a Shepherd Lead Us," or some of those, the young people and the young adults really do miss out on some . . . great theology.[37]

The key to worship is not the songs we sing or the music's beat. The key is not style, although style does matter. The key is spirit. The key is *life.* Over the past decade I have been privileged to speak in some 500 churches, mostly but not exclusively Southern Baptist, in over 20 states. I could share many stories of pathetic churches who are dying. The favorite song of such churches is "Take My Life and Let It Be," and they mean "let it be," as in "don't bother me!" These churches that have confused reverence with rigor mortis are legion. But I would rather note some other churches where life is contagious, where God is

---

[35] "Facts on Growth" at http://fact.hartsem.edu/Press/churchgrowth.htm (accessed October 21, 2008).

[36] T. S. Rainer, *Effective Evangelistic Churches* (Nashville: Broadman & Holman, 1997), 101. Italics added.

[37] Reid, "Impact of the Jesus Movement," 134–35.

at work—big churches, small churches, new missions and some over a century old, rural and urban. Here are some examples:

- A church in Houston, Texas, in a blue-collar neighborhood, with hymns, no choruses, and special music with a southern gospel or country flair.
- An innovative, contemporary megachurch 30 minutes away from the one just mentioned, in an upwardly mobile area, blending old hymns with new hymns and choruses, incorporating drama, and using an overhead.
- A rural church in North Carolina, with a young pastor, singing traditional hymns as though they were written yesterday, filled with the love of Christ.
- A midsized congregation in the northeastern United States, using both familiar songs and new tunes, and occasionally some written by members, with a very free service order.
- A small-town congregation in South Carolina where *contemporary* means songs like "There's Just Something about That Name" and "His Name Is Wonderful." In other words, songs contemporary 25 years ago. But a church full of life and reaching people.

Many more churches could be cited, but my point is clear: No one style of worship is the exclusively biblical approach. The Bible, especially the New Testament, does not give specific instructions about the form of the worship service. This does not mean that anything goes in worship. "Decently and in order" is how Paul told the Corinthians to worship. Some form, tradition, or liturgy gives continuity from generation to generation. There must be an underlying theology of worship and a biblical ecclesiology.

What I am saying is that there is a need for traditional churches, for some people love church like Granny had. But churches that worship in a manner that honors Christ *and* relates to culture are also necessary.

Evangelism and Corporate Worship

People are passionate about what happens in worship services. We must teach our people that worship is not designed to please the congregation but to please God.

There is a tendency to make a strong distinction between worship services for the saved and evangelistic services or weekly seeker services. But there is ample biblical evidence for the concept of open worship—worship that focuses on exalting God, but that draws people into his presence. This includes drawing sinners to salvation. Today we are in the midst of a *worship reformation,* a movement that continues to address the issue of worship form (relevance) stretching beyond form to the core of worship itself—biblical substance. This is a worship movement with more life-reaching, life-changing potential than anything the evangelical church has seen in the last 75 years.

The Lord gave Moses clear instructions about worship: "And if a stranger dwells with you, or whoever is among you throughout your generations, and would present an offering made by fire, a sweet aroma to the Lord, just as you do, so shall he do" (Num 15:14 NKJV). So strangers were expected to worship. Deuteronomy 26:10–11 also mentions how foreign residents worship. The psalmist declared, "Let everything that has breath praise the LORD. Praise the LORD!" (Ps 150:6 NKJV). The presence of unbelievers is also noted in the New Testament (see 1 Cor 14:22–25).

Israel was to be a kingdom of priests and a light to the nations (Isa 51:4). Worship really is an encounter of God with his children. Lost people are potential children of God. The Bible indicates that there is none righteous, but it also says that those who seek God will find him if their search is genuine. In our worship we should not put unnecessary burdens on unsaved people who may be in attendance.

Morgenthaler asks rhetorically, "Just how does evangelism take place in a service that is 'fully worshiped'?" Her reply is worth considering: "It happens in two ways: first, as unbelievers hear the truth about God (through worship songs, prayers, communion, baptism, scripture [preaching!], testimonies, dramas, and so on); and second—and more importantly—as they observe the real relationship between worshipers and God."[38] This can be seen in Psalm 126 in the Old Testament and in the Acts narrative in the New Testament.

Some evangelists, including Franklin Graham and the Harvest Crusades of Greg Laurie, are moving toward a worship experience, even in their evangelistic crusades. Perhaps a miniature example of open worship would be Paul and Silas when they worshipped in the prison at Philippi and their worship drew the prison keeper to want to know Christ (see Acts 16). Gerrit Gustafson gave a definition of

[38] Morgenthaler, *Worship Evangelism,* 88.

worship evangelism, the kind of evangelism that occurs in the context of open worship: "Wholehearted worshipers calling the whole world to the wholehearted worship of God . . . [and] the fusion of the power of God's presence with the power of the gospel."[39]

What then are the characteristics of worship evangelism? Morgenthaler suggested these:[40]

> *Nearness.* Worship evangelism features a sense of God's presence.
>
> *Knowledge.* The worship is centered on Christ. Our worship is not centered on seekers or on us; it is centered on the risen Lord. Some seeker services deny the gospel because they think seekers are offended by it. We should not be offensive in worship or at any other time, but we should not be surprised if the gospel is an offense to some people (see 1 Cor 1)! The fear of offending people with the salvation message may indicate a much deeper problem: We may be willing to do whatever it takes to get unbelievers into church but not to bring them to Christ!
>
> *Vulnerability.* This is an opening up to God. Lost people are not looking for perfect Christians; they are looking for people who are *real,* who open themselves before a holy God and make it clear that they are not God, that they are seeking to worship him. Perhaps we need to talk less about being seeker friendly and emphasize that we are sinner friendly. After all, Jesus was called a friend of sinners. The point of vulnerability is that worship ought to be about honesty. We're not perfect. We need to let the world know we make mistakes. But we have an anchor in Jesus Christ when our ship is adrift.
>
> *Interaction.* Worship evangelism means participating in a relationship with God and others. How can we make the church and worship relevant? The key to relevance is not changing the gospel or our worship to make people happy. God desires not that we be happy—but holy. When we're holy, we find happiness. The only way to be relevant is to be real. The central issue is not to be *relevant* but to be *significant.*

"Contrary to popular belief," Morgenthaler added, "it is not culturally relevant in turn-of-the-millennium America to throw out every

[39] G. Gustafson, "Worship Evangelism," *Psalmist* (February–March 1991), 50.

[40] Morgenthaler, *Worship Evangelism*, 102–28.

single piece of historic Christian communication."[41] Morgenthaler cited a survey that discovered that 47 percent of unchurched people indicated they would like to sing some traditional hymns. Taking the older hymns and updating the music would communicate to the current day. I mentioned I travel with a young worship band ministering to students. We regularly include hymns in the song list. Young adults do not hate hymns; they do tend to be unimpressed with the way many Christians sing them!

Take a few minutes to consider the corporate worship of your church. Does it exalt God? Is it a celebration of the resurrected Lord? Can lost people be saved by participating? Would they want to know the God represented in your worship?

Morgenthaler, whose book is by far the best I have seen on this subject, offers five rudders to guide worship evangelism.

1. Worship first, evangelize second.
2. Never sacrifice authenticity for relevance.
3. Add before you subtract.
4. Be committed to relevance based on your community's culture in the present and its meaningful religious past.
5. Customize your own worship methodology.[42]

Extending Worship Evangelism Beyond the Service

Worship evangelism is really more of a mind-set, a focus of ministry, than a method. It can be conducted in three ways.

1. *Corporate.* The subject of this chapter has been on corporate worship in a local church. Just imagine if your church approached each Sunday morning with great anticipation of encountering God, and with the desire of seeing people apart from Christ reached.
2. *Family.* Worship on various levels helps the unbeliever to see the manifest presence of God. The head of a national organization focused on evangelism came to Christ out of Judaism in the early 1970s. He sensed his need for Christ in part because he had a meal with a Christian family. As part of their routine of worship as a family, they prayed before the meal. In that

[41] Ibid., 128.
[42] Ibid., 284.

simple time, this man sensed God's presence like never before. One of the ways you can teach worship to your children is to have family worship at home.

3. *Personal.* Your personal evangelism will not likely reach past your personal devotion. Gregory said of the Church Father Basil, "His words are like lightning because his life is like thunder." Perhaps no greater power in witnessing exists than a believer whose primary aim is to know and honor God, for out of that personal worship, one learns to think as God thinks, and to want what God wants, which certainly includes the fulfillment of the Great Commission. Further, a lost person can tell if you or I have been walking with God.

Our culture is dry spiritually. We are eroding because of a lack of rain, the rain of the Spirit of God. We need a fresh rain.

Questions for Consideration

1. Do you think of worship more as receiving a blessing from God or offering yourself to God?
2. Does your church's corporate worship exalt the Lord in such a way that lost people who attend can sense the presence of God and see the work of God in the members?
3. Have you been more concerned about your personal preferences in corporate worship than whether or not truth is proclaimed?
4. If someone sang the songs in your church for a year, would they have a decent understanding of key theological concepts from those songs?

Chapter 20

Mass Evangelism

You are not the oil, you are not the air—merely the point of combustion, the flashpoint where the light is born. You are merely the lens in the beam. You can only receive, give, and possess the light as a lens does.[1]

—Dag Hammarskjold

The preaching of the gospel has been and will be central to the expansion of the church until Jesus comes. Hammarskjold's analogy serves as a reminder that the gospel preached through a Spirit-endued vessel has been the tool for the conversion of many from the time of Christ until now.

By mass evangelism I refer specifically to gospel preaching to a group of people, including conventional meetings in local churches or arenas. In a general sense, mass evangelism refers to any gospel message presented to a crowd, including a musical, drama, block party, or some other tool. Mass evangelism has endured as a timeless method ordained by God in Scripture and used with incredible effectiveness throughout history. Also, itinerant evangelists have ministered from New Testament times until today.

[1] D. Hammarskjold, *Markings*, trans. L. Sjonberg and W. H. Auden (New York: Alfred A. Knopf, 1966), 155.

The New Testament affirmed preaching the good news to the masses; however, the approach varied according to the audience. John the Baptist vilified the Pharisees; Jesus preached repentance; Peter began with the Old Testament in speaking to Jews at Pentecost; Paul followed a similar approach with a Jewish audience, but when speaking to Greeks in Athens he began with creation.

Historical Sketch

The most effective times of evangelism throughout history also featured some of the most effective mass evangelists. Some were pastors; some were itinerants; still others were pastor-itinerants. In different eras, different means have been used to proclaim the gospel to a given audience.

In the modern era, gospel preaching marked the evangelical awakening in England, although earlier the Pietists in Europe had preached mass meetings of some kind. George Whitefield, John Wesley, and others preached the gospel outdoors, in the streets and fields, with great success. In fact, John Wesley commented at one point that he thought a person had to come to a church building to be converted (talk about a bad case of institutionalism!). Then he met Christ in a life-changing way, and the churches of his day suddenly became nervous at his preaching. He began to preach in the fields reluctantly and of necessity. As a result, multitudes of people came to Christ that had gone untouched by the established church. The Evangelical Awakening that ensued would never have had the impact it did without the preaching in the fields. In their day, mass evangelism in the outdoors, although controversial, became a novel and effective means of proclaiming Christ.

Congregationalist Jonathan Edwards preached his famous sermon, "Sinners in the Hands of an Angry God," to another congregation in what became a one-service, mass evangelism event. Shubal Stearns, noted Baptist leader of the Sandy Creek Church, utilized protracted meetings, or extended evangelistic services. The camp meetings on the American frontier erupted spontaneously about 1800, providing an avenue for many to preach and thousands to be saved. Methodist circuit riders became the itinerant evangelists on the frontier.

Charles Finney utilized protracted meetings, at first extending services over several nights spontaneously after the fire of God fell in revival. In Rochester, New York, Finney preached 98 sermons from September 10, 1830, to March 6, 1831. Hudson called Finney's meetings "the camp meeting brought to town."[2] By the 1830s, the term *revival meeting* was used to refer to a general protracted meeting, whether it was a camp meeting on the frontier under such men as James McGready or a protracted meeting under Finney in the urban areas of the East. In more recent days some refer to such meetings simply as "revivals." This is unfortunate because (as discussed earlier) revival refers to the work of God among His people, not an evangelistic meeting, which focuses on the lost.

D. L. Moody signaled the next significant shift in mass evangelism. He was the first modern urban evangelist. He planned meetings with great preparation, set the date, stayed for many days, and involved the entire city. He preferred to speak in secular arenas rather than church buildings (not unlike Paul's move from the synagogue in Acts 19 to the school of Tyrannus). A whole caravan of evangelists followed after him, including Wilbur Chapman, R. A. Torrey, Billy Sunday, Gypsey Smith, Mordecai Ham, and Billy Graham—the best-known of all, and the evangelist who has preached to more people than any other in human history. Whether it was field preaching, camp meetings, local church meetings, or citywide crusades, Wood has aptly concluded, "For every age God has a programme of evangelism."[3]

In George Whitefield's day, mass evangelism in the fields was rejected by many church leaders as an innovation unworthy of the church. Today, some church leaders have stopped holding evangelistic meetings because they are considered too traditional! While our society has changed, and expecting people to attend weeklong or two-weeklong meetings may be a stretch given our overly busy, ADD culture, mass meetings still play a vital role in effectively evangelizing an area. On the other hand, some churches who see evangelism as only attractional hold a meeting once a year to focus on getting the unsaved to a church building to hear the gospel, doing very little to be missional in their communities beyond the church property. Both extremes should be rejected, whether one ignores mass meetings of some kind or some do them exclusively. Why should a church consider mass evangelism? And how should the church conduct such meetings effectively?

---

[2] W. Hudson, *Religion in America* (New York: Charles Scribner's Sons, 1981), 143.

[3] A. S. Wood, *John Wesley: The Burning Heart* (Grand Rapids: Eerdmans, 1967), 97.

Why Mass Evangelism?

Mass evangelism and evangelists are biblical concepts. Both were God's idea. Mass evangelism, or the preaching of the gospel to a group, permeates the New Testament. Peter's sermon at Pentecost comes to mind as a famous example. Jesus, Paul, and others preached to large crowds. This doesn't mean that churches that fail to conduct annual or semiannual evangelistic campaigns are bad; it suggests that some have given up on the method prematurely. Unfortunately, some evangelists using manipulative techniques have given evangelistic meetings and evangelists a bad reputation. But there are many godly, effective preachers who are gifted as harvesters.

Mass evangelism reminds believers that people are lost and must be reached. In a day when tolerance is a virtue and conviction is a vice, too many believers have lost a sense of their own lostness apart from Christ. Our culture has robbed us of the sense of people's lostness and the urgency of evangelism. Gospel preaching speaks not only to lost people; Christians need to hear the "old, old story." We need to be reminded of the need of others for Christ.

Mass evangelism still works. While we should never be driven by pragmatism, we should neither ignore approaches that can be both biblical and effective. We can preach the timeless gospel in a changing world. The largest services in the history of Billy Graham's crusades are happening in the early twenty-first century—on youth night! Graham has learned how to preach the timeless gospel in a changing world. Franklin Graham has continued arena meetings with success.

Some of my most precious memories are of evangelistic services: the father of a close friend coming to Christ in deep brokenness and tears; a married couple from different church backgrounds who moved from a religious system to a relationship with God; one-fourth of a junior high school football team coming to Christ in one night; a church transformed by witnessing the power of God changing lives.

A recent study revealed that almost one-half of evangelistic Southern Baptist churches use "revival evangelism" (better, evangelistic meetings) regularly. How has the method been so successful? First, extensive planning is done. Hard work and high expectancy mark these churches. Second, prayer lies not on the periphery in these efforts but marks every step of preparation. Third, these churches generally use vocational evangelists.[4]

[4] Thom Rainer, *Effective Evangelistic Churches* (Nashville: Broadman & Holman, 1995), 33.

As a young pastor, I used such an evangelist. We prepared diligently in our little church, using our Home Mission Board's (now the North American Mission Board) materials. We prayed all night one Friday! We went out into the community again and again. And God blessed! More people came to Christ and were baptized in that church in one week than had been reached for the past eight years. Don't give up on the method; it will reach people in our day if we make the right preparations.

Many evangelists hold crusades in local churches or areas. Some of the most effective evangelists tell me that areawide crusades are still effective in small-to-midsized towns and cities. In modern times, more organized, structured evangelistic campaigns in local churches and great arenas have been the means for the conversion of multitudes. In the Southern Baptist Convention, years marked by simultaneous evangelistic crusades have led to some of the most significant increases in baptisms.

A. W. Tozer is known for his books, including *The Pursuit of God,* which emphasizes godliness and holy living. What many people don't know about him is that as a seventeen-year-old walking home from his job at Goodyear in Akron, Ohio, he heard a street preacher say, "If you don't know how to be saved, just call on God." After that, he called out to Christ to save him. A. W. Tozer came to Christ through a street preacher. We should be careful about throwing out evangelistic methods.

Evangelistic Preaching

In *Effective Evangelistic Churches,* Thom Rainer noted that preaching played an important role in virtually every church surveyed. More important than worship styles or ministries was the role of the pulpit. More than 90 percent of churches surveyed reported that preaching played a major role in the evangelistic growth of the church.[5] Respondents also indicated that almost three out of four pastors of these churches preached expository messages.

Some people believe that to reach the current generation, expository preaching must be abandoned in favor of topical, needs-oriented sermons. However, studies indicate that expository preaching still plays a vital role in many evangelistic churches. In fact, in our day one can see a rise in younger pastors who preach expositionally for

[5] Rainer, *Effective Evangelistic Churches*, 50.

an hour or more to huge congregations in urban centers. We should remember that the Bible speaks to both *felt* needs and *real* needs! It takes more work to exegete a text and apply it to today's world, but the long-term effects are worth it. The Word of God is as relevant as tomorrow, for God already knows tomorrow's headlines! Instead of deemphasizing sound, biblical, expository preaching, we should work to eliminate *boring* preaching and replace it with *effective* preaching. By the way, young people do not hate preaching—they hate preaching that is not challenging and not relevant to them. I had a doctoral student do a survey on application of biblical texts in preaching. He found that adults could make application of a biblical sermon easily, but youth needed the preacher to take a little more time to give specific application to their life. He found that youth do not reject biblical teaching, but they need help to see how it is to be lived out daily.

During my first year as a professor at Southeastern, a pastor from Virginia told the true story about a little boy who came to the evening service at his church. The pastor waxed unusually long that evening, and the child became restless.

"When will he be finished, Mom?" he asked.

"Quiet!" snapped his mother.

Soon the little boy inquired again, "Mom, when will he be done?"

The mother again replied, "Son, sit still and be quiet, or I'll take you out and spank you."

Finally, after the pastor had preached almost an hour, the boy had all he could stand. "Mom," he pleaded, "just take me out and spank me, please!"

The boy thought a whipping was better than the preaching he was hearing! Evangelistic preaching should be marked by effectiveness, earnestness, and biblical fidelity—and it shouldn't be boring.

In a lecture at Southeastern Seminary, Haddon Robinson spoke of four worlds the preacher must know in order to communicate the message to any generation. He should know the world of the Bible, which includes a thorough exegesis of the text. He should also know the current culture in which we live. The third world is the preacher's own, personal world—his strengths and weaknesses. The final world is the immediate world of his local church or the congregation that he is currently addressing. By knowing these worlds and exercising some serious study, preachers can apply the gospel to any generation.

In Jonathan Edwards's day, a literate culture in a Puritan world required depth of thought and profound images. In our day, influenced by television and the Internet, illustrations and media play a larger role than ever. Communicating to this generation requires an understanding of relationship, which is such a vital part of our culture. The exposition of the Word of God must serve as the foundation of our preaching. Evangelistic preaching must be passionate, biblical, urgent, and relevant.

Today, due to the information available online, some have developed the sorry habit of downloading other's messages and preaching them. I like what Jerry Vines said: "I milk a lot of cows, but I make my own butter." Preaching the sermons of others is an echo, not a word from God. If you would preach the gospel, be much a man of prayer and much a man of the Scriptures. Preach a word from God burned on your heart, or stop preaching until you can.

It fascinates me that the preaching during the great awakenings focused not on the need for revival but on the gospel. Teaching and preaching the gospel effectively not only encourages the lost to be saved, but can challenge the saved to keep a focus on what matters. Note the following insights from great preachers:

- Charles Spurgeon: "A burning heart will soon find for itself a flaming tongue."[6]
- Martyn Lloyd-Jones: "Preaching is theology coming through a man on fire. . . . What is the chief end of preaching? It is to give men and women a sense of God and His presence."[7]
- E. M. Bounds: "It takes twenty years to make a sermon because it takes twenty years to make the man."[8]

The Gospel Invitation

Central to the evangelistic service is the public invitation. Because of extremes by some evangelists who are manipulative and insincere, some preachers have moved away from the open invitation. I believe the invitation is essential to effective evangelistic preaching. Whenever the Word of God is preached, it calls for a response. That does

[6] C. H. Spurgeon, *Lectures to My Students* (Grand Rapids: Baker, 1977), 148.
[7] W. Duewel, *Ablaze for God* (Grand Rapids: Zondervan, 1989), 22.
[8] E. M. Bounds, *Power through Prayer* (Grand Rapids: Baker, 1972), 8.

not mean a public "altar call" in every setting; nonetheless, a call to respond matters.

Some people question whether the public invitation remains a viable or even a biblical way to call people to salvation. I would argue that we should, when the gospel is preached, always call for a response. But that does not always mean we do it in a public, come-to-the-front manner. My president Danny Akin always shares the gospel at our graduation ceremonies. We always have graduates who have family members in attendance who know not Christ. But Akin does not stop and offer an opportunity to walk the aisle; instead, he calls people to respond and encourages any who respond to the gospel to tell their graduate, who will of course rejoice in that news. And, on several occasions that is exactly what happened! He gives an invitation to respond, but he applies it in an appropriate way.

If you are a preacher, you will at times be asked to preside at a wedding or a funeral. You can pretty much guarantee that lost people will be at those occasions. You can clearly and appropriately share Christ and call for a decision without taking away from the focus of the day. I always do this. I officiated a wedding for two students in our chapel a few years back. The groom told me of his uncle, a hippie-type who played drums in a rock band. I took a few moments in the context of the wedding and applied the wonder of human relationships in marriage to the greater wonder of knowing Christ. The uncle heard the gospel, something he had avoided. About a month later he came to Christ.

You can share Christ in such settings, calling for a gospel response without stopping the service to call for a physical response. As increasing numbers of people in the United States, not to mention globally, have little knowledge of the gospel or even of church services, our tying the invitation to salvation to a very specific public response could in fact hinder some from understanding salvation. That being said, I am personally troubled by many who move away from calling people to respond to the gospel and believe many times it comes from a lack of conviction about the power of God to save more than from a reaction to a method, or perhaps it comes from a lack of faith.

Biblical Evidence

In his outstanding book *The Effective Invitation,* Alan Streett argued the New Testament consistently demonstrates the necessity of a public call. The following discussion is far too brief, so the interested reader is encouraged to read his fine book.[9] Streett also recognized the consistent call of God to open obedience in the Old Testament. Further, he cited the ministry of Jesus as it relates to the invitation. Beyond the narratives of Jesus and His call of the disciples, Lazarus, and others, the use of the Greek word *parakaleō* is significant in this discussion. Paige Patterson describes one way this word can be translated:

> I have frequently translated it as "give an invitation." Any time you come across the word *exhortation* on the pages of the New Testament, you have, in effect, an appeal made for people to come and stand with the speaker in whatever it is that he is doing. This, of course, could take many patterns. . . . In any case, it is an invitation to decide.[10]

Streett noted that five times *parakaleō* is related to evangelistic preaching. Other expressions of this meaning range from the analogy of sowing and reaping to the call for open acknowledgment of Christ in Rom 10:9–10. Thus, the New Testament teaches the importance of a public call to Christ.

Historical Evidence

Public calls for the converted to proclaim their faith in Christ openly persisted until the time of Constantine, according to Streett.[11] For more than a millennium following Constantine, the emphasis shifted from salvation by grace through faith in Christ to the sacramental system of the Catholic Church. During this era, the public invitation disappeared. Occasionally preachers such as Bernard of Clairveaux would issue a call for some type of public response, but this was the exception, not the rule.

During the Reformation, the Anabaptists were consistent "in calling men to repent of their sins, place their faith in Christ, and present themselves for rebaptism (since their infant baptism was null and void)."[12] In the First Great Awakening, Jonathan Edwards met with persons privately after they responded to his preaching. George Whitefield and others followed this pattern of calling people to repent, then

[9] R. A. Streett, *The Effective Invitation* (Grand Rapids: Kregel, 1995).
[10] Cited in ibid., 63.
[11] Ibid., 81.
[12] Ibid., 87.

meeting with them privately about their spiritual needs. Sometimes Whitefield could not sleep or eat because of the many people seeking counsel. Some churches today have moved to this approach, where the pastor meets interested people after the service to discuss salvation. Other churches utilize a card, where the pastor takes a moment at the end to encourage those who trust Christ that day or who want to know more to indicate it on the card, after which someone speaks to that person personally by phone or personal visit.

Howard Olive discusses four ways John Wesley utilized a public invitation: (1) he used personal workers who sought anxious souls; (2) he called upon seekers to attend a service in the midweek to demonstrate their faith; (3) he invited seekers to step out publicly for church membership; (4) he used the mourner's bench or anxious seat.[13]

Separate Baptists continued the trend of a public call, but Charles G. Finney made the greatest impact in the modern era. He used the mourner's bench, or the anxious seat, and implored people to come forward and kneel at the altar. With mass evangelists such as D. L. Moody, Billy Sunday, and Billy Graham during the past 150 years, the evangelistic invitation has become a staple in the evangelical diet. Moody used inquiry rooms, Sunday exhorted sinners to "hit the sawdust trail," and Graham calls people to come openly "just as they are."[14]

For me the issue has less to do with whether to call for a response when the gospel is preached, as the gospel in its very nature calls for a response. The focus should be more on an appropriate, effective manner to call for a response.

I have been in a few services where the evangelist seemed more interested in a large response than the work of the Spirit. Such abuses should not prevent us from extending the gospel invitation. When you preach the gospel, there are some things to remember.

1. *Give it with a spiritually prepared mind.* At the point of the invitation, the preacher is dependent on the Holy Spirit, so we must be sensitive to his movement.
2. *Give it expectantly.* Believe God will honor the faithful preaching of his Word.
3. *Give it dependently.* Depend on the Holy Spirit.

[13] H. G. Olive, "The Development of the Evangelistic Invitation" (ThM thesis, Southern Baptist Theological Seminary, 1958), 24–25.

[14] For further elaboration, see Streett, *Effective Invitation,* 98–130.

4. *Give it personally.* I try to speak to an audience the same way I would speak to one person. Do not speak at a crowd; speak to people.
5. *Give it clearly.* Be specific in the appeal. Often people do not respond because they are unclear as to what they are called on to do. Do not rush through the invitation; allow time for clarity, and give enough time to it to allow people to respond.
6. *Give it courteously.* Be direct, but don't manipulate the people.
7. *Give it confidently.* After you have faithfully shared the gospel, you must rely on the Spirit to work. That should bring confidence that it is not about you, but about the work of the Spirit.
8. *Give it urgently.* This is not a "no big deal, take it or leave it" proposition. Give it with passion.

Methods can include giving an invitation:

- To come forward to confess Christ;
- To come forward to go to a counseling or inquiry room;
- To raise their hands, indicating a desire to follow Christ;
- To pray at one's seat; or
- A combination of the above.

The best way to learn to give an effective invitation is by observing effective evangelists. I have also learned that the host pastor can extend the invitation with effectiveness as the people there know him. I recall a time in St. Louis where I preached and extended the invitation. A couple of people responded. Then the pastor, who had great respect among the people, extended the invitation. About 19 people that night responded to Christ, including one person who came from Judaism to faith.

Conducting an Evangelistic Meeting

Hosting a Guest Evangelist

One of the most haphazard activities in the local church is the hosting of a guest evangelist for a meeting to reach the lost, or for that matter hosting a guest minister for any occasion. I have spoken at almost 2,000 various events in my lifetime, and I have pretty much seen it all, from staying in a home with enough cats to fill a zoo to a wonderful night at the Embassy Suites. If you are going to hold such a meeting, and I believe churches should, do not be haphazard about it. If reaching people matters, we should go about it with all our hearts! My friend Daniel Forshee, who has years of experience as a pastor, an evangelist, and a seminary professor, offers the following suggestions for hosting an evangelistic team. If you are the host pastor, here are some practical things to do:

1. *Secure an evangelist whom you know to have integrity.* Whenever possible, secure a vocational evangelist. Do not just invite your buddy in to preach so you can play golf together (yes, that actually happens). Ask if he has a music evangelist whom he can recommend. If possible, secure the musician as well, since music plays an important role in a successful meeting.
2. *Set the date.* The best times for a fall revival meeting are August through November; for a spring revival, March through May. It is better to select the speaker you desire, then set the date. Setting a date and then finding someone who fits the calendar is a poor way of selecting a speaker. Choose the man of God, not the convenient time.
3. *Secure a thorough preparation manual.* Some evangelists provide you with a manual. The North American Mission Board (SBC) provides outstanding materials for such meetings.[15] I have used these materials and have found them effective.
4. *Begin preparations three to six months in advance.* Share with the church council, deacons, teachers, and other key leaders with excitement!
5. *Organize a revival planning team to help with preparations.* Most preparation manuals guide this process.
6. *Pastor, be enthusiastic!* You are the key to the involvement of your people.
7. *Select a theme for the meeting.* This will help in your promotions and publicity.
8. *Use budgeted money for incidentals.* The church should budget for travel, lodging, meals, pianist, organist, and so on. *Never* tell the evangelist that the love offering will be given to the team, and then take expenses for the meeting from the offering. This lacks integrity, but it happens too often. House the team in a decent hotel. Reimburse the team for mileage if

[15] See www.namb.net/planit.

they drive. Surely we can treat the called of God on the same level as the IRS does when it comes to reimbursement for mileage! Just a note: while we should never preach the gospel for money, the truth is most churches are pretty cheap. And those churches are the ones with pastors who complain about their low salaries, likely because they taught their people to be cheap! Paul told the Corinthians: "Even so the Lord has commanded that those who preach the gospel should live from the gospel" (1 Cor 9:14 NKJV). I do many events for no financial remuneration at all, such as FCA huddle meetings and college groups. I know those ministries have little or no budget. But a church should be responsible to care for those who minister to them. Particularly if you host a minister of the gospel who gives his life to itinerant ministry, you should be careful to take good care of both he and his family.

9. *Be clear with the evangelistic team about finances.* Provide mileage expense, airfare, and related costs (parking, meals en route). I know from experience how much travel costs. Quality begets quality!
10. *If you use a love offering, extend a thoughtful, prepared request for the love offering in every service, especially Sunday morning.* Use Scripture, illustrations, and personal example. Do not treat the offering haphazardly. Explain that the evangelists are being paid with no set amount—strictly on a love offering basis. Emphasize to your congregation the joy of giving. Remind people on this and every occasion involving finances that we give to Jesus, not to people. It is for His kingdom. Have special love offering envelopes available in every service, including Sunday morning. I know one pastor who used envelopes for registering attendance as well as the offering. He had all the people put their names on the envelope, indicating that no one had to give. But he encouraged those who desired to worship through giving to enclose a gift as well. There was no high pressure, only encouragement. The love offering was extremely high for a church of its size. Give people the opportunity, teach them to give out of love for God, and they will give!
11. *Introduce the team each night.* Guests need some introduction. It is best to do this during the welcome time early in the service.
12. *Take the minister to share Christ in homes.*

13. *Schedule some fun—golf, for example.* If you pastor First Baptist Church of Grand Canyon, then you know where to take your guests! However, some ministers really do not enjoy doing a lot of sightseeing (I am one of those, who has seen a lot of the world, and really does not enjoy coming home to tell my family all they missed), so check with them.
14. *Have trained counselors available, especially for youth night.* This is a *great* time to get laity involved in evangelism. Besides, God is pleased when people prepare for His blessings!
15. *Pastor, extend the invitation.* As noted above, often the response is greater after an additional appeal by the pastor, since the people know him. For example, say, "When Dr. Hunt used the illustration about the young boy, God convicted my heart . . ."
16. *Be a gracious host.* Make sure that the only concerns the evangelists have are preaching the gospel and leading worship.

Preparing for an Evangelistic Meeting

There are two keys to conducting an effective mass evangelism event. One is practical or organizational. The other is spiritual.

As a young pastor I served a church that struggled, and then had a relapse! The church had declined from about 50 in average Sunday school attendance to less than 10 when they called me. I was in seminary and pretty much ignorance-on-fire at the time. I knew nothing better than to cry out to God in fervent prayer and do the best I could to lead our people to prepare for God to move. The church had baptized three people in the previous eight years or so. The baptistry stored the Christmas decorations (I am not making this up). I led the people to follow pretty much the following, and we saw God work in our little church.

Organizational Preparation

A mass evangelism meeting should work from an updated, cultivated *prospect list.* If the meeting is to be a harvest event and not a cultivating event, there must be people in the services who are unsaved. As I write this, the last two places I have preached I had a conversation after the services with men who openly did not believe, but who came to hear me preach because a friend brought them. They each said they were exploring Christianity. Sadly, too many times I speak at an evangelistic meeting where only the active church members attend (which doesn't mean everyone there is a Christian!). In order to see the lost in the services, believers will need to spend much time developing relationships with friends and neighbors. This will take some time in the months and weeks before the meeting.

You will reach some people before the meeting starts if you begin about six weeks ahead. For example, in the church mentioned above which I served as pastor, we saturated the community with copies of the New Testament, we used radio, we updated our prospect list, and we visited many people. The week before the meeting began, our church saw someone come to Christ. I had told the congregation the Sunday before that I would be filling the baptistry the next Sunday and was praying that God would save 10 people. I saw more eyes rolling than bowling balls at the local alley, but I knew if God did not do something, this church might not survive. The Wednesday night before the meeting began a family shared the news that their daughter had trusted Christ and would present herself the coming Sunday for baptism. I confess that gave my feeble faith helpful confidence.

The very Sunday morning the meeting began, a young woman who had not been to church since she was about 12 gave her life to Christ and was baptized that night. This happened because we had met her and established a relationship.

During an evangelistic meeting, make specific appointments with unsaved people for the pastor and the evangelist to visit. If you take the initiative to set such appointments, you will probably win several whom you visit as the Holy Spirit moves in their lives.

In addition, organizational preparation for a meeting requires *publicity*. Use every avenue you can. We tried to touch our community with different approaches: visitation, door-to-door New Testament distribution, door-to-door flyer giveaway the day before the meeting, phone calls, radio spots, and an ad in the newspaper. In one case, our revival meeting was part of the simultaneous crusades that we periodically have sponsored as Southern Baptists. There were television spots as well and a direct-mail flyer available to us. We targeted specific people to visit. Many people in our community were touched by a small, struggling church. As a result, many came to Christ, and we continued to baptize others after the meeting was over.

The third organizational concern for a revival meeting is *attendance*. Sometimes, we don't get the church people to attend. Monday night is notorious as a weak attendance night, for example. Another problem is that we don't get lost people to attend. How can they come to Christ if they're not present to hear the gospel? A key to attendance night is sponsoring special emphases. In previous days in rural churches, pack-a-pew night was a big hit. Groups, classes, or individuals would compete to see who could pack the most pews or pack the pew with the most people. This approach doesn't work as well today, but other emphases are good possibilities. The most significant special emphasis today is youth night. We also had a children's focus.

Spiritual Preparation

How do you prepare the church spiritually for an evangelistic harvest? After all, organizational preparation matters little without the presence of God. First, provide a list of unsaved people to the evangelist and the church several weeks before the meeting. This will allow the congregation and him to pray specifically during your preparation. It will also encourage the speaker to see that the church is serious about reaching people!

Second, organize focused prayer for the church. This includes praying for the meeting in every Sunday school class, each service, and each meeting, beginning at least six weeks before the meeting. God's blessing is often equal to the level of our expectancy. All-night prayer meetings or seasons of fasting and prayer can be effective. The chapter on prayer has a section on a prayer vigil you can utilize. At our meeting I described above, we held an all-night prayer meeting. I figured if Jesus prayed all night before calling His disciples, I should do the same before a critical event.

Finally, encourage special times of prayer during the week of the meeting. Prayer walks through the community are increasingly used as a means to mobilize believers to pray. Have prayer times before each service, and enlist individuals to pray during the service. Evangelistic meetings are an excellent time to deepen the commitment of the church to prayer!

After our four-day evangelistic meeting we had 13 who made public professions of faith. We baptized 10 of those, as I had prayed from the weeks before. That began a growing sense of the Spirit's work in our congregation. There is potency in expectancy!

Innovative Approaches

Some evangelists are using innovative approaches to share the timeless gospel message. An evangelist friend named Kelley Green has used an approach called Frontliners. Each summer he leads crusades at night and involves youth groups from across the country in evangelistic outreach during the day. This combination of a youth mission trip and a harvest meeting has proven fruitful. Such a method utilizes both the attractional element of a meeting and a more incarnational effort to go into the community. We do not only have to have events and meetings to reach the masses in our church buildings. We can use secular venues, or we can simply find places where the masses already are to present Christ through servant evangelism or other forms where the gospel is proclaimed to crowds in the culture.

Wayne Bristow has utilized Total Life conferences in churches with nontraditional worship services. These conferences target young adults in communities where it is difficult to sustain attendance for four or five days and where traditional revival meetings are no longer successful. Total Life events include evangelistic dinners and luncheons; special events for young people, older children, senior citizens, and young adults; and mixed audience rallies.

Words such as *revival* and *crusade* are confusing or even intimidating to unchurched people. Wayne recognizes these terms have lost much of their meaning, so he uses other terminology. He calls his meetings Total Life conferences. Changing the terminology can change the emphasis in some settings. But this may not be appropriate or workable in every church.

Effective Evangelistic Events

Thom Rainer's book, *Effective Evangelistic Churches,* contains several surprises. For example, Rainer found that event evangelism seems to have little impact. This is true, if we define success or effectiveness in terms of immediate conversions. But we need to remember that evangelism is more than harvesting, although this is our ultimate goal. We must plant and cultivate as well as harvest. In our culture today we must give more attention to sowing and watering if we will have the harvest we desire. So many unchurched need the gospel presented again and again in many venues, events being one of those. Event evangelism can be effective in giving people an opportunity to hear the gospel—particularly people that might not hear it in any other way. A recent example that has grown in popularity reaches outdoorsmen—wild game dinners. These meals, featuring examples of trophy animals, and typically with the gospel presented by a believer who has been an effective hunter or fisherman, have made the gospel available to a group of men who rarely ever attend church services.

A neighborhood block party will present Christ to those for whom the doors of the church are not readily accessible. An evangelistic concert in the church building at Christmas or Easter may draw people who might not come at other times to hear the Word of God preached. We should not judge such events strictly on how many people are converted. But when we do such events, we would be wise to register everyone attending for possible times of further relationship-building and follow-up.

The lost and confused people of your community aren't likely to fall into your church in large numbers asking for answers. Thus, we must take the message to them in creative ways. This can be done through event evangelism.

By being sensitive to your community, its needs, and its activities, you can use existing events or develop some new ones to introduce people to Jesus Christ. Is your town having a parade? Have the church build a float, then let members walk along the parade route passing out tracts. A church in our town cancels Sunday night activities for several nights in the spring as the town has a cultural arts event series on Sunday nights with various artists from bluegrass to country to pop. Church members are encouraged to attend, mingle among the people, and build relationships for further witness.

Valentine's Day, Halloween, Christmas, and New Year's provide opportunities for your church to create an event that draws the unchurched. Then you can tactfully share Jesus with them. In developing an evangelistic event, remember that you're trying to attract the unchurched, not the church! This may mean doing things a little differently than fits your style, but this is OK as long as you don't compromise the gospel. It may also mean having the event somewhere besides the church building. Furthermore, in advertising, it may mean focusing on the event or the personality rather than the church. You're not hiding the church or acting ashamed of the gospel; you're just being crafty in your presentation.

A specialized type of evangelistic event is sports evangelism. Eddie Fox, head of world evangelism for United Methodists, says that the roads of Rome carried the gospel in the first century, but sports is the means of carrying it today. The evangelist of the future may look more like Reggie White than Billy Graham. The kingdom of God is awakening to the fact that sports evangelism can be highly effective.

The following is a general breakdown of the types of sports evangelism, although it can take many other forms:

1. *Major event-centered sports evangelism.* This includes potentially thousands of events per year in the United States, including most pro sports and many major college events, as well as the one-time events such as the Olympics. Most churches in most cities don't realize what an evangelistic gold mine is right before them almost every weekend. Using these events to reach the lost is not difficult and complicated; it's a matter of motivating, educating, and enabling our people!
2. *Personality-centered sports evangelism.* This approach is using a famous athlete to draw a crowd. During the meeting, he shares his testimony and the way of salvation. A thread of this runs through all types of sports evangelism, as it is almost always the persona of an athlete or athletes that draws the audience. Networking with churches and associations on whom to use, and how, is crucial. Personality-centered sports evangelism can work in a variety of ways. The athlete may appear live or on video. Tracts with his or her testimony could be prepared specifically for the sport or event.
3. *Competition-centered sports evangelism.* This is based around nonprofessional, club-level league competition, such as ongoing ministry in the adult men's basketball league, in Little League, and so forth. This has commonly been called recreation ministry. We should be sharing the gospel through written materials and events formed around recreation play all across the nation.

The variations go on and on. Groups such as Athletes in Action and Fellowship of Christian Athletes have long been involved in this type of ministry, but even the smallest church can get involved.

Cheryl Wolfinger of the International Sports Federation (ISF), which sends sports evangelism teams around the world, reports that her organization is swamped with domestic requests for sports evangelism teams. This is happening, although ISF makes no effort to procure domestic requests. Wolfinger uses these increased requests to highlight the interest in sports evangelism throughout the United States.

Mark Snowden, media and sports evangelism consultant for the International Mission Board of the Southern Baptist Convention, confirms Wolfinger's analysis of the burgeoning requests for sports evangelism development in the United States. He reports that the IMB continues to use sports evangelism to get into hard-to-reach countries. Snowden said the IMB is beginning to appoint full-time sports missionaries instead of relegating this work to short-term missionaries, as it has in the past.

Tom Felten is publisher of *Sports Spectrum*, a national Christian sports magazine that is a vital tool for reaching athletically minded lost people. Felten says, "What we're seeing right now is more and more parachurch groups and denominations adding full-time sports evangelism personnel to their staff. The growth is phenomenal. An indication would be our Super Bowl Outreach Kit. We started it six years ago with 2,100 churches involved. This year we will have 6,000 to 7,000 churches holding evangelistic Super Bowl parties. Sports evangelism has been and continues to erupt."[16]

Churches must see the big picture and make specific application of the sports evangelism possibilities within the United States. Courtney Cash, Wolfinger's associate, says some churches are taking advantage of sports evangelism, but that the percentage is low. "They are hosting clinics, organizing leagues, supplying chaplains, providing tournaments in multi-housing units, and playing pick-up games with youth in the inner city," Cash says. "However, even though there are almost one hundred sports ministries in the United States, there [are few] networks to help churches utilize the existing new tool, teach them how to reach sports people, or connect them with the necessary materials to be completely successful in their efforts."[17]

Questions for Consideration

1. Did you come to Christ in a "mass evangelism" setting where a preacher proclaimed the gospel to a group or congregation? Do you know people saved that way?
2. When is the last time you attended services like this?
3. Do you see the need for evangelistic meetings in our day?
4. What are some creative ways your church can be effective in mass evangelism?

---

[16] See A. Reid, *Introduction to Evangelism* (Nashville: Broadman and Holman, 1998), 280.

[17] Ibid., 280–81.

PART IV

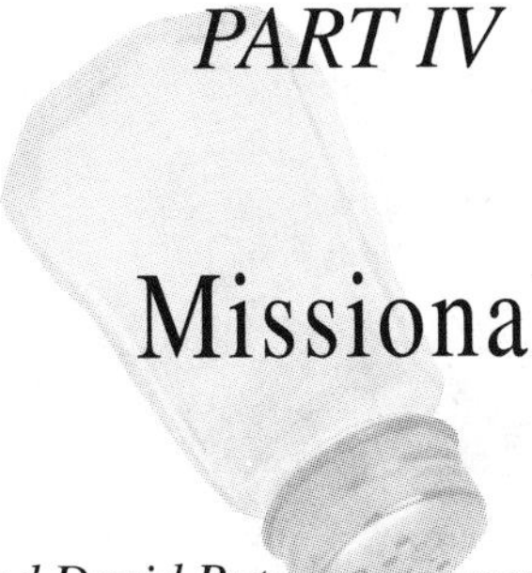

Missional

Ed Stetzer and David Putman argue winsomely for the need of the church today to engage the culture in a missional manner. In their book *Breaking the Missional Code* they note how our culture has become "glocal"—a convergence of the global world with our local communities.[1] Or, as Thomas Friedman would put it, the world has become flat. That is why when you call the toll-free number on your laptop for help you talk to someone from a call center in Bangalore, India. The Internet, among other factors, has shrunk our world.

Before now, in most communities in the West the church was the first choice of the spiritually hungry because the church was the dominant spiritual force in a given area. Now, we must be more proactive, more intentional in stepping into the culture around us and doing what Paul did—reason in the marketplace with unbelievers where they live. Stetzer and Putman argue that we must "break the missional code" in our given contexts to be able to communicate Christ effectively. I think they are right, and I think the shift from an institutional evangelism ("ya'll come") to an intentional, missional approach stands as the greatest challenge facing established churches. Good news: such a change is not only possible for new church plants; conventional churches can change too. They give examples from the young, expansive Mars Hill Church in Seattle (only a few years old) to the First Baptist Church of Woodstock, Georgia (over 150 years old) to demonstrate that both the planting of new churches and the refocusing of established churches can and must occur.

The final section of this book hopes to help believers do just that. We need a new way of seeing the culture, firmly through the lens of Scripture but clear enough to see the culture as well.

[1] E. Stetzer and D. Putman, *Breaking the Missional Code: Your Church Can Become a Missionary in Your Community* (Nashville: B&H Academic, 2006).

Chapter 21

Paradigms

A church which pitches its tents without constantly looking out for new horizons, which does not continually strike camp, is being untrue to its calling.[1]

—Hans Kung

Once upon a time (about AD 1959) in a land called America there lived a group of people who banded together with a common faith, a common culture, and, in so many ways, a common aesthetic. This group proved to be a growing population in numbers and in influence in the land of the free and the home of the brave. If you know much about them and their time, you will recognize them. Here are a few shared features from back in their day:

- white framed or brick building, white steeple, white columns in front, pews, choir loft, piano on the left and organ on the right, carpet often red;
- morning Sunday school, worship service, Sunday evening Training Union and evening service, midweek prayer meeting followed by choir practice, Vacation Bible School in the sum-

[1] Cited in A. Hirsch, *Forgotten Ways: Reactivating the Missional Church* (Grand Rapids: Brazos Press, 2006), 15.

mer, revival in spring and fall (i.e., a four-day to one-week-long meeting);
- leader (pastor) in three-piece suit, always, or so it seemed; choir in robes;
- Sunday services featuring hymns, prayer, offering, a message, invitation, lots of standing and sitting, most folks in suits and dresses.

I am referring of course to the Southern Baptist Convention, my tradition. In the year 1959, however, I could also have been referring to most Protestant churches, from Baptist to Methodist, from Pentecostal to Presbyterian. While some details would have been different, this was the monolithic appearance of the church. This heritage has shaped me, and for that I thank God.

I was born in 1959 in a culture shared by 90 percent of churches, at least in the so-called Bible Belt. Yet it extended further. I realized this more when I served as a home missionary in Indiana. I saw church building after church building (not to be confused with the Church) in the northern part of the state that appeared as if it had been transplanted from the South as southerners had moved north to work in the Rust Belt and took their culture with them.

We had somewhat of a shared faith then. We certainly had a shared aesthetic. Worship services copied one another in style. Just look at the architecture of church buildings and how we programmed our churches. We had a shared life in many ways. And so did America. Life seemed simpler then.

And then along came . . . rock and roll, my generation (those nasty Boomers) who protested just about everything, a huge influx of ethnic friends from many nations, the influence of television and other media like never before, and before you knew it, culture had changed. The nation had changed. The world had changed.

Things *have* changed. We will never go back to that day again. But if the 1950s ever come back, a lot of churches are ready.

We must have a common faith. Truth does not change. God's Word will do. But truth changes us. It must. And culture has radically changed. The United States of America is an international mission field. We are a nation of subcultures. We must "break the code"[2] in the various places we serve to discover how to apply the message to the culture. Too many believers confuse truth with personal preference.

[2] Stetzer and Putman, *Breaking the Missional Code.*

There will always be a place for the type of church I described above. But there will increasingly be a need for many others—those who affirm a common faith, once delivered to the saints, and who likewise take that faith to various subcultures in the same way a missionary overseas would take the gospel to a foreign land.

Paradigms—How We See the World

Every day each of us puts on lenses. I am not referring to the glasses I wear but to the worldview that gives all of us a template through which we live our lives. A few years ago I had to admit I needed new glasses. I had to don bifocals to be able to read easily. I am convinced the church of today, for all of her successes, needs a serious trip to the spiritual eye doctor to look at the way we see the world. In this chapter I hope to show a few examples of changes necessary in how we see the world.

Let's remember that the New Testament teaches this not only in the narratives of the Gospels and the Acts but in the very way it is arranged. We have one message, one time when Christ walked on the earth, was crucified and raised from the dead, and commissioned His followers to reach the world. This happened one time in history. Yet we have four separate Gospel accounts to tell this one story. Three are quite similar (Matthew, Mark, and Luke) because their accounts are close, thus being called "synoptic," which means to "see together." Still, each of those three is written to a different audience, so the same message is applied differently. Then we have the Gospel of John. Same life. Same story but quite different in specifics and focus. Is it not interesting that we tend to present a Gospel of John to people as an evangelistic tool, but so many of us act as if we must all line up together like the first three accounts when many feel a call to be a Gospel-of-John-type witness to the world? Each Gospel writer recorded the story of Jesus from a unique frame of reference.

I am weary of churches fighting over secondary issues like whether or not to clap in church or changing Wednesday night schedules (real examples) as if we are changing the New Testament. By the way, for the most part we got midweek prayer meetings from Pietists on the European continent. I am not opposed to prayer meetings, but I am opposed to the hypocrisy we demonstrate about prayer. Do we have to gather once a week to have an effective prayer ministry? Is that the only way? I know a church with hundreds of weekly small groups praying all week long. Not a bad strategy either. This reminds me of how we complain about prayer being taken from public schools while surveys show only about 12 percent of believers pray *with their families* in a week.

I saw this illustrated recently. I had the honor of preaching in a wonderful church in Springfield, Missouri, at a statewide evangelism conference. This church's pastor not only has shown himself to be an effective preacher and leader, building a wonderful ministry there. He has also, to use the parlance of Stetzer and Putman, "broken the code" for his area. The pastor, along with his family, is a wonderfully gifted singer in the bluegrass/southern gospel tradition. They sang for us. It was wonderful. Not my preference personally but very nice.

This pastor understands the bluegrass, hillbilly culture (that is not a dig; that is an observation) of the area, maybe 35 miles from Branson, and is thus able to reach that culture. If you took that same church and moved to Chapel Hill, North Carolina, in the shadow of the University of North Carolina, you would find such growth the church has experienced much more difficult. Why? Chapel Hill has little resemblance to Springfield, Missouri. If the bluegrass culture of southern Missouri, or the southern gospel culture of the rural south, becomes the dominant aesthetic in America, we are ready to reach the whole nation.

We must affirm the truth more than ever. We must teach our children the best of our heritage, including great hymns and the best of our past—how God has moved in mighty awakenings, how Christianity has influenced society for the better time and time again. We need to keep a love for preaching the Word and a love for the Word and a passion for souls. But we must also be the people of God for this time, in this culture, in a way that brings glory to God and makes disciples of men and women. Here are some key paradigms we must shift to see more clearly how to reach our world.

From Maintaining an Institution to Advancing a Movement

Throughout this book I have argued that evangelism means we are advancing a movement of God, a movement of good news to those in great need. For the church to recover that view we must admit an obsession with institutionalism.

Institutions are not the enemy but excessive focus on them can be. God has given us several, including the home, the local church, and the state. We need institutions to serve as the boundaries of the river of God's movement, keeping us from the excesses of heretical teaching on the one side and ineffective practice on the other. But we have tended to make the institutions the point, with the result of substituting a passion for advancing a movement for the duty of maintaining an institution. Look at how much energy we put into buildings, to getting people at church on Sunday, to convincing people to give up spare time to do church activities. Some churches have become programmed to destroy their families! We need a return to what Thom Rainer and Eric Geiger call a "simple church" with a focus on things that truly matter.[3]

How many people in your church awaken daily thinking something like this: *Today, in my workplace or at school, and in my neighborhood, I get to be a part of something so much bigger than I am! By my character, my words, my deeds, I get to help advance the movement of God on this earth.* On the other hand, how many think something more like this: *I need to be sure I am at the church on time, have my lesson studied, and have my clothes picked out.* Stark difference, I would say.

How do I know we focus more on institutions than on the movement? Because we do not *go* to church; we *are* the church. If every church building in the U.S. burned to the ground today, the church would still be here! Church buildings can be helpful, but our obsession with buildings hinders the movement. We focus far too much on getting people to our buildings and not enough on getting our people into the culture with the gospel.

The local church is not a *hotel for saints;* it is a *hospital for sinners*. Do you see your local church as a birthing center, a spiritual maternity ward? So many youth groups are just that, groups. They should be a youth ministry, focusing on discipling their students so they can go into their schools and reach more who need Christ, instead of planning events to placate the church youth (or more particularly, their parents).

How much of your life do you see as given to advancing a movement? Does that concept appear in your children? Reggie McNeal has given a sober warning for the church:

[3] T. Rainer and E. Geiger, *Simple Church* (Nashville: Broadman & Holman, 2006).

> The current church culture in North America is on life support. It is living off the work, money, and energy of previous generations from a previous world order. The plug will be pulled either when the money runs out or when the remaining three-fourths of a generation that were institutional loyalists die off or both.[4]

We use the term *church* as an adjective instead of a noun. We speak of wearing "church" clothes, of doing "church" activities, or of doing "church" work in a way that separates our Christian lives from everyday living (I am still looking for that concept in the book of Acts).

Please do not hear what I am not saying. The death of a church culture as we know it will not be the death of the church. There are more than a few today who spend most of their time talking as if the church no longer matters or that the Evangelical Church has only caused harm the last generation or so. The church Jesus founded is good; it is right. The church established by Jesus will survive until He returns regardless of what the pundits say. The revolution we need will involve a return to a biblical understanding of the church in culture not an abandonment of it.

But when "church culture" becomes so inward, so separated from a gospel impact in a community, and has become confused with biblical Christianity, it must be challenged. In reality, the "church culture" in North America is a vestige of the original movement, an institutional expression of religion that is in part civil religion and in part a club where its religious people can hang out with other people whose politics, worldview, and lifestyle match theirs.[5] We should be a genuine counterculture, distinguishable from the world not by the clothes we wear on Sunday or our customs but by the character of our lives, the message we share, and the movement we advance.

Steve Addison studies movements. He identified five phases through which ideas spread in missionary movements:[6]

> *White Hot Faith*—Leaders have a direct encounter with God that leads to social change. John Wesley, William Booth, Martin Luther, and others who led movements that lasted, all met

[4] R. McNeal, *The Present Future: Six Tough Questions for the Church* (San Francisco: John Wiley & Sons, 2003), 1.

[5] Ibid.

[6] Only the headings are Addison's, not the commentary.

Christ in a powerful, life-changing way. In his book *Tipping Point* Malcolm Gladwell makes a similar observation of those who lead in times of sudden change, referring to such leaders as Mavens.

Commitment to the Cause—People give their lives to the cause as the center of their lives. This is not only true in Christian movements but also can be seen in movements such as car bombers in the global terrorist network. Similarly, in his watershed book on leadership *Good to Great,* Jim Collins argues that one of the marks of a Level 5 leader in "good to great" corporations is a deeply imbedded commitment to the company.

Contagious Relationships—Ideas become viral expressions traveling rapidly. Networks already existent become the means by which such ideas spread. Again, Gladwell refers to those who have the ability to communicate an idea quickly to many others as "connectors."

Rapid Mobilization—Movements spread quickly by those able to coordinate the efforts of those in it.

Dynamic Methods—Movements tend to be more fluid at accepting and jettisoning methods in favor of those that more effectively spread the message.

Could your church be described more as a movement or an institution?

From Attractional Evangelism to Missional

Most of the evangelism in the current, conventional church has been attractional. This grows directly out of our institutionalism. We have created institutions and thus believe that since we love them so much, if we can only get the lost to them, they will likewise love our institutions and what they stand for. We spend so much time with one another in our institutions that we too often forget what it was like to be lost ourselves. As I said in a previous chapter on mass evangelism, we need not stop our attractional events and equipping. We should not make either-or what is both-and. We can add without subtracting. We do not need to burn down our church buildings and meet under a tree. But we must become living witnesses in the culture. Yet we also must be careful not to depart from the New Testament in our efforts. Show me one place in the book of Acts where a meeting was scheduled and people were invited to attend. That may have been implied at times, but what is obvious in the Acts is that the early church reached people not by attracting them to events but by sharing Christ where the people lived.

When we only focus on attractional witness, we can unexpectedly add an unintended consequence—our witness is not only *attractional;* it is also *extractional:* when someone is evangelized in the attractional mode they are more quickly pulled from their own culture which they are most effective to reach! So, while we win the person, success in this approach to the exclusion of a missional witness can over time also undergird a Christian subculture more interested in distancing itself from the world than actually reaching it.

Driscoll contrasted the "routine" approach of attractional evangelism, in particular mass meetings and weekly personal outreach, with a more missional approach, one he calls "reformissional":

> In both options, the emphasis is on eliciting a swift decision for Christ without taking time to build a friendship. In both versions, those who walk forward, stand up, raise their hand, pray a prayer, sign a card, or indicate by some other means their decision are deemed converts and told to assimilate into churches. Whether they were truly converted is debatable, and the odds of them assimilating into churches are uncertain, unless they already have trustworthy friendships with someone in the church who can serve as a tour-guide, introducing them to the language, values, and systems of the church. While Scripture gives examples of the routine model, the mission model of Jesus may prove to be more faithful to God, more fruit for the lost people, and more appealing to Christians. . . .[7]

To his credit Driscoll also noted the dangers inherent both in attractional and missional witness:

> Attractional churches need to transform their people from being consumers in the church to being missionaries outside of the church. Missional churches need to gather crowds into their church so that hard words of repentance can be preached in an effort to expose people's hearts.[8]

I still knock on doors and preach meetings, but I also seek with my family to reach our neighbors and others in our world with whom

[7] M. Driscoll, *Confessions of a Reformission Rev* (Grand Rapids: Zondervan, 2006), 67.

[8] Ibid., 27.

we can serve as missionaries. We must admit that we have too often created a culture that encourages believers to share Christ with others without getting truly involved in their lives. It is much easier to invite a person to an event at a church or to go out on weekly visitation than to spend the time needed to cultivate relationships with lost people to see God work in their lives. We have taken the path-of-least-resistance approach to evangelism. We can continue to use such approaches, but we must not settle for them or for a paradigm that reduces evangelism to a weekly or annual event.

We must instead take the stance of a missionary in our culture. What if every believer in the U.S. was commissioned in a massive ceremony to live as missionaries in their communities. No one need quit their job or relocate; they would simply live as missionaries, living and sharing the gospel in the workplace and neighborhood, in the marketplace and the school, as if no one else was there to share Christ. We would do more than verbalize the message; we would seek to incarnate it in how we lived in our communities, seeking to live justly, loving our neighbors as Christ loved people.

Well, that will never happen. The massive commissioning thing, that is. But what is clear is that the Most High God of creation has *already* commissioned us to do and be just that! I am not advocating an abandonment of attractional evangelism. But I am arguing the long-term trajectory of the church, if she is not to become increasingly ineffective, is to move to a more missional posture.

From Programmatic to Incarnational

I have been a part of one of the most intense, widely utilized, and extensive efforts to train believers to share their faith in the history of the church. From the 1960s to now, personal witness training through the vehicle of programs in the church has been a hallmark of the conventional church. From Evangelism Explosion to FAITH Evangelism, probably millions have been through a class, and hundreds of thousands have taken what they have learned into communities to share Christ. Some have even taken what they have learned and put it into practice in their daily lives. I have a confession to make: while I have personally benefited from such training and helped write some of the training, I think an honest evaluation would have to say that the long-term result has not been to create an army of soul-winners. No doubt many have been helped. No doubt many have met Christ through this effort. But what it has failed to do is to create a *culture* in which church after church became ignited with an evangelistic passion as a result of the training. I have seen churches become ignited for the gospel where witness-training programs were used, but in every case the leadership of a passionate, evangelistic pastor has been key.

The very approach we used in such training sowed the seeds of its own demise. We pulled out individuals, taught them a specific method, gave them a certain time (usually weekly visitation) to implement what they learned, and awarded them when they finished the course. We expected the minimum of commitment and attempted to make witnessing as painless as possible. But except in those churches where the pastor's leadership led the church to adopt an evangelistic culture, for the most part those trained never spilled over into a movement of personal witness in the congregation. And many I have talked to still never actually think about intentionally speaking to their neighbors about the very things they learned to share one night a week to strangers.

The witness of the early church was viral—it spread like a really good plague. That is the description you get when you read accounts of the great awakenings in history and of the church in China today. I am not opposed to witness training. I hope this book helps to train the readers in witnessing. I would utilize training extensively as a pastor. But I am concerned that we have made evangelism a separate program so that it no longer is seen as at the heart of the church's mission—it is merely one more program we push in our institutions. I know several pastors who regularly offer practical tips on witnessing to the whole congregation on Sundays. I also know some who take their entire message once or twice a year and give instruction to all in attendance on effective witnessing.

By "incarnational" I do not mean we are to be Jesus embodied in the culture. Jesus Christ, the Incarnate One, came to earth once. But as He is the head of the church, we are His body. And as His body, we are to incarnate the reality of Christ's change in our communities. You see this in 1 Thess 1:8–10:

> For the Lord's message rang out from you, not only in Macedonia and Achaia, but in every place that your faith in God has gone out, so we don't need to say anything. For they themselves report about us what kind of reception we had from you: how you turned to God from idols to serve the living and true God,

> and to wait or His Son from heaven, whom He raised from the dead—Jesus, who rescues us from the coming wrath.

The Thessalonians' witness was more than the speaking of a verbal witness, though it certainly included that. The people whom they lived among saw the gospel "ring out," or "thunder," in their culture. As my friend Charles Lyons, longtime pastor in Chicago, told me at lunch recently, "The incarnation is not only theology; it is also strategy."

Bob Roberts described an incarnational church:

> Missional churches become deeply involved in their communities. They are not focused so much on their buildings as they are on living, demonstrating, and offering biblical community in a lost world among a lost people. An incarnational church functions as the "Body of Christ" because it represents the presence of Christ within a community.[9]

Hirsch offered a helpful grid for understanding the incarnational life of the missional believer.

> *Presence*—"There is a time for 'in-your-face' approaches to mission, but there is also a time to simply become part of the very fabric of a community and to engage in the humanity of it all."
>
> *Proximity*—"Jesus mixed with people of every level of society."
>
> *Powerlessness*—Rather than an entitlement attitude toward the world, we must embrace "servanthood and humility in our relationships with each other and the world."
>
> *Proclamation*—"A genuine incarnational approach will require that we be always willing to share the gospel story with those within our world."[10]

From Compartmentalized to Holistic Ministry

This shift ties very closely to the preceding one, as programs tend to separate aspects of the faith that more rightly should be held together. It could be that one of the worst things you do in your church

[9] B. Roberts, *The Multiplying Church* (Grand Rapids: Zondervan, 2008), 11.

[10] M. Frost and A. Hirsch, *The Shaping of Things to Come: Innovation and Mission for the 21st Century Church* (Peabody, MA: Hendrickson, 2003), 133–34.

is have a missions committee that separates missions from the rest of the church. I asked J. D. Greear, lead pastor of Summit Church and a former student, what he thought had to be in a book like this. He answered immediately: "We have to move beyond our understanding of evangelism, community ministry, and church planting as separate ministries to see how they work together." His vision for Raleigh/Durham is preeminently evangelistic. But his method is a church-planting movement incorporating community ministry at the heart. Indeed, his church annually has a weeklong "at home mission trip" called Hope for Durham, where hundreds of church members paint middle school classrooms, help with home repair, and a myriad of other ministries, sharing Christ in the middle of them. Remember the earliest summary of life in the church (Acts 2:41–47) included witnessing, community concern, worship, and instruction all together in a daily context.

Once upon a time life was lived by most in a more holistic manner, where people lived and worked in communities all interrelated. In a more agrarian culture today we see that same integration, in simple villages in the African bush or Amish communities in the West. But with the rise of such things as the 40-hour workweek and urbanization came a separation of life. The result: five-day workweek, one day of worship, and further separation into times for vacation, sports and leisure, and various "times" that vie for attention—work time, family time, church time, leisure time. As a result we find it harder to see our world from a larger, holistic view. "We succumb to the kind of compartmentalization over against an integrated worldview that addresses the entirety of life," James Emory White writes, adding:

> Our thinking about one area never informs our thinking about another. So one can be a Christian and not reflect—or worse, never even think of reflecting—about science and technology in light of the Christian worldview. So issues related to bioethics are seldom met with serious reflection on the nature of humanity and the sanctity of human life in light of the Scriptures. Instead, we let CNN tell us what the scientific and technological breakthroughs will mean for the quality of our life; we marvel at progress, then we privately ponder whether we will be able to afford the procedure. The world of science becomes distinct from the world of faith.[11]

[11] White, *Serious Times,* 101.

The danger from this separation is we begin treating Christianity as a checklist rather than a worldview by which we interpret all of life. As long as we have believers who do the big three (attend, give, and serve in the church building), we assume they are integrating faith into life. As long as churches have the big three (buildings, budgets, and baptisms), we assume our church is influencing culture. Yet many of our churches could vanish from their communities without being noticed.

The saddest part of this for me is to see the impact of this on young people. Because we have not demonstrated to youth the vigor, the risk, the excitement of living out our faith in a culture often opposed to it, in order to connect them with a sense of excitement we take them to theme parks and to play paintball. We see their need to be challenged, but because we have compartmentalized the faith, too many times we separate "fun" from faith. I have seen youth serve and share Christ in their communities who found that such activity was more exciting than playing video games. Thankfully more churches are taking students on mission trips and to places that integrate ministry with life. But these short-term trips, if not wedded to ongoing ministry in their home community, may actually foster further compartmentalization.

The danger of becoming more holistic is the loss of the intentional edge of evangelism. Without care the focus of reaching people for Christ can be lost in the middle of other things. While this is a real danger, so is the danger of *separation* of our witness to the point that many around us may never hear the gospel because of the way we present it.

From Consumerism to Service

The other day I received a postcard from a new church. It said in bold words, "Church Like You've Never Experienced Before!" It had a big bag of popcorn on the front and a subheading "100% boredom free." Really. Seriously? You are guaranteeing you will have such a church that everyone involved will never get bored? Never? No, that church is lying to me. But that is not the real problem. The problem is it appeals to the most base of motivations, consumerism. Church is about me, pleasing me, affirming me. No doubt that approach can draw a crowd. But is that really the point?

What if someone put together a new church advertisement that said, "Becoming a part of this could cost everything you are and would bring with it immense sacrifice, complete surrender, and total devotion, but could also provide for you joy not of this world"? What if we stopped appealing to the consumerism of our culture? What if we boldly declared that a gospel that can be preached in rich and free America but cannot be preached in China or Iraq is a false gospel? What if we proclaimed not how to find "your best life now" but challenged all to lose their life in order to find it in Christ?

Too many churches spend far too much of their money on their church plant. How many times have I met with leaders in cities who could do more with the leftover money of many suburban churches than the latter do with their entire budgets?

"I wonder about our marketing efforts in selling the church rather than lifting up Jesus," McNeal noted. "It seems in the New Testament that Paul's strategy was to preach the gospel. He formed the church as a result of harvest. His goal was converts; the church was the natural byproduct."[12]

Hirsch has observed the consumerism of the Western church:

> Church growth exponents have explicitly taught us how to market and tailor the product to suit target audiences. They told us to mimic the shopping mall, apply it to the church, and create a one-stop religious shopping experience catering to our every need. In this they were sincere and well intentioned, but they must have been also totally ignorant of the ramifications of their counsel—because in the end the medium has so easily overwhelmed the message. . . . Consumerism has actually become the driving ideology of the church's ministry.[13]

Amazingly, as I write this a number of churches are springing up across America, but not just another generation of the megachurch. These are church-planting churches, large to be sure but focused on getting the gospel to the culture more than building an empire. These churches are led by pastors who preach expositional messages of an hour or more in length—hardly giving in to the narcissistic consumerism of our time. And the churches they lead are large, growing, and multiplying, from Summit in Raleigh/Durham, to Harvest Bible Chapel in the Midwest, to Mars Hill in Seattle.

---

[12] McNeal, *Present Future*, 75.

[13] Hirsch, *Forgotten Ways,* 110.

Consumerism in the church has created an entire movement of church swappers, or "church hoppers" as I call them, as they are actually pests. These are professing believers who go from church to church looking for the one with the best approach to meeting their needs. How many times have I met someone like that who says, "I am just looking for a place to get fed." If you have been saved for more than a couple of years, take off your bib and put on an apron and serve! My family moved to Wake Forest in 1995 and joined the first church (a new plant) we visited. In the West far too much church growth comes from these church switchers. But the reality is one cannot consume one's way into discipleship.

From Conformity in All Things to Conformity in Truth, Creativity in Its Application

I have tried to be extremely clear throughout this book that we will not advance the movement of God on this earth by changing the message. But there are those, and the older we get the more of us are like this, who think that the way we do things is about as inspired as the Bible itself. Younger readers may find this hard to believe, but I actually meet people on occasion who believe changing the way a worship service is conducted, or changing dress codes for Sunday, actually means a change of conviction about doctrine. The institutional church confuses outward forms with unchanging doctrine at an alarming level.

A few years ago I spoke at a sweet country church with an emphasis that Sunday on inviting unchurched friends to the service. A sweet, elderly lady came up to me and said, "I knew this was a special day with a special preacher, so I went out and bought a new dress." A new dress? No one brought an unchurched friend. But ladies spent hours the day before or early that morning cooking food for the potluck at lunch, and some bought new dresses. I could have brought 10 unsaved people and all of them could have been saved, but if I had preached in jeans and a tee shirt (as I do often at youth events), that is what would have been the talk of the town. I am not at all saying every country church is like that. I am saying that the institutional church has become too much like that too much of the time.

Over time even the most dynamic movements, from the rise of Christianity to the great awakenings, become more focused on secondary issues, losing their attention on what caused the movement in the first place. This is seen in the rise of Methodism, for example. Birthed in the Great Awakening of the eighteenth century, Methodism spread with great vigor through the work of circuit-riding preachers in the American frontier and missionary preachers in Europe. But today, Methodism is marked far more by decline than growth.

I would argue that discouraging creativity can actually hinder the work of the gospel. So many times in history the fervency for mission came from those pushing the envelope creatively, from the almost scandalous practice of field preaching in the Great Awakening to the novel idea of Carey that believers should take the gospel to the nations. Hirsch argues that effective movements continue to receive energy not from the center, which tends to focus on consensus, but from the fringes. "In the study of the history of missions, one can even be formulaic in asserting that *all great missionary movements begin at the fringes of the church,* among the poor and marginalized, and seldom, if ever, at the center," Hirsch wrote.[14] I would add that while this is true, movements that move too far from the center might end up undermining truth. "Innovation, when not tethered to the truth of the gospel, leads to heresy," Driscoll warned. "Every heretic in the history of the church who took relevance to the culture beyond the bounds of orthodoxy did what Paul, in the opening chapter of Romans, calls exchanging the truth of God for a lie."[15]

There is a tension between living on the edge and standing in the center. But too many churches huddle in the center and have lost the gospel in the process. Hirsch argues, "It seems that when the church engages at the fringes, it almost always brings life to the center."[16]

We walk a tightrope between holding to unchanging truth without reducing truth to formulas or legalism on the one hand and pursuing creativity and encouraging antinomianism on the other. Conformity in essential doctrine, creativity in the application of those truths in a given culture, is the approach we should pursue. In the church today such a pull toward conformity has affected so much of what we do, from discipleship to evangelism.

We have had a tendency to make people clones rather than Christ followers. The Twelve Jesus called could hardly be seen as a monolithic group. Ministry is made easier if we tend to dress alike, act alike, and like all the same things. But that is more of a blueprint for the creation of a cheesy Christian subculture than growing the

[14] Ibid., 25.

[15] Driscoll, *Confessions*, 53.

[16] Hirsch, *Forgotten Ways,* 25.

body of Christ. McManus added: "Christianity as a civilized religion claims to have a group plan negotiated with God. Everybody gets the same package."[17]

A focus on conformity in nonessentials, from clothing style to musical interests, is an easier way to live, but it is also a small way to live. In his fascinating book *Orbiting the Giant Hairball*, Gordon MacKenzie made an observation of elementary school children.[18] MacKenzie worked for decades as a creative expert for Hallmark Cards. His book examined the problems of bureaucracy, in particular the tendency of bureaucracy to suck the creative energy out of people in an institution (in other words, it is must reading for pastors and denominational workers!). In his role as an artist who sketched designs for Hallmark cards, MacKenzie regularly spoke to elementary school classes about art. He developed a simple evaluation that provided a telling insight into how parents in particular and culture in general raise children to seek conformity over creativity. As he spoke to students in each grade, he asked students to raise their hand if they considered themselves an artist:

—First grade: All the children jumped from their chairs, arms waving wildly.
—Second grade: About half the kids raised their hands no higher than their shoulders.
—Third grade: No more than one-third ever raised their hands, and those who did were cautious and self-conscious about it.

"The higher the grade," he observed, "the fewer children raised their hands." He called the pattern "the suppression of creative genius."

Our culture, he observed, categorically raises children to pursue a safe, secure, and sensible path to a career. That has been more pronounced in the church. We have created a culture that celebrates the duty-driven churchgoer and raises eyebrows at the passionate witness on the streets. Every year I take a lot of teens out witnessing in various settings. How many times have I met condescending adults who see the enthusiasm of youth after spending time sharing Christ retort: "They are excited, but they will get over it." That is our problem; we have met Jesus and we have gotten over it. Certainly as we grow older maturity calls for wisdom, restraint, and even silence at appropriate times. But

[17] E. R. McManus, *The Barbarian Way* (Nashville: Thomas Nelson, 2005), 37.
[18] G. MacKenzie, *Orbiting the Giant Hairball* (New York: Viking Adult, 1998).

have we so anesthetized the church that outbreaks of creativity, even those consistent with Scripture, are considered scandalous?

I thank God that as a child about 11 years old, at the time caution begins to overtake enthusiasm, I saw young adults radiantly and unashamedly passionate about their faith. I was a typical good little church kid who knew the right answers in Sunday school and had ribbons for attendance at Vacation Bible School. But I did not know Jesus. Suddenly, the Jesus Movement invaded our church. In 1970 I witnessed many hippie-looking youth become passionate for Jesus. Their passion became mine, for their testimonies helped to lead me to Christ. Our church began creative ministries: a "One Way Christian Night Club" (a converted skating rink for unchurched youth to have a place to gather and meet believers off the church campus, serving only Kool Aid for strong drink), a drama ministry, and ministries at Panama City and other places. I recall one thing in particular about these ministries: they focused particularly on reaching the lost.

We have domesticated the faith. We have turned evangelism into a course, discipleship into a curriculum, and our devotional life into a checklist. Can we recover a Christianity that sees no disparity between biblical conviction and creativity? Can we say to the coming generation that following Jesus does not mean you have to surrender your creative energies and passions for the service of the institution, but that following Christ means unleashing all God has made you to be in service to the Most High?

McManus would agree: "Somewhere along the way the movement of Jesus Christ became civilized as Christianity. We created a religion using the name of Jesus Christ and convinced ourselves that God's optimal desire for our lives was to insulate us in a spiritual bubble where we risk nothing, sacrifice nothing, lose nothing, worry about nothing. Yet Jesus' death wasn't to free us from dying, but to free us from the fear of death. Jesus came to liberate us so that we could die up front and then live."[19]

Creativity in Evangelism

What are ways we can encourage creativity in the cause of Christ without sacrificing the message of the cross? It may be simpler than you think. It starts with a change of mind-set. What if every member of your church thought of himself or herself as a missionary? What if

[19] McManus, *The Barbarian Way*, 48.

every family in your church saw their neighborhood, their workplace, and their school as a mission field? That simple shift in thought could generate many creative ideas.

Here are a couple of rules I follow in thinking creatively as it relates to witness. First, anything, yes, *anything* in culture that is not intrinsically evil can be used for the gospel. We tend to think like Gnostics, who considered spiritual things good and material things evil. Such a mind-set (which is not biblical) leads to the idea that only that which is explicitly spiritual (or "churchy") can be used for spiritual purposes, and anything "secular" (read, "worldly") cannot.

I sat with a group of students once and began to ask them what hobbies they enjoyed. Cooking, running, sports, crafts, and video games were named. I asked the students how they had used such interests for the gospel, whether as a means to build relationships with unbelievers or as a means to share Christ directly. Most had never even thought about doing that. We have so separated our spiritual life (and thus our approach to sharing Christ) from everyday life that we have few creative ideas.

Here are a few examples of everyday interests used for the gospel:

- *Hunters*—Wild game dinners where trophies and wild game for food are shared, featuring an outdoorsman who shares Christ have become a growing example.
- *Sports*—Upward Basketball is a tool used by many churches to relate sports to the gospel.
- *Music and the arts*—I know of several churches in large cities who use art, some even opening art galleries, to engage the culture for the gospel.
- *Crafts*—My family lives in a neighborhood with several unbelieving families. It is our Jerusalem. The greatest impact we have made for the gospel in two families does not come from my great eloquence and wisdom. No, it comes from my wife Michelle, who annually makes a nice craft item as a gift for our neighbors each Christmas. More gospel conversations have come from those gifts than anything else we have done.

Of course there are those who would not enjoy hunting. Not everyone would agree that every issue is "not inherently evil." There are gray areas and some subjects that would vary in a given culture. That being said, I submit there are a multitude of ways Christians can use everyday activities in a more creative way to share Christ.

A second conviction about creativity in witness is this: do not let the gospel be lost in your creative efforts. Some who use drama, for example, love the art form so much that the gospel gets lost in it. Be intentional in bringing creativity and Christ together. Christ must be exalted in all things. And that is exactly why we must sometimes change our paradigms to be effective in a given culture and day.

There are more. Some will be considered in later chapters, such as:

— from church *plants,* (i.e. the physical buildings) to church *planting;*
— from treating youth as children finishing childhood to equipping them as young adults entering adulthood to change the world;
— from Anglo to ethnic in our witnessing focus;
— from rural to urban;
— from families as primarily protecting our children to raising them to become Great Commission Christians; and
— from reaching people like us to reaching the radically unchurched who are not like us.

Questions for Consideration

1. Do you see the need to shift in any of the paradigms mentioned above in your personal life? In your church?
2. What might be some other paradigms in need of changing in our time?

Chapter 22

Church Planting

Following Jesus into the mission field is either impossible or extremely difficult for the vast majority of congregations in the Western world because of one thing: They have a systems story that will not allow them to take the first step out of the institution into the mission field, even though the mission field is just outside the door of the congregation.[1]

—Bill Easum

A few years ago I wrote a book about the need for the church in America to reach the radically unchurched.[2] While I focused on several approaches to penetrate the unchurched culture with the gospel, in the final chapter I argued that most conventional churches will have a difficult time making the necessary shifts to do what it takes to reach large numbers of the unchurched, especially in the cities. Instead, I said, we need those churches to give much time and attention and resources to planting churches that can from the beginning go after unchurched people and subcultures effectively. I believe

[1] B. Easum, *Unfreezing Moves: Following Jesus into the Mission Field* (Nashville: Abingdon, 2001), 31. Italics added.

[2] See A. L. Reid, *Radically Unchurched: Who They Are and How to Reach Them* (Grand Rapids: Kregel, 2002).

that is still the case. The difference between then and now is that many others seem to believe that as well.

While much can be lamented about conventional church life in the Western evangelical church, there have been promising signs of late. One such sign is the renewed vigor and attention given to church planting. Bob Roberts, a leader in the church-planting movement, has seen this shift. "Twenty years ago when I started NorthWood in Texas there weren't a lot of people wanting to start churches—especially the more gifted people. Now there are many," Roberts wrote. He then observed what I see among so many of my gifted students today: "To many, church planting is becoming the 'pastorate of choice' as opposed to taking some existing church filled with other people's headaches!" He then adds a comment that summarizes much of the buzz among students I mentor at Southeastern. "Now, when I hear young pastors talk, they are all talking about wanting to start church planting movements."[3]

"A seismic shift is beginning to rumble in the North American church, especially in church planting," Stetzer observed. "For about twenty years church planting has moved from 'suspicious activity' at best to 'en vogue' in the body of Christ."[4]

WHY PLANT CHURCHES?

Still, many object to the idea. Keller cited three primary reasons many church leaders object:[5]

Objection One: "We already have plenty of churches that have lots and lots of room for all the new people who have come to the area. Let's get *them* filled before we go off building any new ones." I well remember while serving in Indiana a discussion about planting a new church in a town of more than 20,000 with one SBC church averaging in the teens and virtually no other evangelical church. The pastor of the one existing church had a fit. "That is our town to reach," he argued. He had been there more than seven years and had reached about four people.

[3] B. Roberts, *The Multiplying Church* (Grand Rapids: Zondervan, 2008), 47.

[4] E. Stetzer, *Planting Missional Churches* (Nashville: B&H, 2006), 16.

[5] Quotes under the three headings of objections that follow are from Tim Keller, "Why Plant Churches in the City," http://download.redeemer.com/pdf/learn/resources/Why_Plant_Churches-Keller.pdf, Redeemer Presbyterian Church, February 2002 (accessed August 25, 2008).

Objection Two: "Every church in this community used to be more full than it is now. The churchgoing public is a 'shrinking pie.' A new church here will just take people from churches already hurting and weaken everyone."

It is true that some church plants take members from others (that is likely not stealing sheep but growing greener grass). However, if you are the one planting the church, the last people you want to reach are members ready to jump from other churches. If your new church grows by reaching those from other churches, you are reaching the very people who will keep you from going after the unchurched!

Objection Three: "Help the churches that are struggling first. A new church doesn't help the ones we have that are just keeping their nose above water. We need *better* churches, not more churches." First of all, we can do both at once. Second, one of the better ways to help a struggling church is to get it involved in church planting.

One of the roles a new church plant can play in an established church is to refocus the mother church back to her original, biblical focus. The name C. S. Lewis often comes up in discussions of apologetics, philosophy, or literature but rarely in a discussion on church planting. But his words to the church give both an ominous warning to the contemporary church and sound the trumpet for new churches. "There exists in every church something that sooner or later works against the very purpose for which it came into existence." He adds, "So we must strive very hard, by the grace of God to keep the church focused on the mission that Christ originally gave to it." [6] As giving birth to a child often causes a couple to refocus on what matters, birthing a new church can refocus a mother church.

Keller argued winsomely for the place of church planting for those who will study the possibilities:

> The vigorous, continual planting of new congregations is the single most crucial strategy for 1) the numerical growth of the Body of Christ in any city, and 2) the continual corporate renewal and revival of the existing churches in a city. Nothing else—not crusades, outreach programs, para-church ministries, growing megachurches, congregational consulting, nor church renewal processes—will have the consistent impact of dynamic, extensive church planting. This is an eyebrow raising statement.

[6] C. S. Lewis, cited in A. Hirsch, *Forgotten Ways: Reactivating the Missional Church* (Grand Rapids: Brazos Press, 2006), 55.

> But to those who have done any study at all, it is not even controversial.[7]

Roberts, in his typical, unabashed style, offered a changing paradigm for how we define a successful church:

> What if instead of dreaming of a 7,000-seat worship center, I dreamed of clinics, schools, and community centers in the inner city? What if instead of envisioning a 150-acre campus, I saw orphanages around the world and microenterprises? What if instead of longing for about 100 full-time ministerial staff, we had 1,000 staff located all over the world? What if instead of wishing for half the community to attend our local church, the community threw parties to thank our church for all the things it was doing in the community?[8]

I would argue in the cities we need large churches as well, those that can wield much influence. But even in those cases such churches should be building the kingdom more than an empire. Pastor Johnny Hunt of the First Baptist Church of Woodstock, Georgia, leads a massive megachurch in the Atlanta area that also has planted many churches in the United States and across the globe. The future model of success must go beyond simple American utilitarianism ("bigger is better") and see a vision of multiplying churches as well as growth in the mother church.

Why do we need new churches? In many areas there seem to be churches on every corner. The reality is that in the United States there were 28 churches for every 10,000 people in 1900. In 2004, there were only 12 churches for every 10,000 people.[9] While part of that statistic is due to the fact that churches are larger today than a century ago, the U. S. population has quadrupled in that time! We still have not kept up with the population growth.

Actually, church planting is not the point. The Great Commission is the point. But church planting can breed a spiritual movement that helps to fulfill the Great Commission, both in the United States and globally. David Garrison accurately describes the need of the day, for a church-planting movement that will reach multitudes. Garrison

---

[7] Keller, "Why Plant Churches in the City."

[8] Roberts, *Multiplying Church,* 72.

[9] "Are There Enough Churches?" *On Mission*, May-June 1999, 11. See T. Clegg and W. Bird, *Lost in America: How You and Your Church Can Impact the World Next Door* (Loveland, CO: Group Publishers, 2001), 30.

called a church-planting movement "a rapid multiplication of indigenous churches planting churches that sweeps through a people group or population segment."[10] Rather like what you see in Acts. We would all agree this is needed in the 10/40 window. I would submit we need it in the cities of the West as well. He rightly noted that this is not the same as a spiritual awakening, which revives a dozing church. A church-planting movement is a movement of God just as powerful as an awakening; only it sweeps across communities birthing multitudes into the kingdom. Having studied and taught on awakenings for decades, I am convinced we need God to move in the church, and in the culture, through awakening and church planting!

How to Plant Churches

I have taught a number of young students who left the campus ready to change the world by planting a church. Most worked through our denominational system. What I call the "sow lots of seed and some plants will grow" approach basically seeks to get as many church planters as possible, normally a young couple finishing seminary, sending them all over creation with a timetable of typically about three years. At that point or sooner financial support will run out. The young couple goes to the field, excited, often not equipped enough or acquainted with their field, with a ticking clock over their head. I have had many students follow a version of this approach. Some have been quite successful. Many have not. Too many have finished their time not only with no vibrant church planted but also with a sense of failure that clouds their early ministry.

This approach can work in some settings. But in others, especially in large cities with great cultural barriers to cross, it can actually be nothing more than a set up for failure. Pastor Charles Lyons of Armitage Baptist Church in the heart of Chicago has observed this. He told me of a young seminary couple (white, obviously not from the area they sought to reach) who came and worked diligently to start a church there. But alone, with little accountability and few with whom to talk (and a little overconfidence rather than a desire to learn from those who had been there for decades), their efforts were not successful. I have seen this far too often. Such an approach allows large

---

[10] D. Garrison, *Church Planting Movements: How God Is Redeeming a Lost World* (Midlothian, VA: WIGTake Resources, 2004), 21.

numbers of church plants to be reported at national assemblies. But is this really the best way?

A more recent approach is what I would call "find the man of God and turn him lose" approach. This strategy says essentially that the total number of church plants will be determined by how many God-called, gifted men (or teams) are found to plant a church. This approach also tends to put much emphasis on things like internships and ongoing training. Such an approach starts smaller, but I would argue that its emphasis on planting multiplying churches would lead long term to more actual churches being planted that will survive.

Church Planting in Acts

Obviously the early church had to plant churches because there were none when they began their efforts to fulfill the Great Commission. How did the first believers plant churches?

In Jerusalem (Acts 1–7), a movement of prayer (Acts 1:12–14) and the Spirit (2:1–4) birthed the first church. Personal witness and public proclamation in the culture (2:10–39) brought the first converts. They immediately displayed the marks of a church: they were baptized (2:41); there were teaching (2:42), worship (2:42,46), a sense of wonder and God's power (often missed in today's church—2:43), service and ministry (2:44–45; see also 4:34–35), impact in the culture (2:47), evangelism (2:47; see 4:32), and a daily, missional focus (2:46–47).

Following the instructions of Jesus in Acts 1:8, churches were planted soon thereafter in Judea and Samaria (Acts 8–12). Much of this work was begun by regular believers, "laity," rather than the apostles (8:1–4). The movement was led by God (e.g., see 8:26,29; 9:11–17), the gospel was spread personally (8:4,27–40; 10:34–48) and through preaching (8:5; 9:20), miracles were performed (9:35–42), and many were reached, both Jews and Gentiles (9:31).

Finally, churches were planted "to the ends of the earth" in Acts 13–28. Through the leadership of the Spirit (Acts 13:1–3) the gospel again was proclaimed personally (11:19–23) and by preachers; multitudes were reached (e.g., see 11:20–24), particularly in the cities, and churches were begun.

Models

Ed Stetzer has forgotten more about church planting than I know. He offered several models of church planting in his excellent book *Planting Missional Churches:*[11]

Model 1: The Apostolic Harvest Church Planter

Paradigm	Starts churches, raises up leaders from the harvest, moves to new church
Biblical Model	Paul
Historic/Modern Example	Methodist circuit rider, house church movement
Principles	Planter starts church and moves on Planter comes out of the church and returns Pastor may/may not be classically educated New churches provide core for additional churches

Model 2: The Founding Pastor

Paradigm	Starts a church, acts as "church planter" for a short time, and remains long term to pastor the new church
Biblical Model	Peter and the Jerusalem church
Historic/Modern Example	Charles Spurgeon, Rick Warren
Principles	Planter starts and pastors the church long term Pastor often moves from another location Pastor often classically educated Ideally, new church sponsors new congregations

[11] The reader is highly encouraged to examine chapter 4 of Stetzer's book, which I am only summarizing.

Model 3: Team Planting

Paradigm	A group of church planters relocates into an area to start a church. Often the team has a senior pastor.
Biblical Model	Paul (at times)
Historic/Modern Example	Missionaries at Iona, team church plants
Principles	A team relocates to plant a new church (sometimes relocation is not necessary) Church planting vision often comes from one key member of the team Good teams have a gift mix

A team could either divide mother church into multiple daughter churches or become staff members of the founded church.

You can see examples of the first model on the international mission field, and in some cases in the West with catalytic church planters.

My family has been part of the second model for about 15 years now. Only a couple years old when we moved to Wake Forest and meeting on the seminary campus, the church has grown dramatically in its early years. Bill Hybels at Willow Creek, Andy Stanley at North Pointe, Ed Young at Fellowship near Dallas, and Rick Warren at Saddleback Community Church in southern California are only a few of the many examples of this approach today.

Model 3 can be seen in the experience from the 1980s when three young men and their wives graduated from Bible college and seminary and headed to California. They went to Bakersfield, California, each family serving a different church. After an initial time of what could only be described as unsuccessful ministry, they came together to launch Valley Baptist Church. Today Valley stands as a strong megachurch, with two of the three still serving as copastors. They learned well the strength that comes in numbers.

Stetzer gives the historical example of Columba on the island of Iona. I would add the societies of John Wesley. While not begun as a church-planting movement, many of these and those who led them eventually formed into new Methodist churches. Others would argue the house-church approach seen in Asia and other places could be an example of this.

The best strategy for new churches is not a young couple set apart as church planters—it is pregnant churches sending teams to birth new babies. We see this in a sense at Antioch in Acts 13. We see plural being used more than singular: men of Cyprus and Cyrene going to Antioch in Acts 11, Paul and Barnabas and John Mark and Luke and Timothy and others together in various cities.

Bob Roberts in *Multiplying Churches* argued for this:

> Better to be a mother who produces ten than a planter who produces one. The real key to a church planting movement doesn't lie in the individual church that is planted, but in the incubators that produce churches.[12]

Nelson Searcy, founder of Journey Church in New York City, called the three "deadly sins" that kill church planting lack of calling, lack of strategy, and lack of funds.[13] All the passion and idealism in the world still requires these three. Searcy describes in great detail how to launch large and quickly to get a church plant going early and effectively. In some settings, particularly in urban areas with large unreached populations, this can be quite effective. In his case, the massive shift of young professionals into his area over the previous decade provided a demographic to which he could easily relate. For Nelson, his calling, ability to secure funds (which included times of faith-testing!), and a clear strategy to reach those in his area led to great success for Journey.

On the other hand, Joel Rainey provided sage advice on the rigors of church planting in more typical settings. His aptly titled book *Church Planting in the Real World* gives an honest appraisal of the difficulty in planting churches. If you are a young minister who is simply weary of conventional churches and who finds the idea of church planting to be a pretty sexy one, read Rainey's book. Church planting is hard work. It is different than working with an established, more conventional church. But it is not less hard. It will require great faith, the hand of God, sensitivity to the Holy Spirit, and much courage. Rainey gives reasons why *not* to start a church:

—I'm tired of doing church the same old way;
—I'm angry at my deacons;

[12] Roberts, *Multiplying Church,* 17.

[13] N. Searcy and K. Thomas, *Launch* (Ventura, CA: Regal Books, 2006), 19.

> —I'm going to be the next Rick Warren (or, I would add, Mark Driscoll, John Piper, Billy Graham, or whoever you want to pick).[14]

Denominational/Parachurch Approaches

Denominations and other groups can help in the church-planting enterprise. However, one cannot assume that simply because a group has many cooperating churches and resources available that effective church planting can result. Too often well-meaning denominational groups have been guilty of what my former student and current pastor of a church-planting church, J. D. Greear, called "bad parachurch":

> Good parachurch ministries *facilitate* the ministry of the church. A good parachurch ministry attempts to be a resource to the local church through which the church can do *her* ministry more effectively. Bad parachurch *takes* ministry *from* a local church and does it for her. Bad parachurch says, "Give us money and people and we'll do ministry for you."[15]

Greear went on to note that his tradition, Southern Baptists, began with a "good parachurchism"—churches took the initiative, and the agencies of the convention helped them to accomplish their aims. Over time in at least some areas that attitude changed to expect the churches to give resources to the agencies, which apparently knew better how to use them. The result has been a growing bureaucracy and institutionalism that have caused some to question the level to which they will support such agencies in a "bad parachurch" model too often seen today.

The strategy of pooling large sums of money in a denominational agency to use in sending young, barely equipped couples to places with which they are unfamiliar to plant a church in a set period of time (two to three years, normally) has simply not led to vibrant growth across the nation. The obsession with the numbers of new church plants must be supplanted with effective, multiplying churches. Better to take time with a team to plant a healthy congregation which over time will plant many others than to send out numbers of couples prepared more for failure than anything else. Or, much better

---

[14] J. Rainey, *Planting Churches in the Real World* (Missional Press, 2008), 16–18.

[15] http://jdgreear.typepad.com/my_weblog/2008/06/being-young-and-southern-baptist-ed-stetzer-paige-patterson-etc.html (accessed September 25, 2008).

for denominational entities to be less of a sending agency and more of a networking partner (i.e., a midwife) with pregnant churches and potential church plants. There seems to be an increasing move in that direction.

Stetzer noted that whereas in the New Testament one can see teams and individuals and even laity planting churches (he notes Aquila and Priscilla; I would add the spontaneous spread of the gospel leading to the church at Antioch in Acts), and that agencies and denominations can do so, the best way to plant churches is by churches planting new churches. As a historian who has studied for decades the great awakenings, I would argue from Acts and history that the best church-planting movements started with no human agency but by the Holy Spirit. However, I would agree that intentional church-planting efforts are best led by mother churches. The Sandy Creek Baptist Church in North Carolina was founded in the 1700s out of the Great Awakening with two men who were converted through the ministry of George Whitefield and then became Baptists. That one church, today only a tiny congregation, was mother or grandmother to 42 churches in the first 17 years after her founding.[16] Well-known churches today, from Saddleback in California to First Baptist Woodstock in Georgia, have planted many churches in the U.S. and globally. Stetzer cited research that indicates how starting a new church actually helps the mother church in many ways.[17]

Innovative Approaches

Two approaches that are novel in the American church related to church planting are the multisite and house church movements. While on opposite ends of the spectrum, with multisite utilized by larger churches and house churches focusing on smaller gatherings, both have gained momentum in recent days.

The "multisite church" simply means one church in many locations. Sometimes this means locations nearby where the same pastor preaches at one location and then goes to another. Increasingly this refers to the use of videos of the sermon or a team of preachers, so that the same message is preached at each site, the same DNA is being established at each place (with a team or "site pastor" at each

[16] http://www.siteone.com/religion/baptist/baptistpage/distinctives/church/Stearns.pdf (accessed September 25, 2008).

[17] Stetzer, *Planting Missional Churches,* 80.

location). The reason most move to a multisite model is to take the gospel to local areas. For example, in Raleigh/Durham the Summit Church has a main campus in the heart of the city, located between Raleigh and Durham. At the time of writing this they had two other locations, one in northern Durham and a new one at the edge of Duke University where numbers of students actually walk to the service.

Many advocates of the approach argue we see this in the first century either in the Jerusalem church (Acts 2, where there were quickly thousands to be taught) and the church in Corinth. Aubrey Malphurs, notable writer and thinker on church planting and other fields, affirms the concept but warns against the danger of letting multisite take the place of church planting.[18] The vision of Summit Church involves both, with a goal of up to 10 sites in the multisite vein, and planting over 20 other independent congregations as well. The both-and approach makes sense in this day.

Critics warn of the obvious dangers of making this a way to promote the ministry of one preacher and of losing the intimacy in worship by the use of video. Advocates counter by arguing video has become such a part of our culture it does not take away from the effectiveness of preaching, and that some voices should be heard clearly. I would argue that using technology to spread the message of a man of God with a word for our times is not that different in our day from the innovation of publishing sermons in Wesley's day or the building of a great Metropolitan Tabernacle in Spurgeon's. At one level, the use of technology to get the gospel to more people is a good thing. If a multisite campus makes effective use of local staff and, more importantly, of effective small group ministry, this can be a viable approach.

Stetzer offered a summary of the multisite argument:

> If I open a new coffee shop on your side of town, it may take years before people figure out I'm there. Even then, they may never check out my lattes because they already get their coffee at a place called Buckstops. On the other hand, if Buckstops opens a new shop, almost immediately hundreds of people will become regulars. Why? They already know the Buckstops brand. Many congregations are moving to a multi-site strategy for this exact reason: a church plant may take years to get a footing, but an extension site of an established church will grow

[18] http://blogs.lifeway.com/blog/edstetzer/2008/06/malphurs-and-multisite-churches.html (accessed October 10, 2008).

> immediately. Instead of starting with 20 attendees, they may start with hundreds. (When Andy Stanley started the Browns Bridge Campus of North Point, thousands showed up the first day!)[19]

Stetzer warned that the multisite approach could simply be another version of attractional evangelism that has some effectiveness but may end up adding to the consumer culture already too popular in our churches. He offers an evaluation at three levels. First, Pastoral Responsibility: "Despite a church's best intentions at new sites, sometimes certain pastoral duties get lost: scriptural assignments such as praying over the sick (Jas 5:14), watching over those placed in your care (1 Pet 5:1), discipline (1 Cor 5), and breaking bread with the beloved (Acts 2:42). I know that those duties are supposed to be the job of the campus pastor, but we also know it often does not happen." Second, Christian Community: "Connected to pastoral ministry is the community of faith itself. The church is not merely a gathering, but a united people who work together for the glory of God and the good of their neighbors," he warned. "If you are going multi-site, I hope it keeps you up at night, wrestling with ways to build community in a system that can easily discourage it." I have seen such churches approach this issue with an excellent small-group system. Finally, Reproducing New Teachers: "Perhaps my biggest concern is that the multi-site paradigm is that, without intentionality, it will limit reproduction. Let's face it— it's easier to create another extension site than it is to create another Andy Stanley."[20] Stetzer noted he is not opposed to the multisite model, nor am I. But time will tell whether this model truly becomes an entrenched, effective method or a passing approach.

House churches have existed since the New Testament. They have flourished in other cultures globally and have been of particular effectiveness in countries closed to the gospel. But house churches in the West have begun to grow as well. J. D. Payne in his recent work *Missional House Churches: Reaching Our Communities with the Gospel*[21] studied 33 house churches in the United States and found they were quite effective both in reaching the lost

---

[19] http://blogs.lifeway.com/blog/edstetzer/2008/06/questions-for-mcchurch.html(accessed October 9, 2008).

[20] Ibid.

[21] J. D. Payne, *Missional House Churches: Reaching Our Communities with the Gospel* (Carlisle, U.K.: Paternoster, 2008).

and in planting other churches. In an article for the Lausanne *World Pulse* Payne offered five conclusions from his groundbreaking study. First, simple expressions of church life can help penetrate certain sectors of the West with the gospel. Second, biblical ecclesiology and not necessarily Western customs regarding church will guide any effective church multiplication movement brought about by house churches. Third, these churches can teach all churches in the West about evangelism, assimilation, and leadership development. Fourth, they can teach us much about missions and ministry. Many of the churches studied gave between 80 and 90 percent of their budgets to missions and benevolence. Finally, with a proper attitude by house-church leaders, growth of house churches can play a vital role in reaching the West. Payne concluded his article with the salient question: "Will such churches be *missional* house churches?"[22]

Marks of Church Planters

Ed Stetzer listed five marks of a church planter for today: missional, incarnational, theological, ecclesiological, and spiritual. I appreciate these categories as they touch on all the critical factors in our time. "Establishing a missional church means that you plant a church that's part of the culture you're seeking to reach," Stetzer stated, adding, "The goal of church planting is to *reach people.*"[23] "Missional" refers to the posture the church planter takes and the DNA he seeks for his church to have. "Incarnational" more or less describes what happens as the church seeks to be missional. As Jesus came to live among us, we seek to live among others. We as the body of Christ live among people in society, not isolated from them. "But," Stetzer said, "we're changed, transformed; and because of that, we seek to change and transform."[24]

Church planters need a healthy theology: "Some people are, in the name of missional thinking, abandoning basic theological messages. . . . Bible-based theology is the foundation for a successful church plant."[25] Church planters and their plants must be ecclesiological, for the goal is to form biblical, local churches that can transform

[22] http://www.lausanneworldpulse.com/themedarticles.php/990/08–2008?pg=2 (accessed October 20, 2008).

[23] Stetzer, *Planting Missional Churches*, 1. Italics added.

[24] Ibid., 2.

[25] Ibid.

the culture. Finally (and in my view too often overlooked), church planters much be spiritual. Without the Holy Spirit the work of God will fail. I would add that church planters need accountability—to a mother church, a denomination, or a network. And, church planters need encouragement from those same groups.

Bob Roberts has led his church to plant new churches all over the world. He knows well the calling of the church planter:

> No vocational ministry requires more self-initiating skills than that of church planting. First and foremost, this is what church planters must be if they are going to survive. These are the dreamers—the ones who see something no one else does. They want to get out there and try it. The key characteristic I'm looking for isn't as much success or failure as it is the potential that drives them. Church planters are visionaries who lead people to accomplish great things. They not only see the vision for themselves; they get others to see it as well. It causes them to be the kind of risk takers that others want to stand alongside.[26]

Among the many characteristics required of church planters, Roberts observed key components including a commitment to and ability in personal evangelism, including a capacity for apologetics and an understanding of how to apply the gospel in emerging cultures. Church planting may not be the same as meeting regularly with hard-nosed deacons in a traditional church, but it is every bit as difficult, only in different ways. Searcy and Thomas remind the married minister that a call to church planting will be confirmed in the spouse as well. However, they wisely advise three principles: (1) the timing of the husband's call may not match the timing of the spouse's call; (2) the intensity of the call may not be the same for both of you; (3) the spouse must be fully heard, involved, and committed to the task.[27]

Ed Stetzer has conducted extensive research on recent church-planting work. He offers a summary of some of the best practices in recent church-planting efforts.

---

[26] Roberts, *Multiplying Church,* 97.

[27] Searcy and Thomas, *Launch*, 38–40.

Best Practices

Ed Stetzer[1]

Planting Effective Evangelistic Churches

As I look to Scripture, it seems that God has a passion for starting new churches. Much of Scripture shows planting as a biblical priority and practice. As we seek to evangelize every *oikos* and *ethnos,* we must also congregationalize every *oikos* and *ethnos*. The church is not only the natural culmination of evangelism; it is the prime mover.

Church-Planting Systems

The emergence of church planting systems will likely prove to be the most significant contribution of the last quarter of the twentieth century to planting successful new churches. Planters now have access to support systems that did not exist in the 1980s. Church Planter Assessments, Bootcamps/Basic Training, Peer Networks and Mentor Programs/Supervision have all emerged to undergird planters in their endeavor. Furthermore, research shows that planters participating in church-planting systems plant larger and more evangelistic churches than those who do not participate.[2]

According to a study I did in 1984, assessed church planters (as opposed to those not assessed) lead churches that are 20 percent larger during their first year and 27 percent larger by their fourth.[3] Assessed planters also experience more than twice as many conversions by their fourth year.[4] An assessment evaluates potential church planters to identify key qualities needed to plant a church. It helps planters know if they are gifted and called to church planting.

Other components of church-planting systems reveal similar results. Planters participating in bootcamps lead churches that are 30 percent larger by year 4.[5] Planters participating in mentoring have a 12 percent advantage in year 1 and steadily increase to a 25-percent increase by year 4.[6] Finally, church planters who participate in a church-planter peer

[1] Document in the hand of Alvin Reid from E. Stetzer, October 15, 2008.

[2] E. J. Stetzer, "The Impact of the Church Planting Process and Other Selected Factors on the Attendance of Southern Baptist Church Plants" (PhD dissertation, The Southern Baptist Theological Seminary, 2003), 96.

[3] Ibid., 81.

[4] Ibid., 82.

[5] Ibid., 85.

[6] Ibid., 90.

network tend to start much quicker than those who do not. Their churches are more than twice as large during the first year.[7]

Church-Planting Teams

Another significant contribution to church planting during the past 20 years is the emergence of church-planting teams. The reason is obvious—teams are able to share the often overwhelming workload involved in starting a church. Teams can penetrate more of the community and influence more potential converts. They can support and encourage each other in the often lonely task of church planting. Finally, team church planting enjoys tremendous biblical precedent. The book of Acts highlights an entire network of church-planting teams working throughout the Roman Empire.

Church-planting teams also prove to start larger and more evangelistic churches than do lone planters. Churches starting with multiple pastors are almost twice as large after four years as churches with a single pastor.[8] Would two planters working to start two separate churches reach more people and have a greater kingdom impact than those same planters working together? Research reveals that the results are about the same. However, the social, emotional, and spiritual benefits of team planting make it a trend with tremendous appeal.

High Member Standards

Many successful evangelistic church plants have high member expectations. Requiring new members to attend a new member's class, requiring new members to sign a church covenant, having a stewardship plan in place, and conducting intentional leadership training were connected with higher attendance in new church plants.[9] It may seem counterintuitive. It seems lowering standards would encourage more people to participate. The data indicates otherwise.

This is a refreshing insight for those who believe the Great Commission is about making disciples and not just converts. An emphasis on commitment and spiritual depth will pay huge dividends toward the success of the new church. Likewise, lowering standards to appease cultural demands may actually undermine the new church and compromise its success. It is clear that high expectations promote a culture of commitment within a new church that ultimately results in high performance. Members who are

[7] Ibid., 95.

[8] Ibid., 163.

[9] E. Stetzer and P. Conner, "Church Planting Survivability and Health Study," Center for Missional Research, North American Mission Board, 2007, 12.

taught and expected to serve, give, and evangelize will generally live out these values better than those who are not.

Perseverance

Realistic expectations of the church-planting experience are essential. Too often, planters have plans and strategies based on unrealistic expectations. When such strategies fail to produce at the expected level, church planters are often demoralized and discouraged—and the church plant suffers. Realistic church-planter expectations increase the survivability of a church plant by 400 percent.[10]

Helping planters have realistic expectations often helps them have perseverance. Planters who are emotionally and strategically prepared for the long haul are more patient and able to take setbacks and disappointments more readily. Planters with inappropriate expectations often quit too soon when these planters could have grown their church with more time. Church planters must prepare themselves for the rigors of starting a new church.

Conclusion

We have learned a great deal over the past few years about planting successful evangelistic churches—and this short chapter points out some of that learning. Oddly, research on North American church planting is still limited—there are many resources on planting churches around the globe. Missiology primarily focuses on the rest of the world—but more analysis is needed here. Our understanding is still growing as God continues to call men and women toward the sacred task of building His church. Thus, we will press forward in humility, wisdom, and courage to plant new churches that advance the kingdom of God.

[10] E. Stetzer and P. Connor, "Church Planting Survivability and Health Study."

Statistics tell us that church plants are effective evangelistic tools. New churches grow faster and baptize more people than established churches. (In 2007 it took more than 47 Southern Baptists to baptize a single person.[28] Yet, new SBC churches needed fewer than 7 to reach one person.[29])

[28] http://www.usatoday.com/news/religion/2008–04–25-baptists-decline_N.htm

[29] E. Stetzer and P. Conner, "Church Planting Survivability and Health Study," Center for Missional Research, North American Mission Board, 2007, page 5. Note: Dividing the average baptism rate for new churches by the average size of those churches.

Planting new churches is one of the most effective methods in reaching the lost.

Church planting is growing in influence and in focus. During the past 20 years we have witnessed a renaissance of church-planting interest, knowledge, and excitement. That has led to new systems and approaches to planting churches that effectively reach the lost. In this brief chapter, we will look at a few of those systems and approaches that are increasing church-planting effectiveness, including church-planting systems, teams, high membership standards, and perseverance.

Questions for Consideration

1. Is your church currently involved in planting or assisting a new church plant? If not, why not?
2. What can you do personally to help in church planting?
3. If a new church plant were to be started in your area, what would be the most effective way to go about it?

Chapter 23

Reaching the Unchurched

If the culture rejects Christianity, it should be because it has refused to hear the gospel message of Christ rather than that it turned its back on the church's outdated, culturally irrelevant methods.[1]

—Albrey Malphurs

The American church faces an irony; we have developed the most elaborate Christian subculture in history while being less effective than ever in reaching the hardcore unchurched. We must refocus on those who are not like us. To do that we must spend time observing those around us who do not understand our Jesus.

As a child I dreamed of going to Africa. I have always loved animals, and I have especially loved studying the animals of Africa. My first trip there a few years back did not disappoint. I journeyed with fellow professors and students to South Africa, where we shared the gospel and planted a church. I found a green mamba in the wild (I got a stick on it but decided against picking it up since I would only have died had it bitten me so far in the bush) and carefully held a black mamba. But what truly blessed me was the children. The children had

[1] A. Malphurs, *Planting Growing Churches for the 21st Century* (Grand Rapids: Baker, 1998), 14.

never seen anything like the toys we have in the West. They had never seen eyeglasses and were amazed at mine. The students made all the children pipe-cleaner glasses. You would have thought they had all been given a Nintendo Wii. All week they wore those glasses!

Students taught them to play duck-duck-goose, the children's game where you sit in a circle and have one person run around the circle saying "duck-duck-duck" until he taps one person and says "goose," meaning "you are it." That person has to get up and catch the one who tagged her before he sits down in her place. You likely know the game and have played it. There was only one problem. These children had no idea what either a duck or a goose was. So, the whole game made no sense, until a student changed the game to animals they understood. So, the children had a glorious time playing this amazing new game of pig-pig-cow!

We cannot simply teach things to people in a new culture without translating what we teach into a language they understand. This involves more than vocabulary; it involves concepts and subjects to which they can relate. Sometimes we assume people know what we talk about when we say that God loves them, we have all sinned, and Jesus came to offer salvation. But if a person has no biblical concept of God or sin, how can that person understand salvation?

The Radically Unchurched

*By radically unchurched I mean people who live in the West who have no clear personal understanding of the message of the gospel and who have had little or no contact with a Bible-teaching, Christ-honoring church.**

*For more information see A. L. Reid, *Radically Unchurched: Who They Are and How to Reach Them* (Grand Rapids: Kregel, 2002).

Where are those who are willing to confront the contemporary culture with the timeless gospel? While every individual is either saved or lost, there are two groups of people who have not responded to the gospel: (1) those who have heard the message but have rejected it and (2) those who haven't clearly heard. The first group must be confronted at the point of their excuses or objections for rejecting the gospel. The major issue for them is one of *volition.* The second group must hear the gospel in a manner that communicates the message clearly. Their need is for *information.*

What the church needs today is not more buildings, more dollars, or more new ideas—not a marketing strategy or new technology. What the church needs today is an army of apostle Pauls, who serve God with a passion and who are burdened for reaching those who have never clearly heard the glorious gospel.

Let me use the apostle Paul and his time as an analogy. He was called to be the apostle to the Gentiles, although he sought to reach Jews as well. Think of the *Jews* of Paul's day, who had a religious heritage from which Paul could begin his witness, as analogous to the millions of nominal Christians in the United States—those who have been to church and heard about God but who have never been changed by the gospel. Like the first-century Jews, they have some awareness, but they still need the gospel's power.

The *Gentiles* in the first century were those who knew nothing about the gospel message until someone like Paul told them. They had no heritage of Scripture as the Jews did. Some were religious; some were not. They are analogous to the millions of people in our country who have little knowledge of Christianity. They know what a clerical collar is, and they recognize a church building, but they have no functional knowledge of the gospel. I call these people the *radically unchurched*. They may be devoutly religious, as some first-century Gentiles were, or they may be irreligious. They may be Muslim or Hindu or New Age or Mormon, or they may be agnostic.

The difference between these people and the nominal Christians—the "Jews," to use my analogy—is that any idea they have of Christianity is obscure or flawed. These people recognize the golden arches of McDonald's much more quickly than a cross as a symbol with meaning.

The evangelical church has had some success reaching the "Jews"—or those with some knowledge and background in the faith. They are more likely to be like us. Our evangelism tools are almost exclusively geared toward them. Attractional evangelism can reach many of these. Most evangelism methods are geared toward harvesting, and those who have some background in the faith are obviously closer to harvest time. But the "Gentiles"—the radically unchurched—are a different story. Many of them are not ready for the harvest, although some certainly are. They are what Billy Graham called "an unseeded generation." They see the church as irrelevant and an enemy to progress. They are ignorant of the truths of Christianity.

We can honor God by seeking ways to present the gospel in a way that will be understandable to them.

Churches in our nation are much more effective at reaching the "Jews" than the "Gentiles." We have some modest success at reaching those connected somewhat to churches, but we are not reaching the hardcore unchurched. We need more churches who seek to reach the radically unchurched. In doing so we must find ways to communicate effectively the message we cherish when those who hear it do not automatically share our love for it. But first let's consider the importance of confronting the objections raised by the "Jews."

Dealing with Those Who Make Excuses

The reason some people are not saved is that no one ever took the time to explain to them why and how salvation can change their life. But those who have grown up with an awareness of the gospel, the "Jews" in my analogy, often reply to a witness with one excuse or another. This is also true of the unchurched in general. One of the practical things I have learned about witnessing by actually witnessing a lot (novel thought) is that the overwhelming majority of excuses people give initially for rejecting Christ often have nothing to do with the real reason they say no to the gospel! So, answering objections should involve determining the real objection as much as the ability to answer them.

I'll never forget one of the first times I taught evangelism and took people witnessing with me in a local church. That was the spring when a national evangelical religious personality fell into sin. Week after week we would visit, and people would say, "Look at that guy. I don't need to be around a bunch of hypocrites." At first, I was defensive, but then I changed my approach. As we talked to a man whom I'll call Bob, he raised this scenario.

"Bob," I said, "You are right. Not every preacher lives a life that honors Christ. There are hypocrites. In fact, Jesus spoke against hypocrites more than anyone else. Let me ask you a question. How would you describe a real Christian?" Bob's reply was *not* that he believed Christianity was false due to the testimony of a fallen preacher. Rather, he replied that a Christian is someone who goes to church, is moral, and so forth. He did not disbelieve the faith; he was only using this fallen preacher as an excuse.

I then said to Bob, "Can I explain to you what a real Christian is according to the Bible?" He then allowed us to share Christ. He did not respond, but the gospel was proclaimed.

Most people have never been confronted with the truth of the gospel in a personal encounter with a loving witness. But most have wondered about spiritual issues that cause them to think about ultimate realities. From tragedies to cults to psychic hotlines, various events cause everyone to think about God at some point. When an objection is raised, we have to ask, "Are they rejecting Christ based on a clear knowledge of the gospel, or are they ignorant or misinformed about Christianity?" We must get beyond the excuses that people give to the real reason they object to the claims of Christianity.

I'm convinced that many of the objections people raise are smoke screens. They are attempts to set aside the main issue—a volitional commitment to God—under the guise of intellectual excuse. This is not new in our day. Michael Green, in *Evangelism in the Early Church,* described a street preacher of the second century who was talking to a group of philosophers. One of them asked him why a small mosquito has six feet and wings while the elephant, the largest of all animals, is wingless and has only four feet. The question was an attempt to stump the preacher much as some questions are asked in our day. But listen to Green's comment on his response:

> The preacher is unabashed. "There is no point in telling you the reason for the different structure of mosquito and elephant, for you are completely ignorant of the God who made both." He could . . . answer the frivolous questions if they asked them sincerely, but he refuses to get sidetracked by bogus issues like these impelled as he is by the concern to fulfill his commission. The preacher says further, "We have a commission only to tell you the words of him who sent us. Instead of logical proof, we bring before you many witnesses from among yourselves . . . it is of course open to you either to accept or disbelieve adequate testimony of this sort but I shall not cease to declare unto you what is for your profit: for to be silent would be loss for me just as to disbelieve would mean ruin for you."[2]

Part of the struggle we face as witnesses is dealing with questions we can't answer. I heard a student say he hated door-to-door

[2] M. Green, *Evangelism in the Early Church* (Grand Rapids: Eerdmans, 1970), 199.

evangelism because he feared being confronted with an issue for which he had no reply. But note this: *nowhere in Scripture are we told that we must answer every question a person has.* Even the Bible doesn't do that! It doesn't tell us everything we *want* to know but everything we *need* to know. It doesn't tell us where Cain got his wife; that is not a significant issue. It does tell us how sin entered the human race because this is important! We can spend so much time trying to be relevant that we fail to be significant. We may not be able to tell people all they *want* to know about spiritual things, but we can tell them what they *must* know to be converted.

I have learned that the best way to deal with objections is through a Socratic method, as opposed to the rote memorization of pat answers to complex questions. Here are four general principles to keep in mind:[3]

1. Recognize the objection while keeping the conversation focused on the gospel.
2. Remember, the Holy Spirit will give you guidance. Trust Him.
3. The gospel itself will answer many honest questions.
4. Many objections will not be raised *if* you maintain a proper attitude.

Here are five guidelines to help you avoid emotional confrontations without compromising the gospel:

1. *Negotiate; do not argue* (think win/win). Whenever possible, we should agree with the person raising the objection to make it a win-win situation. For example, R. A. Torrey said he was talking with a man who said he was too great a sinner to be saved. Instead of talking him out of that sentiment, Torrey agreed with him and directed him to 1 Tim 1:15 where Paul said he was the chief of sinners but Christ came into the world to save sinners. The man replied, "Well, I am the chief of sinners." Torrey said, "Well, that verse means you then."[4] If it is a legitimate concern that people have when you agree with them and show them the scriptural answer, this makes all the difference in the world as you lead them toward conversion.
2. *Avoid emotional confrontations.*

---

[3] Much of this has been adapted from excellent materials I first learned in the method known as Continuing Witness Training.

[4] R. A. Torrey, *How to Bring Men to Christ* (Pittsburgh: Whitaker, 1984), 33.

3. *Accept the other person as an equal.* Remember that we are not *better* than unsaved persons; the difference is that we have met Jesus! And so can they! A holier-than-thou attitude is quickly discernible.
4. *Exercise gentleness.* The goal is to present truth, not win a debate.
5. *Check your motivation.* Love should be your guide.

The material used with Continuing Witness Training has helped many witnesses in dealing with objections. The basic approach can be summarized in the following steps:

1. *Use a transition statement.* "You've obviously given this some thought." Most people have given some thought to spiritual matters, so your first statement is affirmative, not confrontational. Then you can address the specific objection.
2. *Convert the objection to a question.* The question should deal with the objection raised, as illustrated below. If you are not sure what to ask, two general questions are, "When did you begin believing this?" and "Why?"
3. *Answer the person's question.*
4. *Continue with the gospel presentation.*

Example 1: "The church is full of hypocrites. I don't need it."

Transition: "You've obviously given this some thought. I would agree that hypocrisy does exist in churches. Jesus warned against hypocrisy."

Convert to a question: "Let me ask you a question. What is a real Christian like?"

Typical answer: "Lives a good life, not judgmental, etc."

Answer: "The only way to discover what a real Christian is would be to see what the Bible says."

Example 2: "I believe there are many ways to God."

Transition: "You've obviously given this some thought. I would agree that there are many religions with many devout followers."

Convert to a question: "Let me ask you a question. Have you ever considered the unique claims of Christianity?"

Answer [following their response]: "The Christian faith is unique in that it is less a religion than it is a relationship."

R. A. Torrey used a similar approach. If he encountered a skeptic who said, "I don't believe the Bible," he would ask, "Are you saying the Bible is foolishness?" And if he said yes (by the way I've met people like that), you can say, "Well, that's what the Bible says about itself. First Corinthians 1:18 says the preaching of the cross is to them that perish foolishness." And then you can say, "But you don't have to be perishing."[5]

If someone says the Bible is full of contradictions, the best thing to do is hand a Bible to him and kindly ask him to show you one.

An excellent resource for answering the most asked questions in a helpful, pastoral manner is Tim Keller's book *The Reason for God.*[6] Keller answers the most common excuses raised by unbelievers in a manner that is both intellectually stimulating and biblically sound.

Reaching the Radically Unchurched

There are over 120 million functionally secular people in the United States. Millions are caught up in cults and other religious systems. How do we communicate the gospel to them? Before dealing with specific groups, let me say again that any witness is better than no witness. A friend of mine named Saleim grew up a Muslim. He knew Christians in high school, but they never witnessed to him. They apparently thought he was unreachable. Saleim finally came to Christ in college. He told me he could have been saved earlier if someone had taken the time to share the gospel with him!

The landscape of American culture has changed radically over the last generation. In our day we are called to share Christ in a culture with no consensus on *heritage,* as seen in our ethnic diversity; no consensus on our *moral code,* as evidenced by debates over abortion, homosexuality, and euthanasia; and no consensus on *religious belief,* as seen in the growth of other world religions and the explosion of cults.

In any generation, apologetics—or the defense of the faith—has a role in evangelism. The two were combined in the lives of Paul, Justin Martyr, and Augustine, and in our day we see them wed in the lives of such people as Ravi Zacharias and the late Francis Schaef-

---

[5] Ibid., 59.

[6] T. Keller, *The Reason for God: Belief in an Age of Skepticism* (Dutton Adult, 2008).

fer. Apologetics has been founded on propositional truth, and this remains essential. Increasing numbers of unchurched young adults are not only asking, "Can you prove it?" They also want to know if we can live it.

Mormonism's impact in contemporary culture is not due to success on epistemological grounds. They use the arts well (their TV commercials are without peer in touching the emotions). They don't reach people with *truth* claims; they use sensory appeal. Now just imagine if the church, without compromising any commitment to the epistemological basis of the faith, were to appeal to the arts to help declare its truth.

This is why drama and multimedia have become effective in many churches. We live in a sensory, TV-dominated age. How can we share the timeless truths with a postmodern culture? We must do it the same way the Bible does it. The Bible is primarily narrative, easy for a person to relate to. It is *relational*—the story of how God relates to man. For example, the story of the prodigal son may be more effective in reaching some people than the Roman Road witnessing approach. The truth is the same, but the approach is different.

In the sixties, some people said, "God is nowhere." Now God and gods are everywhere. In the sixties secular people were turned off by the church because it was too spiritual; now they are turned off because it is not spiritual enough.

Unchurched people can and do wonder about Christianity. They generally have three responses to Christians:

1. Do Christians really believe this?
2. Do Christians really live this?
3. Does it really matter?

How do we relate to changing culture and the people in that culture? We must distinguish between pop culture and traditional culture. George Hunter defines pop culture as much the same everywhere; it varies little across space but changes rapidly across time. Some popular music in Tokyo can be found in Chicago. Changes are called *fads.* Traditional culture varies greatly across space, but it changes very little across time. Changes do occur and are called *trends.* In relating to a changing culture, Hunter states:

- Some things should be abandoned—hymns that are not understandable, mimeographed bulletins, irrelevant announcements.
- Some things should be kept—preaching, singing, prayer, giving.
- Some things should be repackaged—worship style, worship order.[7]

Imagine that you are in a community with 5,000 homes that you want to touch with the gospel. Using mass evangelism, the Sunday school, small group, visitation, outreach—all of these viable, traditional tools—you will reach many. But how many will you truly impact? There is a significant percentage of people you will never touch—the radically unchurched. We tend to rate our success based on who we are reaching without evaluating all those we are not touching with the gospel.

Let's assume you have a fruitful Sunday school campaign. You go out and enroll 10 percent of the population in Sunday school in three years (500 of those homes). Then you have evangelistic crusades each year. In three years 50 people a year (150 people) come to Christ. So you have reached 650 homes in three years.

Statistics show that one out of three unsaved people in our Sunday schools will eventually come to Christ. So out of those 500 people whom you enrolled in Sunday school, about 170 would come to Christ.

Now we have 150 people reached with the gospel through mass evangelism and 170 reached through Sunday school for a grand total of 320. Add to that the 80 who came to Christ by other means in three years. Four hundred people have come to Christ out of 5,000 homes. Outstanding, yes, but literally thousands of people in that community have still not heard the gospel of Christ.

Without taking anything away from these methods, the truth is the greatest single missing element of evangelism is a missional witness, the very means to reach the unchurched. We must get involved in the lives of the millions of unchurched people all around us if we are to reach America and the world. And when we do, we must tell them the timeless, unchanging gospel in a manner that they can understand.

Perhaps the best place to learn how to reach the unchurched of our time is to see how they were reached in the early church. As a

[7] G. Hunter, "The Rationale for a Culturally Relevant Worship Service," *Journal for the American Society of Church Growth* 7 (1996): 137–38.

case study let us look at Paul's visit to Philippi in Acts 16 where three diverse people were reached. The first, Lydia, could be considered a "Jew" at least in her understanding by my earlier analogy. She had a hunger for God and an understanding of Judaism. The slave girl and the jailor offer two examples of unchurched people. Lydia was Asian and a professional, a moral person and a God-fearer who immediately showed interest in the gospel. The slave girl was a spiritually bankrupted youth who had been used by adults. Yet she is the one who ran after Paul! The jailor was a blue-collar worker, seemingly neither interested nor opposed to the gospel, only indifferent. How were they reached?[8]

Lydia came to Christ mainly through an *explanation.* While not explicitly stated it seems clear by implication and by Paul's ministry elsewhere that she simply needed to have the message clarified. She was ready! When I am randomly witnessing in restaurants or in neighborhoods I always pray for "Lydias."

The slave girl came to Christ mainly through a *demonstration of kindness*. Paul's deeds paved the way for her to hear the words. She was oppressed spiritually and economically, and Paul helped her to be released from both. There are many unchurched youth who will not quickly hear our words if they do not first see our deeds. They are wary of moving from exploitation from the world to another form of exploitation in churches who do not deliver on their promises. An amazing movement has spread through contemporary youth culture with the twin themes of "Love Is the Movement" and "To Write Love on Her Arms" stemming from one person's compassion to a 19-year-old named Renee who was cutting herself and addicted to drugs. I have seen more than a few youth come to Christ because of Renee's story.[9]

The jailor was reached because of a *demonstration of character.* Stunned by their singing of songs of praise while yet in jail, he turned out to be more in prison than the inmates. Freedom involves more than physical access, as he witnessed in the lives of Paul and Silas. When Paul and Silas had the opportunity to flee they refused, demonstrating character like that of their Lord. Uncommon character in the workplace can make a huge impact. I worked in college and seminary with construction crews and in factories. The work is blue collar,

[8] I am indebted to Tim Keller for helping me to think through this passage in Acts 16 for our day. See http://www.redeemer2.com/themovement/issues/2004/april/advancingthegospel_4_p3.html (accessed August 28, 2008).

[9] See http://www.twloha.com.

hard, and often unappreciated. I was often the youngest and more then often ridiculed for my faith. Yet I tried hard to display a life that honored Christ, which led to some remarkable doors of witness and at least one case of a coworker coming to Christ.

The church that will effectively reach the unchurched has members filled with a passion for Christ and whose lives demonstrate that Christianity is more than serving on a church committee—it is a radically changed life through Christ! To state it simply, the key to communicating the gospel to the unchurched is to be *real*, to let them see the genuine change Christ has made.

One of the ways we can become more effective in reaching the unchurched is by identifying subgroups, pockets of the unchurched, and developing effective ways to penetrate those groups. I have a friend in our church who came to Christ as an adult from a very unchurched background. He is a skydiver both from his military days and as a hobby. He tells me the overwhelming majority of skydivers are unbelievers, many of whom talk about the free-falling experience as the greatest spiritual experience of their life. They need to be reached and most likely will be reached by people like my friend who know them in their culture. There are many subgroups that can be classified in many ways: ethnic communities in the cities, homosexual groups (many of whom increasingly live in urban areas in the same proximity), or even the unchurched population involved in the sex industry, from escort services to pornography.

Other groups are linked more by affinity, from NASCAR followers to hunters, from artists in the city center to bikers living on the road. Many churches have in fact launched successful ministries to such groups. My friend David Wheeler has reminded me of a group too often overlooked by the church, those with special needs. David has a precious special needs daughter and has given much time and effort to reaching those with such needs.

One of the most practical efforts you can have in your church is to identify those groups in your community for whom no one cares, begin to care for them, and from that to share the gospel. No doubt in your community there are those who have some reason to identify with one another but who have few in their group who know Christ.

Evangelizing People in Special-Needs Situations

David Wheeler

Individuals with special needs and their families easily represent one of the largest unreached people groups in America. In fact, according to statistics gathered by Joni and Friends Ministries, the divorce rate of families dealing with special-needs children is over 85 percent. In addition, less than one out of ten of these individuals (approx. 5%) or families are associated with church at any level.

Consider some other alarming statistics from Joni and Friends Ministries:

- 54 million or 20.6 percent of people in the United States live with some level of disability.
- Nationally, 4 million of these people are under 18 years old.
- Abuse in families with a disabled child is twice that of typical families.
- Nine out of ten women who find out their unborn baby has Down Syndrome will eventually abort.
- The handicapped and their families represent the largest unreached and unchurched people group in America!

With this in mind, it is imperative that local congregations catch the vision to reach this group with the gospel. According to special education teachers and those fluent in this kind of ministry, the most effective approach is family-to-family contact through genuine concern and servant-oriented ministries.

As the parent of a special-needs child, please allow me to point out several misconceptions relating to special-needs individuals. First, most people tend to lump all impairments into the same category with the assumption that physical needs are always related to mental deficiency. Nothing could be further from the truth. Like everyone else, special-needs children and adults must be dealt with individually. The truth is, those with physical or mental challenges need the saving grace of the gospel message. In many cases, these individuals will excel beyond their supposed difficulties and often become bold, personal witnesses themselves.

This leads to the second misconception that somehow special-needs individuals must always have limitations placed upon their activities and behavior. This is a wrong assumption. If you are the Christian parent of a special-needs child, please know that, like all other Christians, those with impairments must also be obedient to the call of evangelism. This means that families of special-needs children must not limit their community involvement in evangelism for the "sake" of the child or the parent. In most cases, special-needs individuals can be very effective in evangelism and often become an asset in doing family-to-family ministries.

Suppose there is a family dealing with a special-needs situation in your community. Who could be better prepared to minister to this family evangelistically? You already understand many of the difficulties and challenges. It only takes a sacrifice of time, a strong trust in God, genuine concern, and a willingness to listen and get involved in kingdom business. In the end, this will build family togetherness, create memories, and develop a greater confidence among both the physically and mentally challenged, as well as the family members involved.

For instance, one family of a child with cerebral palsy spoke of how they participated in door-to-door servant evangelism projects by allowing their excited young girl to be the first person met at the door bearing gifts. In one case it was fudge at Christmas; in another instance it was batteries for smoke detectors or bags of microwave popcorn with a card attached stating "pop in and visit our church sometime." Those visited were introduced to each participant, given a special gift by a "special" child, then told that "Christ loves them." In some of those cases they prayed with individuals; in others, they were able to share the gospel. In every instance, the participants learned the same important lessons about fulfilling the Great Commission, regardless of physical or mental limitations. Both the young girl and those visited received an extraordinary blessing.

As far as ministering family to family within special-needs situations, consider several options like providing "parents night out" opportunities, especially where the needs are chronic and demand around-the-clock care. I recently heard of a family like this where the parents hadn't been alone in over three years! No wonder the divorce rate is so high!

In some cases, the situation may demand the securing of a nurse who is trained to administer proper care. In many other situations you may only require a mild dose of patience, a listening ear, and a special ability to administer the love of Christ. Ask the Lord to show you how to proceed.

You might also consider preparing meals or providing some new clothes. If they are of good quality, consider offering some of the slightly used clothes that your children have outgrown. In addition, one person expressed the need for volunteers to do grocery shopping. By the way, always be careful to respect handicap parking places and never stare at those who are impaired. Relax and be yourself!

Most importantly, do not give up even if the special-needs family does not respond immediately. Remember, above all people, they know the difference between loving concern and pity. These individuals do not need pity. On the contrary, they need Jesus and the affirmation of dignity and self-worth that is inherent to the gospel.

Five suggestions to remember when ministering to people affected by special-needs situations:

1. Ministering to the disabled is not complicated; always remember there is no one-size-fits-all solution.
2. You must plan to minister to the whole family, not just the person with the disability.
3. Begin by researching community-based opportunities for ministries. Start by asking questions . . . CARE!
4. Be honest about your attitudes and prejudices. According to Joni & Friends, "the disability community feels *attitudinal accessibility* is of greater concern than physical accessibility."
5. As a goal, seek to include and engage the disabled and their families in the harvest. In other words, help them find their ultimate fulfillment in Christ!

Reaching Those in Cults and Other Religions

While identifying unchurched people groups noted above may take some work, it does not take much effort to see the impact of cults and other religions in communities in the West. America has become a microcosm of the world—a place of thousands of religious systems. How do we reach them?

The proliferation of cults and new religious sects has been an unmistakable part of American society during the past 30 years. Thousands of new religious groups, ranging in membership from less than fifty to hundreds of thousands, have sprung up. Other groups such as Mormons and the Jehovah's Witnesses have been around much longer. Other world religions are also growing in the United States. In particular, the rise of Islam has caused a great rise in pluralism and syncretism, with the merging of faiths and other challenges to the Christian faith.

What is a cult? Brooks Alexander, cofounder of the Spiritual Counterfeits Project in California, gave a theological definition of a cult.

1. A cult has a false or inadequate basis of salvation. In other words, their soteriology is wrong. This comes out of a faulty Christology.
2. A cult has a false basis of authority. Biblical Christianity is founded on the Bible as the Word of God, while a cult looks for other authorities—a messianic figure, a David Koresh-like leader, or other writings such as *The Book of Mormon* or *The Pearl of Great Price*.[10]

There are certainly other religious sects as well: Zen Buddhism, Hare Krishna, and the Unification Church. Evangelicals in America must confront Mormonism and Jehovah's Witnesses more than any other single group or groups. We must admit that cults represent "the unpaid bills of the church."[11]

Principles of Witnessing

Here are five principles for witnessing to people in cults and other religions:

1. *Commit to a relationship with this person whenever possible.* Such a person, if devout, will not be won to Christ upon first contact with the gospel. As a pastor, I had the privilege of leading a Mormon to Christ, but I led her to Christ out of a relationship that I had established with her family. I have also led Muslims and one Buddhist to Christ. In every case, I got to know them and spent time with them. They saw the change Christ has made in my life.
2. *Know your faith and theirs.* None of us can be an expert in all the different cults. But if there is a dominant religious group in your area—Mormonism for example—you ought to know something about their beliefs so you can talk intelligently with them. The Interfaith Witness Department of the North American Mission Board and the Spiritual Counterfeits Project have excellent materials to help. My friend John Avant led a Mormon missionary to Christ. He knew Mormon beliefs, and he was able to demonstrate weaknesses in their theology. However, he didn't do this initially. After spending time talk-

[10] B. Alexander, "What Is a Cult?" *Spiritual Counterfeits Project Newsletter* 5, no. 1 (January–February 1979).

[11] J. K. Van Baalen, *The Chaos of the Cults* (Grand Rapids: Eerdmans, 1938).

ing with the missionary, finding points in common, he began to show the errors in Mormonism and was able to lead this person out of Mormonism into genuine Christian faith.

3. *Do not begin your witness by attacking the other person's beliefs.* This may seem contradictory to the example of John Avant, but the principle stands. If you start witnessing to a person involved in a cult by attacking the cult, for example, the person is not likely to have any respect for your views. Begin your witness by affirming anything you can about the group, building rapport as you would in any other witnessing situation. Then move to God's truth.
4. *Share your own testimony.* This is critical. I have had students from a Mormon background who were very effective in winning people to Christ out of Mormonism. One student, Larry, was a fourth-generation Mormon. He has won several to Christ over the Internet by sharing his testimony and telling how he came out of Mormonism.
5. *Explain the gospel clearly, noting especially the reality of sin and the need of a Savior.* Their soteriology is almost always a works-oriented view of salvation. They need to hear the gospel of grace.

Biblical Model

There is a biblical paradigm that helps us in dealing with cults and other religions. The apostle Paul went to Athens to preach the gospel. The number of idols in that city overwhelmed him. The religious pluralism was abundant. How did Paul share Christ in a culture filled with religious belief but empty of the gospel?

First he was provoked when he saw the city was given over to idols. Are we aware of and brokenhearted by the idolatry of our age? He reasoned in the synagogue with the Jews and the Gentiles and in the marketplace, talking to them about their relationship to God and their need for him (Acts 17:17). Then he was taken to Mars Hill and asked to speak on what he believed.

Second, he acknowledged their religious search. Paul said, "Men of Athens, I perceive that in all things you are very religious" (NKJV). The King James Version translates that last word as "superstitious," but the term is less one of condescension than one of recognition. Paul affirmed the reality of their search for God, building a common ground with them. He affirmed their search, recognizing they were seeking truth. Of course if he stopped there he would have been a pluralist. But he did not.

Third, Paul knew their beliefs. He even quoted two of their poets (see Acts 17:28).

Fourth, Paul moved from their error to the truth. He noticed an inscription on an idol—"To an Unknown God" (Acts 17:23). He started talking about God in general terms as Creator and moved on to the specific reality of Jesus as the Son of God. Paul did not compromise the gospel. Instead, he began where they were and took them to the place where they could be.

Finally, Paul clearly presented the gospel. If he had not done this, we could accuse him of selling out the gospel by speaking of a general god. He moved from a general understanding of God to the specific claims of the cross. He also talked about the judgment of God and the resurrection (Acts 17:23–31). At Paul's mention of the resurrection, the people began to respond in the three ways people inevitably respond to the gospel. Some believed the gospel, others rejected it, while others sought to know more. That's the way people respond. If we follow these principles in witnessing to people in cults and other religions, or in sharing with the unchurched in general, we can expect these same kinds of responses.

Questions for Consideration

1. Have you encountered an excuse for rejecting Christ by anyone recently? How would you use the process explained above to deal with that excuse and ensure the gospel is proclaimed?
2. Do you know anyone in a cult or another religious system? How might you share with that person?
3. Do you have personal friends who would be described as radically unchurched?

Chapter 24

Reaching Children and Families

Many men and women of the age of 60 and 70 years have been disciples of Christ from childhood.[1]

—Justin Martyr

Roughly half the people who come to Christ do so before age 13. How we evangelize children matters greatly. How we reach families does as well.

In his book, *The Bridger Generation,* Thom Rainer reminded us that 80 percent of people who are saved come to Christ before age twenty.[2] From the early church to the contemporary setting, reaching the young has been a critical need for the church.

There are few resources that give sound, detailed counsel concerning the evangelization of children. Yet in many circles, about one half of those making professions of faith are under the age of 13.

---

[1] M. Green, *Evangelism in the Early Church* (Grand Rapids: Eerdmans, 1970), 219.

[2] T. S. Rainer, *The Bridger Generation* (Nashville: Broadman & Holman, 1997).

The Age of Accountability

Roy Fish, the dean of evangelism professors, having taught at Southwestern Baptist Theological Seminary for more than 40 years, offered sage counsel on this vital subject.[3] Fish notes certain assumptions from Scripture concerning children. First, infants and young children are safe within God's care. Second, if they die, they will go to heaven. Delos Miles, my predecessor at Southeastern Baptist Theological Seminary, stated:

> The child is not a "miniature adult." Infants and young children who die before they are capable of conversion go to heaven. They are a part of God's kingdom. Based upon what the Bible tells us about the nature of God, He will not hold a young, immature child responsible for making a decision of which he is incapable.[4]

Fish's third assumption is that there is a time when children become accountable to God. In other words, we must confront the issue of the "age of accountability." Miles defined this term: "Infants are safe in God's care until they become capable of responsible decision-making."[5] William Hendricks defines the age of accountability as "the moment of grace when one is brought to a decision for or against Christ by the Spirit."[6]

Of course, various traditions deal with this matter in different ways. Sacramental theology focuses on the role of sacraments such as infant baptism. However, the biblical text indicates a conversion theology, regardless of the age of the individual. I agree with Fish, Miles, Hendricks, and others that there is no set age of accountability.

Because of biblical teaching on conversion and the practice of believer's baptism following conversion, the age of accountability is an important concept. Yet we must admit there is no singular biblical passage that clearly elaborates this concept. We get a glimpse in passages such as Rom 14:12, which perhaps implies the idea: "So then,

---

[3] R. Fish, *Introducing Children to Christ,* TC1794, Southwestern Baptist Theological Seminary, 1997. Unless otherwise noted, all references to Fish in this chapter are from this excellent audiotape.

[4] D. Miles, *Introduction to Evangelism* (Nashville: Broadman and Holman, 1981), 325.

[5] Ibid., 325.

[6] W. Hendricks, *A Theology for Children* (Nashville: Broadman, 1980), 15.

each of us will give an account of himself to God." Other passages worthy of examination include:

> **Deuteronomy 1:39:** "Your little children who you said would be plunder, your sons who don't know good from evil, will enter there. I will give them the land, and they will take possession of it." In this passage we see the children were not held responsible for this sin that led the people into the wilderness.
>
> **2 Samuel 12:23:** "But now that he is dead, why should I fast? Can I bring him back again? I'll go to him, but he will never return to me." David, referring to his infant son who died, stated he would go to where the baby is, implying life beyond this life.
>
> **Romans 7:9–10:** "Once I was alive apart from the law, but when the commandment came, sin sprang to life and I died. The commandment that was meant for life resulted in death for me." Paul seems to say there was a time he did not stand as guilty before the law, that is, in his infancy.

Part of the reason for concern about evangelizing children is the alarming number of people who say something like this: "I didn't know what I was doing at age nine. I joined the church, but I didn't have the capacity for making an intelligent decision. When I was seven or eight nothing really happened, so I needed a later saving experience to be a real Christian." The fact that increasing numbers of adults have done this has caused some people to look suspiciously at the possibility of child conversion.

Further, increasing numbers of children being baptized at earlier ages has caused some to be alarmed at the rate at which we are baptizing children. The issue raises genuine concerns. This is reflected in the extremes that exist on this subject. On the one hand are those who question the possibility of evangelizing children. An example of one who looked suspiciously at this issue is Sam Southard in his book *Pastoral Evangelism.*[7] Relying heavily on the findings of both psychologists and theologians, Southard concluded that conversion requires a responsible, repentant attitude that is not possible until adolescence or the early teenage years.

On the other hand, some groups seek to evangelize children at a very early age. Fish noted that a former head of the Child Evangelism Fellowship (CEF) wrote that children should be evangelized from

---

[7] S. Southard, *Pastoral Evangelism* (Nashville: Broadman Press, 1962).

three to five years of age. The idea of a three-year-old understanding even the simplest implications of the gospel is extremely problematic, and this seems to me to be very close to infant baptism. And yet, at the other pole, there is too much reliance on psychology to the neglect of the Spirit. Hear Fish at this point:

> We ought not to pay a great deal of attention to secular psychologists who have no knowledge of the work of the Holy Spirit in Christian conversion. Conversion or regeneration is a miracle which defies explanation on a psychological basis. To declare that the Holy Spirit cannot convict children of sin, cannot reveal Christ savingly to them, and cannot work the miracle of regeneration in them is a prerogative no psychologist or theologian ought to assume.[8]

Scripture and Children

We must admit that the Bible says very little explicitly about the evangelization of children. The Old Testament offers examples of children serving the Lord. Samuel was quite young when he began to minister to the Lord under the tutelage of Eli. During the Old Testament era, the idea developed that Jewish children became responsible members of the worshipping community at age 12. This is why Jesus was taken to Jerusalem to worship when he was 12. This was not specified in the Old Testament; it simply evolved during the Old Testament era.

Certain passages in the New Testament are helpful on this subject. There is the implication that Timothy followed Christ from childhood (see 2 Tim 3:15). Jesus said, "Let the little children come to Me. Don't stop them, for the kingdom of God belongs to such as these" (Mark 10:14).

But the most definitive passage relative to the conversion of children in the New Testament is found in Matt 18:1–4. In this passage, Jesus used two words to describe little children. One of the words is *paidion* (vv. 2,4,5). The other is *mikros* (vv. 6,10,14). The first word refers to a very young child and periodically refers to infants. It was used of Jesus as an infant. The second word, *mikros*—the word we use in English in such words as microscope and microcosm—also refers to children of a young age.

[8] Fish, *Introducing Children to Christ.*

Fish on Matthew 18

Roy Fish offered the following commentary on this passage.[9]

1. *Conversion occurs on the level of a child.* Jesus says, "Except you be converted and become as little children, you will by no means enter the kingdom of heaven." We typically think of salvation as something of an adult experience to which children must attain. But this passage indicates just the opposite. Not only is conversion possible for the child, but also any adult who would enter the kingdom must first become as a child. We say to children, "Wait until you're adults; then you can become Christians." Jesus said, "Oh, no, you've got it in reverse. You adults become little children, and then you can become Christians."
2. *Humility, the essential quality of greatness in the kingdom, already belongs to the child.* Jesus said, "Whoever will humble himself as this little child, the same is the greatest in the kingdom of heaven." The word *humility* refers to a state of weakness and dependence that determines greatness. The older we grow, the more proud we become.
3. *A little child can believe in Jesus.* Jesus warned those who "offend one of these little ones who believe in Me." Fish is correct when he says this is the most important statement in Scripture concerning evangelizing children. It should settle the question once and for all as to whether a child can be saved. The word Jesus uses for *believe* here is the same word found in John 3:16; Acts 16:31; and Rom 10:9–10.
4. *Jesus says that to cause a child to stumble is an extremely serious thing.* If a person should cause those who believe in him to stumble, it would be better for him if a millstone were hung about his neck and he were drowned in the depths of the sea. How serious it becomes to reject a child who truly seeks Jesus. What a sobering word to a parent who would treat with indifference the spiritual interest of a little child.
5. *We should seek a little child, for the Lord Jesus as a shepherd seeks a stray sheep.* The sheep in this context refers to children, not adults. Both the preceding and following verses refer to a child. Jesus is saying that we should seek and find

[9] Ibid., used with permission. Cf. A. Reid, *Introduction to Evangelism* (Nashville: Broadman and Holman, 1998), 248–50.

children for Him as straying lost sheep are sought out by the shepherd.

6. *The Father's will is that no child should perish.* Although the phrase is couched in negative terms, if we turn it around, it declares that the Father desires that every child should be saved. This should cause us to double our efforts in prayer and tactful, careful evangelism that seeks to lead children to the Savior.

I want to conclude this final section by quoting Fish at length:

> In summary, there is a time when children do not need conversion, a time of innocence when they are not accountable or responsible to God. But if the Bible teaches that children, along with adults, respond to God negatively, they respond to what they know about God with rejection, it might be that *negative* and *rejection* are words all together too mild. They respond by rebellion against God. And the New Testament teaches that when a man or a child responds negatively to God or what he knows about Him, he becomes accountable or responsible to God. In my thinking, this certainly is possible for children.
>
> God does not have two ways of saving people—one way for saving adults and another for saving children. To what extent, then, should we attempt to put a child through the hoop of a dramatic adult experience of conversion? The answer is very simple. Only in the proportion as the child is an adult. The essential ingredients must be present in the salvation experience of a child, however minutely they might appear. Repentance to a child, though based on a limited awareness of sin, will involve a rejection of what in himself is displeasing to God. He should be taught some idea of the cost of following Christ, but to expect all characteristics of a dramatic adult conversion in the conversion experience of a child is being unrealistic. I would not want to soften the line of the necessity of a conversion experience for children. However, we must keep in mind that the New Testament demand is not so much for dramatic conversion as it is for repentance and faith.[10]

[10] Ibid.

Children in History

There are notable examples of childhood conversion in Christian history. Polycarp, bishop of Smyrna, was converted at age nine, during the first century. He testified at his martyrdom in about AD 160 that he had been a believer for 85 years. He was martyred at age 95. He may have been converted through the ministry of John the Apostle.

Isaac Watts, the father of English hymnody, came to Christ at age nine. Some of Jonathan Edward's biographers contend his salvation came at age seven. Commentator Matthew Henry was ten; Baker James Cauthen, for many years head of the Foreign Mission Board of the Southern Baptist Convention, was six. W. A. Criswell of the great First Baptist Church, Dallas, Texas, was under ten when he met Christ.[11]

Principles for Dealing with Children

1. *Deal with each child individually.* This principle is true of adults as well but is so critical with children. Perhaps the reason many children make spurious decisions, or are unsure of genuine commitments, is because of the poor way they were counseled. Some children may in fact be ready, but others simply want to please others around them. Utilizing trained workers to deal at length with each child is essential. If children come forward as part of a group, some would do so because of peer group pressure. A large number of children are not coming because they are ready to make their commitment to Jesus Christ. But some are coming who are willing to make that commitment if only someone would counsel with them and show them the way.
2. *Avoid asking questions that expect a yes or no answer.* Children want to please. They will likely give you the answers they believe you want to hear.
3. *Consider the child's religious background.* My son Joshua at age six and one half understood more about the gospel than many unchurched teenagers I have met. He had been nurtured in a Christian home where the Bible is read daily, where spiritual matters are discussed regularly, and where church

[11] The last two paragraphs are from Fish, *Introducing Children to Christ.* Cf. Reid, *Introduction to Evangelism*, 250–51.

involvement is a central part of our family life. In fact, by the time he was eight, he beat me in Bible Trivia (OK, I did ask him the children's level questions)!

If a child has no religious background, the first time he expresses interest in becoming a Christian, there's a high probability he or she is not ready to make that commitment. Very few children are truly converted the first time they hear the gospel (or adults, for that matter).

4. *Do not use fear as a primary motivation.* I believe fear is a viable part of the gospel for a person of any age. Many people come to Christ because they are afraid of the consequences if they reject Him. But extreme methods should not be deliberately used to produce this fear. We must refrain from severe efforts to produce fear in the lives of boys and girls as a motive to get them to Jesus.
5. *Explain the gospel on a child's level.* A few times each year, I will have a small child shake my hand following a sermon delivered in his or her church. The child will say something like, "I really liked your sermon," or "I understood that." These compliments mean more to me than anything anyone else could say. If I speak in such a way that a child cannot understand me, it is not a sign that I am deep or profound; it means I'm a poor communicator!

   You do not have to use terms like *reconciliation, justification,* or *repentance.* You need to explain such terms on a child's level. The meaning you communicate is more important than the specific words you use.

   When you talk to boys and girls about becoming Christians, also talk to them in terms of Christian responsibility. Talk in terms of the lordship of Christ. If they're old enough to accept Him as Savior, they're old enough to understand something of the responsibilities of the Christian life. The obligation to obey Jesus belongs as much to the young child as to the aging adult. Those who are old enough to trust are old enough to obey. The claims of the gospel, the law of God, and our need for Him must be clearly stated to any person regardless of age.
6. *Affirm the child regardless of his or her level of understanding.* You should *never* present a child as having received Christ if you have doubts about the genuineness of his or her confession. But we can affirm the child at some level. W. A. Criswell

affirmed children who come forward as taking a "step toward God."[12] When a child comes forward in a service, regardless of age, he or she ought to be greeted with these words: "I'm so glad you've come forward today." If an adult refuses to do this and ignores a child's interest, this can be devastating to a child's growing faith as well as to his trust in adults.

Expression of interest on the part of a child does not mean he or she is ready for an experience of conversion. We must remember that the Holy Spirit can lead a person a step or two nearer to Christ without bringing him or her to new life. Preparatory work is sometimes long, but it's just as much the work of the Holy Spirit as regeneration.

7. *Distinguish between the internal experience of conversion and external expressions associated with it.* Children easily confuse the symbol for the real thing. The real thing happens when they trust the Lord Jesus as their Savior. But the symbol, the external expression, happens when they walk down an aisle and present themselves for church membership and baptism. Some boys and girls are prone to equate salvation with baptism and joining the church.

   This is how it is when most children make a public decision: Little Johnny comes down the aisle. We're glad. He's age 10, but we haven't had a chance to talk with him about this matter. We ask him why he's coming, and he says, "I want to join the church." We quickly explain that he must trust in Jesus to be his Savior, and then we begin asking him questions before the congregation. "Johnny, you know you're a sinner, don't you? You know that Jesus died for you, don't you?" And we begin to nod our heads in an affirmative fashion. "And Johnny today you are trusting Him as your Savior, aren't you?" By then our head is bobbing like a fishing cork when the fish are biting.

   When children come forward, why not say something like this: "Johnny, I'm so glad you've come forward this morning. As best you can, tell me why you've come." Let him express to you his feeling about the matter. Don't rush in to counsel him or her at the altar. Schedule some time for this after the service. The salvation of a child is too important to rush. Use questions like these: "Tell me what you've been thinking about in regard to becoming a Christian. Why do you want to become

[12] Miles, *Introduction to Evangelism,* 328.

a Christian? What made you start thinking about it? What do you think a person has to do to become a Christian?"

Keep in mind that children need only to receive Christ. They don't have to explain the gospel in detail. Children may not be able to explain why they have this need, but they must sense a need for Jesus. They must understand that God's provision for meeting the need they feel is Jesus. They don't have to have all the theological answers, but they must understand that it is through Jesus that God meets the need they are experiencing. They also must know how to appropriate or to claim God's provision—through faith by trusting Him as they commit their lives to Christ.

Opportunities to Evangelize Children

As you will read below, I believe the best people to evangelize children are their parents. For those who do not have believing parents we should take advantage of appropriate opportunities to share the gospel.

- Vacation Bible School
- Children's Night at evangelistic meetings
- Sunday School teachers
- UPWARD Sports

The Place of Families in the Spread of the Gospel

We have a tendency in the Western church to focus excessively on protecting our children and far too little on preparing them and challenging them to live valiant lives for Christ. While it is vital for parents to protect their children, especially when they are small, do we really protect them if we shield them from biblical teaching on such subjects as persecution for the sake of the gospel? Do we help our children by rearing them in a Christian subculture that elevates the institution and minimizes the gospel?

McNeal observed:

> Churches are so busy getting people involved at the church that they've neglected this fundamental agenda of spiritual

> formation. The typical church family leaves spiritual stuff to what happens at the church, thereby delegating spiritual formation to the institution. And the institution encourages it! What if churches cut down on church activities so people could have some conversations within their own families? What if we facilitated this even at church as a beginning point? What if parents spent as much time with the children's minister as the children do? What if student ministers spent as much time with students' parents as they did with the students? This would be a shift from most church expectations of staff.[13]

For a little dose of perspective, consider for a moment the ministry of Adoniram Judson. One of the earliest in the modern era to leave the comfort of the West for the international mission field, Judson understood to some extent the hardships ahead of him. He met Ann Hasseltine and sought to marry her. He wrote a letter to her father to ask for her hand in marriage but did not minimize the cost of marriage to a man compelled to go overseas. "I have now to ask whether you can consent to part with your daughter early next spring, to see her no more in this world!" he wrote, adding, "Whether you can consent to her departure to a heathen land, and her subjection to the hardships and sufferings of a missionary life?" He concluded with a question: "Can you consent to all this, in hope of soon meeting your daughter in the world of glory, with a crown of righteousness brightened by the acclamations of praise which shall redound to her Saviour from heathens saved, from her means, from eternal woe and despair?"[14]

Ann did in fact die on the mission field. Most of us will not face such a decision about one of our children. But it breaks my heart to see students of mine sitting in my office, called to the mission field, weeping because their Christian parents are unhappy that God is taking their child overseas. But even that does not affect personally every believer. The most pressing question is, are we raising our children in our churches to love and proclaim the gospel?

I ask in churches regularly how many in the congregation were raised in Christian homes. I ask the same of my students. Normally the response is around 90 percent. Then I ask all those raised in Christian homes how many of them recalled their parents ever discussing

---

[13] R. McNeal, *The Present Future: Six Tough Questions for the Church* (San Francisco: John Wiley & Sons, 2003), 88.

[14] Cited in D. L. Akin, *Five Who Changed the World* (Wake Forest, NC: Southeastern Baptist Theological Seminary, 2008), 23.

the need to reach their neighbors, or any attempt to share Christ with neighbors? Typically the response is less than 3 percent. We raise our children in neighborhoods acting as if we were atheists. We expect the local institution to do the work. Further, recent studies show that only 12 percent of Christian families pray together regularly. We can complain about prayer being taken out of public schools legally, but we have taken prayer from our homes willfully!

I believe for the gospel to become effectively shared once again in our day, it will take families living and sharing Christ missionally in neighborhoods. It will take children being raised to be more committed to making an impact for the kingdom of God than getting a good job and paying the bills. It will take a renewed passion by Christian parents to leave a legacy of the gospel for their children.

Inheritance: Passing Down a Legacy of Faith

The family has been rightfully one of the most common points of emphasis in the modern church. Seminars, parenting training videos, books, sermon series, and a litany of parachurch ministries have at various levels focused on the family. This is right and good. But I believe a vital element has been missing from most of these. Over the past few years I have asked my students how many remember their church hosting any of the above—marriage retreat, and so forth, or a sermon series on the home. Virtually all recall such a focus. Then I asked, "How many of you recall an emphasis in these events or resources which specifically dealt either with evangelizing your children or with raising children in the Christian home to be evangelistic?" Very few. I think we would agree that nothing matters more to Christian parents than their children becoming passionate followers of Christ. Yet we hardly ever talk about that in the church. I believe part of the reason for this stems from the institutionalism in our churches, as if evangelizing children were the job of the church rather than of parents. Perhaps it is also because we assume parents will do this.

As a young pastor I taught the parents of older children (grades 4–6) how to share Christ with their children. As a result, over the next few months several children were led to Christ by their own parents. As parents, Michelle and I have sought both to teach and model a love for the gospel whether in our home, the neighborhood, or a local restaurant. We have been blessed with a son and a daughter who get this, both of whom have led people to Christ and who love Jesus and

His gospel. We have seen a love for the gospel affect every aspect of their lives from how they relate to friends to how they treat strangers. You can raise your children to do more than survive in a wicked culture. You can raise children who love God's truth and share it, and who pass that legacy to their children as well.

I believe the Scripture gives clear guidelines to Christian parents regarding the importance of raising children not only to love and follow God, but also to share the gospel with others. We see the heart of this in Deut 6:4–9; this passage is the most quoted in the New Testament. While ceremonial laws and certain customs passed away from the Old Testament to the New, this passage endures. In fact, Jesus called the truth in this passage "the Great Commandment." We would do well to teach this truth and to follow the pattern in our homes we see described in these verses.

Being a parent must be the most exciting . . . and frightening . . . and inspiring . . . and upsetting . . . and amazing . . . and routine . . . and joyful . . . and at times sorrowful . . . experience in life. I spend much time with youth. Many of them do not have a close relationship with parents. Many have hardly ever seen a family who loves one another. So many long for nothing more than a family that stays together and loves God and one another. I have yet to meet a young lady who longs to look back at age 45 and describe her life like this: three divorces, two kids by two different men, neither of whom will pay child support. So many would rather break the cycle. A gospel-centered home is the cure!

If you are a parent, how will you leave a legacy to your children that will lead the generations following to love God?

Demonstrate Godliness—Moses is addressing the parents and adults when he gives this message. "Listen, Israel: The LORD our God, the LORD is One. Love the LORD your God with all your heart, with all your soul, and with all your strength." This, the Greatest Commandment as Jesus deemed it, should be central in any Christian home. In your decisions as a family, do you seek first to listen to God? Does your family put following what God says above all else? If so, does a passion for the lost have a central part in your home? Do we sometimes miss the centrality of loving God above all when we tell our children to get a good education, good job, but fail to place as much emphasis on hearing and loving God? Do we affirm in our teaching and our living that there is only one God, and only one way to have a right relationship with that God?

Educate in Godliness. Verses 6–9 tell us the responsibility of parents:

> These words that I am giving you today are to be in your heart. Repeat them to your children. Talk about them when you sit in your house and when you walk along the road, when you lie down and when you get up. Bind them as a sign on your hand and let them be a symbol on your forehead. Write them on the doorposts of your house and on your gates.

We have developed an institutional mind-set in the church that has compartmentalized our lives. So, many parents see spiritual training as primarily the job of the church. In particular with teens that job goes to the youth pastor. Unfortunately that is exactly what the Scripture does *not* teach. Think about the marriage seminars, sermon series on families, or parenting classes you have had at your church. Most of them never talk about sharing Christ with your children. Yet nothing is more important than that to a believing parent. Why the omission? Because we have given the serious spiritual matters to the "professionals" at the church.

This passage puts the spiritual training of a child squarely on the shoulders of parents. We are to instruct them, literally "sharpen the knife," and live truth before them. How does this look practically? It certainly involves active participation in a gospel-centered local church. It includes imparting a vision for the salvation of both the neighbors and the nations. I like to think about this passage in this way:

These words that I am giving you today are to be in your heart—my children should see me spending time in God's Word, actively sharing my faith, and demonstrating Christlike character daily.

Repeat them to your children—I should be instructing my children, particularly when young, about the things of God. I should help them see how to live out a biblical worldview, making decisions in all arenas of life from a biblical perspective.

Talk about them when you sit in your house—Family mealtime provides a great avenue for teaching everything from civility to life lessons. Shared activities with children provide further opportunities for instruction.

When you walk along the road—The church and the home are not the only places to learn how to live and share Christ. Our activities, from talking to the waitress at the restaurant to being courteous at the mall, help to show how to live out our faith rather than compartmentalizing it in the confines of our house and the church house.

When you lie down and when you get up—Bedtime, especially for younger children, provides a great time for prayer and instruction in spiritual things.

Bind them as a sign on your hand and let them be a symbol on your forehead. Write them on the doorposts of your house and on your gates—I suppose this could include Christian symbols and expressions at our homes, but more than that it is vital that we incorporate the gospel into the fabric of our lives. Our interaction with our neighbors should bring glory to God and communicate Christ to those who need Him.

Questions for Consideration

1. What priority does your church place on reaching children and their families for Christ? What priority do you place?
2. If you have children at home, have you talked to them about the gospel or have you considered that to be the church's role?
3. What can you do to help raise children who not only embrace Christianity intellectually but also to become Great Commission Christians?

Chapter 25

Reaching the Next Generation

The work has been chiefly amongst the young; and comparatively but few others have been made partakers of it. And indeed it has commonly been so, when God has begun any great work for the revival of his church; he has taken the young people, and has cast off the old and stiff-necked generation.[1]

—Jonathan Edwards, commenting on the First Great Awakening

The above quote by Jonathan Edwards, a man of God and leader in the First Great Awakening, demonstrates the powerful role young people can have in the movement of God. But in our day we rarely hear this from church leaders. Instead, those outside the church often see the influence of young people spiritually. Note the following:

[1] J. Edwards, *Some Thoughts Concerning the Present Revival of Religion,* in *The Works of Jonathan Edwards,* ed. S. E. Dwight (Edinburgh: The Banner of Truth Trust, 1834).

> I call this population of fierce young Evangelicals the "Disciple Generation."
>
> An awakening entails young people reinventing traditional rituals, making the faith of their forefathers their own. This isn't just an observation on the MTV age—it's been the final stage of every awakening before a national transformation is complete. To hit critical mass, it takes a youth movement.[2]

The above quote comes not from an evangelical "youth expert" but from an unbeliever, a secularist who spent a year among evangelical youth to study their passion and conviction. Lauren Sandler is convinced this movement of evangelical youth is having a significant impact. And she, being a leftist, is none too happy about it.

I have spent much of my ministry in churches the past few years with a focus on young people. In addition, I have spoken to college students on dozens of campuses. I love young people. The older I get the more I love them. What saddens me is that the most optimistic people I find regarding young people, and in particular those who follow Christ, are actually unbelievers. Not only Sandler, but Naomi Schaffer Riley, writing about religiously committed college students in *God on the Quad;*[3] Andrew Beaujon, who writes about the influence of Christian rock music in *Body Piercing Changed My Life;*[4] and the first of its kind, *Millennials Rising: The Next Great Generation*[5] by generational experts Howe and Strauss all paint a positive image of many young adults, particularly those with religious convictions. Negative images of youth sell well at church youth events. But too few are those who believe in youth and challenge them to be radical, fanatical followers of Jesus! Certainly, there will always be more than enough youth in trouble, youth at risk, who need our attention. But I meet so many young adults who simply want to know their lives can matter, that Christianity is more compelling than doing their church duty, that Jesus Christ is who He says He is.

What might happen if the church began to see the potential of youth as a missionary force? What if we treated our youth in churches

---

[2] L. Sandler, *Righteous: Dispatches from the Evangelical Youth Movement* (New York: Viking, 2006), 5, 12.

[3] N. S. Riley, *God on the Quad: How Religious Colleges and the Missionary Generation Are Changing America* (New York: MacMillan, 2005).

[4] A. Beaujon, *Body Piercing Changed My Life: Inside the Phenomenon of Christian Rock* (New York: De Capro Press, 2006).

[5] N. Howe and W. Strauss, *Millennials Rising: The Next Great Generation* (New York: Vintage Books, 2000).

like young adults rather than like third graders as so many churches do? What if college students became a priority of ministry rather than a sidebar of the church? What if we turned our youth groups and their YMCA-like programming into youth ministries focused on penetrating public schools and universities with the gospel?

The news is not all good for this generation. It is the most unchurched in history. It will not be reached by merely hosting a youth rally and offering a paintball tournament. Some plant churches today to reach the increasing numbers of unchurched young adults. "It seemed that young people went to church with their parents but upon graduation from high school often dropped out of church altogether, with some returning once they were older, married, and had children," Driscoll observed. "The Holy Spirit burdened me to start a church for the people who had fallen into that drop-out hole. Over the years, the statistics have further verified the need for this focus."[6] He noted Barna's research finding that more than four out of five or 81 percent had gone to a Christian church, but a 58-percent decline in church attendance happened when these youth became ages 18 to 29. Thus, about 8 million 20-somethings who were active churchgoers as teenagers will no longer be active by their thirtieth birthday.

I am grateful that I grew up in a church with a strong youth group. Because of its influence, I was able to begin, with a Methodist friend, a Fellowship of Christian Athletes chapter and a Christian club at our public high school. I attended youth retreats that made a life-changing impact on my life. I participated in choir and mission tours across the country. Young people were important in our church, and we knew it.

I believe the greatest challenge confronting the church in the new millennium relates to youth ministry. We must address the issue of youth evangelism, both in terms of evangelizing teenagers and equipping students to witness to their peers. There is a critical need for youth ministry built on relevant, conviction-laced biblical teaching. The church has an open door to feed the idealism of youth with Christian truths and values.

The Potential of Youth

Biblical Perspective on Youth

I began to pay attention to youth ministry in particular when my son Josh, now nearly done with college, entered the youth minis-

[6] M. Driscoll, *Confessions of a Reformission Rev* (Grand Rapids: Zondervan, 2006), 10.

try at our church. I eventually wrote a book on the subject, *Raising the Bar: Ministry to Youth in the New Millennium,* in which I argued youth should be treated like young adults entering adulthood rather than children finishing childhood.[7] Response, especially from veteran youth ministers, has only confirmed my conviction. More importantly, Scripture and history weigh in against the modern approach toward youth as goofy and unable to make commitments. I speak annually to thousands of youth, who love the fact that a guy with a PhD will push them to believe deeply and live fervently. They long to be pushed, to be encouraged, for someone to believe in them.

Part of our problem comes from how we look at young adults as a group. There is no notion in Scripture that advocates the idea of adolescence as seen in American culture, at least in terms of the low expectations of youth. My colleague and Greek scholar David Alan Black, in *The Myth of Adolescence,* noted three categories in the Bible for people: (1) childhood/pre-adulthood (ages 1–12); (2) emerging adulthood (ages 12–30); (3) senior adulthood (ages 30-death).

He noted that these stages could be seen in the life of Jesus (Luke 2:41–52; 3:23; and the remainder of the Gospel, respectively), and in the persons John describes in his first epistle (little children, young people, and fathers). It is also true that in the Old Testament youth could not fight in war and do certain other duties (like give an offering on one occasion) before age 20, but the distinction hardly rivals that of modern day adolescent thought.

The view of adolescence practically speaking has led to an assumption in and out of the church that teenagers go through a lengthy process (much longer than puberty—roughly ages 12 to 18 or 19) where they are expected to be silly, love games more than learning, and play more than being serious. This view has led our culture, both in the church and outside, to become systematically organized to fabricate two myths about youth. *First, it encourages teenagers to behave like grade-school children instead of young adults. Second, it perpetuates the notion that the teenage years of necessity must expect rebellion, sarcasm, narcissism, and general evildoing.* "Sowing wild oats" has become a popular term for what is expected of youth, including churched youth, during their young adult days. Certainly hormonal changes and rapid maturation over a brief time open the opportunity for such behavior if left unchecked. But that is my point: we must not

[7] See A. L. Reid, *Raising the Bar: Ministry to Youth in the New Millennium* (Grand Rapids: Kregel, 2004).

let the bar of expectation be set so lowly. I have had two children, a boy and a girl, go through puberty. I have watched the mood swings and the physical changes. But we act as though such a transition lasts for many years rather than a much briefer time, and often we use such changes as an excuse to allow bad behavior. We pattern our attitude toward youth more from MTV and less from the Word.

Look at the young people who stood valiantly for God, often at critical times in the history of God's people: Isaac respected and listened to his father when Abraham almost sacrificed his son (Genesis 22); Joshua served as Moses' assistant as a young man; Samuel as only a lad heard the voice of God when His voice was rare in the land; David killed Goliath as a young man; Jeremiah served as a prophet and Josiah led a revival while young; Daniel and his friends were possibly middle school aged in Daniel 1 when they stood up for their convictions; on and on the examples go. In fact, in the Bible the examples of youth who were knuckleheads are far more remote than examples of young people standing for God.

Historical Examples

One of the overlooked features of modern spiritual awakenings is the vital role played by young people. While significant revivals were cited earlier, the following survey examines specifically the role of youth in these acts of God.

Pietism, the experiential awakening of the eighteenth century, grew through the impact of students who graduated from the University of Halle, then spread the experiential emphasis to points across the globe. Zinzendorf graduated from Halle. The 100-year prayer movement begun through his influence at Halle was essentially a movement among young people.

The role of youth is abundantly clear in the First Great Awakening. Jonathan Edwards, commenting on the revival in 1734–35 under his leadership, referred to the role of youth in its origin: "At the latter end of the year 1733, there appeared a very unusual flexibleness, and yielding to advice, in our young people."[8] This happened after Edwards began speaking against their irreverence toward the Sabbath. The youth were also greatly affected by the sudden death of a young man and a young married woman in their town. Edwards

---

[8] J. Edwards, "Narrative of the Surprising Work of God," in *The Works of Jonathan Edwards,* ed. S. E. Dwight (Edinburgh: The Banner of Truth Trust, 1834), 1:348.

proposed that the young people should begin meeting in small groups around Northampton. They did so with such success that many adults followed their example. Concerning the revival's effect on the youth, Edwards commented,

> God made it, I suppose, the greatest occasion of awakening to others, of anything that ever came to pass in the town . . . news of it seemed to be almost like a flash of lightning, upon the hearts of young people, all over town, and upon many others.[9]

In England, the Evangelical Awakening featured such notable leaders as the Wesley brothers and George Whitefield. Their ministries grew out of a foundation built in college through the Holy Club. Whitefield was only 26 when he witnessed remarkable revival in the American colonies. These young men never let their youthfulness hinder their impact.

The Second Great Awakening featured powerful revival movements on college campuses. Hampden-Sydney, Yale, Williams, and others serve as bold reminders of what God can do in our day as well. Churches could not have experienced the depth of revival they felt apart from youth. Bennett Tyler collected 25 eyewitness accounts of pastors during the Second Great Awakening. Twenty of these revival reports described the important role played by young people. Ten accounts noted that the revivals began with the youth, and five documented the fact that revival in their area affected young people more than any other group. Only one account out of 25 asserted that no youth were involved.[10]

Colleges experienced revival in the 1857–59 Layman's Prayer Revival as well. One pivotal feature of this revival in relation to young people was the impact it had on Dwight Lyman Moody, who was 20 years old at the time. In 1857 Moody wrote of his impression of what was occurring in Chicago: "There is a great revival of religion in this city. . . . [It] seems as if God were here himself."[11] Biographer John Pollock reports that "the revival of early 1857 tossed Moody out of his complacent view of religion."[12] Moody went on to make a dramatic impact for Christ during the rest of the nineteenth century.

---

[9] Ibid.

[10] B. Tyler, ed., *New England Revivals as They Existed at the Close of the Eighteenth and the Beginning of the Nineteenth Centuries* (Wheaton: Richard Owens Roberts, 1980).

[11] J. Pollock, *Moody* (Chicago: Moody, 1983), 34.

[12] Ibid.

An aspect of Moody's influence regarding students that cannot be overlooked was his leadership in the Student Volunteer Movement. Although this movement's roots have been traced to the Second Great Awakening and the Haystack Prayer Meeting of 1806, it was Moody who invited 251 students to Mt. Hermon, Massachusetts, for a conference in 1886. As a result of those meetings, highlighted by A. T. Pierson's challenging address, 100 students volunteered for overseas missions. In 1888 the Student Volunteer Movement was formally organized with John R. Mott as chairman. Over the next several decades, literally thousands of students went to serve as foreign missionaries.

According to J. Edwin Orr, the Welsh Revival of 1904–1905 was greatly influenced in its beginning by a church in New Quay, Cardiganshire, and the testimony of a teenage girl. Pastor Joseph Jenkins led a testimony time in a service in which he asked for responses to the question, What does Jesus mean to you? A young person, 15-year-old Florrie Evans, only recently converted, rose and said, "If no one else will, then I must say that I love the Lord Jesus with all my heart."[13]

For more information on the role of youth in historical movements see Alvin Reid, Join the Movement: God Is Calling You to Change the World *(Grand Rapids: Kregel, 2007).*

Her simple testimony caused many people to begin surrendering to Christ, and the fires of revival fell. The revival spread as young people went from church to church testifying. An itinerant preacher named Seth Joshua came to New Quay to speak and was impressed by the power of God. He then journeyed to speak at Newcastle Embyn College. The next week he spoke at nearby Blaenannerch, where a young coal miner named Evan Roberts, a ministerial student at the college, experienced a powerful personal revival.

Roberts felt impressed to return to his home church to address the youth. Seventeen heard him following a Monday service. He continued preaching and revival began there. The revival spread across the country, and news of the awakening spread worldwide. Many colleges reported revival. A good example was the revival reported at Denison University in Ohio.

[13] W. T. Stead, *The Story of the Welsh Revival* (London: Revell, 1905), 42–43.

Many colleges witnessed revival in the 1950s as well. In Minnesota, Northwestern School, St. Paul Bible Institute, and the University of Minnesota were touched. The year 1951 saw a notable spiritual stir on the campus of Baylor University. President W. R. White commented favorably about revival at this school.

A powerful campus awakening was experienced at Wheaton College in February 1950. After numerous prayer meetings were inaugurated by student leaders the previous fall, the revival began when a student shared a testimony of his changed life in an evening meeting. Others began testifying, and this continued for more than two days. Asbury College in Kentucky experienced revival as well.

Finally, the Jesus Movement described was actually a youth awakening. Many of the leaders of churches, denominations, and parachurch organizations were touched by this revival. A significant number of evangelistic pastors and other leaders trace their zeal for the Lord to the impact of the Jesus Movement on their life.

Students are perhaps the most fertile field for the working of the Spirit of God. If only churches would tap into the zeal of youth!

Reaching Young Adults Today

I would submit at least two things must happen before we can reach the massive numbers of young adults in our day, whether in secondary schools or universities. We must retool youth ministry with a perspective of raising an army of missionaries instead of creating a culture of games with a little Bible sprinkled in. Second, we must find effective ways to reach youth while they are young.

Time to Retool Youth Ministry

First, we need a reformation in student ministry at the youth and college levels. Some have gone to the more extreme approach of abolishing youth ministry altogether, creating "family integrated churches" that focus more on the family unit than a separate youth ministry. While that may be a viable model, I believe there is hope for youth ministry, especially as it relates to reaching unsaved youth and their families. In fact, if your youth ministry is not focused on penetrating the youth population with the gospel, I wonder why you have it. A youth *group* is focused on the churched youth and is inward focused. A youth *ministry* emphasizes reaching students who need

Christ. A youth *group* is institutional and easily becomes boring. A youth *ministry* seeks to advance the movement of God among the youth in a community and is compelling. Such a youth ministry can actually help fuel the flame of evangelism throughout the church body.

Youth ministry as we know it today came of age over the past generation. Focusing on activities and separation from the life of the church, it has hardly as a movement turned a generation of young adults into missionaries to their generation. Over the past three decades the number of vocational youth ministers has grown while at the same time effectiveness in reaching students has declined. This is not an indictment of youth ministers, but it may indicate that the growth of youth ministry as an entity of its own has helped to take young people out of the mainstream of the church. In many churches with significant youth ministries, the only time young people are noticed is when they return from camp or when a youth emphasis is scheduled during revival services.

Here are some fundamental elements for effective youth ministry from my book *Raising the Bar.*

1. Recover the Biblical Place of Parents (Deut 6:4–9)

For Christian families, youth ministry should be gravy, nothing more. Youth should learn by teaching and by example how to follow Christ from believing parents. Should youth ever be segregated? I believe so. But I also believe most churches segregate too much. When do we segregate youth? First, when it can be justified biblically. You can have a youth meeting focused on issues related to students, for instance. Second, it should be limited to those times when absolutely necessary. That would not include a separate Sunday morning worship experience that turns youth ministry into a parachurch ministry on the church campus. Third, when it occurs parents and other key adults should be encouraged to participate as much as possible.

This is a fatherless generation. Young people crave godly adults. As a young lady said on the back cover of my book *Raising the Bar:* "We know how to be teenagers; we want the church to teach us how to be adults." One of the reasons I have such a great rapport with youth and spend much time on Facebook answering questions is so many do not have a father, and I represent at least a glimpse of a father figure. I minister often with my whole family to students, and in particular with my son Josh as he drums in his band. That means a great deal to the students to whom I minister.

The acrostic SOAP—Significant Other Adult Person—is used to note the importance of only one adult in the life of a troubled young person. Adults who demonstrate a proclivity for Christian maturity and also relate well to youth should be active in the youth ministry. Adolescent adults who never grew up (I have met men in their thirties who act like they are in their terrible threes) should not be the sponsors on the youth trips. As I am writing this, I am responding via Facebook to a young lady who by age 20 had been molested, raped, contracted a STD, and cut herself many times. She has met Christ and has begun a wonderful process of growth, but she really needs some adults in her life who will not use her. These students are everywhere, and it is time to get outside our youth rooms and into the lives of these precious young adults.

2. Building a Foundation for Youth Ministry, Not a Youth Group

Sadly, the greatest hindrance to moving a youth group to become a youth ministry is the group of parents of the churched students! Four keys to developing a youth ministry focus on reaching lost students:

(1) Biblical Truth—young people do not hate preaching. They hate preaching that is either condescending on the one hand or fails to challenge them on the other. They can handle the truth! Games are fine in their place. I love roller coasters and games. But after more than 50 DiscipleNows, dozens of youth camps, and hundreds of rallies, not to mention immense time interacting personally with youth, I am more convinced than ever that youth hunger for truth that is taught in a way that helps them to apply it to where they live. Present compelling truth, the great idea of the faith, not just a first-grade version surrounded by games.

(2) Passionate Evangelism—youth pastors must ask the sobering question of whether they are passionate for the lost students in their area. Teach youth to witness, take them out into the community. Call them to accountability to share with their friends, and be willing to go with them.

(3) Authentic Worship—young people hunger for God. Worship means more than a few posters of the latest "Christian" band and background music. It means teaching them to encounter God corporately and personally. I take a wonderful worship band with me because I know the role of corporate worship that connects with

students matters much. Too many adults sadly confuse their preference in music with biblical truth and are sacrificing the future of their children on the altar of their musical preferences. By the way, young people do not hate hymns, just the way many of us sing them!

(4) Bold Prayer—challenge students to pray boldly for lost friends, to pray God-sized prayers. Let them see their leaders as men and women of prayer more than organizers of events.

Reaching Students Today

This kind of youth ministry can be a formidable force for the gospel in a given community. At the same time, we should be aware of effective ways to reach youth.

The first step in reaching youth is simply this: try to reach them. Is it possible that we have lost ground in evangelism in America because we are always playing catch-up? Do we work too hard to gear worship services to adults, provide materials for adults, and focus all our energies on those who pay the bills while neglecting the younger generation? No doubt this is true of college students, who are almost totally neglected by most churches. If you are a youth pastor or a pastor for that matter, how much time, effort, and energy do you give to reaching lost students?

We must see technology as our friend in evangelism. The Internet affects this generation of youth the way television affected Boomers. Throughout history, the church at its best has been at the forefront of technology. Think of how the printing press was used to publish the Bible and how trade routes helped in worldwide missions expansion. In recent history, we have lagged behind. I have been privileged to lead someone to Christ through the Internet. The technology is available. Compare TV evangelists to MTV in terms of influencing culture! The Internet may become one of the most viable tools for reaching the Millennial generation. Facebook, Myspace, and other social networks are filled with students. This can become a vital tool for connecting with and reaching out to students.

We must use the media and the arts in biblical ways to declare Christ to this generation. If we are going to reach this generation, we may have to sing the gospel to them. Can we not use the arts to reach this group? Must we only expect them to like our music when so many portals allow for an amazing diversity of musical styles in which to connect with them? There is a reason I take a band with me to do youth and college events who are themselves young people. This provides another means to connect with students.

Hold to the cross and the truthfulness of Scripture. Young adults today are immersed in a sea of relativism. An uncertain ocean requires a strong hand and a sound rudder. We must confront the pluralism of the age with courage, not compromise.

Demonstrate intimacy with God and people. Youth crave intimacy. The Millennials are a fatherless generation. We must minister to youth, and to college students for that matter, in the context of the many difficult families in which they have lived. Young adults yearn to be around and to see families who love each other. Strong families involved with students can be a powerful demonstration of the gospel.

The numbers of fatherless children (homes with no father present) grew from 14 percent in 1970 to almost one third by 1993. Further, the percentage of mothers, with school-aged children, who work outside the home has increased from 39 percent in 1960 to 70 percent by 1987. Today, 50 percent of marriages end in divorce.[14] The crumbling of the home, coupled with the rise of youth gangs, points out the desire for intimacy.

Churches must place a higher priority on youth. They are not the church of the future; they are the church of today. Churches need both the wisdom of mature believers and the zeal of youth. During the Jesus Movement and the years following, youth choirs filled hundreds of churches. They were a focal point of the service and a source of great inspiration. Surely there are ways students can be brought into the heart of church life.

Your church bears a responsibility to guide students. Mature Christians should help young people channel their zeal in ways that honor Christ. We can affirm their concern for unsaved friends and encourage them to maintain convictions. The True Love Waits campaign is a beautiful illustration of the multitude of godly young men and women who seek to honor God with their bodies. The author is grateful to God for a church that affirmed and encouraged him to make a radical commitment to Christ as a teenager. In your church, delegate responsibilities to mature youth in the worship service. They can help take the offering, lead in prayer, and do dramatic presentations. An occasional word of affirmation from the pastor in the service is very affirming.

[14] T. S. Rainer, *The Bridger Generation* (Nashville: Broadman & Holman, 1997). 54–56.

Finally, those of us who are older can listen to young people. They, too, can hear from God. At times they are more sensitive to the voice of the Spirit than many of us. May the following words remind us of the importance of youthful zeal, regardless of age:

> If we look at the ranks of middle-aged men and women we observe that there is all too often no spiritual fire, no urge to achieve things for God. That condition does not suddenly come upon people at that age; you need to be on guard against it now, whatever your age. *It is when one has found his niche that imperceptibly zeal flags and lethargy creeps in.* Oh, to keep burning brightly to the end![15]

Questions for Consideration

1. Do you see youth as children finishing childhood or as young adults entering adulthood? What difference does it make?
2. Would you describe your church's attitude toward ministering to youth as a youth group (focusing on the churched youth) or as a youth ministry (focusing on those yet to be reached)?
3. Do you have any college students in your area? If so, what can your church do to minister to them?

[15] A. J. Broomhall, *Time for Action* (Downers Grove, IL: InterVarsity, 1965), 132, italics added.

Chapter 26

Reach the Cities, Reach the Nations

Christianity was an urban movement, and the New Testament was set down by urbanites.[1]

—Rodney Stark

The single most effective way for Christians to "reach" the US would be for 25 percent of them to move to two or three of the largest cities and stay there for three generations.

—Tim Keller

So there was great joy in that city. (Acts 8:8)

I have many people in this city. (Acts 18:10)

But they now aspire to a better land—a heavenly one. . . . for He has prepared a city for them. (Heb 11:16)

---

[1] R. Stark, *The Rise of Christianity* (New York: HarperOne, 1997), 147.

In 1974, Ralph Winter presented an address at the Lausanne Congress on World Evangelization entitled "The Highest Priority—Cross-Cultural Evangelism." Winter's address led to a growing focus on the identification of unreached people groups around the world. As these groups became identified worldwide, it became apparent most of them live in one large region in the East. In 1990, Luis Bush coined the term the "10/40 window," referring to the area in the Eastern Hemisphere between 10 and 40 degrees north of the equator. Since then, the growing awareness of this region's need for the gospel has had a profound effect on the development of international mission strategy. Of the 55 most unreached countries, 97 percent of their population lives in that window. Hardly a day goes by on our campus without mention of this designation. Much energy and urgency for the unsaved has been generated because of this focus.

The time has come for a Western version of the 10/40 window. Whereas the 10/40 window refers to the area demanding the greatest cause for urgency, the window to which I refer holds as much promise as it manifests great need. I am referring to a revolutionary call to reach the great cities of the West, and of the world.

Arguably no one has championed the city as a place of promise and need as much as Tim Keller, pastor of Redeemer Presbyterian Church in New York City. Read Keller's resources (www.redeemer.com) and you may join me in a conviction that the time has never been more urgent to reach the cities.

Why the Cities?

Over the years I have tried to write about areas where I believe the church today has failed to be effective as it relates to reaching people. I have written on spiritual awakenings because I am sure we cannot reach the West or the world without a God-intervention. I have written on reaching the unchurched because we mostly are not, and on students because we tend to treat them like kids instead of radicals. So in this book I am including chapters related to areas the church must refocus. Areas like church planting. And the cities. Why a chapter on the cities?

Biblically, the gospel spread via the cities of the Roman world. Simply study the book of Acts to see the priority given to cities. Large cities influence the culture like never before in history. In *The Rise of Christianity* Stark argued, "Within a decade of the crucifixion of

Jesus, the village culture of Palestine had been left far behind, and the Graeco-Roman city became the dominant environment of the Christian movement."[2] In fact by AD 300, the urban areas of the Roman Empire were 50 percent Christian, but the countryside remained 90 percent pagan.[3]

Strategically, commerce and culture flow through the cities. The flattening of the world has given large cities global ties and national influence. Now more than ever a teenager in rural North Carolina decides everything from musical tastes to future plans based more on urban America than from his local community. As a young adult I know in New York City recently observed, "Everything that will happen in the U.S. happens first in New York." As the city goes, so goes the nation. Keller argues that large cities have as much or more power than states or nations today.

Globalization has caused large cities to be more similar than different around the world. In the past few years I have spent time in cities in several nations: Kiev, London, Paris, Florence, Rome, Chiang Mai, and Bangkok, among others. Add to that ventures to large cities in the United States, and having lived in medium to large metropolitan areas from Birmingham and Raleigh-Durham to Indianapolis, Dallas-Fort Worth, and Houston, and a common theme is apparent. In most if not all of these cities I just named, one can go to a major shopping district and grab a quick meal at McDonald's or a sit-down meal at Hard Rock, grab a latte at Starbucks, and shop for Prada. I have done all the above except shop for Prada.

Major cities have more in common with each other from nation to nation than they do with rural areas in their own country. Pop culture, which changes little over space but rapidly over time, has increased in influence, while traditional culture, which changes slowly over time but varies greatly over space, has lessened in influence. We may reach Warsaw and Tokyo more by studying New York than by taking knowledge gained from village evangelism (overseas or in the U.S.) to the cities.

Cities are changing. This past spring I spoke at a college in Dallas, Texas. On the flight home I sat next to a middle-aged divorcee who had recently moved to the city-center in Dallas, the downtown area that had recently undergone a major revitalization, replete with loft apartments and the opportunity to live a complete life never driving

---

[2] Ibid., 160.

[3] http://www.redeemer2.com/themovement/issues/2004/april/advancingthegospel_4_3.html (accessed August 28, 2008).

a car or traveling far from home. She loved her life. She epitomized what so many have found—the city can be a place of greatness, where excellence in the arts and education is appreciated, where energy and life pulsate 24/7.

Keller has observed the rise of the city-center as key to understanding the city:

> The center city, unlike the "inner city" (where the poor live) or where the working-class live, is where there is a confluence of a) residences for professionals, b) major work and job centers, and c) major cultural institutions—all in close proximity.[4]

Keller notes who lives there; people who have immense influence live in these centers—young professionals, mostly single; creative professionals; corporate leaders; leaders in the arts and education; new immigrant families; second-generation Americans; students/academics; and the gay community.

Anglo evangelicals have been fascinated with the suburbs for decades but must begin to see the importance of the city-centers. As a child I remember when a trip across Birmingham to the zoo seemed like a forever-long excursion. Then Interstate 59 was built in the 1960s. Suddenly the zoo was closer! We trace the rise of the (mostly suburban) megachurch to the year 1970 due in no small part to the ease of travel afforded by the interstate. But today the suburban-inner city dichotomy I hear so many use to categorize the city must be changed. The city-center and its holistic life view have replaced the suburbs and the shopping mall as the locus of influence, and we must realize that *city* is not synonymous with *inner city.*

In 2000 80 percent of people in the U.S. lived in metro areas, but only 50 percent of Southern Baptist churches are there.

We are losing the cities. My young adult friend in New York City would argue we have already lost them. We must go after them with the aggression of pioneer missionaries in an unchurched land, for that is where we are. In 2000 the Census Bureau reported that 80 percent of the United States lives in metropolitan areas. Yet Anglo evangelicals in particular tend not to be there. Only 50 percent of Southern Baptist churches are in metro areas.

[4] http://www.redeemer2.com/themovement/issues/2005/may/ministry_in_globalculture.html (accessed August 26, 2008).

Perhaps we could begin a serious conversation about whether the key to reaching the cities, the nation, and the world might be to offer a vision to believers to move to the cities. In particular, what if we began a call to the Millennials (those roughly 25 and under) in the United States who love Jesus and want to be part of something that matters to include in their career plans the idea of spending their lives in the great cities? I cannot help but believe that if 30 percent of Southern Baptists, for instance, shifted to the cities and at the same time took a missional, passionate, evangelistic heart for those cities with them, things might be different in a generation.

The cities of the West have been immersed in postmodern thought. Pluralism, tolerance toward other faiths (except for Christianity), relativism, and experientialism thrive in such contexts. Cities teem with young postmoderns who are not uninterested in spiritual matters; conventional, institutional Christianity however generally does not sway them.[5]

The nations of the world are in the cities of the West. When my family lived in Houston, our street included Anglo, Chinese, Hispanic, and African-American families. A few blocks away the street signs in one area were printed in English and Mandarin Chinese. Even in the town of Wake Forest, North Carolina, where we currently live, our street is multiethnic and includes one mixed-race marriage. Over 40 percent of the new students at New York University in 1996–1997 had other than English as their first language, while 50 percent of the PhDs granted in engineering and science in the United States are to "foreign nationals," mostly Asians. Some 13 percent of Americans speak another language at home besides English. The twentieth century was dominated by the mainly Anglo (at least in terms of influential leaders) United States, but the twenty-first century is the ethnic century, or even the Asian century. Globalization has shrunk the world and shifted influence.

One of the most remarkable shifts in the last few decades has been the dramatic rise of Hispanics in the United States, particularly in the cities. Half the U.S. population growth since 2008 came from Latinos, a remarkable statistic and one the church should know. By mid-2007, Hispanics accounted for 15 percent of the U.S. population. We may see the day when Spanish becomes a required language for ministry students! Fastest growth has come in Texas, on the West Coast

[5] For more on postmodernism and reaching unchurched postmoderns, see my book *Radically Unchurched.*

(particularly the cities of the Pacific Northwest), Florida, and remarkably, North Carolina.[6]

However, the effect of postmodernism has not been to bring all ethnic groups together. Only the gospel can truly break down the walls of race or class. Read the book of Acts to see how quickly the gospel collapsed numerous barriers. On the surface, while the multicultural emphasis of postmodernism seems to liberate all in the name of tolerance, it in fact leads to the destruction of various cultures, as Veith notes:

> The fact is, real cultures promote strict ethical guidelines. From Mexico to Africa, family ties are strong and sexual promiscuity is strictly forbidden. No culture (other than our own) would teach that there are no absolutes. Contemporary Western culture with its pornography, consumerism, and all-encompassing skepticism toward authority and moral traditions is ravaging traditional cultures.[7]

Rather than lifting up all people by praising their differences, postmodernism leads to fragmentation. Any common ground for discussion is destroyed by a multitude of competing groups. As Veith notes, "People are finding their identities, not so much in themselves, nor in their communities or nation, but in the groups that they belong to."[8]

We should continue to press for more and more to go to the nations in international missions. We cannot take away from this call. We may never catch up with the need. But need alone does not determine God's call; if it did we should all start packing for China tomorrow. We must be driven by the Spirit and captivated by a strategy that sees not only the need of the times, but the perspective of long-term change as well. And in fact our focus, in addition to an urgent call to the nations, will have the serendipitous effect of reaching the nations as well, since those from virtually every tribe and tongue live in the great cities of the West.

Urban Leaders

In a two-day period recently I had meals with two men who in many ways represent the great need of our time in the West—to go

[6] http://pewhispanic.org/reports/report.php?ReportID=96 (accessed November 1, 2008).

[7] G. E. Veith, *Postmodern Times: A Christian Guide to Contemporary Thought and Culture* (Wheaton: Crossway, 1994), 144.

[8] Ibid., 146.

back into the cities and reach them for the gospel. One of the men was a younger church planter named Darrin Patrick. Darrin had planted the Journey church six years earlier in the city of St. Louis. A church already with alliances with the Southern Baptist Convention, the Acts 29 Network, and including a relationship with Covenant Seminary (Presbyterian), Journey had in six years become the largest SBC church in the city. The next day I had lunch with Charles Lyons, pastor for three decades of the Armitage Baptist Church in Chicago. Lyons was the first person to get the wheels spinning in my mind about the need and opportunity of the city.

These men came from two different generations, two different backgrounds, and two different cities, albeit both were Midwestern. One was a church planter who had quickly developed a church-planting network, the other an established pastor who had given his life to the city of Chicago. But both of these men, neither of whom knew the other, said so much of the same thing. They both described the need of the city. They recognized what Tim Keller of Redeemer Presbyterian in New York City has been saying, that the cities of America are revitalizing, that many young, ethnic, single, and spiritually unaligned people are flocking back into the cities, and we have done little to reach them. They spoke in similar terms of what it would take to turn the tide of (being generous) modest success (if any) in church planting efforts in the cities around. They spoke of the need of interns and the failure of sending young couples to the cities to plant churches only to be chewed up and spat out due to isolation. They spoke of the need of suburban and other churches thriving outside the cities to help fund such internships.

The American church has tended to see cities as dangerous places, places to be avoided. Suburbs have become the haven of many evangelicals. And we wonder why the church has lost so much influence in our day? Influence comes from the cities.

Cities in the Bible

A quick scan of the Bible reveals 724 references to the term "city" (HCSB). As early as Gen 4:17 we read of Cain establishing a city and naming it after his son Enoch. Why do we avoid the cities? Cities are places of great sin. In Genesis 11 we read of the effects of sin, when men gathered in a city and longed to make a tower up to the sky to "make a name for ourselves" (Gen 11:4). Later, Sodom was a city filled with gross immorality, where Abraham could not find as many as 10 righteous men (Gen 18:32).

But cities also provide great opportunity. Read Joshua and see that the conquest centered on the cities of the region. The conquests of the Old Testament and the spread of the church in the New focused on cities. Influence lies close to cities, as cities hold many people!

In 1 Samuel 9 we read of a city where a man of God resided, none other than Samuel. His reputation is known throughout the region. A respected man of God in the city can have much influence. It was the city of Jerusalem chosen by God to be the place where His temple would be built (1 Kings 8). This city would be known as the city of David. After the exile, Ezra and Nehemiah gave much attention to rebuilding the city as the key to rebuilding all aspects of society, spiritual or not. The psalmist (Ps 46:4) described the dwelling place of God as a city (see also Psalm 48). Similarly the writer of Hebrews described heaven as a city (11:16), and John in Revelation did so as well.

The cities need the Lord! Read Ps 127:1. Proverbs 11:11 tells us "a city is built up by the blessing of the upright, but it is torn down by the mouth of the wicked." The prophets speak much of the judgment of God on the cities. God judged Jerusalem, allowing her to be overtaken by pagans because of her sin (Jer 33:4). And yet, the Lord promised a day of future restoration: "This city will bear on My behalf a name of joy, praise, and glory before all the nations of the earth, who will hear of all the good I will do for them. They will tremble with awe because of all the good and all the peace I will bring about for them" (Jer 33:9).

Would that God would give us the same burden for the lostness of the cities He gave to Jeremiah in the book of Lamentations: "My eyes are worn out from weeping; I am churning within. My heart is poured out in grief because of the destruction of my dear people, because children and infants faint in the streets of the city" (Lam 2:11).

Read Acts and see how the spread of the gospel followed the path of cities. Paul's epistles were written to one of two groups: some addressed individuals (Timothy, Titus, Philemon), but for the most part they addressed churches in the cities (Rome, Corinth, Ephesus, Philippi).

We cannot underestimate the role Antioch played in the expansion of the Christian movement. "Antioch is of special interest because it was unusually receptive to the Christian movement, sustaining a relatively large and affluent Christian community quite early on," Stark argued, noting that the urban conditions, replete with overcrowding, disease, sanitation issues, and the like, "gave Christianity the opportunity to exploit its immense competitive advantages vis-à-vis paganism and other religious movements of the day as a *solution* to those problems."[9]

By the end of the first century, Antioch had about 150,000 residents, making it the fourth largest city in the empire, Rome being the largest. That means those who lived inside the city walls constituted about 117 people per acre. Compare that to New York with 27:1 and Chicago with 21:1. A transient and multiethnic population filled the city. "Any accurate portrait of Antioch in New Testament times must depict a city filled with misery, danger, fear, despair, and hatred," Stark observed. "A city where the average family lived a squalid life in filthy and cramped quarters, where at least half the children . . . died at birth or during infancy. . . A city filled with hatred and fear rooted in intense ethnic antagonisms and exacerbated by a constant stream of strangers."[10] "And surely," he observed, "too they must often have longed for relief, for hope, indeed for salvation."[11]

Stark argued that Christianity in Antioch literally revitalized the city by "providing new norms and new kinds of social relationships able to cope with many urgent urban problems."[12] Disease, earthquakes, ethnic strife, poverty, and the like existed prior to Christianity's appearance in Antioch; but the Christians showed a new way to cope. His observation should be heeded by those who seek to move out of the Christian subculture with signs on the church property as a primary means of "outreach." The residents of Antioch warmly received the missionaries as recorded in Acts 11. They brought a message of hope, but more than words—they brought "a *new culture* of making life in Graeco-Roman cities more tolerable."[13]

"Within a decade of the crucifixion of Jesus, the village culture of Palestine had been left far behind, and the Graeco-Roman city became the dominant environment of the Christian movement." —Rodney Stark

[9] Stark, *Rise of Christianity*, 147 and 149 respectively.

[10] Ibid., 160.

[11] Ibid., 161.

[12] Ibid.

[13] Ibid., 162.

The Cities Today

People today, especially in the cities, identify themselves less by broad categories (political parties, grand ideologies, etc.), and more by subcultures, or as some would put it, by tribes. "On one occasion," Hirsch observed, "some youth ministry specialists I work with identified in an hour fifty easily discernible youth *subcultures* alone (computer nerds, skaters, homies, surfies, punks, etc.). Each of them take their subcultural identity with utmost seriousness, hence any missional response to them must as well."[14]

In 2008 the ten largest cities of the world were these:[15]

1. Tokyo
2. Mexico City
3. Mumbai, India
4. Sao Paulo
5. New York City
6. Shanghai
7. Lagos, Nigeria
8. Los Angeles
9. Calcutta
10. Buenos Ares

The largest cities in the U.S.:[16]

1. New York City
2. Los Angeles
3. Chicago
4. Houston
5. Phoenix
6. Philadelphia
7. San Antonio
8. San Diego
9. Dallas
10. San Jose

However, when you include the larger metro areas the cities in the top 10 change dramatically:

[14] A. Hirsch, *Forgotten Ways: Reactivating the Missional Church* (Grand Rapids: Brazos Press, 2006), 61.

[15] http://www.worldatlas.com/citypops.htm (accessed September 23, 2008).

[16] http://en.wikipedia.org/wiki/List_of_United_States_cities_by_population (accessed September 23, 2008).

Largest metro areas in the United States (July 1, 2007 U.S. Census estimates)[17]

1. New York Metro
2. Los Angeles Metro
3. Chicago Metro
4. Dallas-Fort Worth Metro
5. Philadelphia Metro
6. Houston Metro
7. Miami Metro
8. Washington, DC Metro
9. Atlanta Metro
10. Boston Metro

A little closer look at the numbers reveals the following: About 162 million (58% of the population) live in the 50 largest metros in the United States. Over 100 million lost people at a minimum live there. The fastest growing metros are in the southern and western parts. The 50 largest metros account for 63 percent of the nation's population.[18]

Las Vegas (83%), Austin (48%), and Phoenix (45%) were the fastest growing metros in 1990–2000. However, a study of Southern Baptists and the cities revealed only 50 percent of Southern Baptist churches are in the metros where 80 percent of the population lives. But the numbers are actually even worse because only 25 percent of SBC churches are in the 50 largest metros, where 63 percent of Americans live. There is a great and open door for the gospel in the cities of the United States. We are indeed a mission field.

Darrin Patrick and Charles Lyons agreed that the best way to plant churches in the city involves bringing interns alongside effective churches (whether new churches like Patrick's or established churches like Lyons's). These interns can live for a time among the people of an urban church in order to learn the culture of the city. Cities are so multiethnic and so diverse that one cannot expect to take a seminary diploma and a young wife and be effective among the unchurched without learning from people already there. We often set up young church planters for failure before they begin. Further,

[17] http://en.wikipedia.org/wiki/United_States_metropolitan_area (accessed September 23, 2008).

[18] R. Stanley, "America's 50 Largest Metropolitan Areas," North American Mission Board, 2002.

a team approach works far better than a couple in the urban setting. Read Acts and see how often Paul traveled with others in his church-planting efforts. Some groups and denominations focus far too much on the numbers of new churches (sowing grass seed) and not enough on planting strategic, exponentially growing churches (planting a garden). The latter takes more time to see an impact, but long term is much more effective.

No one demonstrates this better in the cities than Tim Keller and Redeemer Presbyterian Church in New York City. Begun in 1989 with 15 people and a desire to reach professional New Yorkers in Manhattan, Redeemer now has more than 4,500 gathering weekly in at least four sites. In 1993 she began a church-planting ministry and has planted churches in other cities and nations. Her church-planting center has helped many church planters learn effective church planting in the cities.

Darrin Patrick relayed to me a simple approach to church planting in the cities which seems to be effective in other places:

Local Church → Networks (within a denomination) → Alliances (like-minded groups across denominations) → church-planting movements result.

This is the approach of Redeemer Presbyterian:

> The vision of Redeemer's Church Planting Center (RCPC) is to ignite and fuel a city-focused, gospel-centered, values-driven church planting movement in New York, in cooperation with the wider Christian church, and to assist national leaders and denominations to plant resource churches in the global centers of the world.[19]

You can see in this description recognition of the need to move beyond traditions for the sake of the gospel. However, it does not include surrender to those traditions and their distinctives. I would argue that a group of, say, Southern Baptist churches intent on planting new churches in the city could work together and then network with other evangelicals to pool their resources. The net result would be more, not less, Southern Baptist churches, along with others as well, all sharing Christ in the city. We see this in international missions all over the world as different groups work together and yet do not lose their identity.

---

[19] http://www.redeemer.com/about_us/church_planting/ (accessed April 24, 2009).

A sectarian, parochial mind-set will never reach the cities. On the other hand, the surrender of conviction will not lead to long-term, biblical effectiveness. These two extremes must be avoided. The need is great, the gospel is our only hope, and church planting is the means to get the gospel to the cities.

A Vision for the Cities

The cities of America influence the entire nation and the world. The entertainment centers of Los Angeles, New York City, and increasingly Nashville affect cities globally. Other world cities like Chicago wield great influence as well. But one does not reach a world city in our time in a year or a decade. One must look at a generation, or maybe two, to see real change. Boston is the major city of New England. When the Great Awakening hit Boston and New England, the colonies and ultimately the young nation reaped the benefit. As secularism and its impact have spread in Boston, one can see its growing influence. San Francisco comes to mind when one thinks of the homosexual agenda, but we make a mistake if we underestimate the impact of Boston. Massachusetts, after all, has been in the headlines as much as any place on the issue of gay marriage. A student of mine who plans to go to Boston and has studied the city told me this week that from kindergarten on, public school children are taught the homosexual agenda. Just think about the impact of that one reality on a generation.

We are too like politicians looking for a quick fix to solve issues that may take a generation to change. Are we willing to say, for example, that we will go after the five most influential cities in America for a generation? If we cast a vision for our best and brightest believers to move to New York, Boston, Chicago, Los Angeles, and Washington, D.C., for a generation, we just might affect the whole world. While the United States has experienced what some call urban sprawl, the church has exhibited an urban crawl.

In 1906, San Francisco was hit by one of the most destructive earthquakes in history. In his book on the earthquakes, Simon Winchester argues that San Francisco was the major city on the West Coast, much more influential than Los Angeles, for example.[20] But after the earthquake, the City of the Angels soon began to grow in influence. One hundred years later, the media capital of the world,

[20] S. Winchester, *The Crack in the Edge of the World* (San Francisco: HarperCollins, 1998).

which arguably exerts more influence in popular culture than any city on earth, is Los Angeles. If we took a century-long look into the future and seriously sought to reach the major cities of the United States, it just might change the whole world. And we may not need an earthquake to see it happen.

In the summer of 2008 I took Hannah on a trip to Thailand. Spending time in Bangkok and Chiang Mai reminded me how similar cities are globally. Seeing the vast numbers of people so in need of Christ is staggering. While there I caught up with a former student who spent time in Pattaya, Thailand. She told me the wickedness there was visceral. I observed the child prostitution and glimpses of the awful sex trade industry. She informed me Pattaya led the world in sex change operations.

Earlier a British band called Bluetree had come to Pattaya to be part of an event with their church, featuring everything from live worship to cleaning the streets. More than 30,000 prostitutes fill this city, and the band saw the wickedness all around them. On one of the more vile streets a club called the Climax Club advertised the need for a band to play. Aaron, the bandleader, explained what happened there:

> We got the chance to play in this bar, a two-hour worship set in this bar. I don't think the people in the bar spoke a word of English but we basically got to go in. The deal was that we play and we bring a following of people with us; so we're there, set up, really good gear! Amazing drums, the biggest drum kit you've ever seen in your life. . . . So we all set up and there was like 20 Christians all standing in front of us, and the deal was we play, they buy lots of drinks, alright? I don't think the place has ever sold so much Coke in its whole life in one night![21]

As they played they watched people weep while they sang songs about Jesus. In the midst of their worship, Aaron began singing "greater things" over and over, broken for this wicked city. That night, in a club, they penned the words to a song that has reminded me many times that our God is Lord of the cities:

> You're the God of this city
> You're the King of these people
> You're the Lord of this nation
> You are___

[21] http://octagus.typepad.com/steph/2008/01/god-of-this-cit.html (accessed October 28, 2008).

For there is no one like our God
There is no one like our God

Greater things have yet to come
Great things are still to be done in this city
Greater things are still to come
And greater things are still to be done here

Perhaps it is time to think about a Western window, playing off the 10/40 concept, which should still receive priority. Reach the city, reach the nation. No, reach the city, reach the *nations.*

Questions for Consideration

1. Do you think of cities as (a) a place of crime, crowds, and noise; (b) a place to visit but not to live; (c) a place full of life, culture, and vitality; (d) an amazing opportunity for the gospel? (You can choose more than one.)
2. What would happen if the majority of believers in the United States saw themselves as missionaries and moved to the cities for a generation?

Conclusion

Missional Living Realized

A *few years ago my family moved.* When we first moved to Wake Forest in 1995, we built a house in a neighborhood populated mostly by seminary faculty. I do love my colleagues, but living in a Christian ghetto never quite fit us. So when we got a chance we moved into the country to live on seven acres, with a swimming pool and beautiful trees. While there we helped a neighbor become an active follower of Christ and plug into our church. But while we enjoyed the space, we missed the impact we could make. So we sold the place, moved back into Wake Forest, and bought a house in a subdivision. On our street where we now live there are about a dozen houses. Only one family on the street is originally from North Carolina. Our closest neighbors are from California (two families), Rhode Island, and Pennsylvania. Most are from outside the south. Most are unchurched. We have a couple who live together, an interracial couple, and a variety of political and social views, not to mention religious ideas.

We have seen God at work here. We have seen a few come to Christ, and some are active in our church now. But the work is slow. These are very successful people, several of whom own their own businesses. Most got enough conventional Christianity, usually of the mainline Protestant variety, to make them think they could do better without it. It has been quite a laboratory to help me think through how America must be reached. My family lives as missionaries in the community. We have shared Christ intentionally with most if not all and have spoken to neighbors on many occasions on spiritual issues.

I believe more than ever the secret to reaching America is helping believers to live missionally in their communities, workplaces, and schools. We must keep the gospel ever before us.

After a speech, an older man approached pro-life activist Penny Lea. Weeping, he told her the following story:

> I lived in Germany during the Nazi holocaust. I considered myself a Christian. I attended church since I was a small boy. We had heard the stories of what was happening to the Jews, but like most people today in this country, we tried to distance ourselves from the reality of what was really taking place. What could anyone do to stop it?
>
> A railroad track ran behind our small church, and each Sunday morning we would hear the whistle from a distance and then the clacking of the wheels moving over the track. We became disturbed when one Sunday we noticed cries coming from the train as it passed by. We grimly realized that the train was carrying Jews. They were like cattle in those cars!
>
> Week after week that train whistle would blow. We would dread to hear the sound of those old wheels because we knew that the Jews would begin to cry out to us as they passed our church. It was so terribly disturbing! We could do nothing to help these poor miserable people, yet their screams tormented us. We knew exactly at what time that whistle would blow, and we decided the only way to keep from being so disturbed by the cries was to start singing our hymns. By the time that train came rumbling past the churchyard, we were singing at the top of our voices. If some of the screams reached our ears, we'd just sing a little louder until we could hear them no more. Years have passed and no one talks about it much anymore, but I still hear that train whistle in my sleep. I can still hear them crying out for help. God forgive all of us who called ourselves Christians, yet did nothing to intervene.
>
> Now, so many years later, I see it happening all over again in America. God forgive you as Americans for you have blocked out the screams of millions of your own children. The holocaust is here. The response is the same as it was in my country—Silence![1]

---

[1] From the brochure, "Sing a Little Louder," by Penny Lea.

While Lea applied this tragic story to the abortion holocaust in America, it also speaks to the negligence of the church to seek to save lost souls from hell. May our generation not be so busy spending time in activities at the local church building that we miss the cries of the hurting. Tell someone about Jesus, won't you?

Afterword

When Alvin Reid first asked me to do the afterword for this book, he referred to it as his magnum opus. His use of the word *magnum* was no exaggeration. This is easily the most comprehensive book on the subject of evangelism I have ever read.

Again and again I was impressed with the minute details of virtually every aspect of evangelistic ministry. The reader cannot help but be impressed with the soundness of the biblical and theological aspects of this book. But Alvin has a way of making theology come alive, and one of the strengths of this book is the combination of inspiration and theology. The illustrations employed in the book are to the point and gripping in their interest.

Another significant fact about the book is that to Alvin, evangelism is more than some mechanical operation which is humanly contrived. The Holy Spirit's work and the prayer factor on the part of the church are constant themes on these pages.

It is refreshing to read a book that comes to the rescue of what some regard as obsolete methods in evangelism. The author still strongly believes in assigned visitation as a part of the evangelistic planning of a church. He is unashamed to say that most churches that are strong in evangelism are churches that are unafraid to knock on doors with a view to sharing the message with those within. Chapters on the evangelism of children and young people are especially strong.

There is an unusual fairness in assessment of what is workable in contemporary evangelism and what is not. As far as telling the truth about evangelism today, this book certainly carries with it the ring of the real.

Roy Fish
Distinguished Professor of Evangelism Emeritus
Southwestern Baptist Theological Seminary

Name Index

Subject Index

Scripture Index